Brands

Branding has emerged as a cornerstone of marketing practice and corporate strategy. In this book, Jonathan Schroeder brings together a curated selection of the most influential and thought-provoking papers on brands and branding from *Consumption Markets & Culture*, accompanied by new contributions from leading brand scholars Giana Eckhardt, John F. Sherry, Jr., Sidney Levy and Morris Holbrook.

Organized into four perspectives – cultural, corporate, consumer, critical – these papers are chosen to highlight the complexities of contemporary branding through leading consumer brands such as Disney, eBay, Guinness, McDonald's, Nike and Starbucks. They address key topics such as celebrity branding, corporate branding, place branding and retail branding, and critique the complexities of contemporary brands to provide a rich trove of interdisciplinary research insights into the function of brands as ethical, ideological and political objects.

This thought-provoking collection will be of interest to all scholars of marketing, consumer behaviour, anthropology and sociology, and anyone interested in the powerful roles brands play in consumers' lives and cultural discourse.

Jonathan E. Schroeder is the William A. Kern Professor of Communications at Rochester Institute of Technology in New York. He is editor in chief of the interdisciplinary journal *Consumption Markets & Culture*.

Routledge Interpretive Marketing Research
Edited by Stephen Brown
University of Ulster, Northern Ireland

Recent years have witnessed an 'interpretive turn' in marketing and consumer research. Methodologies from the humanities are taking their place alongside those drawn from the traditional social sciences.

Qualitative and literary modes of marketing discourse are growing in popularity. Art and aesthetics are increasingly firing the marketing imagination.

This series brings together the most innovative work in the burgeoning interpretive marketing research tradition. It ranges across the methodological spectrum, from grounded theory to personal introspection, covers all aspects of the postmodern marketing 'mix', from advertising to product development, and embraces marketing's principal sub-disciplines.

Brands

Interdisciplinary perspectives

Edited by
Jonathan E. Schroeder

Routledge
Taylor & Francis Group

LONDON AND NEW YORK

First published 2015 by Routledge

2 Park Square, Milton Park, Abingdon, Oxfordshire OX14 4RN
52 Vanderbilt Avenue, New York, NY 10017

Routledge is an imprint of the Taylor & Francis Group, an informa business

First issued in paperback 2019

British Library Cataloguing in Publication Data
A catalogue record for this book is available from the British Library

Library of Congress Cataloging-in-Publication Data
Brands: interdisciplinary perspectives/edited by Jonathan E. Schroeder.
  pages cm. – (Routledge interpretive marketing research)
  Includes bibliographical references and index.
  1. Branding (Marketing). 2. Brand name products. 3. Product management.
  I. Schroeder, Jonathan E., 1962–.
  HF5415.1255.B734 2014
  658.8′27 – dc23
  2014024844

ISBN: 978-1-138-78796-4 (hbk)
ISBN: 978-0-367-87017-1 (pbk)

Typeset in Times New Roman
by Florence Production Ltd, Stoodleigh, Devon, UK

Contents

Acknowledgements

Thank you to editor Jacqueline Curthoys who supported this project, to editorial assistant Sinead Waldron for attention to detail, and to Kerrie Loyd and Jennie Ellis for marketing support. Also, thank you to the team at Taylor & Francis that publishes *Consumption Markets & Culture*, including Mathew Derbyshire, Rachael Arbon, Zoe Sternberg, Stephen Kirton, Harriet Canavan, Jasper Navarez and Rebecca Gelson. Thank you to Andrew Craddock for copy-editing and to Amy Wheeler at Florence Production. Thanks to CMC's founding editors, Fuat Fırat, Nik Dholakia and Alladi Venkatesh, and former editor Lisa Peñaloza, whose efforts have helped pave the way for inter-disciplinary work on brands. Some of the contributions in this book appeared in distinguished special issues of *Consumption Markets & Culture*; thank you to guest editors Paul du Gay, Teresa Davis, Greg Patmore, Samantha Warren, Alf Rehn, Fuat Fırat, Simone Pettigrew and Russell Belk. I also thank CMC editorial board members, reviewers, authors and faithful readers. Appreciation goes to Morris Holbrook, Giana Eckhardt, Sidney Levy and John Sherry, who kindly agreed to write brand new commentaries for this volume. I also thank graduate assistant Gelsey Randazzo for help on the manuscript, and administrative assistant Cassandra Shellman. This project has been supported by the William A. Kern endowment at Rochester Institute of Technology.

About the editor

Jonathan E. Schroeder is the William A. Kern Professor of Communications at Rochester Institute of Technology in New York. He has published widely on branding, communication, consumer research and identity. He is the author of *Visual Consumption* (2002), co-author of *From Chinese Brand Culture to Global Brands* (2013), editor of *Conversations on Consumption* (2013), and co-editor of *Brand Culture* (2006) and *The Routledge Companion to Visual Organization* (2014), as well as a special issue on 'Being Branded' for the *Scandinavian Journal of Management* (June 2013). He is editor in chief of the interdisciplinary journal *Consumption Markets & Culture*, and serves on the editorial boards of the journals *Advertising and Society Review*, *Critical Studies in Fashion and Beauty*, *European Journal of Marketing*, *International Journal of Indian Culture and Business Management*, *Journal of Business Research*, *Journal of Historical Research in Marketing*, *Journal of Macro-marketing*, *Marketing Theory* and *Visual Methodologies*. He has held visiting appointments at Wesleyan University, Göteborg University, Sweden, University of Auckland, New Zealand, Bocconi University, Milan, Indian School of Business, Hyderabad, and the Shanghai International Business and Economics University. He is a Fellow of the Institute for Brands and Brand Relationships.

About the contributors

Aaron Ahuvia is Professor of Marketing at University of Michigan-Dearborn, USA.

John Amis is Associate Professor of Management at University of Memphis, USA.

Russell W. Belk is the Kraft Foods Canada Chair in Marketing at Schulich School of Business, York University, Canada.

Anders Bengtsson is CEO of Protobrand Consulting, Boston, USA.

Amanda J. Broderick is Dean of Salford Business School, UK.

Maaike Broos is a Filmmaker at Broosdoc, Amsterdam, Netherlands.

Robert Crawford is Associate Professor and Head of the School of Communication at University of Technology, Sydney, Australia.

Catherine Demangeot is Senior Lecturer in Marketing at University of Strathclyde, UK.

Giana M. Eckhardt is Professor of Marketing at Royal Holloway, University of London, UK.

Charlene Elliott is Associate Professor of Communication Studies and Canada Research Chair at University of Calgary, Canada.

Patricia Gayá Wicks is Senior Lecturer in Management at University of Bristol, UK.

Christine Griffin is Professor of Social Psychology at University of Bath, UK.

Morris B. Holbrook is the William T. Dillard Professor Emeritus of Business at Columbia University, USA.

H. Rika Houston is Professor of Marketing at California State University, Los Angeles, USA.

Elif Izberk-Bilgin is Associate Professor of Marketing at University of Michigan-Dearborn, USA.

Eva Kipnis is Senior Lecturer in Marketing and Advertising at Coventry University, UK.

Dannie Kjeldgaard is Professor of Consumer Culture at Southern Denmark University, Denmark.

Maria Kniazeva is Associate Professor of Marketing at University of San Diego, USA.

Sidney J. Levy is the Coca-Cola Distinguished Professor of Marketing at University of Arizona, USA.

Alfons van Marrewijk is Professor of Business Anthropology at VU University Amsterdam, Netherlands.

Laurie A. Meamber is Associate Professor of Marketing at George Mason University, USA.

Sofie Møller Bjerrisgaard is Head of Partner Relations at Business Kolding, Denmark.

Agnes Nairn is Professor of Marketing at EM-Lyon Business School, France.

Lisa Peñaloza is Professor of Marketing at Kedge Business School, Bordeaux, France.

Lynne Pettinger is Assistant Professor of Sociology at University of Warwick, UK.

Jonathan E. Schroeder is the William A. Kern Professor of Communications at Rochester Institute of Technology, USA.

John F. Sherry, Jr. is the Raymond W. & Kenneth G. Herrick Professor of Marketing at University of Notre Dame, USA.

Michael L. Silk is Reader in Education at University of Bath, UK.

1 Introduction

Jonathan E. Schroeder

This book brings together a curated selection of papers on brands and branding published in the innovative, interdisciplinary journal *Consumption Markets & Culture*, together with four new chapters by leading thinkers in brand research. The goal is to provide an overview of important developments in branding and brand research over the past 15 years, as well as a close look at creative thinking about brands and their role in consumption, markets, and culture. With contributions from marketing academics, consumer researchers, management scholars, sociologists, branding consultants, anthropologists, and a filmmaker, the book reflects the wide-ranging interest in branding.

Branding has grown tremendously in the past decade. Branding has emerged as a cornerstone of marketing practice and corporate strategy. In addition, researchers in sociology, geography, anthropology, history, marketing, management, organization, and even literature have embraced branding as a key imperative of our era, and are eager for ideas and insights. Whereas there are a growing number of handbooks, companions and encyclopedias of branding, this book provides a diverse look at branding processes and practices from four distinctive perspectives – cultural, corporate, critical, and consumer – in ways that expand the ways that brands can be thought about and managed. *Brands: Interdisciplinary Perspectives* offers a significant contribution by organizing brand research into the four perspectives – cultural, corporate, consumer, and critical – in one volume. As far as I know, this is the first use of such a typology, which should prove useful for synthesizing the burgeoning literature on branding, and spurring creative insights into brands.

Overview of the book

This collection takes advantage of the enormous interest in brands and branding, and capitalizes on *Consumption Markets & Culture*'s rich trove of interdisciplinary research insights. The individual chapters were chosen to highlight the complexities of contemporary branding, as well as to introduce the four perspectives on brands. The authors hail from the US, Canada, the UK, Denmark, Finland, France, the Netherlands, and Australia.

This book offers the reader a topical introduction to research and thinking on branding from interdisciplinary perspectives. The chapters deal with leading consumer brands such as Disney, eBay, Guinness, McDonald's, Nike, and Starbucks, as well as key branding topics such as celebrity branding, corporate branding, place branding, and retail branding. This collection should be of interest to scholars, MBA students, and researchers in branding, marketing, consumer research, communication, sociology, anthropology, management studies, and media studies, as well as brand managers and anyone interested in the role brands play in our lives and in culture. It might also serve as a supplemental introductory branding text for courses in branding, brand management, and consumer behavior.

The book is divided into four parts – cultural perspectives, corporate perspectives, consumer perspectives, and critical perspectives – each representing a different perspective on branding. Part I showcases four chapters that look at brands from a cultural approach (i.e., they consider brands part of culture, rather than primarily a management tool). Part II presents four chapters that start with a traditional corporate approach, informed by cultural issues. Part III focuses on brands from a consumer perspective, foregrounding consumers' experiences and relationships with brands. Part IV provides an important critical perspective, revealing how brands function as ethical, ideological, and political objects, beyond their strategic roles. This part is not merely critical for critique's sake; rather, it demonstrates that a critical perspective on brands remains essential for understanding brands' powerful roles in consumers' lives and cultural discourse.

Each part includes a new chapter written by an expert in the area, which reviews the chapters and places them into a wider context. These chapters provide useful commentaries with revealing connections and insights to the four brand perspectives. For an overview of the cultural branding approach, and probing critical reflection of the cultural-oriented chapters, we turn to Giana Eckhardt, Professor of Marketing at Royal Holloway, University of London. Eckhardt is a leading scholar within the cultural approach to branding, with particular expertise in global branding and ethical consumption (Devinney, Auger, and Eckhardt 2010). Her work on Asian and Chinese brands has made substantial contributions to the branding literature (e.g., Cayla and Eckhardt 2008; Eckhardt and Bengtsson 2010; Eckhardt, Dholakia and Varman 2013). She brings significant international experience to her role as commentator, as she places the cultural perspective chapters into the context of the flourishing literature of consumer culture theory, within which her work plays important roles. In closing, she offers trenchant thoughts on the future of branding.

Sidney Levy focuses on the three chapters that represent the corporate perspective on brands. Levy, Coca-Cola Distinguished Professor of Marketing at University of Arizona, and Professor Emeritus of Marketing and Behavioral Sciences at Northwestern University's Kellogg School of Management, produced many of the foundational articles on branding, including the classic "The Product and the Brand" with Gardner, from 1955, and the brilliant

"Symbols for Sale," from 1959, which is one of the most read and cited papers to appear in *Harvard Business Review*. Sixty-odd years into his research career, he continues to make contributions to the field (e.g., Levy 1999, 2003, 2014), and he remains a cherished mentor for many scholars around the world. He brings a wealth of wisdom to his commentary on corporate brands, and his perceptive insights help us understand the corporate perspective via his distinctive approach to the "technology of branding." We are truly fortunate to benefit from his vast experience – he has been thinking profoundly about brands for a long time.

Morris Holbrook is a legend within consumer research. His prolific output mapped much of the contemporary intellectual landscape of marketing and consumer behavior scholarship. Among his many, many scholarly contributions include a number of classic papers on branding (e.g., Berthon, Holbrook, and Pitt 2007; Chaudhuri and Holbrook 2001), as well as foundational work that helped prepare the groundwork for the consumer perspective, shifting attention away from producers and toward consumers as objects of interest for brand researchers (e.g., Holbrook 1987). After a long, illustrious, and productive career at Columbia Business School, Holbrook recently retired, but remains active, as his wonderful, winsome, and witty commentary on the consumer perspective chapters attests.

Anthropologist John F. Sherry, Jr. has produced an interdisciplinary body of work at the center of contemporary consumption studies. He has successfully managed two worlds – the corridors of academic research and realms of practical consulting. In addition, he has made substantial contributions to both anthropology and marketing; indeed, he holds concurrent appointments as Professor of Anthropology and the Raymond W. & Kenneth G. Herrick Professor of Marketing at University of Notre Dame. He has been a pioneer in bringing anthological insight into consumer research. Among his many publications, his work on service branding (Kozinets et al. 2002; Sherry 1998), brand meaning (e.g., Sherry 2005), and brand strategy (Brown, Kozinets, and Sherry 2003) are particularly noteworthy in the branding context. His eloquent assessment of the critical chapters highlights his intellectual vision, and provides rich insights into how multiple perspectives illuminate brands and branding.

Brand research: four perspectives

Brands and branding occupy key roles in marketing, management, and strategy. Furthermore, branding, referring to the process of bringing attention to a product, company, concept, person, or cause, has become an everyday term. The American Marketing Association defines brands as a "name, term, sign, symbol, or design, or a combination of them, intended to identify the goods and services of one seller or group of sellers and to differentiate them from those of competition." However, brands and branding are not just managerial tools or marketing concepts; they represent a contested cultural, managerial, and scholarly arena. Understanding brands and branding implies an awareness of basic cultural processes that affect contemporary brands, including historical context, ethical concerns, consumer response, and regulation.

Recent research on brands and branding has opened up to encompass cultural, sociological, and theoretical analysis that both complements and complicates corporate, economic, and managerial approaches. Brands can be seen to have representational and rhetorical power both as valuable cultural artifacts and as engaging and deceptive bearers of meaning and value, reflecting broad societal, cultural, and ideological codes. From a cultural perspective, brands are not only mediators of cultural meaning; brands themselves have become ideological referents that shape cultural rituals, economic activities, and social norms. For example, strong brands develop normative ideals for the way people talk, think, and behave – their goals, thoughts, and desires. Brands may pre-empt cultural spheres of religion, politics, and myth, as they generally promote an ideology linked to economic, political, and theological models that equate consumption with happiness (Schroeder 2009).

Research and thinking about brands and branding can be divided into four perspectives: corporate perspectives, consumer perspectives, cultural perspectives, and critical perspectives. These four perspectives demonstrate the growing interdisciplinary interest in brands, and how brand research sheds light on basic issues of consumer agency, consumer behavior, and consumer culture. They also signal a move away from a focus on the consumer-brand dyad, toward broader social, cultural, and theoretical concerns. Studies that extend brand research into cultural and historical realms may provide an essential bridge between our understanding of, on the one hand, value residing within the product or producer intention, or, on the other, value created by individual consumers or brand communities.

Central issues in contemporary research in brands and branding include: (1) conceptual and ideological tensions between corporate brand management and research into brand culture; (2) theoretical issues of brands from interdisciplinary perspectives; (3) brands in transition economies such as China, India, and post-Soviet Russia; and (4) debates over consumer agency, co-creation, and consumer exploitation within global brand culture. Greater awareness of the associations between the traditions and conventions of culture and the production and consumption of brands helps to position and understand branding as a global representational system.

The cultural perspective

The cultural perspective considers brands part of culture, rather than primarily a management tool. A cultural perspective reveals how branding has opened up to include cultural, sociological, and theoretical inquiry that both complements and complicates economic and managerial analysis of branding. In addition, cultural research on branding values historical perspectives, often missing from managerial research (e.g., Bently, Davis, and Ginsburg 2008; Manning 2010; Moore and Reid 2008; Schroeder and Salzer-Mörling 2006). An emphasis on culture forms part of a larger movement within the brand research canon, reinforcing a basic premise that culture and history can provide necessary context to corporate perspectives of branding's interaction with consumers and society. A key aspect of contemporary thinking from this perspective revolves around co-creation processes, and how brands interact with labor (e.g., Carah 2014; Sullivan, Gosling, and Schroeder 2013), thus overlapping with critical approaches.

Brand research from a cultural perspective occupies the theoretical space between strategic concepts of brand identity and consumer interpretations of brand image, shedding light on the gap often seen between the corporate and consumer perspectives. The cultural perspective emphasizes brand heritage, history, and legacy, and how these create associations, meaning, and value. Brand culture focuses on how brands share stories, build community, and solve problems. As cultural forms, brands evolve in accordance with changes in the historical, geographical, and social context (e.g., Aspara et al. 2014; Cayla and Eckhardt 2008; Parmentier, Fischer, and Reuber 2012). From this perspective, cultural, ideological, and political environments influence the process of building brands, brand meaning, and brand value. Along these lines, brand culture has been defined as "the cultural codes of brands – history, images, myths, art, theatre – that influence brand meaning and value in the marketplace" (Schroeder 2009: 124). Brands, understood as cultural forms, reflect people's ideologies, their lifestyles, and their cultural values.

The corporate perspective

The corporate perspective represents the majority of branding research and thinking. Many of the world's biggest companies and highly rated brands, such as Apple, Disney, Google, and McDonald's, are seen as corporate brands rather than corporate entities, each valued more for their intangible brand attributes than for any other assets. These brands are an increasingly important, powerful, and visible part of culture. Within the corporate perspective, models of brand equity, brand identity, and brand image are central to understanding issues such as brand DNA, brand essence, and brand valuation. Brand value remains a core concern for the corporate perspective (e.g., Foster 2013; Madden, Fehle, and Fournier 2006). Also, one can speak of a brand culture within a corporation, referring to how closely the organization aligns with brand values, "living the brand."

Basic branding strategy generally implies that branding decisions work together with a number of other branding elements, including the brand's essence, the brand's personality and positioning, and the brand's execution, which may include advertising, promotion, and social media. From a corporate perspective, branding is largely about communicating a message interpreted in line with the brand owner's intention. Within the corporate perspective, global branding marks an increasingly important topic. Although branding experts often agree on which features make a brand global – the use of same name worldwide and similar positioning strategies and marketing mixes in target markets – there exist some disagreements about the limits to which a brand must go before it can be christened "global." Some maintain that absolute, undiluted standardization of brand strategy and marketing mix is essential.

"Brand identity" refers to the strategic intention of the brand – what the brand manager imagines brand to be. Brand identity contributes to models of brand equity, strategic brand management, brand leadership, and "living the brand" programs (e.g., Hatch and Schultz 2008). "Brand image" concerns the image of the brand in the minds of the customer and in the marketplace. Brand image forms the basis for understanding advertising, brand community, and market segmentation models. "Brand equity" refers to the value of the brand, generally considered a function of the awareness of the brand and the positive attitudes, beliefs, and feelings about the brand. Counterfeiting and intellectual property issues remain significant concerns within the corporate perspective.

The consumer perspective

Consumer research has shown that brands are interpreted in multiple ways, prompting an important and illuminating reconsideration of how branding works. The consumer perspective has shifted attention from corporate perspectives toward a consumer perspective to understand the roles of brands and branding in the everyday lives of consumers, and the roles brands play in consumer culture (e.g., Schroeder 2009). Consumers are seen to construct and perform identities and self-concepts, trying out new roles and creating their identity within and in collaboration with brand culture. From a consumer perspective, brands can be understood as communicative objects. Cultural codes, ideological discourse, consumers' background knowledge, and rhetorical processes have been cited as influences in branding and consumers' relationships to brands.

Key concepts within the consumer perspective include brand relationships, brand community, and brand tribes. Brand relationships encompass how consumers form relationships and attachments to brands, fostered by strategic brand communication, and negotiated by consumers (e.g., Fournier 1998; Kornberger 2010; Luedicke, Thompson, and Giesler 2010; Pongsakornrungsilp and Schroeder 2011). Brand communities and brand tribes refer to groups of followers of a brand, who often get together, online or in person, to celebrate their favored brand. Brand communities are marked by shared ideals about the brand, brand routines and rituals, and a sense of obligation to the brand (Muñiz and O'Guinn 2001; Schau, Muñiz, and Arnould 2009).

Global branding and the consumer perspective often overlap. From the consumer perspective, a global brand is one interpreted by brand actors worldwide, including employees, consumers, and the media. In other words, the global status of brands is constituted by worldwide recognition, sales, or brand awareness. Accordingly, global branding refers to brand discourses on a global scale. These discourses include advertisements, brand communities, fan blogs, investment analyses, media commentaries, official brand websites, and trade fairs (Zhiyan, Borgerson, and Schroeder 2013).

The critical perspective

Critical perspectives on brands provide an important, reflective point of view, revealing how brands function as ethical, ideological, and political objects, beyond their strategic roles. This perspective is not merely critical for critique's sake; a critical perspective on brands remains essential for understanding brands' powerful roles in consumers' lives and cultural discourse (e.g., Aronczyk and Powers 2010; Arvidsson 2006; Moor 2007).

Key critical concepts include aesthetic labor, double exploitation and working consumers, and globalization. Aesthetic labor involves how consumers co-create brand meaning and value through owning, displaying, discussing, and promoting brands (Zwick, Bonsu, and Darmody 2008). Further, consumers produce much labor reviewing brands, often via online platforms, such as Amazon, Facebook, TripAdvisor, Twitter, and Yelp!. This labor has led to concerns over "double exploitation" of workers, in that first their labor is exploited for pay, and then their aesthetic labor is exploited for free, turning them into "working consumers." From this perspective, if brands are co-created by consumers and companies, then consumers ought to benefit economically from the value they help create for brands (Cova and Dalli 2009).

A common criticism of brands and branding focuses upon globalization and its homogenizing effects on local and indigenous economies and markets. Global brands often represent imperial desires, from a critical perspective, colonizing weaker, local brands without global budgets or brand strategists, leading to a global brand landscape in which Western brands dominate (e.g., Foster 2008). In addition, the rise of super brands such as Amazon, Facebook, and Google may lead to less consumer choice. Conspicuous consumption of brands, including luxury brands, may lead to consumer discontent by social inequality more visible in daily life, particularly for young consumers. Another line of criticism concerns the expansion of brands and a branding logic into a wide range of institutions, including hospitals, nations, politics, and personal lives. Social media tends to encourage branding in one's own online life, via Facebook, Twitter, and many other platforms. Brand relationships and brand communities have been criticized as fostering relationships with corporate, for-profit entities, as well as celebrity brands, rather than with friends and family, promoting online brand communities over local communities.

Conclusion

These interdisciplinary perspectives encompass how brands articulate, embody, and embrace cultural contradictions and existential tensions (Holt and Cameron 2010). Furthermore, as can be seen in Western brands' impact on global culture, global branding practices influence local culture. A thorough analysis of brands derives not only from networks of users, producers, and other brand builders, but also from local and global events, such as definitive moments in a nation's history, consumer boycotts, and anti-globalization movements.

This collection reveals how brands, brand meanings, and brand values can be understood as cultural, consumer, corporate, and critical objects. Together, the chapters offer a perceptive map for future thinking about brands. Everyone who is interested in brands is encouraged to develop multiple perspectives in order to understand brands as a fundamental aspect of contemporary consumer culture and corporate strategy. Crucial concerns for future work on brands and branding include the growth of social media and digital culture, co-creation of brands, brand measurement and value, brands in emerging economies, and the psychological, interpersonal, and cultural effects of consumers' relationships with brands.

References

Aronczyk, Melissa, and Devon Powers, eds. 2010. *Blowing Up the Brand: Critical Perspectives on Promotional Culture*. New York: Peter Lang.

Arvidsson, Adam. 2006. *Brands: Meaning and Value in Media Culture*. London: Routledge.

Aspara, Jaakko, Hanna-Mari Aula, Janne Tienari, and Henrikki Tikkanen. 2014. "Struggles in Organizational Attempts to Adopt New Branding Logics: The Case of a Marketizing University." *Consumption Markets & Culture*. Available at: www.tandfonline.com/doi/full/10.1080/10253866.2013.876347#.VA83Iecbr7c (accessed September 10, 2014).

Bently, Lionel, Jennifer Davis, and Jane C. Ginsburg, eds. 2008. *Trade Marks and Brands: An Interdisciplinary Critique*. Cambridge: Cambridge University Press.

Berthon, Pierre, Morris B. Holbrook, James M. Hulbert, and Leyland F. Pitt. 2007. "Viewing Brands in Multiple Dimensions." *MIT Sloan Management Review* 48 (2): 37–43.

Brown, Stephen, Robert Kozinets, and John F. Sherry, Jr. 2003. "Teaching Old Brands New Tricks: Retro Branding and the Revival of Brand Meaning." *Journal of Marketing* 67 (3): 19–33.

Carah, Nicholas. 2014. "Brand Value: How Affective Labour Helps Create Brands." *Consumption Markets & Culture* 17 (4): 346–366.

Cayla, Julien, and Giana M. Eckhardt. 2008. "Asian Brands and the Shaping of a Transnational Imagined Community." *Journal of Consumer Research* 35: 216–230.

Chaudhuri, Arjun, and Morris B. Holbrook. 2001. "The Chain of Effects from Brand Trust and Brand Affect to Brand Performance: The Role of Brand Loyalty." *Journal of Marketing* 65: 81–93.

Cova, Bernard, and Daniele Dalli. 2009. "Working Consumers: The Next Step in Marketing Theory?" *Marketing Theory* 9 (3): 315–339.

Devinney, Timothy, Pat Auger, and Giana M. Eckhardt. 2010. *The Myth of the Ethical Consumer*. Cambridge: Cambridge University Press.

Eckhardt, Giana M., and Anders Bengtsson. 2010. "A Brief History of Branding in China." *Journal of Macromarketing* 30 (3): 210–221.

Eckhardt, Giana M., Nikhilesh Dholakia, and Rohit Varman. 2013. "Ideology for the 10 Billion: Introduction to Globalization of Marketing Ideology." *Journal of Macromarketing* 33 (1): 7–12.

Foster, Robert J. 2008. *Coca-Globalization: Following Soft Drinks from New York to New Guinea.* New York: Palgrave Macmillan.

Foster, Robert J. 2013. "Things to Do with Brands: Creating and Calculating Value." *HAU: Journal of Ethnographic Theory* 3 (1): 44–65.

Fournier, Susan. 1998. "Consumers and Their Brands: Developing Relationship Theory in Consumer Research." *Journal of Consumer Research* 24 (March): 343–373.

Gardner, Burleigh B., and Sidney J. Levy. 1955. "The Product and the Brand." *Harvard Business Review* 33 (March–April): 33–99.

Hatch, Mary Jo, and Majken Schultz. 2008. *Taking Brand Initiative: How Companies Can Align Strategy, Culture, and Identity Through Corporate Branding.* San Francisco, CA: Jossey-Bass.

Holbrook, Morris B. 1987. "What Is Consumer Research?" *Journal of Consumer Research* 14: 128–132.

Holt, Douglas, and Douglas Cameron. 2010. *Cultural Strategy: Using Innovative Ideologies to Build Breakthrough Brands.* Oxford: Oxford University Press.

Kornberger, Martin. 2010. *Brand Society: How Brands Transform Management and Lifestyle.* Cambridge: Cambridge University Press.

Kozinets, Robert V., John F. Sherry, Benet DeBerry-Spence, Adam Duhachek, Krittinee Nuttavuthisit, and Diana Storm. 2002. "Themed Flagship Brand Stores in the New Millennium: Theory, Practice, Prospects." *Journal of Retailing* 78: 17–29.

Levy, Sidney J. 1959. "Symbols for Sale." *Harvard Business Review* 37 (July–August): 117–124.

Levy, Sidney J. 1999. *Brands, Consumers, Symbols and Research: Sidney J Levy on Marketing.* Compiled by Dennis W. Rook. Thousand Oaks, CA: Sage.

Levy, Sidney J. 2003. "Roots of Marketing and Consumer Research at the University of Chicago." *Consumption Markets & Culture* 6 (2): 99–114.

Levy, Sidney J. 2014. "Olio and Intègraphy as Method and the Consumption of Death." *Consumption Markets & Culture.* www.tandfonline.com/doi/full/10.1080/10253866. 2014.908287#.VCTRFOckMoY.

Luedicke, Marius K., Craig J. Thompson, and Markus Giesler. 2010. "Consumer Identity Work as Moral Protagonism: How Myth and Ideology Animate a Brand Mediated Moral Conflict." *Journal of Consumer Research* 36: 1016–1032.

Madden, Thomas J., Frank Fehle, and Susan Fournier. 2006. "Brands Matter: An Empirical Demonstration of the Creation of Shareholder Value Through Branding." *Journal of the Academy of Marketing Science* 34 (2): 224–235.

Manning, Paul. 2010. "The Semiotics of Brand." *Annual Review of Anthropology* 39: 33–49.

Moor, Liz. 2007. *The Rise of Brands.* Oxford: Berg.

Moore, Karl, and Susan Reid. 2008. "The Birth of the Brand: 4000 Years of Branding." *Business History* 50 (4): 419–432.

Muñiz, Albert M., Jr., and Thomas C. O'Guinn. 2001. "Brand Community." *Journal of Consumer Research* 27 (4): 412–432.

Parmentier, Marie-Agnès, Eileen Fischer, and A. Rebecca Reuber. 2012. "Positioning Person Brands in Established Organizational Fields." *Journal of the Academy of Marketing Science* 41 (3): 373–387.

Pongsakornrungsilp, Siwarit, and Jonathan E. Schroeder. 2011. "Understanding Value: Co-Creation in a Co-Consuming Brand Community." *Marketing Theory* 11 (3): 303–324.

Schau, Hope Jensen, Albert M. Muñiz, Jr., and Eric J. Arnould. 2009. "How Brand Community Practices Create Value." *Journal of Marketing* 73: 30–51.

Schroeder, Jonathan E. 2009. "The Cultural Codes of Branding." *Marketing Theory* 9: 123–126.

Schroeder, Jonathan E., and Miriam Salzer-Mörling, eds. 2006. *Brand Culture.* London: Routledge.

Sherry, John F., Jr. 1998. "The Soul of the Company Store: Nike Town Chicago and the Emplaced Brandscape." In *Servicescapes: The Concept of Place in Contemporary Markets*, edited by John F. Sherry, Jr. Chicago, IL: NTC Business Books, 109–150.

Sherry, John F., Jr. 2005. "Brand Meaning." In *Kellogg on Branding*, edited by Alice M. Tybout and Tim Calkins. New York: John Wiley, 40–69.

Sullivan, Katie, Jonathan Gosling, and Jonathan Schroeder. 2013. "On Being Branded." *Scandinavian Journal of Management* 29: 121–122.

Zhiyan, Wu, Janet Borgerson, and Jonathan Schroeder. 2013. *From Chinese Brand Culture to Global Brands: Insights from Aesthetics, Fashion and History.* Basingstoke: Palgrave Macmillan.

Zwick, Detlev, Samuel K. Bonsu, and Aron Darmody. 2008. "Putting Consumers to Work: 'Co-Creation' and New Marketing Govern-Mentality." *Journal of Consumer Culture* 8 (2): 163–196.

Part I
Cultural perspectives

2 Brand culture and branded workers

Service work and aesthetic labour in fashion retail

Lynne Pettinger

Introduction

The retail sector lies on the blurred boundary between production and consumption, and hence plays a critical role in mediating between buyers and sellers of goods. This article explores one significant aspect of branding in the retail sector: the extent to which store brands influence the work done by retail sales assistants to produce and promote consumption of the products on sale in these stores. It focuses on two main elements of sales assistants' roles in clothing chain stores: the provision of customer service and the embodiment of the workers, arguing that these are both influenced by the brand strategy of the employing organisation and hence how the market and the "lifestyle retail brand" define the context of retail service work. It uses ethnographic data gathered through working and shopping in retail clothing chain stores to contribute to understanding the labour of producing and promoting consumption. While advertising has more often been the focus of academics researching the promotion and selling of commodities (e.g. Nava et al. 1997), marketing, in particular the current fashion for branding, is of great relevance to competition in the retail marketplace.

Studies of consumption have tended to focus on the role of shopping in creating identities, positioning the shop as a site for leisure and pleasure, reflecting a traditional separation between consumption and production. Despite interest in shops as sites for consumption, pleasure, and identity development (Chaney 1990; Falk and Campbell 1997; Miller 1998), insufficient attention has been paid to work and workers in this sphere. Examinations of contemporary and historical retailing and consumption have neglected the changing nature of work for those responsible for selling and serving, and the consumption spaces they describe appear curiously empty of workers. Bowlby (2000), for example, in her important account of the development of self-service, does not consider the impact on employees of the "work transfer" (Glazer 1993) from employee to customer that is involved here. McRobbie (1997) criticises this dominance in studies of consumption of the notions of pleasure and enjoyment, noting particularly that consumption is not equally open to all, and that "those who work at producing consumption" (McRobbie 1997: 73) are often ignored. There are some notable exceptions to this (du Gay 1996), but retail work remains under-examined.

Studying the work that occurs in the spaces of consumption offers insights into both work and consumption, and the relationship between these. I argue that sales assistants are components of how store brands are performed for consumers, along with the inanimate store design, layout, and marketing and advertising practices (Birtwistle, Clarke, and Freathy 1999; Nixon 1996). By focusing on those who work at sites of consumption, locations for other people's leisure activities, it is possible to explore the relationship between production and consumption, and how consumption relations are influenced by, and in turn influence, those of work and production. By taking the store brands as a starting point and asking how these relate to the nature of work being done, the marketplace is recognised as significant for work, as well as for consumption. The study draws on a theoretical approach to the market derived from Slater (2002a, 2002b), Cochoy (1998), and recent explorations of the "cultural economy" (du Gay and Pryke 2002).

The interlinking of production and consumption in the retail marketplace is explored in two ways. First, the tendency of studies of consumption to ignore work is dealt with by asking how service work influences consumption, by reflecting marketing and branding and influencing shoppers' behaviour. Second, the tendency of studies of service work to sideline consumption and the market is addressed by examining work and consumption through the lens of branding. It is argued that efforts to sell products to customers using branding techniques to stratify shops by age, gender, class, and "lifestyle" are what brings production and consumption together in retailing. It is imperative to understand how retail sales work is located in a market environment structured around the selling of goods, and the impact this has on the work itself and who is doing it.

Methodology

The empirical data comes from a two-stage ethnographic study, involving a period spent doing participant observation as a temporary employee of Distinction[1] (referred to as "worker observation"), and a subsequent period spent visiting seven major high street chains as a customer, observing and interacting with workers (referred to as "shopper observation"). This article draws on just three of the stores studied. Both forms of observation were conducted covertly. The chains were purposively sampled to reflect a range of target customer profiles, although all were selling primarily to consumers under the age of 40. Shopper observation was conducted chiefly at two sites: a large suburban shopping centre, in South East Britain, and an area of Central London and involved over 100 visits to the sample of stores. The observational data is supplemented by "key informant" interviews with shop floor retail workers at the shopper observation stores. Company documentation was used to identify brand strategies. As such, the method reflects what Baszanger and Dodier (1997) call "combinative ethnography," which entails looking in at the research field and gathering data in different ways to produce an "inventory of possible situations" (Baszanger and Dodier 1997: 17). The ethnographic research is reported predominantly through the use of vignettes to encapsulate a particular phenomenon that was witnessed on numerous occasions. Such vignettes are indicative of observations and are not the only possible examples that could have been given. On occasion, when general tendencies are being discussed, a suitably short vignette was not available or appropriate, and here several observations have been summarised.

The dual ethnography is a particularly appropriate methodology for understanding customer service work, as recognition of the multiple competing roles and identities that coexist on the shop floor is built into the research design. The focus here is on workers and customers, rather than on the organisation and management. Ethnographies situated in shops have been used to research customers rather than workers (DeNora and Belcher 2000; Miles 1996; Miller 1998). The "success" or otherwise of customer service initiatives and brand strategies is dependent upon their impact on customers and consequent contribution to sales, and therefore understanding the customer's perspective is essential to making sense of customer service work, as acknowledged by organisations themselves in their use of "mystery shoppers." However, the interactions between workers and customers are critical here, and I make use of the contrasting images that can be produced of the same site when viewed from the perspective of different players.

Production and consumption

Bauman suggests that society is dominated by consumption. He argues for a strict partition between production and consumption, and argues that con-sumerism has taken the place of production and wage labour (Bauman 1998: 23). Individuals interact with society and the social system as consumers rather than producers (Bauman 1992: 49). The separation of production and consumption transforms consumption into something that enables self-expression and is comfortable and pleasurable (Leach 1994: 148). Consumption has been thought of as cultural, part of a system of signs (Baudrillard 1988: 47), distinct from social structures with aesthetic criteria dominating (Bauman 1998; Lash and Urry 1994).

However, seeing consumption as purely "cultural" is problematic, as work is involved in every aspect of consumption (Burrows and Marsh 1992). Furthermore, consumption is mediated by the market, particularly by corporations (Slater 1997). This means that consumption cannot be separated from the economic sphere. The changing nature of work and the prevalence of service sector work at the juncture between production and consumption problematise any tendency to make sharp distinctions between these. A divide between production and consumption ignores the complexity of interactions between work and consumption: consumers are workers at different moments, and consumption relies on production, production on consumption.

On the other hand, an excessive focus on production and concomitant relative neglect of consumption, as implied by Sayer and Walker (1992), for example, in their analysis of the place of retail in the service sector, is also problematic. The work of consumption is sidelined, as the only work that matters in this view is that done by paid workers in the public domain. Furthermore, the role of consumption in influencing production is also sidelined (e.g. in terms of how "just in time" production allows supply to respond to demand) (Cheng and Podolsky 1996). Particularly in the field of retail, production and consumption have been seen as coming together, for example: "[w]e are increasingly implicated in producing what we consume, as the line between production and consumption blurs" (Leadbeater 1999: 25) (i.e. the customer becomes more involved in the production process). Such general statements require empirical investigation, which this article seeks to provide.

Culture and economy

Recent academic work has begun to acknowledge the contribution of the cultural to the economic domain, although this has been seen as taking different forms. An essential division lies between those who conceptualise culture and economy as distinct concepts (Bradley and Fenton 1999; Ray and Sayer 1999; Warde 2002) and those who argue for the existence of a "cultural economy" (i.e. an economy performed through cultural means) (du Gay and Pryke 2002; Slater 2002a, 2002b), presented by Slater as meaning "economic and cultural categories are merged within the structures of market relations and micro-economic action" (Slater 2002b: 60). Du Gay and Pryke (2002) stake a similarly strong claim for this relationship between culture and economy – that economies are "performed and enacted by the very discourses of which they are supposedly the cause" (du Gay and Pryke 2002: 6). In this account, economy and culture coalesce in such a way as to force the inclusion of culture in consideration of the economic domain. Slater (2002b) uses the example of marketing to illustrate this, which I consider in detail in the section on branding, below.

Not all agree with conceptualising the relationship between culture and economy as a blurring of boundaries or coming together of the two fields. Ray and Sayer (1999), for example, contend that economic logic is distinctive in having an instrumental element: "the existence of activities . . . which are simultaneously economic and cultural does not mean that the distinction is no longer valid, for it is primarily about logics and purposes of action rather than about different spheres of everyday life" (Ray and Sayer 1999: 7).

Thus, "economy" and "culture" operate in different ways, even when occurring in the same place. This is a position supported by Warde (2002), who argues that "unless we can distinguish clearly between economic activity and cultural activity, culturalization would be unidentifiable" (Warde 2002: 185).

In the empirical instance being examined here, I explore the extent to which competition in the retail marketplace, structured through marketing and branding, is enacted using cultural means, drawing on shared meanings and norms (Slater 2002a). In the sphere of branded clothing retail, the economic activities of buying and selling are influenced by the social and cultural construction of the retail market (and the work done within these stores). Before considering these questions in the light of empirical research, I will explore branding in more detail.

Marketing and the silent salesman

The branding of goods and companies have, to some extent, reduced the need for active "selling" by workers; customers, in many instances, already know what products they want, from which stores. Within the self-service system that operates in chain store clothing retail (see below), the "silent salesman" replaces a human relationship between customer and retailer: "[i]nstead of speaking, the silent salesman unchangingly is, shows, subtly presents and offers" (Bowlby 2000: 37). Forms of promotion, such as advertising and marketing, are thereby important components of the selling process, involving assessing and meeting the "needs" of the buyer (Gilbert 1999: 27), even if those "needs" are created by marketing itself.

Marketing, alongside selling techniques, visual display, product design, and advertising (Mort and Thompson 1994: 107), is integral to retailing. Marketing is a part of a "promotional culture," where "the boundary between sign and object is blurred" (Wernick 1991: 184). It involves creating, assessing, and meeting consumers' "needs" for products. Cochoy talks of the mediating role played by marketers themselves as "halfway between producers and consumers . . . disciplining (mastering/codifying) the market economy" (Cochoy 1998: 125). He examines the historical evolution of the discipline of marketing as a "science" of distribution (Cochoy 1998: 204). Cochoy suggests that marketing entails "performing" the economy (i.e. influencing profit and sales) "without direct use of economic frameworks" (Cochoy 1998: 216), even if always in the service of the economic.

Marketing operates at the level of both production and consumption, argues Slater, its central aim being to make an object "meaningful and desirable within specific social relations" (Slater 2002a: 247), hence creating a cultural "value" for the product. Yet, this cultural value, given the centrality of the profit motive to the firm, has an economic motivation. Slater (2002a, 2002b) argues that markets are not comprehensible to economic actors (in this case, those who produce advertising and marketing) without cultural knowledge and calculation, even if these cultural knowledges are disguised by economic discourses. Similarly, it might be argued that consumers' "reading" of marketing signals are also key. Marketing is thus a bridge between economic discourses (of sales, of profit motives) and efforts to encourage sales of goods on the shop floor.

Marketing thus requires that attention is paid to the social and cultural context of products: the object/product, the social relations of consumption and the social actors for whom the products were constructed (Slater 2002b: 73). I would add the social, cultural, and economic relations of production and of retailing must also be incorporated. I contend that the point of selling – the shop, the shop workers – contribute to the creation of meaning and context for the products being sold (i.e. the brand extends from product, to store environment, to employees). Marketing and branding are closely related, with the brand being created to market the product or company (Randall 1994: 84). Brands operate through the "forging of links of image and perception between a range of products . . . to achieve repeated exchange in a predictable manner" (Lury 1993: 87), and it is to branding that I now turn.

Branding

Brands are cultural artefacts, defined as "the process by which the cultural work is designed to function as its own advertisement . . . to create an audience for itself" (Lury 1993: 207). In the context of retail, this implies that the image of the store presented to the customer tells them about the nature of goods to be found in that store. However, this characterisation of the brand in cultural terms is somewhat deceptive, requiring an extrapolation of the brand from its social and economic context, in particular the role of the brand in structuring competition in markets. How brands are positioned as different to each other and hence how they contribute to competition in the retail sector is of particular importance.

Branding has long been a feature of the retail sector, developing from 1850 (Alexander 1970: 136), and particularly significant since the 1920s (Lancaster 1995: 141). Branding contributed to guaranteeing the markets for mass-produced goods (Jefferys 1954: 12) and relates to the growth in chain stores. The branding of organisations, products, ranges, and services is increasingly pervasive,[2] reflected in an ever-burgeoning business literature directed at "creating powerful brands," to borrow the title of one book (de Chernatony and McDonald 1998). Branding is endemic in retail and is currently the dominant strategy around which retail competition is structured. Branding is a way in which the market uses cultural means for promotion, and particularly for selling, and hence one way in which the economic is influenced by culture. In the case of the retail sector, products, ranges, and the company itself may be branded. The department store Debenhams, for example, includes all of these forms of branding. It markets itself as differentiated by "our unique combination of own-bought brands, exclusive designer ranges and leading international brands."[3] In contrast to Lury's (1993) definition of a brand, quoted above, that reflects how consumers witness the brand, the business literature stresses the brand as economic, with a brand being: "an identifiable product, service, person or place, augmented in such a way that the buyer or user perceives relevant, unique added values which match their needs most closely" (de Chernatony and McDonald 1998: 20).

The stores I have concentrated on in this article are marketed as "lifestyle retail brands," defined by Helman and de Chernatony as: "a focused retail brand, targeted at a specific market segment defined by lifestyle. The basic retail proposition is augmented with a set of added values that have symbolic value and meaning for the lifestyles of a specific consumer group" (Helman and de Chernatony 1999: 49).

The brand is aimed at a particular social group and tries to reflect the cultural values of this group. "Added values" are the cultural and symbolic associations created. "Lifestyles," a somewhat nebulous idea, are defined by the juxtaposition of elements such as education and affluence, family life cycle, urbanisation, race and ethnicity, and mobility (Kotler 1999), a combination of social and psychological concepts. Lying behind the word "lifestyle" are more sociological markers of difference, most notably social class and status. I turn now to examining the brands that form the basis of this study.

Each retail firm discussed here operates with a brand strategy. This section draws on the participant observation described in the methodology section and on textual analysis of the organisations' websites and publicly available documents, looking, as suggested by Atkinson and Coffey (1997), at the language and rhetoric that is used to signal the brand. The three stores I focus on are chain stores selling to particular segments of the mass market. Each has a presence in the shopping centres and major high streets in the UK. "Distinction," the store where worker observation was conducted, is "targeted at the top end of the mass market" (Company Accounts 2001), and analysis of official company documents reveals the prevalence of a discourse of "style" and "quality." This impression is reinforced by the aesthetics of the brand, performed through store design and layout, with fittings a mixture of pale wood and black metal, and a universal cream and black logo, and by the style and price of the garments for sale.

Cheap Chic, in contrast, selling young women's clothing, targets the "value fashion market." Here, rather than the aspirational "style" and "quality," the focus is on "fashion" and "value." For example, "value-conscious customers demand inspiring stores, competitive prices and, critically, the speedy passage of new trends from catwalk to high street" (Report and Accounts 2001). This is reflected in product style and price, and in design and layout of the store. Cheap Chic stores are large, crowded with often untidy rails, described by my key informant working at this store, Becky, as "just a nightmare, the clothes were really packed in tightly and things were constantly on the floor." The difference between the two can be conceived of in class terms, with Cheap Chic being aimed at a working-class clientele. Alternatively, the difference can be seen as one of lifestyle and age, with Distinction selling to an older, family-oriented social group, and Cheap Chic to young, fashion-conscious women.

Fashion Junction is different yet again. Retaining the explicit fashion orientation of Cheap Chic, but with a more expensive "design-led" product range, stores are styled as boutiques, smaller in size than the other stores discussed, with sparse layouts and smaller ranges. Fashion Junction's status as an aspirational lifestyle brand is strongly signalled by its ability to sell logo products. These three brands are manifested differently on the shop floor in two key ways: in terms of the customer service offered, and through the workers' style of embodiment. The next section explores customer service.

Customer service

Customer service has been studied by sociologists primarily in terms of interactions between workers and customers that are seen as characterising this form of employment (e.g. in the highly influential "emotional labour" perspective of Hochschild (1983)). The extent and nature of emotion work required of workers by customers and managers has been well documented and well rehearsed (e.g. Abiala 1999; Macdonald and Sirianni 1996; Tyler and Taylor 1998). Emotion work involves inducing or suppressing feelings in order to affect the feelings of others (Steinberg and Figart 1999: 22). Its predominance in customer service work, argues Bauman (1998), reflects a consumer society that stresses the aesthetic value of interactions, and where consumer choice is a dominant ideology. However, overemphasising the centrality of emotional demands placed on workers as the dominant feature of service work can risk neglecting other aspects of the work (Wolkowitz 2002: 499). Customer-worker interaction, and hence emotion work, happens within an intricate context of market, store, product, and non-interactional work tasks (such as setting out stock). This wider context must be taken into account. I explore first what customer service entails in the retail sector and how it relates to selling and consumption, and second how the different aspects of customer service vary according to the brand of the retail store being studied.

The expression "customer service" tends to be used as though its meaning is self-evident. Phrases such as "the company's commitment to the highest standards of customer service"[4] are common. However, it is worth asking quite what customer service entails. Even literature directed at enhancing customer service (Cook 2000) does not always provide a clear definition of what customer service means, arguing that "it is the perception of each customer that counts . . . it is often a subjective and intangible experience" (Cook 2000: 11). Good service is here defined only as "exceeding customer expectations" (Cook 2000: 25). Broadbridge includes "product knowledge, efficiency, patience, submissiveness, pleasantness, friendliness, and an attractive appearance" (Broadbridge 1991: 46) in her typology of customer service, but this still does not fully clarify what customer service work involves.

In this section, the phrase "customer service" is unpacked to show it is not a constant phenomenon, but variable and contingent on an organisation's sales strategy (as well as on training and the proximity and effectiveness of management, though these are not the focus here). Selling in the retail clothing sector involves filling in with some form of customer service where self-service is not possible. The relationship between services provided by workers and self-service done by customers is critical, a reflection of the retail "service culture," a term I use to refer to the nature and extent of customer service provision. Service culture is defined as the mix between three distinct components of customer service – self-service, routine service, and personal service – that dominates at a store and varies with the store brand. While there is a standard baseline of routine services that all stores must fulfil (to meet the exigencies of the economic exchange), the precise balance between the types of service depends upon the brand, with some stores stressing high levels of service as an aspect of their competitive strategy.

Self-service

Self-service, which developed in the post-war period (Bowlby 2000), dominates chain store retailing. It changed the nature of working and shopping by requiring customers to work in gathering together potential purchases. In a self-service system, selling is conducted predominantly by the "silent salesman" (Bowlby 2000), manifested in the retail brand and associated with marketing and advertising, rather than by the shop-floor sales assistants. Self-service entails the customer "working" in selecting products, a process described by Glazer (1993) as a "work transfer" from paid employee to unpaid end user, although this "work" is also a form of consumption "spectatorship." Hence, here, there is a blurring between "work" (loosely defined) and consumption for consumers. Later, I demonstrate how there is also a blurring between work and consumption for retail workers.

However, self-service by customers relies on work having already been carried out by sales assistants, who unpack, arrange, and tidy the rails of clothing. Worker observation revealed that the work that facilitates self-service – cleaning, tidying, preparing, and setting out stock – took up a large proportion of sales assistants' time. The work of cleaning, tidying, and replenishing stock has a dual function. Sales assistants prepare the store as a branded environment. They also do the necessary work to enable customers to serve themselves. The productive work done by shop-floor workers is prescribed by the chain store, which sets down design and layout specifications to communicate the image of the brand. Zoë, an interviewee, described how Head Office managers came into the store she worked in[5] to test that specifications had been met. The different store brands are reflected in how the stores appear, from the clean, white, and pale wood lines of the sparsely arranged, highly designed Fashion Junction, to the neon-lit, crowded rails of the value fashion Cheap Chic, to the carpeted, more sophisticated Distinction.

By setting out the branded products in order to make it possible for the majority of customers to browse and select the products they want without needing to interact with shop-floor employees, sales assistants facilitate consumption. This implicates the customer in the work of selling, as they search for the correct size of garment, carry it to the fitting room, and to the till. In summary, therefore, the work done by sales assistants to present the store involves them in manipulating the branded products, fixtures, and fittings of the store in order to produce the branded consumption space and to enable customers to easily select and purchase these branded products.

Routine service

Self-service by customers is limited by stores needing to control and monitor customers and meet the demands of economic exchange. "Routine service" refers to the essential service work that keeps the shop functioning.[6] Such services, most notably processing transactions on the till, but also monitoring fitting rooms, are described as "customer service," even though highly routinised. Routine services are combined with other functions such as control, surveillance, and monitoring customers, in particular to prevent theft. They are necessary within a self-service system to mediate customers' relationships with the products on offer, especially the till, where ownership of goods is transferred through an exchange dictated by EPOS[7] technology. The repetitive nature of routine services mean they do not vary greatly from customer to customer, or between stores, comparable to the routinised service provision in fast food and insurance sales discussed by Leidner (1993). Routine services thus play a minimal role in branding and are relatively consistent between organisations, occurring where self-service must end. Routine services can segue into more personal services or can involve personal interactions between workers and customers, brief conversations as the routine transactions are processed. I now discuss personal service, arguing that service cultures vary in the extent to which personal service replaces self-service.

Personal service

"Customer service" usually refers to more than routine services. It describes personalised interactions between unequal individuals, customers, and workers, where workers, as representatives for the branded organisation, tread a delicate line between service and selling. Personal service is the aspect of service that is most variable according to the brand strategy, seeming, in many cases, to be the marker of difference between stores. The character of personal service depends on customer demands within the more or less codified service regime of the store. While stores may have "rules" about the sorts of personal service they expect sales assistants to provide, to which customers must conform to some extent, within this personal service can be negotiated and (if the worker is amenable) pushed beyond the store rules. Services may be offered as part of a worker's routine: at Distinction (worker observation), workers were told what services they were expected to offer customers at different moments (e.g. offering further assistance to those trying on clothes). However, service provision itself is personalised, based on the interaction between worker and customer. It may move outside company strictures, into territory that cannot be directly monitored by management. During shopper observation, I explored the limits of this negotiation, demanding advice and opinions on my personal appearance. I discuss below how workers differed in their ability and willingness to provide extra services, focusing on how this varied between brands. It is worth noting, however, that this also varies between individual workers and according to how busy the store was. On some occasions, a worker may refuse to provide a particular service that on other occasions had been willingly offered. For example, during shopper observation at Distinction, where sales assistants were usually very willing to search for garments in different sizes, workers might occasionally say they were too busy, or even forget to get products they had promised to fetch.[8] There is therefore a considerable degree of scope for the extent of personal service to vary. The negotiations over personal service may produce tensions between the interests of the customers and those of the organisation (e.g. when the services being demanded by customers did not result in sales),[9] or, on the other hand, when organisational policies denied customers certain services that they requested (e.g. not allowing them to order stock at very busy times).

The range of personal services sales assistants may offer includes: looking in the stockroom, taking orders, reserving goods, exchanging, and refunding, as well as more intimate services such as giving advice. During worker observation, many customers were aware of these services and did not hesitate to ask. Others seemed surprised to be offered, or reluctant to accept. Personal services play an important role in the selling process. Services that were regularly offered were personalised in the way they are presented to the customer: "I can keep this on one side 'til later for you." "Do you want me to see if I can order one for you?" The worker made it clear that they are putting in effort on behalf of the customer. However, personal service may go beyond store prescriptions and common practice, and involve a unique and private service given to a particular customer. Giving advice is one instance of this. As a worker, I was often asked for advice on how things looked: "Is this top too tight?" "Do the colours match?" Similarly, as a shopper, I used this approach to compare customer service provision at the different stores, finding that, within the variations between individual workers, between stores at different locations and between different times of the day, reasonably systematic differences between different brands were discernible, which I discuss below. These services were variable, unpredictable, and beyond the direct control of management, as evinced by how different workers provided different levels of service to different customers.

The provision of personal service requires the worker to perform emotional labour, and demands social and cultural skills and knowledge. However, it occurs within a context of self-service, where most customers "work" themselves in facilitating their own consumption. The wider context of the stratified high street is also relevant, where stores' "service cultures" are related to their brand and marketing strategies. I explore this using the examples of Distinction and Cheap Chic, stores at different ends of the mass market.

Service cultures and store brands

In this section, I argue that the service culture of a store is influenced by its sales strategy, as manifested in its brand. The brand orientation, specifically which customer segment of the mass market a store is aiming at, affects how far self-service dominates over personal service (although routine services are largely consistent between stores). I show how personal service is more extensive at stores at the top end of the market. Throughout this section, the focus is on how the service culture is manifested to the customer, rather than the managerial ideas that lie behind it.

Stores such as Cheap Chic emphasise value and tend to provide minimal personal service. At Cheap Chic, rails were usually messy because not enough workers were employed to keep them tidy. This meant fewer people were available on the shop floor to provide personal service. Where workers were available during the shopper observation period (e.g. on the fitting room), on three of the four occasions I asked for a different size, they declined to assist and did not offer to find someone else to help, as elsewhere. Instead, they answered, "You'll have to go and look yourself" or, "I'm sorry, I can't leave the fitting room."[10] My requests were out of step with the service culture of the store, based as it is in a brand that emphasises "value," and hence limits costs to keep prices low. Workers at stores with relatively low-key service cultures may be prepared to provide customer service, but many are not experienced in dealing with demands and rarely offered assistance spontaneously. This reflects not only the store's service culture, but also its recruitment of workers. Employees at Cheap Chic were usually young and had not built up communication skills, nor were there more experienced workers to learn from. Workers here were not trained or encouraged to offer personal services that would detract from their general stock-processing and routine service duties. This leaves customers to do more of the consumption work apart from the routine till transactions. Personal interaction with workers rarely mediates between customer and products, and shoppers operate unfettered by offers of service, browsing through rails themselves and accepting low prices for the cheap fashion on offer as a trade-off against the absence of personal service.

Stores such as Distinction, in contrast, aiming at the upper end of the mass market, have service cultures that stress personal service. Workers here are trained and encouraged to perform personal services. Workers present on the shop floor tidying rails (and hence facilitating self-service) provide customers with someone able to give individualised customer service. Each hour I spent tidying during worker observation at Distinction saw several customers asking for stock in other sizes to those out, or in other colours, or for information. Personal service provision was not confined to bringing products, but involved more micro-interactions, including offering advice and being friendly. These personal services were directed at enhancing sales by providing the customer with otherwise unavailable products, and by creating goodwill between store and customer. The greater attention to personal service at Distinction in comparison to Cheap Chic was reflected on many occasions (e.g. workers offering to contact other stores in the quest for garments in the correct size).[11] By way of a caveat, it is important to note how this personal service at Distinction was not always consistent or absolute: customer demands were not always met.

The prevalence of personal service provision at Distinction, and stores similarly branded by discourses about "quality" and "service," stands in marked contrast to the relative absence of such services in value fashion stores such as Cheap Chic. Here, the service culture is dominated by self-service. The differences between Distinction and Cheap Chic reflect the continuum stores may be positioned on, between low product cost/low service and high product cost/high service outlets. However, it is not only service cultures that vary between stores. The aesthetics of the store also differ, both in terms of the design and layout (which reflect the brand and the service culture), and the way the sales assistants themselves are aestheticised.

The embodied worker

All workers are embodied in some way (Wolkowitz 2001). In the case of the clothing chain store employees studied here, this embodiment takes a particular form, often dominated by a fashion aesthetic where the retail product is worn by employees. In this section, I explore the extent to which workers embody the marketing and branding strategies through the clothing they wear at work, and through their own consumption behaviour. In embodying the brand, workers are selling in the way distinct from any form of customer service they may also provide. I use the example of Fashion Junction, contrasting the aesthetic labour performed here to the more corporate style of embodiment prevalent at Distinction and Cheap Chic. Fashion Junction is an example of a store targeting a particular market niche, offering more expensive products in highly designed environments. Its marketing strategy is mirrored by an emphasis on employee aesthetics as an extension of the aesthetics of the products and store environment.

Wolkowitz (2002) argues that the distinctive feature of service work is its relationship to the body, both the body of the service provider and the service recipient, rather than (disembodied) social interaction. The expression of branded corporate identities through aesthetics, encompassing not just the design of products and environment, but embodied in employees, has been examined in research into service organisations in the "style" service sector (Warhurst and Nickson 2001; Warhurst et al. 2000). Here, workers are seen to perform "aesthetic labour," defined as "a supply of 'embodied capacities and attributes' possessed by workers" (Warhurst et al. 2000: 4). Implicit in the definition, and explicit in the reported data, are the connotations "aesthetic" has with beauty and attractiveness. These attributes possessed by workers are mobilised by employers to contribute towards the service encounter, and their presence or absence can lead to exclusion from certain jobs. Aesthetic labour skills or attributes are reflections of particular forms of social and cultural capital and are structured via gender, age, class, and ethnicity. Aesthetic labour is a specific instance of the more general issue of the embodiment.

Corporate embodiment

The embodiment of retail workers can be seen to vary between store brands. Whether workers wear a form of uniform (Distinction and Cheap Chic) or model current stock (Fashion Junction), the embodiment of workers is part of the branding of the stores. In some instances, uniforms demarcate workers precisely as workers; they impose a corporate identity that indicates their function as a worker. Distinction and Cheap Chic both required some form of uniform, although the ultimate result is a very different form of embodiment. At Cheap Chic, the predominantly young (under 20) and entirely female workforce wear coloured shirts and black trousers or skirts, supplemented by hair and make-up styles that reflect the class, age, and gender backgrounds of the workers, a form of working-class femininity (Skeggs 1997). This reflects the customers at this "value fashion" store, and the trading style that minimises service. It manifests the low-cost brand through the lack of attention paid enforcing appearance "rules." My informant at Cheap Chic, Becky, describes how she rarely had to wear her uniform, except when the area manager was due to visit, as the store manager was happy for her "girls" to dress as they wish, and this was borne out by shopper observation.

In contrast, at Distinction, workers are embodied as "professional" working women. They must wear suits (from current stock), and are highly styled and made-up. This is reinforced by their job title ("consultants," not "assistants") and reflects Distinction's orientation towards the upper end of the mass market and service culture that stresses personal service. The limits set on the acceptable range of current stock from which workers must choose their clothes (these were restricted to the formal "business" ranges) involved a worker in promoting a corporate, not fashion, style, but still one that reflected both the Distinction brand and demonstrated part of the clothing range to customers. The appearance of workers was policed by management at Distinction (e.g. preventing workers from purchasing outfits already owned by several of their colleagues), so a wider range of current stock was demonstrated. Workers who wore inappropriate clothing risked being sent home; Jenny, the assistant manager at Distinction, was consulted by a manager at another branch where someone arrived for work in sandals, pedal pushers, a little top, and blue hair, and had wanted to know whether to let her work.[12]

Style and fashion

At Fashion Junction, on the other hand, the store and worker brand is more of a "style" identity than a corporate one, related to the products and lifestyles on sale. The worker, wearing current stock and with appropriately fashionable hairstyle and make-up, appears as a consumer as well as a worker, signalling what is fashionable to customers, and how they might look in the "right" clothes. Workers at such stores are not only fashionably dressed; they are young, usually slim, with "attractive" faces. This was not so true in Distinction or Cheap Chic, where workers did not always fulfil the "aesthetic" labour criteria of Warhurst and Nickson (2001).

Some variations in the workers' aesthetic form were discernible, according to gender and occupational position. Notably, the local labour market has an impact on who is employed: metropolitan stores tended to have a workforce that was more ethnically diverse, and with a style aesthetic that was more distinctive. For example, at Fashion Junction, hairstyles might incorporate bright colours – blue or pink – and asymmetric fringes, suggesting that the workers were less conventional and more directional than at the suburban store, where almost all female employees had long blonde hair and the men short, spiky, gelled styles. Thus, not only do aesthetic(ised) labour demands vary between organisations; geography affects taste for fashion and the precise market niche is subtly different in different places. The implications of this for the brand is that there is some flexibility within the brand that allows it to suit local conditions while retaining a recognisable core.

In all instances, sales assistants' cultural capital and social attributes of gender, age, class, and ethnicity and lifestyle are appropriated by employers, as is any tacit knowledge about clothes and customers that such workers have, in order to enhance the brand aesthetic and sell more effectively. Workers do not have autonomy over their own appearance at work, but must display a fashion competency. Different consumer behaviours are demonstrated by employees in different brands. I discussed in the previous section on customer service how consumers are implicated in the labour process. The reverse is also true: workers are also consumers. In modelling the clothing range sold by their employers, sales assistants are selling and consuming at the same time. Workers' attitudes to fashion, to shopping for clothes, and to the products sold are a diverse, but important, part of the coming together of production and consumption in retail.

Workers as consumers

Several respondents were very interested in fashion and clothes, and it mattered to them what they sold. Chris, now a manager at Fashion Junction, previously worked in two independent designer shops and described working at Fashion Junction as "this is really the basement I'd go to, I wouldn't go any lower" (Chris). Chris stridently preferred more expensive stores that were not part of the mass market ("I do like Harvey Nichols"). These tastes contrast with his current situation as a chain store employee. He was not alone in this; his colleague Phil had never been into several of the mass-market chain stores in his home town and described the clothes at Fashion Junction as "bland."

While still interested in fashion and clothes, Becky at Cheap Chic and Beth at Distinction talked about the products they sold and their own consumption behaviour in very different ways to Chris and Phil. Both shopped at mass-market stores, predominantly those similar to the store they worked at, although they may go to the more expensive Fashion Junction or similar for "something special" (Becky). They were thus very aware of the branding of the stores they worked in and of other stores on the high street. As the target market for many of the stores, it is to be expected that they were aware of the differences between them and that this awareness will influence their own consumption behaviour, both of the products they were selling and of products sold by competitors. Workers exhibit different modes of identification with the product and different consumption behaviours that, in some ways, reflected aspects of the marketing of the stores they worked in.

Conclusions

Analysis of ethnographic data on sales assistants in retail chain stores illustrates two interesting phenomena. First, it shows how there is a relationship between work and consumption: consumers work and workers consume. Both influence the selling environment. Second, it relates the construction of competition in the retail sector at the macro level, through branding, to the micro level of the shop floor. This occurs through consideration of the contribution made by workers to how the brand is presented to consumers, the labour that goes into producing and promoting the consumption of branded stores and branded products. Looking at one specific empirical context, as recommended by Bradley and Fenton (1999: 122), reveals how, in this instance, the symbolic form of the brand is executed by social actors, in pursuit of economic success. The creation of cultural meanings in the economic sphere is actively pursued. The remit of branding in influencing work and workers includes the work that is done to present the branded store and branded products, customer service, and how workers are embodied. Branding can thus be seen as a cultural tool used to enhance organisational economic performance, in a way akin to the role Slater (2002a, 2002b) suggests marketing takes, indeed as a specific instance of marketing. However, it is worth noting how the operationalisation of the brand is contingent on the social actors at the sharp end, in this case the retail workers. The discourse of the brand may therefore not be fully put into practice.

Customer service is, in part, an interaction between worker and customer but is framed by the "service culture" of the brand, expressed through the products, the store, and the work that is involved in enabling service and resulting from the economic impetus of the organisation to sell. There are significant tangible and intangible elements of the retail experience, relevant to understanding retail selling, including the nature of the service culture and the extension of the branded, designed environment to incorporate the sales assistants themselves. The relationship between workers, consumers, and the store brand is revealed through consideration of sales assistants' embodiment. The clothing worn by workers is part of the performance of an organisation's brand image, and workers' bodies are part of how the brand is communicated. Work and consumption in retail are entwined most clearly on the bodies of sales assistants. The visible consumption of the products they sell illustrates one aspect of how work and consumption coexist and bring the worker's body into the selling process. This supports du Gay and Pryke's argument that "service work is a contingent assemblage of practices built up from parts that are economic and non-economic (but always already cultural) and forged together in pursuit of increased sales and competitive advantage" (du Gay and Pryke 2002: 4).

The role of sales assistants in promoting consumption would tend to support the idea that production and consumption coexist and are co-produced. It involves reclaiming work as a critical part of consumption and market relations, operating against both Bauman's (1998) contention that work does not matter in a consumer society, and Sayer and Walker's (1992) reduction of retail to an addendum to the production process. Recognition of this must impact on studies of service sector work that do not contextualise the work within the marketplace and also studies of consumption where notions of work or selling are absent. Instead, work and consumption interact constantly in the sphere of retail.

The examination of work and consumption in retail their relation to selling is rendered especially acute when the market is included explicitly in the analysis. The links that can be traced between the brand and embodiment and the service culture reflect in this instance how forms of culture, both material and symbolic, contribute to the economic through contributing to the performance of the brand, and thereby enhancing selling. This implies that sales assistants, and the work they do, are also part of how the store is constructed as a branded environment and as an economic entity. Marketing and branding thus provide a useful framing device for the study of retail service work. Examining consumption environments such as shops from the perspective of productive work in a market environment adds a new perspective to studies of consumption. It overcomes the tendency for consumption to be abstracted from wider social relations by reminding us what others must do to enable consumption. There is scope for further research in this area (e.g. to research customers' own perceptions and attitudes to branded service cultures and the workers who provide the services).

Notes

1 A mid-market store selling men's, women's, and children's clothing and products for the home. Further details are given in the section on branding, below. Stores and workers have been given pseudonyms for reasons of confidentiality. More detailed reference details for company documents are not given, also for reasons of confidentiality.

2 Branding has spread into voluntary sector organisations (de Chernatony and McDonald 1998: 21); "employer branding" is used by companies to recruit the "right" sort of graduates (Sykes 2002). There have also been attempts to "rebrand" countries. See, for example, www.wolffolins.com (accessed 31 October 2014).
3 See www.debenhams.com/about-debenhams (accessed 31 October 2014).
4 See www.monsoon.co.uk/discover/heritage (accessed 31 October 2014).
5 Not one of the three stores referred to in this paper.
6 Although Sayer and Walker (1992) deny that it makes sense to called this service, seeing this function as "sales and maintenance work," an extension of the production and distribution of products (Sayer and Walker 1992: 61).
7 Electronic Point of Sale.
8 Distinction, Shopping Centre, 8 September 2000.
9 During worker observation, I served several customers whose demands for assistance seemed unlikely to result in a sale, and who appeared to be looking for social interaction rather than goods. In another era, such customers would have been referred to as tabbies (Rappaport 2000: 206).
10 11 October 2000, Central London; 8 October 2000, Shopping Centre.
11 For example, Distinction, 25 September 2000, Shopping Centre.
12 Worker observation, 15 December 1999.

References

Abiala, Kristina. 1999. "Customer orientation and sales situations: Variations in interactive service work." *Acta Sociologica* 42: 207–22.

Alexander, David. 1970. *Retailing in England during the Industrial Revolution.* London: The Athlone Press.

Atkinson, Paul, and Amanda Coffey. 1997. "Analysing documentary realities." In *Qualitative research: Theory, method and practice*, edited by David Silverman. London: Sage.

Baszanger, Isabelle, and Nicolas Dodier. 1997. "Ethnography: Relating the part to the whole." In *Qualitative research: Theory, method and practice*, edited by David Silverman. London: Sage.

Baudrillard, Jean. 1988. *Jean Baudrillard: Selected writings*, edited by Mark Poster. Cambridge: Polity Press.

Bauman, Zygmunt. 1992. *Intimations of postmodernity*. London: Routledge.

Bauman, Zygmunt. 1998. *Work, consumerism and the new poor*. Buckingham: Open University Press.

Birtwistle, Grete, Ian Clarke, and Paul Freathy. 1999. "Store image in the UK fashion sector: Consumer versus retailer perceptions." *The International Review of Retail, Distribution and Consumer Research* 9 (1): 1–16.

Bowlby, Rachel. 2000. *Carried away: The invention of modern shopping*. London: Faber & Faber.

Bradley, Harriet, and Steve Fenton. 1999. "Reconciling culture and economy: Ways forward in the analysis of ethnicity and gender." In *Culture and economy after the cultural turn*, edited by Larry Ray and Andrew Sayer. London: Sage.

Broadbridge, Adelina. 1991. "Images and goods: Women in retailing." In *Working women: International perspectives on labour and gender ideology*, edited by Nanneke Redclift and M. Thea Sinclair. London: Routledge.

Burrows, Roger, and Catherine Marsh, eds. 1992. *Consumption and class: Divisions and change*. Basingstoke: Macmillan.

Chaney, David. 1990. "Subtopia in Gateshead: The MetroCentre as a Cultural Form." *Theory, Culture and Society* 7 (4): 49–68.

Cheng, T. C. Edwin, and Susan Podolsky. 1996. *Just-in-time manufacturing: An introduction*. 2nd ed. London: Chapman & Hall.

Cochoy, Frank. 1998. "Another discipline for the market economy: Marketing as performative knowledge and know-how for capitalism." In *The laws of the markets*, edited by Michel Callon. Oxford: Blackwell.

Cook, Sarah. 2000. *Customer care: How to create an effective customer focus*. 3rd edn. London: Kogan Page.

de Chernatony, Leslie, and Malcolm McDonald. 1998. *Creating powerful brands in consumer, service and industrial markets*. 2nd ed. Oxford: Butterworth Heinemann.

DeNora, Tia, and Sophie Belcher. 2000. "'When you're trying something on you picture yourself in a place where they are playing this kind of music': Musically sponsored agency in the British clothing retail sector." *Sociological Review* 48 (1): 80–101.

Du Gay, Paul. 1996. *Consumption and identity at work*. London: Sage.

Du Gay, Paul and Michael Pryke, eds. 2002. *Cultural economy: Cultural analysis and commercial life*. London: Sage.

Falk, Pasi and Colin Campbell, eds. 1997. *The shopping experience*. London: Sage.

Gilbert, David. 1999. *Retailing marketing management*. London: Pearson Education.

Glazer, Nona Y. 1993. *Women's paid and unpaid labour: The work transfer in healthcare and retailing*. Philadelphia, PA: Temple University Press.

Helman, Deborah and Leslie de Chernatony. 1999. "Exploring the development of lifestyle retail brands." *The Service Industries Journal* 19 (2): 49–68.

Hochschild, Arlie. 1983. *The managed heart: Commercialization of human feeling*. Oakland, CA: University of California Press.

Jefferys, James B. 1954. *Retail trading in Britain 1850–1950*. Cambridge: Cambridge University Press.

Kotler, Phillip. 1999. *Kotler on marketing: How to create, win and dominate markets*. New York: The Free Press.

Lancaster, William. 1995. *The department store: A social history*. London: Leicester University Press.

Lash, Scott, and John Urry. 1994. *Economies of signs and spaces*. London: Sage.

Leach, William. 1994. *Merchants, power and the rise of a new American culture*. New York: Vintage Books, Random House.

Leadbeater, Charles. 1999. *Living on thin air: The new economy*. Middlesex: Penguin.

Leidner, Robin. 1993. *Fast food, fast talk: Service work and the routinization of everyday life*. Berkeley, CA: University of California Press.

Lury, Celia. 1993. *Cultural rights: Technology, legality and personality*. London: Routledge.

Macdonald, Cameron Lynne, and Carmen Sirianni, eds. 1996. *Working in the service society*. Philadelphia, PA: Temple University Press.

McRobbie, Angela. 1997. "Bridging the gap: Feminism, fashion and consumption." *Feminism Review* 55 (Spring): 73–89.

Miles, Steven. 1996. "The cultural capital of consumption: Understanding 'postmodern' identities in a cultural context." *Culture and Psychology* 2: 139–58.

Miller, Daniel. 1998. *A theory of shopping*. Ithaca, NY: Cornell University Press.

Mort, Frank, and Peter Thompson. 1994. "Retailing, commercial culture and masculinity in 1950s Britain." *History Workshop Journal* 38 (Autumn): 106–27.

Nava, Mica, Iain MacRury, Andrew Lake, and Barry Richards, eds. 1997. *Buy this book: Studies in advertising and consumption*. London: Routledge.

Nixon, Sean. 1996. *Hard looks: Masculinities, spectatorship and contemporary consumption*. London: UCL Press.

Randall, Geoffrey. 1994. *Trade marketing strategies: The partnership between manufacturers, brands and retailers*. 2nd edn. Oxford: Butterworth Heinemann.

Rappaport. 2000. *Shopping for pleasure: Women in the making of London's West End*. Princeton, NJ: Princeton University Press.

Ray, Larry, and Andrew Sayer, eds. 1999. *Culture and economy after the cultural turn*. London: Sage.

Sayer, Andrew, and Richard Walker. 1992. *The new social economy: Reworking the division of labor*. Oxford: Blackwell.

Skeggs, Beverly. 1997. *Formations of class and gender: Becoming respectable*. London: Sage.

Slater, Don. 1997. *Consumer culture and modernity*. Oxford: Polity Press.

Slater, Don. 2002a. "From calculation to alienation: Disentangling economic abstractions." *Economy and Society* 31 (2): 234–49.

Slater, Don. 2002b. "Capturing markets from the economists." In *Cultural economy: Cultural analysis and commercial life*, edited by Paul du Gay and Michael Pryke. London: Sage.

Steinberg, Ronnie J., and Deborah M. Figart. 1999. "Emotional labour since the managed heart." *Annals of the American Academy of Political and Social Science, Special Edition: "Emotional Labour in the Service Economy"* 561 (January): 8–26.

Sykes, S. 2002. "Talent, diversity and growing expectations." *Journal of Communication Management* 7 (1): 79–86.

Tyler, Melissa, and Steve Taylor. 1998. "The exchange of aesthetics: Women's work and the gift." *Gender, Work and Organisation* 5 (3): 165–71.

Warde, Alan. 2002. "Production, consumption and 'cultural economy'." In *Cultural economy: Cultural analysis and commercial life*, edited by Paul du Gay and Michael Pryke. London: Sage.

Warhurst, Chris, and Dennis Nickson. 2001. *Looking good, sounding right: Style counselling in the new economy*. London: The Industrial Society.

Warhurst, Chris, Dennis Nickson, Anne Witz, and Anne Marie Cullen. 2000. "Aesthetic labour in interactive service work: Some case study evidence from the 'new' Glasgow." *The Service Industries Journal* 20 (3): 1–18.

Wernick, Andrew. 1991. *Promotional culture: Advertising, ideology and symbolic expression*. London: Sage.

Wolkowitz, Carol. 2001. "The working body as a sign: Historical snapshots." In *Constructing gendered bodies*, edited by Kathryn Backett-Milburn and Linda McKie. Basingstoke: Palgrave.

Wolkowitz, Carol. 2002. "The social relations of body work." *Work, Employment and Society* 16 (3): 497–510.

www.debenhams.com/about-debenhams
www.monsoon.co.uk/discover/heritage
www.wolffolins.com

3 Packaging as a vehicle for mythologizing the brand

Maria Kniazeva and Russell W. Belk

> And yet it seems clear that a poet two millennia hence would certainly learn more about our world by looking at cans from a supermarket than canvases from a museum.
>
> (Hine 1995: 237)

A visit to any local supermarket reveals that the surfaces of paperboard cartons, aluminum cans, and plastic grocery bags are being used by marketers as narrative vehicles whose purposes far exceed meeting labeling requirements to provide nutritional descriptions of their content. These packages bear stories that celebrate brand origins, echo advertising campaigns, and spin autobiographical tales of the companies they seek to animate. Even a cursory look at modern supermarket shelves demonstrates that a supermarket has become a storehouse of literary text rich in motivational stories, historical tales, and artistic renderings of heroic and romantic myths. For example:

White Wave Foods' Silk Soymilk carton reminds us of a time when American women could not wear trousers. The carton glorifies "an American hero" Amelia Bloomer for popularizing the Turkish-style pants that later became a symbol of women's rights of self-determination. And a packet of Celestial Seasonings' Honey Vanilla Chamomile Tea preaches the power of persistence that may turn "hopeless failure" to "glorious success." We approach our study of packaging stories—narrative literary texts that go beyond labeling requirements—with the premise that food packages act not only as protective containers, but as important tools for marketing communications that convey values, ideas, associations, and messages to the consumer (Santino 1996; Simonson and Schmitt 1997). Our attempt at unpacking packages is long overdue because the power and signification of packaging is an under-explored topic in consumer research. Thus, although the informational function of packaging labels and its power to influence immediate purchase decisions have been examined (e.g., Mazis and Raymond 1997; Nayga, Lipinski, and Savur 1998; Lin and Lee 2004; Wachenheim 2005), the role of packaging stories as symbolic communication remains to be addressed. As a cultural phenomenon, packaging is under-acknowledged (Hine 1995; Simonson and Schmitt 1997; Escalas 1998).

This paper aims to develop our understanding of the role of packaging rhetoric and to offer a theoretical framework that will explain how packaging contributes to brand conceptualizations (Fournier 1998; Brown, Kozinets, and Sherry 2003; Holt 2004). We treat packaging stories as cultural productions, similar to those of art, literature, and advertising. As such, we examine these texts as carriers of mythic content, and our inquiry concerns packaging as a vehicle for mythologizing the brand. Specifically, we address two research questions: (1) How do brands seek to mythologize themselves through the packaging stories? (2) What can consumers learn about their world from the "poetry" of packaging? To answer these questions, we will discuss how mythological structures are used in packaging texts, what myths they invoke, and what messages they convey.

In doing so, we join a stream of research into marketplace mythology, which has offered strong theoretical foundation for understanding the role of myths circulating in the marketplace (Levy 1981; Stern 1995; Holt 2004; Thompson 2004). We intend to fill in two gaps in this theoretical domain. First, because studies in this area have been mostly conducted from the consumers' perspective, we will now go "backward" and focus on how those myths offered by marketers are responsive to what consumers find absent in contemporary culture. Second, because of our emphasis on packaging stories, we will add a missing piece to studies of meaning transfer (McCracken 1988) that have neglected packages in favor of advertising. For example, work on brands (e.g., Aaker 1995; Fournier 1998) and brand personality (e.g., Aaker 1997) has largely ignored the communication function of packaging in favor of advertising claims. Research that uses the Zaltman Metaphor Elicitation Technique (ZMET) involves consumer storytelling about brands, but does not focus on stories offered to these consumers through packaging (e.g., Zaltman and Coulter 1995; Zaltman 2000). The marketplace mythology literature (Stern 1995; Holt 2004; Thompson 2004) has also neglected packaging. When Thompson (2004) discusses the primary means through which cultural meanings are conveyed into the lives of consumers, he talks about media, advertisements, conversational discourses among consumers, and practitioner narratives. Stern's (1995) study of consumption myths examines how they appear in consumer narratives and surface in advertisements. While theorizing the mechanism of iconic brand building as being rooted in storytelling and mythology, Holt (2004) emphasizes advertising campaigns as makers of mythic cultural images for brands. We seek to expand these perspectives on marketplace mythology, starting from the assertion that "prior conceptualizations of consumer myths have largely ignored the interrelationships between cultural mythologies, marketplace structures, and the interpretive predilections of key consumer constituencies" (Thompson 2004: 163). The following sections clarify terminology, provide a brief review of academic research into marketplace mythology, and present our methodology and findings.

Narrative, myth, consumer myth

From narratives to myths

Consumer researchers have borrowed from anthropology, folklore studies, and literary studies to define the three terms popular in marketplace mythology studies: narrative, myth, and consumption myth (Stern 1995). Narrative is the broadest of these and encompasses the other two. Narratives (stories) involve a structural sequence of cause-and-effect-related events. They usually have a plot and a central character (the hero). The key structural element of a narrative is a conflict that is resolved by the hero's actions and results in a state of equilibrium. Several forms of narratives are distinguished, including folk stories, historical accounts, personal accounts, and myths.

The term myth derives from the Greek word *mythos*. It is a modern prejudice that sometimes equates myth with "untruth." Myth originally referred to an authoritative speech or story and later came to be associated with ancient tales about the gods. The supernatural forces in these narratives helped people make sense of the surrounding world. Explaining the world and our place within it was, and has remained, the major function of myth (Campbell 1988). According to Campbell, there are two orders of mythology—nature-oriented and socially oriented—and both of them "teach you about your own life" (Campbell 1988: 11). From a structuralist perspective, myths also follow certain patterns: (1) they are highly symbolic; (2) they are rich in mythic archetypes such as familiar story patterns, characters, images, and experiences; and (3) they convey deep meanings (Levi-Strauss 1963).

Different academic traditions emphasize various aspects of myths; the theological approach views myths as "ideology in narrative form" (Lincoln 1999), while cultural critics and anthropologists examine myths as powerful traditional stories unfolding a culture's beliefs and worldviews (Levi-Strauss 1969; Campbell 1988). Myth was first formulated in marketing by Sidney Levy using a sociological viewpoint that a myth is "a tale commonly told within a social group" (Levy 1981: 51). This approach is enriched by a cultural perspective in Barbara Stern's (1995) definition of myths as "the culture's story stock" that derives from the culture's past and is represented by different narratives, including consumption stories (Thompson 1997).

Consumer myths

Together, Levy and Stern offer a broad structural perspective for understanding consumer myths. Levy defines consumer myths as "consumer protocols . . . that use a sociocultural vocabulary" (Levy 1981: 60). He also calls them "little myths that organize consumer reality," as opposed to traditional or "grand myths" (Levy 1981: 53). While employing Levy's definition, Stern (1995) stresses the explanatory function of consumer myths is not different from that of general myths. Thus, Stern sees the tales of consumer myths as very much "a part of the cultural fabric" (Stern 1995: 184). She also views consumer myths as "a literary production we might interpret in ways comparable to those of . . . literary critics" (Levy 1981: 49).

Levy's structural approach analyzed binary oppositions found in consumer stories about food consumption and treated them as descriptors of the mythic patterns. This approach to consumer myths derives from Levi-Strauss (1963). Stern (1995) instead borrowed from structural and poetic literary criticism and especially classifications of Northrop Frye ([1957] 1973). Her analysis of consumer myths associated them with archetypal themes such as nature's four seasons and the human life cycle.

Prior analyses of consumer myths are predominantly concerned with the content of mythic narratives (Belk, Wallendorf, and Sherry 1989; Wallendorf and Arnould 1991; Thompson 2004). This research adds to our understanding of consumer behavior by articulating mythic themes circulated in the marketplace. For instance, Thompson (2004) discusses mythic constructions of nature, technology, and science and develops the construct of marketplace mythology. Still, these approaches remain largely structural. As Brown observes: "Passé though they are, it cannot be denied that structuralist or para-structuralist approaches to literary criticism are inherently appealing to marketing researchers. Let's be honest . . . marketing is a structuralist academic discipline, or semi-structuralist at least" (Brown 1998: 154). Alternative approaches, including the more post-structural analysis of metaphors (e.g., Zaltman and Coulter 1995), do not as readily lend themselves to understanding the mythic nature of consumer and marketing tales.

The most common unit of analysis in research on consumer myths is that of oral consumer stories (Levy 1981; Stern 1995; Thompson 2004), also called consumption stories (Thompson 1997), consumer texts, consumer protocols, consumer narratives, and consumption tales (Stern 1995). Both approaches to studying consumer myths—structuralist and post-structuralist—have also been used in analyzing texts crafted by marketers. However, these analyses are focused on advertising copy and illustrations only (Stern 1995, 1996; Thompson 2004) and have yet to embrace narratives found on goods' packages. The focus on advertising texts has nevertheless made progress. These studies have identified links between myths, consumer values, and advertising (Stern 1995), articulated the relationship between marketplace mythologies and ideological agendas (Thompson 2004), and explored how myths come to be used, and not simply which myths are used in advertisements (Johar, Holbrook, and Stern 2001).

Consumer stories versus packaging stories

Consumer stories elicited by in-depth interviews represent the most common texts in analyses of consumer myths (e.g., Stern 1995; Thompson 2004). Although these stories are often examined as literary texts (Levy 1981; Stern 1995), the consumers themselves hardly regarded their words as well-crafted stories. This makes consumer tales different from purposely created works of literature such as advertising copy (Johar, Holbrook, and Stern 2001) or packaging stories. Anonymous writers of advertising and packaging narratives take time to craft their texts and invest them with meaningful messages that their companies wish to convey (Holt 2004). Consequently, we can expect these narratives to be more calculated and to offer a conscious reflection of brand personalities and consumer values (Mick and Buhl 1992; Stern 1996). This development can also be seen in the evolution of packaging.

The very first stories appeared on packages of patent medicines sold in London in the seventeenth century (Hine 1995). For instance, the container for Anderson's pills introduced their inventor and presented him as a former personal physician to King Charles I. In addition to making this royal connection, the container told that the physician learned of this remedy while on a trip to Italy, adding a more exotic foreign flavor and some magic to the pills. In America, containers with patent medicines claimed ties with secret Indian remedies, similarly investing a sense of adventure and exoticism to otherwise dull pills. The end of the nineteenth century marked the widespread use of packages for marketing products, which was evidenced by the revolutionary makeover of the mundane product of oatmeal. The transformation of what used to be a feed for horses into a desirable human food ("a delicacy for the epicure, a nutritious dainty for the invalid, a delight to the children") was "alchemy through packaging": putting oatmeal into a small box, investing the box with personality (Quaker Oats), and outfitting it with recipes (Hine 1995: 77). In a similar manner, "it was the package that raised a humble, ordinary food—the biscuit—into a position of importance on the tables of the Victorian diner" (Sacharow 1982). Thereby did Uneeda Biscuit end the bulk packaging of the old cracker barrel.

Historically, packages radically changed the marketplace into one where the selling, once done by people, was increasingly done through packaging narratives, and the package progressively had to take on the selling function in order to create consumer appeal. The immediacy and intimacy of the package to brand image and brand choice is why interest in packaging looms large in marketing research (Teague and Anderson 1995; Loureiro, McCluskey, and Mittelhammer 2002; Wansik 2003). But the focus of such efforts is on the effects of information presented in the form of labels, claims about fat content, nutritional value, eco-labels, and warning messages, and on claims related to the absence of genetically modified ingredients, not on the stories that many labels help to tell.

Methodology

In this paper, we aim to understand the power of specific marketplace structures—stories that product packages offer—which we treat as cultural productions. The context of packaging lets us explore the communication qualities of a largely ignored marketplace vehicle of meaning transfer

(McCracken 1988). Our qualitative methodology includes a close reading of narratives on food product packages that go beyond mere statements such as "fat free" and offer stories and descriptions that may engage the consumer's imagination (Stern 1995; Grayson 1997; Escalas 1998). For example, this text comes from a bag of popcorn: "Better Than Food. In 1963, Grandpa Po invented Nutra Nuts for his children as an alternative to candy. Family and friends went 'nutty' for the irresistible, all natural snack. You'll go 'nutty' for Nutra Nuts too. Enjoy!" We provide an etic analysis of packaging narratives and employ procedures for developing grounded theory (Strauss and Corbin 1998). Our initial analysis of the extensive set of over 100 narratives was conducted using several coding techniques, beginning with open coding, line by line, and by whole sentences. Axial and selective coding then led to building a better understanding of the mythological structures on which these stories draw. This helped us generate initial concepts, define starting points for the research, and center our analysis on 11 stories containing mythic themes common to our pool of narratives.

Data have been collected from food packages bought in the US supermarkets Ralphs and Wild Oats over the last two years. Products were chosen to represent a wide variety of categories purchased by consumers on a regular basis. They included popcorn and jerky snacks, crackers, rice cakes, cookies, cereal, baby food, taco shells, tea, and peanut butter (see Table 3.1). In addition, so that our stories had a common general theme, we considered only those packages that prominently contained the word "natural."

We focus purposely on food packages that make use of the highly popular claim of naturalness. From a marketing perspective, being natural is an emotionally charged category, and not a physical quality of the product. Unlike claims such as "organic" or "fresh," whose use is regulated by the Food and Drug Administration, the label "natural" lacks any specific requirements and has no official definition. It is a mythical construct that is constantly created by marketers and recreated by consumers (Kniazeva 2002; Thompson 2004). According to *Marketing News* (2004), "natural" was the most popular tag that fruit juice marketers used on their product introductions in 2004—three times as often as the label "organic."

We see naturalness as an important cultural concept. Regard for nature has changed considerably from a time when it was seen as wild, savage, and uncultured, full of dirt and primitives, and "red in tooth and claw" (Coward 1989: 148). Instead, in the West, nature has become the emotional source of all that is good (Kniazeva 2002; Thompson 2004). As such, our study focuses on appeals employing what Thompson (2004) labels the romantic metaphor of "nature as maternal power" engendering a myth of magical regeneration.

Reading packaging narratives

The main motif of the myths always relates to power, and in ancient myths the presence of gods, demons, and other supernatural forces was needed to

Table 3.1 Sample of data set

Category	Product	Parent company	Store
Snack	The Original California Natural Gourmet Turkey Jerky	SnackMasters	Ralph's
Snack	Grandpa Po's Original Popcorn Snack with Soy Beans	Nutra Nuts, Inc.	Ralph's
Snack	TLC Original 7 Grain Tasty Little Crackers	Kashi Company L.L.C.	Ralph's
Snack	Lundberg Family Farms Whole Grain Organic Salt Free Brown Rice Cakes	Lundberg Family Farms	Whole Foods
Snack	Back to Nature Chocolate & Mint Crème Sandwich Cookies	Back to Nature Foods	Whole Foods
Snack	Garden of Eatin' Yellow Corn Taco Shells	Garden of Eatin', a division of the Hain Celestial Group, Inc.	Whole Foods
Snack	Brent & Sam's Chocolate Chip Pecan All-Natural Gourmet Cookies	Brent & Sam's Cookies, Inc.	Whole Foods
Cereal	Whole Kids Organic Rainbow Rings	Whole Foods Market	Whole Foods
Tea	Celestial Seasonings Natural Honey Vanilla Chamomile Caffeine Free Herb Tea	Celestial Seasonings, a division of the Hain Celestial Group, Inc.	Ralph's
Butter	Maranatha Crunchy Organic Peanut Butter	Maranatha Natural Foods, a division of nSpired Natural Foods	Whole Foods
Baby food	Earth's Best Organic Whole Grain Oatmeal Cereal	The Hain Celestial Group, Inc.	Ralph's

symbolize the ultimate authority responsible for the social and natural order. On the surface, such supernatural forces disappeared from many contemporary myths. However, this does not diminish the importance of power. In the packaging analyzed, we find old wine in new bottles.

Many of the packaging stories position the brand through a personal brand biography that seeks to convey to the consumer that it is a warm sympathetic character. Rather than providing impersonal information, the packaging narratives offer a dialog with the customer. "I personally guarantee this tea will meet your highest expectations . . . let us know how we can serve you better," says the founder and chairman of Celestial Seasonings, who leaves his signature on the package of Honey Vanilla Chamomile Tea. "Enjoy!" invites the package with Lundberg Family Farms' rice cakes, concluding the narrative with the names of four members of the Lundberg family. But it is not a friend-friend relationship that is invoked between the two sides; it is more of a self-imposed servant-master connection. The master here is the consumer, whom the companies address not only as a familiar "you," but also with self-deprecating adjectives that, in turn, flatter and elevate the customer's majesty:

Thank you! We appreciate your purchase of SnackMasters "The original California" Natural Gourmet Turkey jerky. It's our sincere promise and commitment to provide you, our sacred customer with the finest whole-some, high quality Natural Gourmet Turkey Jerky products possible. Our SnackMasters processing facilities are located in the heart of Northern California's San Joaquin Valley. Our secret family recipe supported by our time tested "old fashioned" processing technique, emphasizing very strict quality control standards, guarantees you, our valued customer, an authentic natural gourmet meat snack that not only tastes great but is also nutritionally good for you. Our Natural Gourmet Turkey Jerky is sliced from 100% natural turkey breast meat that is 98% fat free. We have exercised every precaution humanly possible to insure your confident snacking pleasure and satisfaction. You can see, feel and taste the SnackMasters advantage.

(Quote from the package of SnackMasters Natural Gourmet Turkey Jerky)

The discourse of inverted power is strong in this narrative and implies three influential forces: a born-to-enjoy-life master, a subordinate servant, and an indifferent or deceitful surrounding world whose malevolence and carelessness can be resisted through the idealized servant-master union, in which the protective servant exercises "every precaution humanly possible," or, as the box of Whole Kids Organic Rainbow Rings cereal promises, always uses "all organic ingredients available." This is necessary to shield the master from the vices of the modern world. Thus, a mythological role of being a master is assigned to a consumer by marketers of the products, which echoes foundational writings about mythology. But while Campbell (1988) talks about mythological roles human beings have to play when they move between stages of life or enter into new professions, mythological roles of the marketplace are appointed in a symbolic response to the realities of the surrounding world. To justify such role allocation, marketplace mythology as exemplified in packaging narratives centers around the theme of the world condition—as it is viewed nowadays, as it supposedly was in the past, and as it ideally should be in the immediate future. Consequently, while playing their own role of brand signifiers, packaging stories participate in grander postmodern mythical narratives like that of the Macintosh computer as rebellious trickster (Belk and Tumbat 2005).

Myth of the world in the past

Packaging narratives depict the modern world as a deeply distorted reflection of what it originally was—the garden before agro-chemical technology. While the values of the past include family, tradition, authenticity, peace, and simplicity, the current era is associated with broken family ties that need to be restored, scientific "advances" that pose threats, constant pressure on the well-being of humans, and unnecessary complexity in everyday life.

The time motive—venerably old versus dangerously modern—strongly permeates the packaging narratives. For example, Garden of Eatin' counts the years separating it from a glorified past while announcing that it has been making its finest tortilla chips "for over a quarter of a century." The word "century" by itself carries the ponderous importance, adding momentous significance to the company's products. But it seems it does not really matter how far in the past the reader is invited to travel. As soon as the packaging narrative is able to indicate the product's ties with older times, meaningful weight is added to its content because it ceases to be just a food item and becomes a symbolic bridge between a romanticized yesterday and a prosaic present. This nostalgia theme leads us to the complexity of the relationship between the sacred and profane in the contemporary world (Belk, Wallendorf, and Sherry 1989).

"When you find a quiet moment, ease into a cup of contentment with Honey Vanilla Chamomile Herb Tea," invites the packet of Celestial Seasonings' tea. Thus, it is not the tea that the company is offering to its consumers, but a cup of gratification and soothing pleasure. This pleasure, the narrative implies, is much needed in a hectic world where a person needs to put effort into finding a moment of calm, which is necessary to survive everyday challenges.

"At Kashi," claims the narrative on the package of Original 7 Grain Crackers, "we know there's a time in the day when we need to take a moment to give ourselves some tender loving care: a minute to refuel bodies and our spirits. So, we're offering you a great-tasting snack you can feel great about." The company's crackers even come under the brand name "TLC." But this abbreviation officially means "Tasty Little Crackers," one learns from the fine print on the package. Offering a double reading of the popular acronym, the packaging narrative makes a connection between its material content and the mythical meanings it conveys. In a world where humans are forced to act and be like machines, where both the people and technology share the same need for refueling, TLC crackers stand out not as a source of necessary physiological energy, but as a means of spiritual rejuvenation. And while the package describes crackers as having attractive taste properties such as being crunchy, being "the right size for popping in your mouth," and "baked to crispy perfection," it is the constellation of metaphorical words that elevates the snack to the position of "heavenly" food. When the story repeats the word "heart" and its variation "hearty," it is not talking about the physiologically vital part of the body, but builds upon the symbolic connotations of the word as meaning love and vitality. The "heart" is used to describe the incredible efforts put into creation of the snack ("we put our hearts into bringing you . . ."). In a similar manner, when the snack is described as "hearty," it is presented as jovial and energetic.

Even TLC's combination of ingredients appears to be sacred, as it consists of seven whole grains and sesame seeds. The number "seven," long endowed with religious and mystic connotations in the West, was believed to be a magic number by the Greeks (Crump 1992). As for sesame seeds, besides their nutritional value as a good source of protein and fat, they too carry mythical associations. For example, according to an Assyrian myth, the gods drank sesame wine the night before they created the earth. And it was the now familiar exhortation, "open sesame" that Ali Baba uttered to open the treasure cave in *The Thousand and One Nights*.

The exploitation of a spiritual vocabulary can also be seen in brand and company names. Thus, the Hain Celestial Group offers a wide variety of Celestial Seasonings teas, and its "Garden of Eatin'" division makes transparent reference to the Garden of Eden. The latter, the original beautiful and worry-free home of Adam and Eve, links with the creation myth of Christianity, Judaism, Islam, and earlier religions. By marking their messages with religious connotations through the packaging rhetoric, branded food products equip their consumers with powerful tools. Religious motifs have been found to be central among loyal members of brand communities who adopt them to sustain their brand faith (Muñiz and O'Guinn 2001; Belk and Tumbat 2005), to resist the disappearance of brands (Muñiz and Schau 2005), and even revitalize them (Brown, Kozinets, and Sherry 2003).

Myth of the corporate world

The Back to Nature cookies' narrative offers a glimpse into the history of the company:

> It began very simply. In 1960 in the back of a small health food store in Pasadena, we created something people really liked: a delicious, naturally low-fat granola. Soon it was our most popular item, and health food stores across California were asking for it.

The story puts emphasis on the simplicity of the birth of the company's products, an inauspicious beginning "in the back" of an unknown local store, and the "small is beautiful" philosophy that eventually resulted in well-deserved recognition across the state.

This account goes on by indirectly contrasting the company with other firms representing the big corporate world. The latter are implied to offer unnecessarily complex products with ingredients that consumers cannot even pronounce, and to go after customers by boasting about their companies' size and making a lot of marketing noise. Here, bigness is posited as the enemy of moral goodness, and the narrative hints at the irresponsibility of the corporate world that Back to Nature positions itself against. Compromises are the province of global corporations, which estrange themselves from nature. Corporate farmers, reports the Lundberg Family Farms Rice Cakes' narrative, "burn entire fields of rice straw after harvest, polluting the air and depleting soil nutrients." They use potentially harmful pesticides and herbicides, adds the package of Earth's Best Whole Grain Oatmeal Cereal. Conventional manufacturers sabotage your health, implies the story on the package of Kashi's Original 7 Grain Crackers. It describes most conventional snack choices as being full of highly refined sweeteners, artificial ingredients, hydrogenated oils, and cholesterol. Conventional products are made with genetically engineered ingredients, warn the packages that prominently display "No GMO" labels. This critical packaging chorus is very much in line with how Thompson's (2004) informants perceive conventional medicine (i.e. represented by grim and emotionally detached doctors imposing doctrinaire, draconian, disempowering, and degenerative treatments and making the whole medical system even more adversarial and alienating).

Back to Nature's self-described mission silently declares opposition to all the negatives imposed on consumers by large corporations. Myth making in the company's narrative draws a clear line between "us" and "them" where the "us" is positioned as not being threatening, greedy, or profit-driven, much in contrast to the "them." Moreover, our analysis reveals the deliberate exploitation of the words "only," "always," and "never" that are frequently used in packaging narratives—as if sending a strong message to the reader that there is no place for compromises only in the natural world.

Myth of the natural world

The package of Lundberg Family Farms Whole Grain Rice Cakes portrays its idealized relationship with nature. Its commitment to nature extends to multifaceted framing: political, economic, and psychological. In presenting such an encompassing construct of nature, this company is not alone. All narratives from the packages selected carrying the label "natural" participate in creating the world they claim to be natural. True, real, pure, simple, wholesome—these are the meaningful descriptors that are used in the narratives while distancing the "natural" world from a fake, artificial, tainted, and mechanistic world. The truly natural world is the one providing the greatest similarity to long-gone "simpler times"; it is the world that appreciates purity of nature and that generously offers "truly flavorful, wholesome foods made with simple ingredients." Here, the reader can also hear strains of Henry David Thoreau: "Back to nature; simplify, simplify, simplify; nature is full of genius, full of divinity" (Thoreau 1947: 344).

Naturalness appears as a rich emotional construct that connects with positive contemporary images of nature. For instance, ostensibly negative descriptors obtain a positive connotation among Kniazeva's (2002) informants: brown spots on tomatoes are romanticized for being caused by insects, creatures of nature, and scarcity and seasonality of fruit are linked with the pleasure of anticipation of favorite mangos ripening. People "do not want to remember that nature can also be destructive as in deadly hurricanes and poisonous mushrooms," reports Kniazeva (2002: 101). In a natural health context, Thompson (2004) also finds nature to be a positively framed powerful mythic construction, and his informants attribute magical, regenerative powers to nature. They firmly believe that aligning with what nature has to offer for one's health lets them assert control over their lives and bodies versus losing control by being complicit in a scientized medical system.

We can see here the spiritual treatment of nature that Coward (1989) found pervades alternative medicine, vegetarianism, voluntary simplicity philosophies, the natural childbirth movement, and dietary beliefs linking food to health with a resulting reverence for magical, harmonious, whole, natural foods free of herbicides, pesticides, and genetic modification. These beliefs are, in turn, linked to puritanical American beliefs that we must take responsibility for our bodies, work hard to perfect our health, cleanse our environment and system of pollutants, and choose the foods that will make us healthy. At the same time, Coward (1989: 148) concludes that these choices embrace a purely fanciful myth of achieving health through eating. Too much is out of consumer control and dependent on the environment, so that only collective and political actions are likely to alter the food production system. But as Franklin, Lurry, and Stacey (2000) point out, "natural" is being reconfigured by branded food corporations and others in ways that serve their ends. Just as other "organic" street styles have been co-opted and appropriated for commercial ends (Frank 1997), so too have nature, natural, ecology, and environmentalism been co-opted, appropriated, commodified, and transformed in order to sell brands. Rather than attempting to fill cultural needs like Volkswagen or Apple as valiant underdogs (Holt 2004), or early Kellogg's cereal or Graham Crackers as health foods to suppress carnal urges (Wyman 1993), this is trendy opportunism.

Myth of the idyllic world

Many packaging lyrical stories collectively build up a mythical idyllic world in which not only are fields never burned, they are anthropomorphized and treated as live creatures. They are a part of Mother Earth. Our fields, describes the Lundberg Family Farms Rice Cakes package, are periodically kept out of production "so the soil may rest." In this perfect world, rice straw is chopped, rolled, and turned back into the soil to replenish organic matter, and there is no place for pesticides, herbicides, or commercial fertilizers. Like the body's purported desire to heal itself (Coward 1989), the earth is alleged to be regenerative if it is not poisoned with chemicals, scarred by burning, or tricked by genetic meddling. This is the symbolic paradise where harmony thrives and all living creatures peacefully coexist and take care of one another. "Our fields furnish essential winter habitat for thousands of migratory waterfowl. Not only are the majestic flocks beautiful to behold, they help the rice straw decompose and provide natural fertilizer"; so culminates the story from the Lundberg Family Farms package showing an exquisite appreciation of nature in its wild state.

The processing techniques are no less celebratory of the triumph of tradition. These ideal manufacturers not only would not call themselves manufacturers. They appear to enjoy living in the past; they stone-grind their grains, mill their own rice, pop their rice cakes right at the farm, and bake their cookies to crispy perfection. They "minimally process," treasure original recipes, refrain from using preservatives, and slice their jerky from "100% natural turkey." Their final products are not mechanically or automatically made, but thoughtfully invented and crafted. And if in some rare instances they are made, they are handmade from scratch. For example, the TLC crackers, asserts the narrative, are not manufactured; they are created, as from the onset they were "dreamed up," which brings them farther and farther away from a profane, mechanically calculated product and closer to that of a "fantastic" creation. To think of these snacks as manufactured is an inappropriate intrusion of the profane machine into the sacred garden (Marx 2000). This idyllic world downgrades the role of technology, elevates "from scratch" to the pedestal of ultimate naturalness, and invokes the words "nothing added" as a symbol of utmost authenticity.

Discussion

As literary productions, our packaging stories follow the basic structure of the narrative (Grayson 1997). They have a formal main character, represented by a company or a product inventor, and offer plots that take readers from their initial setting's state of chaos and crisis to the final destination of satisfaction and happiness. As cultural constructions, these stories are full of mythic archetypes: they make use of culturally familiar symbols and carry along mythic meanings reflective of cultural values. When a package informs that "the irresistible, all natural" snack was originally invented by Grandpa Po for his children as an alternative to candy, it implies how careless the world was in failing to take proper care of its children until Grandpa Po offered his solution. "Grandpa Po," here, is a metaphor for a strong traditional, extended family, the ultimate family authority, a cornerstone, the one who cements all its units together. And although packaging stories provide various metaphors and symbols, they are all utilized to arrive at the same destination—that of harmonious existence. Harmony is a desired outcome, culmination of these packaging narratives.

Our analysis of these stories leads us to conclude that marketers heavily exploit the notion of myth to give a grand sense of purpose to their otherwise mundane and commoditized products. They mythologize their ordinary staple foods by fitting them in the surrounding world. This is why myths of the world—past and modern—are so prominent in contemporary story-telling. They implicate the consumer in glamorization of the past, criticism of the present, and idealization of the desired future. Like myths of the past, they help us dream of a better world. The mechanism of such a mythologizing movement includes employing narrative structures, filling them with mythic archetypes, and thereby constructing messages full of hope and deep meaning (see Table 3.2).

Empowering and ennobling consumers through myths

We support findings by other researchers that commercial storytelling is not an innocent exercise in word crafting, but an important brand-building function (Holt 2004; Thompson 2004). In that sense, we extend the latest and most comprehensive examination of commercial storytelling offered by Holt (2004), in which he focused on advertising texts and concluded that they contribute to myth making by providing what is needed or eroded in everyday beliefs. Companies play significant roles in creating these myths by shaping the meanings of their brands to offer that which consumers find missing or threatened in their culture. Crafting their packaging stories, firms mythologize their brands by poetically reflecting societal dreams, hopes, and wishes. Moreover, we propose that contemporary commercial storytellers revisit traditional mythology in order to make an illusion of empowering and ennobling consumers as masters served by subservient, if not worshipful, brands. By doing so, they collectively create a new grand postmodern marketplace myth—that of a powerful regal consumer.

As a first step in this process (see Figure 3.1), a traditional myth of an ultimate authority is used to offer a contemporary vision of power distribution in the marketplace. This action gives birth to the myth of inverted power, which suggests the master–servant relationship as that of being reflected by the consumer–firm relationship. The myth-making process then centers on this newly created myth of inverted power and continues by embedding products with mythical meanings meant to magnify mythological roles allocated to products. Finally, when the two—products and their consumers—meet, all the significance attached by storytellers to the products transforms otherwise powerless consumers into powerful marketplace players. As a result, newly empowered consumers can temporarily escape imposed world conditions by shaping their personal myths and servicing their individual lives. Thus, myths of the past are meaningfully used to serve the present.

Specifically, our findings reveal two major contributions offered by packaging narratives: they empower consumers by providing spiritual rejuvenation and representing an antidote to all the forces threatening to destroy nature. In truth, there may be little that an individual consumer can do about global warming, threats to endangered species, and the proliferation of chemical and genetic uncertainties in the world. But packaging narratives offer a clear and simple symbolic affirmation of values that oppose such ominous trends: buy this product. All these myths are communicated by utilizing archetypal symbols associated with a romanticized past where harmony thrived, relationships were personal, corporate compromises were

Table 3.2 Marketplace myths as cultural constructions

	Myth of the world in the past	*Myth of the modern world*
Archetypes	Gods	Corporations
	Garden	Agro-chemical farms
	Paradise	Labs
	Nature	Technology
	Mother and father	Strangers
	Peace	Stress
	Soul	Dollar
	Heart	Robots
Descriptors	Wholesome	Chaotic
	Romantic	Prosaic
	Slow	Hectic
	Happy	Worried
	Small	Large
	Pure	Tainted
	Natural	Artificial
	Idyllic	Sinful
	Magical	Scientific
	Quiet	Noisy
	Generous	Greedy
	Creative	Mechanistic
	Safe	Dangerous
	Real	Fake
Values	Tradition	Science
	Authenticity	Change
	Simplicity	Complexity
	Centered coexistence	Survival
	Modesty	Success
	No compromises	Compromises
	Harmony	Profit
	Relationship	Partnership
	Family	Business
	Eternity	Now

unheard of, technology had not come to dominate, and families were strong. These myths are offered by the companies to counterbalance the social realities of the contemporary world, which are far from the intimate paradise of an idyllic past and desired future.

When Campbell talked about the meaning of "being mythologized," he explained it by making reference to people: "When a person becomes a model for other people's lives, he has moved into the sphere of being mythologized" (Campbell 1988: 15). Our study supports this mythologizing mechanism in relation to brands that are being made to exemplify life-motivating models. Similarly to Campbell's interpretation of myths as offering life models, those myths that we detected in the packaging narratives aim to provide meaningful guidance and become directing agents (Campbell 1997).

From our analysis of these narratives, it is clear that myth-making activity engages two major participants—companies and consumers—and that it is the consumer who finishes the challenging postmodern marketplace activity described by Firat and Venkatesh:

> Marketing is the major practice in society that consciously resignifies words, terms, and (brand) names. Consider the use of words, such as, "natural," "unique," "individual," and "you!" in the context of representing brand images for products that are used to change one's "natural" features and convince "individuals" into buying and consuming the same products that millions of others use, yet make them feel "unique" or "you!" (that is, themselves).
>
> (Firat and Venkatesh 1993: 230)

It also follows from our analysis that the process of corporate myth making offers consumers the building blocks necessary to make sense of the fragmentary postmodern age (Firat and Venkatesh 1995).

As a result of such collaborative myth making, it is becoming increasingly challenging for marketers to craft textual stories that link together the personalities of products (Aaker 1997) to the personalities of those consuming

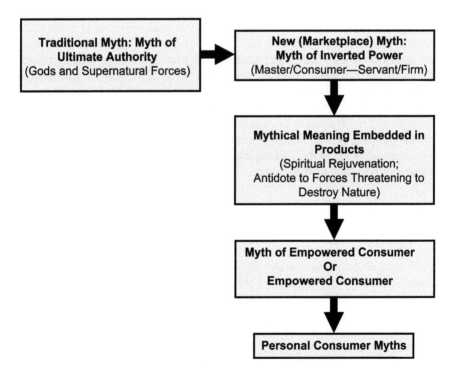

Figure 3.1 Empowering consumers through packaging narratives

them. The myth of being natural is just one such example. It is created not only by descriptions of the heavenly delicious taste of the product, but also by opposing multiple countermyths. Marketers explicitly or implicitly refer to these countermyths on their packaging. By stating that their foods contain no genetically modified material, they promulgate the countermyth that other brands do. By stressing that they are, for example, "Lundberg Family Farms," they suggest a countermyth that other brands are mechanistic corporate farms and factories. By glamorizing the natural origin of their ingredients, they oppose a countermyth that other brands use artificial components in their products. By simultaneously addressing numerous countermyths in one packaging narrative, marketers offer a multidimensional poetry of packaging that helps their ultimate readers—consumers—finish the myth-making process by subconsciously screening the literary material in a search for desired symbolic cues and by creatively inventing and reinventing multiple myths.

A multiplicity of building material for creating desired consumer myths is what a postmodern consumer arguably needs. These building materials are not the uniform myths of Holt's (2004) iconic brands, the singular brand personalities of Aaker (1997), nor the deep self-transformative myths of Thompson (Thompson and Troester 2002; Thompson 2004). Rather, "mythology is the song. It is the song of the imagination" (Campbell 1988: 22). In the world where "there is no longer a metanarrative, one dominant ideology, philosophy or agenda" and where fragmented and heterogenized markets and consumers rule (Fırat and Venkatesh 1993), there is no such thing as a monomyth regarding nature that marketers can borrow, dust off, embellish, and multiply. As previous studies have demonstrated, to associate the product with the mythical natural world, one consumer may need to envision a grandfather guardian, another a bruised tomato representing the non-GMO natural product (Kniazeva 2002). But as soon as marketers manage to invest their brands—through either advertising or packaging narratives—with multiple seeds that creative consumers can skillfully cultivate into desired plants of their own, the communicative job of the postmodern marketer will be done. The myth-making consumer will take it from there.

Conclusion

By examining the packaging narratives as a means of mythical meaning transfer, our study has focused entirely on the verbal "seeds" disseminated by marketers. But current research suggests there is a necessity for marketers to more holistically recognize that consumers are not just markets and segments, but whole people. Consumers negotiate their lives while making sense of commercial messages, assert Mick and Buhl (1992), in their meaning-based model of consumers' advertising experiences. As such, they "do not choose brands, they choose lives," concludes the study of consumer brand relationships (Fournier 1998) that defines a brand as consumers' collections of perceptions and a source of added meanings in consumers' lives. Moreover, consumers manipulate and hybridize marketer-created brand narratives (Muñiz and Schau 2005) and use them to sacralize, individualize, and build brand communities (Brown, Kozinets, and Sherry 2003). That is why the next logical step should be to examine how the verbal seeds planted by marketers are metaphorically cultivated by consumers.

References

Aaker, David A. 1995. *Building strong brands*. New York: The Free Press.

Aaker, Jennifer. 1997. "Dimensions of brand personality." *Journal of Marketing Research* 34 (August): 347–57.

Belk, Russell W., and Gülnur Tumbat. 2005. "The cult of Mac." *Consumption Markets & Culture* 8 (3): 205–17.

Belk, Russell W., Melanie Wallendorf, and John F. Sherry, Jr. 1989. "The sacred and the profane in consumer behavior: Theodicy on the odyssey." *Journal of Consumer Research* 16 (June): 1–38.

Brown, Stephen. 1998. *Post modern marketing two: Telling tales*. London: Thompson.

Brown, Stephen, Robert V. Kozinets, and John F. Sherry Jr. 2003. "Teaching old brands new tricks: Retro branding and the revival of brand meaning." *Journal of Marketing* 67 (July): 19–33.

Campbell, Joseph. 1988. *The power of myth*. New York: Doubleday.

Campbell, Joseph. 1997. *The mythic dimension: Selected essays 1959–1987*. San Francisco, CA: HarperCollins.

Coward, Rosalind. 1989. *The whole truth: The myth of alternative health*. London: Faber & Faber.

Crump, Thomas. 1992. *The anthropology of numbers*. Cambridge: Cambridge University Press.

Escalas, Jennifer. 1998. "Advertising narratives: What are they and how do they work?" In *Representing consumers: Voices, views and visions*, edited by Barbara B. Stern. London: Routledge.

Fırat, A. Fuat, and Alladi Venkatesh. 1993. "Postmodernity: The age of marketing." *International Journal of Research in Marketing* 10: 227–49.

Fırat, A. Fuat, and Alladi Venkatesh. 1995. "Liberatory postmodernism and the reenchantment of consumption." *Journal of Consumer Research* 22 (December): 239–67.

Fournier, Susan. 1998. "Customers and their brands: Developing relationship theory in consumer research." *Journal of Consumer Research* 24 (March): 343–73.

Frank, Thomas. 1997. *The conquest of cool: Business culture, counterculture, and the rise of hip consumerism*. Chicago, IL: University of Chicago Press.

Franklin, Sarah, Celia Lury, and Jackie Stacey. 2000. *Global nature, global culture*. London: Sage.

Frye, Northrop. [1957] 1973. *Anatomy of criticism: Four essays*. Princeton, NJ: Princeton University Press.

Grayson, Kent. 1997. "Narrative theory and consumer research: Theoretical and methodological perspectives." *Advances in Consumer Research* 24: 67–70.

Heath, Joseph, and Andrew Potter. 2005. *Nation of rebels: Why counterculture became consumer culture*. New York: Harper Business.

Hine, Thomas. 1995. *The total package: The secret history and hidden meanings of boxes, bottles, cans, and other persuasive containers*. Boston, MA: Back Bay Press.

Holt, Douglas B. 2004. *How brands become icons: The principles of cultural branding.* Cambridge, MA: Harvard Business School Press.

Johar, Gita Venkataramani, Morris B. Holbrook, and Barbara B. Stern. 2001. "The role of myth in creative advertising design: Theory, process, and outcome." *Journal of Advertising* 30 (2): 1–25.

Kniazeva, Maria. 2002. "Naturalness as a frame of reference for consumer perception of food." In *Enhancing knowledge development in marketing.* Vol. 13, edited by William J. Kehoe and John H. Lindgren, Jr. Chicago, IL: American Marketing Association.

Levi-Strauss, Claude. 1963. *Structural anthropology.* Translated by Claire Jacobson and Brooke Grundfest Schoepf. New York: Basic.

Levi-Strauss, Claude. 1969. *The raw and the cooked: Introduction to a science of mythology.* New York: Harper Torch Books.

Levy, Sidney J. 1981. "Interpreting consumer mythology: A structural approach to consumer behavior." *Journal of Marketing* 45 (Summer): 49–61.

Lin, Chung-Tung Jordon, and Jong-Ying Lee. 2004. "Who uses food label information: A case study of dietary fat." *Journal of Food Products Marketing* 10 (4): 17–37.

Lincoln, Bruce. 1999. *Theorizing myth: Narrative, ideology, and scholarship.* Chicago, IL: University of Chicago Press.

Loureiro, Maria L., Jill J. McCluskey, and Ron C. Mittelhammer. 2002. "Will consumers pay a premium for eco-labeled apples?" *Journal of Consumer Affairs* 36 (2): 203–19.

McCracken, Grant. 1988. *Culture and consumption.* Bloomington, IN: Indiana University Press.

Marketing News. 2004. "Random sampling. Apples and oranges." Editorial. October 15, 3.

Marx, Leo. 2000. *The machine in the garden: Technology and the pastoral ideal in America.* New York: Oxford University Press.

Mazis, Michael B., and Mary Anne Raymond. 1997. "Consumer perceptions of health claims in advertisements and on food labels." *Journal of Consumer Affairs* 31 (1): 10–26.

Mick, David Glen, and Claus Buhl. 1992. "A meaning based model of advertising experiences." *Journal of Consumer Research* 19 (3): 317–38.

Muñiz, Albert M., Jr., and Thomas C. O'Guinn. 2001. "Brand community." *Journal of Consumer Research* 27 (March): 412–32.

Muñiz, Albert M., Jr., and Hope Jensen Schau. 2005. "Religiosity in the abandoned Apple Newton brand community." *Journal of Consumer Research* 31 (March): 737–47.

Nayga, Rodolfo M., Jr., Daria Lipinski, and Nitin Savur. 1998. "Consumers' use of nutritional labels while food shopping and at home." *Journal of Consumer Affairs* 32 (1): 106–22.

Sacharow, Stanley. 1982. *The package as a marketing tool.* Radnor, PA: Chilton.

Santino, Jack. 1996. *New old fashioned ways: Holidays and popular culture.* Knoxville, TN: University of Tennessee Press.

Simonson, Alex, and Bernd H. Schmitt. 1997. *Marketing aesthetics: The strategic management of brands, identity and image.* New York: Free Press.

Stern, Barbara. 1995. "Consumer myths: Frye's taxonomy and the structural analysis of a consumption text." *Journal of Consumer Research* 22 (September): 165–85.

Stern, Barbara. 1996. "Textual analysis in advertising research: Construction and deconstruction of meanings." *Journal of Advertising* 25 (3): 61–73.

Strauss, Anselm, and Juliet Corbin. 1998. *Basics of qualitative research*. London: Sage.

Teague, Jacqueline L., and Donald W. Anderson. 1995. "Consumer preferences for safe handling labels on meat and poultry." *Journal of Consumer Affairs* 29 (1): 108–27.

Thompson, Craig J. 1997. "Interpreting consumers: A hermeneutical framework for deriving marketing insights from the texts of consumers' consumption stories." *Journal of Marketing Research* 34 (November): 438–55.

Thompson, Craig J. 2004. "Marketplace mythology and discourses of power." *Journal of Consumer Research* 31 (June): 162–80.

Thompson, Craig J., and Maura Troester. 2002. "Consumer value systems in the age of postmodern fragmentation: The case of the natural health microculture." *Journal of Consumer Research* 28 (March): 550–72.

Thoreau, Henry David. 1947 *The portable Thoreau*, edited by Carl Bode. New York: Penguin Books.

Wachenheim, Cheryl J. 2005. "Changing consumer perceptions about genetically modified food products." *Journal of Food Products Marketing* 12 (1): 30–44.

Wallendorf, Melanie, and Eric J. Arnould. 1991. "'We gather together': Consumption rituals of Thanksgiving day." *Journal of Consumer Research* 18 (June): 13–31.

Wansik, Brian. 2003. "How do front and back package labels influence beliefs about health claims?" *Journal of Consumer Affairs* 37 (2): 305–29.

Wyman, Carolyn. 1993. "I'm a Spam fan: America's best loved foods." Stamford, CT: Longmeadow Press.

Zaltman, Gerald. 2000. *The dimensions of brand equity for Nestle Crunch Bar: A research case*. Cambridge, MA: Harvard Business School Press.

Zaltman, Gerald, and R. Coulter. 1995. "Seeing the voice of the customer: Metaphor-based advertising research." *Journal of Advertising Research* 35 (4): 35–51.

4　Just doing it

A visual ethnographic study of spectacular consumption behavior at Nike Town

Lisa Peñaloza

We shouldn't be wasting your time *telling* you about NIKE TOWN, *showing* you little pictures. That's fine and all, but *it doesn't even come close.* You know? You gotta *go.* You gotta *see* for yourself. You gotta *feel* it. You really do.

(Caption, Nike Town brochure, emphasis added)

Introduction

Fifteen years ago, Holbrook and Hirschman (1982) called for studies of experiential consumption behavior. Within this realm, they located entertainment, arts, and leisure, as well as day-to-day product usage and related activities. The authors emphasized multi-sensorial properties of consumers, nonverbal stimuli, symbolic meanings, and hedonic tasks, in contrast to previous work emphasizing cognitive information processing, decision-making, verbal stimuli, and problem-solving tasks. This paper is located within the experiential tradition in its *topic of study* and *research approach.* Whereas Holbrook and Hirschman distanced their work from "directly observable buying behavior" (Holbrook and Hirschman 1982: 137), emphasizing instead the mental events surrounding the act of consumption (i.e., subjective states of consciousness evident in narratives and aesthetic judgments), this study emphasizes directly observable buyer behaviors. Specifically, this research explores consumers' behavioral motor and visual activities and related spacial and symbolic aspects of consumption environments *in conjunction with* mental, subjective processing of cultural meanings.

Consumers' bodily motor and visual capabilities are important parts of the consumption experience of newly emerging product showcases such as Nike Town, as stated in the quote above. They are also under-investigated aspects of consumption behavior. In our literature; with few exceptions, consumers are virtually bodiless. In fact, focusing on differences between interpretive and positivist work (Hirschman 1986; Belk, Sherry, and Wallendorf 1988) has blinded us to their commonalities in emphasizing *narrative* aspects of consumer behavior. With the exception of work on visual (e.g., Mick 1986; Scott 1993) and tactile (Hornik 1992) processing, existing work on the body has focused on its *representations* in advertisements and other social discourse, particularly the way they reflect and rework particular social relations (Joy and Venkatesh 1994; Peñaloza 1994; Thompson and Hirschman 1995). This research extends previous work on the body by exploring spatial and kinetic aspects of consumers' behavior.

This paper *investigates* the consumption of *spectacle* at Nike Town Chicago. This consumption venue, a fastidiously designed five-story compilation of merchandise, celebrity athlete memorabilia, and corporate tribute, is one of the most popular tourist destinations in the city. More importantly for our purposes, that this product showcase has become a consumption Mecca renders it a virtual lab of postmodern consumption phenomena with theoretical significance to the field of consumer behavior.

In developing its theoretical framework, the paper draws from and contributes to literature in consumer behavior, marketing, museum studies, and postmodern cultural theory. Such issues as definitions of spectacles, their components, and specific processes of cultural meaning making provide background for the questions addressed in this research. In the field of consumer research, there has been no empirical work regarding the actual processes through which consumption spectacles take on cultural meanings, despite scholarly and popular sentiment that spectacles are an important and pervasive marketplace phenomena.

In the consumer behavior literature, the word spectacle has been used in reference to a type of performance (Deighton 1992) and to the contemporary postmodern condition (Fırat and Venkatesh 1995). In a conceptual paper, Deighton (1992) characterized spectacle as a particular type of market performance that involved consumer participation, exaggerated display, and the amplification of social values, with an emphasis on knowledge of its mechanics of production as part of the experience. The focus of his work was not on spectacle per se, but rather on highlighting the performative quality of many consumption behaviors. In contrast, this work empirically examines the consumption of spectacle with attention to the nature of its consumption processes and cultural meanings.

Spectacle has been identified as the predominant mode of consumption in postmodernity, based on a wide range of marketplace examples, including film, theater, theme parks, advertising, and cyberspace (Debord 1977; Baudrillard 1988; Ewen 1988; Denzin 1995). Fırat and Venkatesh (1995) described spectacles as rich, complex visual images and environments, which conveyed cultural meanings that were integrated into consumers' understandings of reality. The focus of this work was not on spectacle either, but rather on articulating the philosophical underpinnings of postmodern thought and sketching out criteria for appropriate research. Nevertheless, it was useful in addressing the impact of marketplace spectacles on consumer behavior, and its postmodern epistemology was useful in formulating the research design.

In the methods section, visual ethnography is compared to other forms of ethnography, with attention to their objectives, strengths, and weaknesses. The visual ethnographic design is then mapped out and linked to the particular research questions of interest: (1) What is the nature of spectacular consumption processes? (2) What cultural meanings are conveyed at the site? (3) What role does the environment play in affecting spectacular consumption processes? (4) How does one particularize questions one and two to the Nike Town Chicago site as a corporate collection of sports memorabilia and products? (5) What are the *effects* of spectacular consumption in producing particular subject positions?

Participant observation and photography were *well tailored to these research questions*, given the visual nature of spectacle. *Researcher participation* with the store design, displays, and consumers, together with interviews with consumers and observations of their behaviors, were valuable sources of data, given its experiential qualities. The spatial and multi-sensorial features of the consumption environment, particularly its *architecture, furnishings, displays of artifacts, images, sounds,* and *textures* in relation to consumers' behaviors were well suited to the use of photographic records. Supplementing these data were interviews with consumers and employees, and corporate documents. As checks on the accuracy and insightfulness of the interpretive analysis, split samples of visual findings were compared, and findings were subjected to consumers and employees in member-checking dialogues.

I began by personally experiencing the site, and then proceeded to document the architectural design, furnishings and fixtures, *product and celebrity displays*, and products. At this point, I was particularly *interested* in the display *conventions*, and pictorial and verbal narrative *contents* as mechanisms of cultural meaning production. Nike Town provided consumers with an orchestrated, visually oriented feast of artifacts and images, which I initially organized into four categories of cultural meanings: competition, beauty and aesthetics, desire, and performance. Further work was required to decipher how meanings were consumed at the store, however, and consumers' comments that it was "cool," "not what I expected," and "like a museum" only partially illuminated the spectacular consumption process.

In subsequent fieldwork, I shifted my focus to observing and talking with consumers in the store, and photographing their activities. In coding these data, I realized that it was in the interactions of consumers with the site and its accoutrements, including products, fixtures, other consumers, and employees, that the spectacular consumption experience was *enacted*. Initial themes were reformulated in conjunction with additional data, as I worked to refine the analysis of substantive themes and understand their relation to processes of meaning making. Processes of spectacle consumption became more intelligible as I learned which aspects of the store were of interest to informants, and as I coded the photographs, gaining greater appreciation of consumers' physical positions relative the products, displays, and to each other. At this point, competition, performance, style, and recreation were identified as themes, while desire was reclassified as an outcome of the spectacular consumption process.

Together, the interspatial design and intertextual displays were critical in making meanings. Interspatialities refer to mapped paths of consumers through the site. The most crucial factor was the sequence of visuals produced by their physical movement, as these trajectories played a key role in producing meaning. At Nike Town, its architectural design employed high ceilings, narrow passageways, circular rooms, and theatrical props, which placed consumers in varied spatial and visual relations with the displays. Intertextualities refer to the principles by which displays of celebrity sports memorabilia, images, and products were arranged at the store so as to encourage some meanings and preclude others. Ultimately, it was consumers whose physical mobility through the store put them in relation to its design and displays, which were visually processed as an artifact of passage in producing meanings.

Nike Town is an important site of cultural construction, conveying cultural meanings throughout the store in its design and displays. The architectural space was ideological, in the sense that its design and displays placed consumers in particular relations to meaningful symbols and artifacts. Architecturally, the high ceilings and larger-than-life celebrity displays diminished consumers, creating feelings of awe potentially associated with the company, just as mountain bikers suspended above the flow of entering consumers produced a sense of action and adventure. Glass cases containing the artifacts of professional and amateur athletes positioned them as celebrities, just as the ample lists of their accomplishments positioned them as exceptional. Products were billed as celebrities in their own right through the same display techniques used with celebrity memorabilia, and in the positioning of autographed merchandise in the celebrity cases. Captions featuring celebrity and amateur athlete lore (e.g., the story of Gale Devers racing the boys home and playing with dolls, or Michael Jordan not lacing up his shoes) personalized these exceptional athletes, and encouraged consumers to identify with their more mundane qualities.

By empirically investigating spectacular consumption processes, this research contributes to our theoretical understanding of experiential consumer behavior. At Nike Town, consumers' spectacular consumption processes inherently involved exploration, discovery, suspended disbelief, and pleasure, each of which actively involved consumers. Fundamental to spectacular consumption were consumers' bodily and visual activities. These data demonstrate consumers' symbolic and evaluative processes operating in tandem, in contrast to the bifurcation between the two domains of hedonistic and traditional problem-solving/decision-making consumption behaviors that permeate our field.

Second, this research builds upon previous work positing the environment as endogenous to many types of consumption behaviors (Sherry 1995). In this case, the store design and displays were much more than mere context, functioning as both consumption objects and vehicles of cultural consumption meanings. In previous work, carriers of cultural meanings have been limited to products, such as fashion, and media, such as television programming and advertisements (McCracken 1986; Shrum, Wyer, and O'Guinn 1998).

Third, this work explores the theoretical significance of this hybrid consumption venue. As a combination of store and museum, this retail site was situated between consumers' categories. This hybrid status rendered the site distinctive, memorable, and slightly confusing to consumers, whose frequent questions of employees included whether they could buy anything and whether they should pay to enter. In exploring the implications of institutional hybridity, this research extends work on incongruent consumption schema beyond products (Cohen and Basu 1987; Meyers-Levy and Tybout 1989) to include consumption institutions.

Traditionally, museums have been the quintessential modern institutions whose collections are revered parts of a culture (Karp, Kraemer, and Levine 1992). Similarly, at Nike Town, Nike displayed some of our most highly revered artifacts and images within a distinctively designed facility. Yet this was not a museum. In understanding the theoretical significance of this consumption site, it is important to emphasize that it was a store. As a retail showroom, the site provided Nike with a fully vertically integrated distribution channel, such that monetary profits accrued to Nike in the form of direct sales, even as it built the value of retailers' and distributors' inventory and of the many cooperative corporate and educational ventures also promoted here (e.g., collegiate and professional sports programs, sports equipment, and media companies).

Spectacular corporate showcases are not new; businesses have used spectacles to build brand equity and corporate image for almost 150 years (Palmade 1976; Fox and Lears 1983). What is new is the increasingly comprehensive and conscientious way in which companies go about designing their architectural and display combinations, the increasing numbers and types of stores using this strategic format, and the particular symbols and meanings employed. As such, Nike Town is part of larger trend of major consumer products companies, joining Coca-Cola, Sony, Time Warner, Land Rover, and REI in developing multi-sensorial, experiential venues in major upscale locations such as Madison Avenue in New York, Michigan Avenue in Chicago, and downtown Seattle (Gantenbeim 1996; Pacelle 1996). These are private spaces, with private ownership or copyright of the products, celebrities, and images displayed to the public, unlike the public collections of cultural icons at the museum.

Finally, in conveying complex cultural meanings via spectacle, particular forms of consumer subjectivity were constituted at Nike Town. By constituted, I mean the ways in which consumer subject positions were produced as the *effects* of intertextual discursive practices and interspatial design. This is not to suggest that the design, decor, and artifacts determined subjectivity, since consumers brought a wide array of associations to any particular symbol. Rather, this research highlights the ways in which the design and display elements of the retail space placed consumers in particular relations with them, which facilitated consumers' movement, gaze, and positioning. These forms of subjectivity are theoretically significant given scholars' repeated assertions that consumption is an increasingly important mode of enfranchisement in capitalist society (Giroux 1991; Lee 1993). The research concludes with discussion of the forms of subjectivity produced at Nike Town in comparison with our existing conceptualizations of consumer behavior.

Theoretical framework

In the spectacle, one part of the world represents itself to the world and is superior to it. The spectacle is nothing more than the common language of this separation. What binds the spectators together is no more than an irreversible relation at the very center, which maintains their isolation. The spectacle reunites the separate, but reunites it as separate.

(Debord 1977: 29)

Historical precedents

Contemporary spectacles may be traced to early religious rites, royal processions, museums, and public exhibitions (Barry 1991b). Religious examples include symbolic re-enactments of prophets' births and deaths interpreted by religious leaders. A key feature of spectacles is the stories they tell. Spectacular stories may be acted out or narrated, yet always incorporate the tensions between superhuman qualities or events and normality.

The regal processions were elaborate dramatizations of current issues of the day, typically using physical archways, fireworks, and other props to create the illusion of superhuman powers (Campbell 1923). Additionally, kings and queens borrowed religious symbols and reinvested them with new thematic associations (Barry 1991b). The processions culminated in a positive outcome for the king and/or queen, and in this way encouraged people to believe in and to support the crown, thus further legitimating the monarchy (Yates 1975).

The museum spectacle was quite relevant given consumers' repeated comparisons of Nike Town to one. The first museum was the Medici Palace in Florence, which has been traced to 1440 (Hooper-Greenhill 1992). Medici was a very successful trader who accumulated a collection of objects from all over the world, which he showed publicly. In doing so, the Medici family gained social power, as it was believed at that time that special powers were transferred from the artifacts to their owners.

Spectacle was a feature of early retailers, who used elaborate storefront displays of art and other novelties to pull passersby into the store. The first department store, the Bon Marche, was opened in Paris in 1852 by Aristide Boucault in an indoor version of the earlier outdoor marketplaces, the arcades

(Palmade 1976; Slater 1993). The emergence of these department stores and of mass consumption, like the public walkways that accompanied them, has been linked to the Industrial Revolution and the rise of mass labor (Palmade 1976; Barry 1991a). By the mid-1800s, urban development resulted in the replacement of narrow streets with wide boulevards and walkways necessary for public transportation. Significantly, this newly emergent public transportation, which offered cheap access to the cities, was underwritten by merchants. The early markets were located at the center of town, and here people of previously separated stations in life came to work and to stroll, to see others, and to be seen (Benjamin 1973). To this day, the abstract, rationalized neo-classical version of the market contrasts with the boisterous and dynamic cultural activities upon which it depends (Slater 1993).

The most heightened spectacles were the public exhibitions held at the turn of the century. London's Crystal Palace, the Chicago Exhibition and the World Fairs in New York and Paris were noted examples (Rydell 1993). These festivals featured spectacular collections of people and artifacts from the "new" world that most people had never seen before (Karp and Levine 1991). Significantly, they were funded by the state primarily, with some corporate support, as in the case of the J. W. Skiles Company sponsoring an Eskimo exhibit at the World's Columbia Exposition in Chicago in 1893 (Hinsley 1991). By showcasing people from the new world, nations conveyed their dominion over these faraway lands to their publics. As importantly, the exhibits cast their visitors into new relations with the world in which they lived.

Components

The first component of market spectacles is their draw. These are distinct, highly valued agents, stories, and/or novel objects. Agents range from early religious deities and prophets and state dignitaries to contemporary actors, musicians, athletes, and even criminals. Stories generally feature themes of adversity, conquest or moral triumph, and love, and it is these activities that imbue the actors with heroic qualities. Objects typically become highly valued as a function of their association with a valued person or deity. Examples include religious relics, royal jewels, state papers, art, and celebrity memorabilia. Valued objects function as a source of power in their possession and use; specifically, there is totemic power in the processes of transference from the original person to object to other persons that endows later owners and possessors of the items with social value (Belk, Wallendorf, and Sherry 1989). Additionally, power and value may be transferred from the object to the place housing it. Examples include religious shrines and temples, places of birth of political leaders, museums, and celebrities' homes.

At Nike Town, sports celebrity memorabilia and art were the primary spectacular objects. McCracken (1989) noted that celebrities encapsulate the values of a culture. Celebrity athletes date at least to the Olympics, and continue to signify the spirit of the games, of competition, and of winning, as resonant with national, town, or school teams or players. Further, athletes connote rich imagery of sexual prowess (Paglia 1992).

Art objects have an equally spectacular historical trajectory, dating to early religious imagery, portraits of religious and royal leaders, landscapes of property holdings, and still life representations. The modernist art movements called attention to art as a way of seeing, and challenged representational practices and conventions of patronage and access, such that art was diffused to a greater degree among the populace. This work raises questions regarding the types of objects at Nike Town, and how they compare to other contemporary objects of value (e.g., religious icons, national treasures, art and artifacts).

The second component of spectacle is its *audience*. From the spectators of the early Olympics in Athens and the coliseum of Rome, to the monarchs' kingdoms, religious congregations, citizenry, and, most recently, consumers, popular audience support and participation is required. Most critically, this participation plays a key role in legitimizing the social institution (Foucault 1980). Various levels of audience participation include *being there*, experiencing the event with others, *beholding* the spectacular sights and objects, and actively taking part in the rituals. The audience may be live and/or convened through the media.

The third component of spectacles is their *institutional sponsor*. Early patrons included the church, the state (monarchy, democracy, and socialist alike), and, most recently, the corporation. Key institutional issues include mode of acquisition and use, with patronage a useful measure of social resources and their corresponding social power (Hooper-Greenhill 1992). In the case of religious institutions and nation states, cultural icons were acquired by conversion, purchase, or conquest. The collections were used to glorify the institutions and, in turn, socially legitimated them.

With corporations, acquisition is generally the result of purchase, and the social power accorded to corporate institutions is not insignificant. Corporate art patronage has played a formative role in building consumer culture (Fox and Lears 1983; Harris 1985). As early as the eighteenth century, Englishman Josiah Wedgwood used the art of John Flaxman, Joseph Wright, and William Hackwood to design and decorate his pottery, and of painters George Romney and George Stubbs in early trade promotions (McKendrick, Brewer, and Plumb 1982). In the US, commercial art was rare prior to World War I, and consisted of architectural design and furnishings. Notable examples were Frank Woolworth's lavish corporate headquarters in New York, the glass mosaics of Louis Comfort Tiffany, and John Wanamaker's department store in Chicago that contained French paintings (Harris 1985). By the 1920s and 1930s, artwork was used to sell products ranging from hosiery and luggage to housewares. Renowned artists such as Marc Chagall and Guy Arnoux worked for retailers, publishers, and advertising agencies such as Saks, Conde Nast, and J. Walter Thompson (Harris 1985). Commercial art became an increasing part of product design and packaging in the 1950s (Lorenz 1990).

Significantly, corporate patronage raises distinct concerns from that of religious or state institutions. Chief among these was that corporate sponsored art and social icons would become mere public relations agents advancing the interests of the firms. Noted artist and social critic Hans Haacke, "The choices of works to place on exhibition and their very forms of presentation create a climate that supports prevailing distributions of power and capital and persuades the populace the status quo is the natural order of things" (Haacke 1984: 15).

Even so, there is some evidence that even when commissioned, art and artifacts can retain a critical edge, challenging the social conventions of religious, state, and even corporate institutions. Much of the art commissioned by the Container Corporation of America from 1930 to 1980 was highly critical of the modern state and corporation. The collection is impressive, containing the work of over 200 prominent artists, such as Rene Magritte, Andy Warhol, Man Ray, and Rufino Tamayo (National Museum of American Art 1985). Ironically, the collection was donated to the National Museum of American Art in 1986. What was once private is now public, as has been the case historically with numerous private collections, as the result of institutional shifts of power. Of interest in this research was the significance of the corporation Nike as owner and curator of some of our most highly valued social icons.

Contemporary market spectacles typically combine both market and non-market features, as the result of institutional precedents and shifts in institutional power. The joint trends of increasing commercialization and privatization of culture have alarmed cultural theorists such as Henry Giroux (1991) and Herb Schiller (1992), who see them as fueling corporate power. These concerns are not new, but rather date to the beginnings of modernity itself (Schudson 1984; Scott 1993), even as their relevance continues in the present. This research questions the market and non-market forms of spectacular consumption at Nike Town. Business institutions' role as vanguard of our collective social icons is a consumer research issue of increasing importance given the dual, global trends of commercialization and privatization. As institutional patron, business retains a distinct social contract as compared to the church or state. Further, as democratic-capitalist forms of political economy diffuse throughout the world, it is important for consumer researchers to consider the significance of corporations, such as Nike, in proliferating artifacts of value, a role historically held by their institutional predecessors, the church and state.

The fourth component, *processes of meaning making*, is most critical to advancing our understanding of spectacular consumption. Scholars have distinguished spectacles from festivals, contests, and ceremonies, emphasizing the consumption of performance across these venues (Deighton 1992). Specifically, spectacles have a narrow focus, separation between actors and audience, and *audience participation within a small set of approved responses* (Dayan and Katz 1985), whereas festivals are unframed, with no sharp division between audience and performers, and unlimited audience participation.

Further, spectacles feature exaggerated display and rhetorical amplification of a moral concept, with value assessed in their process, whereas contests assess value in the outcome (Barthes 1972). Ceremonies share a narrow focus and division between actors and audience with spectacles, yet differ with the audience a part of the performance, and their timing in the here and now, as compared to the otherworldly sense of spectacle (Deighton 1992).

This research brings empirical data to bear on Deighton's (1992) dichotomous conceptualization of consumption performances as involving *either* observation *or* performance, and realism *or* fantasy. Previous conceptualizations portray the consumption of market spectacles as involving *combinations* of observation *and* behavior, fantasy *and* reality (Debord 1977; Baudrillard 1983). Further spectacular consumption may not be as clearly distinguished by structural differences in market spectacles as Deighton (1992) suggested. That is, some contests, ceremonies, and festivals may become spectacular as a function of the consumer behavior they engender. Examples of spectacular contests include the Super Bowl, the Olympics, and the Miss Universe Pageant; spectacular ceremonies include the Presidential Inauguration and royal weddings; and spectacular festivals include Cinco de Mayo, Mardi Gras, and Gay Pride celebrations. Importantly, this work directs attention from the type of market spectacle to the characteristics of spectacular consumer behavior processes.

At its most basic, the market spectacle accomplishes *focused collective attention*. Yet, spectacular consumption entails much more in its experiential sense of transcending one's immediate physical circumstances and interjecting oneself into the story via imagination and fantasy. This is its most distinguishing characteristic and perhaps the greatest challenge in empirically studying spectacular consumption behavior processes.

Given the fantastical, imaginative qualities of spectacular consumption across a realm of market phenomena, including advertisements, film, theme parks, and retail stores, a key issue for researchers is understanding how they achieve *credibility* and *perceived meaningfulness* (Crew and Sims 1991) as spectacular. Some cultural theorists have argued that people cannot distinguish reality from spectacle (e.g., Debord 1977; Baudrillard 1983) to the point that images have become the desired end in themselves (Ewen 1988). Yet, this may refer to consumers' abilities to interject the fantasy of the market spectacle into their own reality via their imagination in incorporating elements of it into their own experience. Thus, spectacular literacy draws from traditional models of literacy, even as it is extended to new visual and participative communication forms (Scott 1993). Like reading a book, knowledge of spectacle conventions in film, advertisements, and retail stores is required to make them work.

In sum, visual and spatial processing of cultural meanings are necessary, but not sufficient components of spectacular consumption. For example, Mick (1986) demonstrated the benefits of semiotic analyses in investigating advertising meanings, while Scott (1994) noted that both visual symbols and words in advertisements communicated rhetorically. Of central importance in this work is the way visuals tell stories. While much of it has focused on *still images* in advertisements, other scholars have focused on *moving images* in film and television programming. Examples include the work of Hirschman (1986) and Shrum, Wyer, and O'Guinn (1998) in demonstrating the cultural meanings and values inherent in these media, and, more importantly, documenting their effects on how we see ourselves and others, and conceptualize reality.

The study of spectacular consumption processes must of necessity extend our understanding of visual consumption to the domain of material consumption environments for they are important parts of the spectacle. In our literature, the environment is most typically operationalized as an *exogenous* influence on consumers' behavior (Belk 1975; Lynch 1983; Stayman and Deshpande 1989). Yet, the environment *is endogenous* to spectacular consumption processes in a range of marketplaces, including tourist destinations, theme parks, and museums, as well as department stores, malls, and restaurants (Sherry 1995).

The consumption of space has been articulated clearly by urban architectural scholars. De Certeau (1984) wrote at length of *pedestrian speech acts*, the symbolic meaning process consumers engaged in while walking through the city. Key was making sense of perceptions of physical characteristics as architectural design, human density, and movement patterns. Barry (1991a) focused on consumers' processes of making meaning at a mall, emphasizing the ways in which consumers experienced the string of images and sensations they produced as they moved through store designs and product displays. Viewing spatial dimensions of the environment as integral aspects of consumption alters our conceptualizations of consumer behavior to include more explicitly important motor and visual activities in relation to architectural design.

Yet, understanding symbolic meaning processes does not go far enough in understanding how consumers animate the spectacle. Additionally, there is a willful act of *believing in the spectacle* on the part of consumers. Termed *suspended disbelief* or *catharsis* in film and theater viewing, this part of the process is most controversial, as it relates to the place of consumers' conscious understanding of how the spectacle was constructed in making meanings. That is, we must forget that it is a book, movie, or mall in constructing the spectacle, even though it is our very knowledge of the conventions of spectacular texts, film, or stores that enables us to do so.

Effects on consumer subjectivity

While generalized consumer subjectivity would refer to people's sense of themselves as consumers, their abilities and the implications of their consumption behavior in society, in this work I was interested in the particular forms of subjectivity produced in the consumption of market spectacles. Early on in this research, I came across consumers' repeated characterizations of Nike Town as a museum. Museums differ from stores in the forms of subjectivity they engender. Museums have been recognized for producing cultural knowledge and representing what is beautiful, true, and good in society (Karp 1991). In classifying and displaying cultural artifacts and in their forms of presentation, museums challenge and alter our way of seeing the world (Hooper-Greenhill 1992). Most important is the wonder and resonance of the spectacular museum (i.e., the ability of its displayed objects to "stop the viewer in his or her tracks, to convey an arresting sense of uniqueness, to evoke exalted attention," and to "reach out beyond its formal boundaries to a larger world . . . of complex, dynamic forces from which it has emerged") (Greenblatt 1991: 42).

Indeed, analogous forms of subjectivity may be constituted in spectacular stores. Barry (1991a) argued that the process of producing meanings at the mall played a formative role in constituting consumers' desire:

> The activity of shopping directly engages the shopper in the generation of a complex narrative all her own. In a sense she is the protagonist of the detective story, following her own desire as she moves through the store, but not to the scene of the crime. Access to her desire is so difficult, so mysterious . . . Hence the difficulty for each of us in finding out what really interests us.
>
> (Barry 1991a: 17)

Her conclusion was stark: "Shopping is an activity that consists of predictable yet indeterminate activities, where, as in the cinema, what we go to see, what we experience over and over again, is *our own desire*" (Barry 1991: 35, emphasis added). Yet, Barry was less than explicit regarding the actual proceses by which consumers constituted desire in walking through the mall, and the specific meanings attached to consumers' desire. The last issues addressed in this work relate to the forms of subjectivity produced at Nike Town and how they compare to those represented in the consumer behavior literature.

Visual ethnographic research design

> In moving to understand the systematic character of the life of a community the student cannot begin everywhere; he must begin at some point. Commonly the beginning is made with things immediately *visible*.
>
> (Redfield 1955: 19, emphasis added)

Visual methods

Visuals are pervasive as both metaphor and epistemology in society. The words "I see" are used interchangeably for "I understand." Visual methods have a rich tradition in anthropology and sociology, and consist of a wide array of methods, including observation, photography, documentary film, and archaeological artifact and site studies.

In a classic article, Becker (1974) noted that photography and sociology shared a common interest in the social. Visual records include photographs, maps, artifacts, and other documents (Collier and Collier 1986; Hodder 1994).

In the field of consumer behavior, the use of visuals has been limited to content analysis of advertisements (Kassarjian 1977), eliciting experimental responses (Edell and Staelin 1983; Mitchell 1986) and interview data (Heisley and Levy 1991), and illustrating interpretive findings (Wallendorf and Belk 1987; Belk, Sherry, and Wallendorf 1988). These predominant uses in generating other forms of data and in communicating research findings belie the strength of photographs in providing a valuable record of observable consumption behavior and contextual factors characterizing the physical world consumers inhabit (Collier and Collier 1986).

It is a paradox in our field that we have a sophisticated sense of consumers' use of visuals, yet a very limited sense of visuals' usefulness as data on consumption. Even ethnography, which specializes in fieldwork, has relied more on interviews than observation as primary data (Belk, Sherry, and Wallendorf 1988; Arnould 1989; Peñaloza 1994; Holt 1995). In doing so, we have privileged what consumers *say* over what they do in operationalizing consumption phenomena, and limited our ability to compare the two, which is a key strength of ethnography (Spradley 1980). When used at all, observation most often has set the context, framing the research for the "real" events to follow. As a result, we have imposed a distinction between consumption phenomena and its context, and missed important ways in which the "context" operates.

Two seminal works begin to lay the methodological groundwork for visual studies of consumer behavior: Heisley, McGrath, and Sherry's (1992) study of a farmers' market, and Scott's (1994) rhetorical analysis of advertisements. Heisley, McGrath, and Sherry (1992) investigated the physical site using photographs, and noted their use led to greater appreciation of physical changes in people and products over time, which were missed in observations because of their gradual nature. Citing historical studies of literacy, Scott (1994) challenged notions that pictures were less cognitively processed than words. Of particular importance in generating advertising meanings were the *viewing context* and *consumers' attributions of marketers' intentionality*.

Like traditional forms of ethnography, the overall goal of visual ethnography is building social theory. It entails the systematic collection, analysis, and communication of visual records of human behavior and culture (Collier and Collier 1986). Visual methods are well suited to behavioral studies of consumption in situ, as they attend to activities, physical features, and spatial proximities. As a part of culturally informed observation, their strengths lie in providing detailed and complete physical records, integrating the study of culture through investigating images and text, and communicating the context of phenomena. Bateson and Mead (1942) referred to the latter as "aspects of culture never successfully recorded by the scientist, although often caught by the artist" (Bateson and Mead 1942: xi). Notably, even after 10 years of field work in Bali, Bateson and Mead gained new insights through the use of photographs. Visuals are limited in studying consumers' scripts, motivations, and other cognitive processes, although these limitations are lessened when visual data are used in conjunction with interviews, as was done in this research.

The most serious limitation of visual data, however, is associated with the selective perception and intentionality of its collection (Collier and Collier 1986; Harper 1994). While these concerns apply to field notes as well, they become more evident in photographs as the result of the manner in which they are understood to represent reality. Sontag (1977) noted how photographs were a presumed measure of veracity, even as they were recognized to idealize, both in their way of seeing and the substantive content they represent. Photographs both certify and refuse experience, as their conventions influence people's judgments of what is worthy of remembering and what is not. Photographs communicate based on a visual code, Sontag continued; they "alter and enlarge our notions of what is worth looking at and what we have a right to observe" (Sontag 1977: 3). As with other research methods, making their conventions explicit is important in anchoring meaning, yet should not overwhelm the content of the research.

There is a sense in which writing field notes and taking a picture are similar. When used in research, both are used to learn about a particular consumption phenomenon, and both aspire to accurate representations. Like field notes, the rigorous use of visuals requires the researcher not only become aware of his or her own way of approaching, accessing, and representing a social phenomenon, but alter each to examine the phenomena more fully. With photographs, attention is directed to their contents, as well as the ways in which they were taken, to purposely incorporate other viewing angles and additional content. As an example, in the present work, the early photographs were focused on the displays and fixtures. In later photographs, I gave more emphasis to consumers, examining where they stood and how they interacted with the displays, the products, and each other. By taking photos of the same displays from different distances and perspectives, with and without flash, I gained appreciation of the effects of lighting and shadow in focusing consumers' attention to the displays, and routing them through the site.

Researcher as primary data collection instrument

As in more traditional forms of ethnography, the researcher takes the primary role in data collection in visual ethnography. Ethnographies vary in their degree of self-reflection, however, as the result of the type of study and philosophy of the researcher (Wallendorf and Brucks 1993). Marcus (1994) contrasted feminist ethnography, which uses reflexivity to exploit the subjective and experiential aspects of gendered phenomena, with its postmodern counterpart, which uses reflexivity to situate the work within an intertextual matrix of alternative representations and subject positions. In both cases, reflexivity is tied to a commitment to theoretical abstraction by challenging the naive objectivity of non-reflexivity texts and by revealing their authorial conventions and situated subjectivities. The present work uses self-reflection to locate its author's perspective relative to other consumers, as a means of explaining its analytical techniques and reasoning, and in the provision of substantive data.

My personal experience with sports is rather extensive. I lettered in basketball, golf, and tennis in high school. Our basketball team won the state title undefeated twice in a row, and my senior year I was selected to the All State team. I attended college on a basketball and golf scholarship, but left competitive sports after one year. As a doctoral student, I taped a "Just Do It" sticker to my computer screen as an affirmation to stay focused and finish writing the dissertation. Presently, I play basketball and soccer in organized women's leagues, and sporadically run, ride mountain and road bikes, and lift weights for pleasure, to keep in shape, and relieve stress. My weight room at home is decorated with posters purchased at Nike Town featuring beautiful landscapes and inspiring captions, such as "You gotta believe" with Deion Sanders and "Little goals add up" with Stacy Allison. For me, athletic shoes and clothing are matters of function and style, and I am price-sensitive. Of the five athletic shoes in my closet, only the running shoes are Nike.

Over the years, sports have been a source of joy and disappointment, in winning and losing, playing well and making mistakes, working out for self-improvement, and in competition with others. Playing sports is exemplary of consumption. There is the anxiety before a competitive match and the disappointment of not doing better or seeing a teammate not give their all, sprinkled with the ultimate rewards, that sense of timing and flawless performance and winning. That is what brings me back. I received a college scholarship in the wake of Title IX; at that time, women's participation in sports was much less common than it is today, just as wearing sports attire in public and sports recreation were less common practices. Though more people are active, and an even greater number dress casually, one-third of Americans are overweight, suggesting that not all "just do it." It is often said that sports help prepare people to deal with life, but I truly did not see the connections among individual and team sports, work, consumption, and our political-economic system until doing this research.

Data record

The qualitative data that formed the basis of this study were collected via the ethnographic methods of participant observation and photography at Nike Town, supplemented with interviews with employees and consumers at the site, corporate documents, and ethnographic reflections of my experiences in and outside the store with sports and with Nike merchandise. The qualitative data record consisted of 148 pages of field notes, 58 pages of journal entries, and 357 photographs from 24 hours of field observation at the store. In addition, 98 pages of notes were compiled as I made coding sheets of descriptive and summary data from the photographs. Artifacts included corporate annual reports, a nine-page history of the company, 11 brochures, a series of advertisements, and a thick folder of newspaper clippings.

In the field notes, I sought detailed documentation of consumers' activities and the displays at the store. Participant observation activities included tracing my path through the store, with attention to feelings and memories of past sports activities triggered by the design and displays, observing consumers, and documenting my participation with consumers and employees, soliciting their comments, reactions, and answers to specific questions.

Photographs were taken of all rooms and displays, and a sampling of consumers' and employees' activities. Photos were taken late mornings and afternoons, on weekdays and weekends. During low traffic times, it was easier to observe consumers and document displays, and during high traffic times the photographs were less obtrusive. I used standard 50 mm, wide angle, and zoom lenses to provide detailed records of the agents, displays, and artifacts. The wide-angle lens provided good coverage of displays, the zoom lens provided close-up detail, and the 50 mm lens standardized the size of persons and objects relative to the displays. Attention to figure/ground contrast helped study depth and the shifting positionality and perspective of consumers moving through the site. I shifted the focus from figure to ground, and from consumers/displays in the foreground to consumers/displays in the background to recreate the depth of visual fields at the site. Importantly, the photographs enabled written records of greater detail of what was viewed at the time and described in field notes. Their subsequent viewing provided additional information regarding consumers' activities and physical characteristics.

In drawing data from the photographs, I first made impressionistic notes of their contents, and then developed detailed coding sheets. Each photograph was numbered, and its location and the types of social groups and interactions were listed. Socio-demographics, activities, positions, and focal points were then detailed for each discernible individual. Given the visual nature of the data, the codings should be viewed with attention to the range of employees' and consumers' characteristics and activities, rather than their statistically representative occurrence.

Unstructured interviews were used to dialogue with consumers and employees regarding findings and interpretive themes derived primarily from the visual data, in reversal of their customary role as primary data. Pseudonyms were used for consumers and employees to maintain their anonymity and confidentiality, although employees were most vulnerable due to job concerns. Of interviews with 26 consumers in the store, 14 were male and 12 female. Regarding race/ethnicity, three were African American, four were Latino, and 18 were White. Customers were asked how they had heard about the store, whether they had been here before, their reactions, what they liked best, and whether they had bought anything. I approached most of the consumers, although some contacts were initiated by consumers interested in my activities taking notes and pictures.

Twenty-two employees were interviewed. Ten were women, 12 were men; and three were Latino, five were African American, three were Asian, and 11 were White. Five were managers, while 17 were sales associates. Employees were asked how long they had worked here and which celebrities they had seen as icebreakers. Additional questions included what their experiences had been here, what kind of training they had received, the questions they were most frequently asked by consumers, how they were paid, and their sales record. As with consumers, employees' questions regarding what I was doing gave me the opportunity to dialogue with them.

Finally, comparative site visits were made to the Nike Town in Orange County, California in 1995 and 1996. One hundred photographs and 33 pages of field notes were compiled from the field visits. Of interest were similarities and differences between the two field sites in their design, displays, and consumer and employee characteristics and activities.

Corporate field site

A fundamental characteristic of ethnography is the study of social phenomena in situ (Belk, Sherry, and Wallendorf 1988; Sherry 1995). In consumer behavior, there are a range of relevant sites, with phenomenological differences that require modified research practices. For example, stores are characterized by short stays relative to homes. Relevant in this study were neighborhood, company, and in-store behaviors. Nike Town is located in the heart of Chicago's finest shopping area, far from the inner city and suburbs surrounding it. This was prime real estate, afforded by Nike's 1996 sales totaling $6.4 billion (Nike 1996). Neighboring stores included Saks, Marshall Fields, and Neiman Marcus, and within a few blocks were a growing number of concept stores and restaurants, including Sony, Time Warner, Planet Hollywood, Walter Payton's Café, and Michael Jordan's Restaurant.

Nike was started as Blue Ribbon Sports in the early 1960s as the partnership of University of Oregon track coach, Bill Bowerman, and runner-turned-business-professor Phil Knight. Knight's MBA marketing research paper mapped out the basic strategy the company would follow over the next 25 years, namely low-cost athletic shoes produced in Asia. Paid endorsers were first used in 1973, led by world class runner Steve Prefontaine, and by the next year the waffle sole led the market for running shoes. Since then, the company has extended to different sports in shoes and attire, and currently one-third of sales are outside the US. Their promotional budget was $643 million in 1996 alone. Nike has been at the center of two major controversies, the first linking the style of its shoes to gang violence, and the second as the result of its low-cost production in Third World countries (Enloe 1995).

Nevertheless, the company has helped bring about and benefited from the trends toward wearing casual clothing and sports attire. Strategically, Nike Town is a new product showcase, representing the latest marketing trend of the company. There are other Nike Towns in Portland, near Nike corporate headquarters, as well as in Atlanta, Georgia, Costa Mesa, California, and, most recently, New York. Construction or plans are for others in Seattle, San Francisco, Denver, and Dallas.

Emergent design

I began this research with the general question: How do people consume at Nike Town? Initially, I took notes of my impressions and consumers' activities. Subsequent visits were more systematic, as I used notes and photographs to map the site (i.e., the building, furnishings, displays, products and captions), and document people's activities. Field notes were made in the store and completed after each visit. Reviewing the photographs, I made additional notes. Additionally, I compiled a separate journal of reflections and research questions.

Data were then organized into topical categories. The first category, Nike Town, dealt with the store itself, in its combination of retail outlet, new product showcase, and museum. The second category, displays, consisted of the merchandise, celebrities, sports memorabilia, and photographs. The third category, furnishings, included such items as the computer registers, the merchandise transporter tubes, the benches, guardrails, video screens, and packaging. The fourth category, sports, consisted of the range of activities represented—basketball, football, running, tennis, golf, hiking, soccer, volley-ball, biking, and cross-training. The fifth category, consumers, focused on their activities flopping, browsing, and buying, as tourists and as locals, in groups, and alone. The last category consisted of employee activities.

The second iteration of analysis consisted of review of field notes, journal entries, and photographs, together with further reading in the literature on spectacle and visual methods. More directed questions were formulated: (1) the nature of spectacle consumption; (2) the cultural meanings conveyed at Nike Town; (3) the role of environment in influencing spectacle consumption; (4) how to particularize (1) and (2) to Nike Town, as a corporate showcase of consumer objects; and (5) the effects of spectacle consumption on consumers' subject positions.

In reviewing the data, I concentrated on each of the research questions in turn. I was particularly puzzled by the overlaps among three dimensions of the data: content and meaning of the displays, context/environment, and processes of meaning making. I developed a coding scheme to draw further data from the photographs, and began to link the consumer activities I had observed, photographed, and participated in with the research questions.

I returned to the field site in September 1996, where I first documented the changes in the displays, before turning my attention to consumers' behavior.

Upon my return from the field, I added questions to the coding form for the photographs to assess what people were doing, where they were looking, and their positions relative to the displays, products, employees, and each other. In bringing data to bear on each of the research questions, I came to see the role of the environment as both context and content of spectacle consumption, and to appreciate consumers' behaviors within the interspatial design and intertextual displays. I reformulated thematic interpretations to more closely summarize the data, and developed the theoretical contributions.

Credibility assessment

From the onset of this research, I worked to dialogue with consumers and employees. This was unsuccessful at first, generating such comments as, "It's cool!" "It's not what I'd expected!" and "I like it." By the end of my first few field trips to the store, I had moved beyond the exclamations to gaining more insight as to what consumers liked about the store and why (e.g., Carlos (Latino, 30s) from Dallas, who wanted to see Emmet Smith in a Nike jersey because he was a "Reebok man," or William (Anglo, 40s) from Pennsylvania, who had come with his wife and two sons and was looking for Penn State merchandise).

The primary goal of the second iteration of fieldwork was dialoging with consumers. Issues discussed went beyond the basic questions I had listed, to include such topics as consumers' sentiments on the company's marketing activities, on high-paid endorsers, and on the products' high prices. Through conversations regarding the store design and display, the athletes as role models, and the use of the shoes by youth to distinguish themselves at school, I came to view consumers' purchases in the larger context of their lives. In bringing the two sets of comments together, I gained greater appreciation of spectacle consumption at Nike Town.

A second form of credibility assessment was the comparison of split samples of visual data. I compared the coded visuals from the 1994 and 1996 data sets with each other and with those from the Orange County California store. Based on review of this data, I noted differences and similarities across time and across sites, and linked them to product introductions and regional celebrity athletes, sports teams, and events.

Ethnographic writing and representation

In ethnography, writing is an important part of the research act. Through detailed ethnographic description, the researcher transforms observation, participation, and interviews into data for analysis. As importantly, by providing detailed descriptions of the physical site and activities of interest, the researcher strives to transport readers into the story. The primary goal of the ethnographic account that follows is the presentation of data in addressing the nature of spectacular consumption at Nike Town. Detailed description of store designs and displays are provided because they were important parts of the spectacular consumption experience. The data are presented in the form of a simulated visit to Nike Town, beginning with description of the 1994 store, interspersed with informant testimony and ethnographic reflections, and ending with changes in the 1996 store.

Visual ethnographic account

> To everyone who ever succeeded despite conventional wisdom; to everyone who ever took a risk, lost and took another one; to all athletes and the dreams they chase—we dedicate Nike Town.
> (Cornerstone, Nike Town Chicago)

Walking down Michigan Avenue in downtown Chicago in early November 1994, I first observed Nike Town nestled among Brooks Brothers, Saks 5th Avenue, Cole Haan, and the other upscale department stores, boutiques, and luxury hotels that make up the Magnificent Mile. It was a brisk Thursday afternoon, bustling with cars and pedestrian traffic. I had driven two hours north from the university town in central Illinois where I was teaching, having been informed of the store by my students.

The building was a five-story stark off-white structure, with the name and a large trademark "swoosh" in white letters that turned to cool blue neon at night (Figure 4.1). Offsetting the austere facade were large banners

Figure 4.1 Nike Town, Chicago

running the full height of the building, decorated with pictures of athletes, shoes, and the trademark "swooshes." The bottom three floors housed the retail space, while the top two floors were corporate offices and merchandise storage space.

Approaching the store, I was intrigued by four sculptures extending from the building—the front wheel of a mountain bike, the lower body of a man running, the upper body of a man tipping a basketball, and a full length of a woman running—as if they were bursting from the wall. I joined a steady stream of people entering the store. Once inside the foyer, I confronted a life-sized white plaster sculpture of Michael Jordan, suspended three feet above the ground. His accomplishments were listed in black letters on the glass front of the display. Though I played basketball in school, I had not followed the game in years, and was impressed at the extent of his awards (eight time NBA All Star, three time Most Valuable Player, six time scoring champion, Defensive Player of the Year, and Rookie of the Year). On both sides of the sculpture were full-length photographs of athletes, one running and the other lifting weights. Below were diagrams of Nike's new product lines, the Air Max 2, offering low pressure, 15 pounds per square inch soles, and Air Trainer Max 2, offering high pressure, 25 pounds per square inch soles.

Across from these displays were others featuring the new shoes, with a special display in the middle of colorful Nike shoes that had been custom decorated by customers. The shoes were cordoned off from the public with a velour rope that was very similar to those used in theaters and museums; above them was the caption, "There is no Finish Line." The two sides of the rectangular-shaped foyer were covered with framed *Sports Illustrated* magazine covers.

Next, I passed under an archway, above which were three large photographs of Michael Jordan, and into a corridor, beckoned by a dramatic, black-and-white photograph of Gail Devers (Figure 4.2). Her taunt body was crouched in the starting blocks, ready to run. The display also featured smaller photographs of her in a time-lapse sequence blasting from the starting blocks, and stretching, her hands alternatively relaxed at her side or adamantly set on her hips. Accompanying the images was a list of her feats (two time world champion in the hurdles, NCAA champion in the 100 meters, Olympic Gold Medalist, world indoor champion in the 60 meters) and curious stories that she used to race the boys home and played with dolls as a child.

Between the images of Devers and Jordan, and scattered through the building, were compasses cast in concrete in the floor, marking the four directional poles of north, east, south, and west, with Nike Town spelled out in a map of the world, the US at its center (Figure 4.3). At the opposite end of the corridor, a 7 × 3 feet toe of a Nike shoe *extended from the wall* above the sales counter, its angle suggesting a runner traversing this physical constraint and trampling those standing below. Gesturing to the shoe, Martha (Asian, 40s), a manager, stated, "I've never really understood it, but it fascinates the kids!" Two sleek black computer registers were located on either

Figure 4.2 Gail Devers

Figure 4.3 Nike Compass

side of a translucent blue counter, each encased in a black hood, and mounted on wheeled carts. These "product locator terminals" separated employees from consumers, and displayed prices from a small box extending from the counter.

Passing the entryway, I entered the main atrium of the store. Above me, *and apparently descending upon me*, were two white sculptures of mountain bikers, one in pursuit of the other. To their side were another two sculptures, one of a person taking a jump shot, while another defended, arms extended. These athlete-angels were suspended from the ceiling, their white plaster contrasted with the real Nike shoes they wore. Looking up at them and into a series of lights, I was awed and paused momentarily before reorienting to the stream of people around me, and joining them in moving past a large video screen set into the floor.

The video was comprised of nine adjacent screens; like puzzle pieces, they displayed underwater images giving the *impression of being underwater* to viewers standing on them or sitting on two benches strategically placed at its sides to try on shoes. As I sat observing, two junior high school age boys stood at its edge, reluctant to step on it, then hesitatingly testing it with a toe before walking over it. Next to the video was a huge aquarium literally built into a sidewall, where an Asian man in his 30s pointed out various saltwater fish to a child, about 2 years old. The aquarium served as backdrop for a large display of sports sandals.

Rejoining the flow of consumers, I stepped onto an escalator to the second floor that went past a wall-sized image of women doing step aerobics. Its cubist style was reminiscent of Marcel Duchamp's "Nude Descending a Staircase." As I looked back down the rising escalator, I saw an image of an African-American woman lifting weights. Both images were comprised of panels, such that only one was visible on the way up, the other on the way down.

On the second floor, consumers were no longer following an orderly route, but rather winding through the passageways and milling about, taking in the displays of celebrities and products or seeking out particular items. The second floor featured tennis, basketball, and aerobics areas. In each were shoes, clothing, and accessories attractively displayed amidst photographs of celebrity and amateur athletes and glass cases of their memorabilia.

Of the scores of photographs and displays of celebrity athletes, those of Michael Jordan predominated. "They treat him like a god," Lili (Latina, 60s) told me during her first visit. Initially, I was puzzled at her invocation of deity, but as I reviewed the data I noted many references to superhuman feats. The most dramatic display was a two-story length photograph behind the full-sized backboard of Michael Jordan coming down from the clouds to dunk a basket (Figure 4.4). Beneath the image were the words of William Blake, "No bird soars too high if he soars with his own wings." I was taken aback by the magnitude and serenity of the image, and I was not alone in this reaction. I watched as a middle-aged Anglo couple stood before the photo, their voices dropping to a whisper.

Figure 4.4 Michael Jordan in the clouds

Completing the tribute to Jordan were five displays in a room on the third floor, each contained in glass cases and separated from consumers by velour ropes, like those used in a museum or theater. One case displayed the 10 styles of Air Jordan shoes from 1985 through 1994, with a listing of his individual and team accomplishments each year. A caption described Jordan's role in designing the shoes from the beginning:

> Because Michael doesn't tie the top eyelet, his shoes have been specifically designed so they perform with or without the top eyelet laced. Michael soars toward the basket, and just when gravity would pull down most mortals, *he* changes directions in mid-air and jams it home. Because he spends *so much* time in the air, his shoes are designed for high flyers who want a soft and stable landing. Michael and his Air Jordan shoes— intense, sophisticated, without equal.

Next to the display of the shoes were two glass cases of boxes of Wheaties cereal, each featuring Michael Jordan on the front and signed. The caption under one of the boxes read:

> Wanna play hoops with Mike? Better eat your *Wheaties*. Since 1988, when Jordan's indomitable smile first graced a box, millions of future All-State, All-American, All-Neighborhood hoopsters have slammed down the breakfast of champions. Michael joins the company of some of the *greatest athletes* of the 20th century, including Babe Ruth, Walter Payton, and Pete Rose in endorsing a product as All-American as basketball itself.

A fourth case featured a claymation rendition of Jordan, while the fifth case contained a set of his golf clubs. The claymation display was designed by Will Vintion Studios, creator of the California Raisins, and featured a scaled-down Michael in a circle of his shoes, balancing a basketball on one index finger, and that year's Air Jordan shoe on the other.

Elisa (Latina, 20s) gave her reactions to the Jordan displays: "It's kind of a cult. It's fun." This was her second visit, and she had brought her parents who were visiting from Venezuela. "It's beautiful," her mother Lydia (Latina, 50s) told me, "so expansive." Next through the room was an Anglo family who lived in the area—parents, grandma, two boys, and an 8-year-old girl who had come to shop. Mark (White, 30s), the father, played basketball in college, and described the store as amazing: "I didn't expect this. It's *like a museum*. This is great," he said, pointing to the display cases of Air Jordans. William (White, 40s), who had come from Pennsylvania with his wife and two sons, described the store as follows: "It's a whole different shopping experience," the man told me. "The majority of stores are chains, with merchandise all packed in. This is *not even like you're in a store*." Then, pointing to the black and red 1985 and 1986 shoes, he added, "*these are collectors' items*."

As William said this, I recalled the display of Jordan's 1990 NBA All-Star uniform I had passed earlier. All the items were signed and set in glass cases—the red jersey with number 23, shorts, and Air Jordan Shoes, white with red and black trim that year. The caption listed Jordan's accomplishments since he had joined the NBA in 1984, and noted that "his baggy shorts have quickly become a trend in and out of the league. For Michael, it is a matter of function rather than fashion, since he wears his University of North Carolina game shorts underneath."

Other celebrity displays featured Andre Agassi, Pete Sampras, Monica Seles, Charles Barkley, Jackie Joyner Kersee, Joan Benoit Samuelson, Bo Jackson, Curtis Strange, David Robinson, and Chris Webber, among others. The celebrity displays varied in size, sport, and content, although they all featured a beautiful image, an impressive list of accomplishments, and some personal information. The human interest stories, such as David Robinson's interest in philosophy or Monica Seles' comeback, personalized the athletes and invited consumers' identification, even as the displays rendered them larger than life. One display featured the hand and footprints of Charles Barkley cast in concrete, inviting children and adults alike to compare features. I did, and was amazed at how they dwarfed my own. Barkley's statistics were listed: 6'6" tall, 260 pounds, and size 15 shoe, with a caption detailing his strong dislike of losing.

Betty (White, 50s) was inspired by the display of the zen philosophy of Phil Jackson, coach of the Chicago Bulls. She had come to Chicago from Tennessee on business, and said the store reminded her of her daughter, a former professional skater. As we stood reading the display, she explained to me that you could apply his philosophy not only in sports, but also in business. The display featured excerpts from Jackson's book, *Sacred Hoops*, kõans such as "Being aware is more important than being smart," and "The secret is in not thinking, quieting the endless jabbering of thoughts so that your body can do instinctively what it's been trained to do without the mind getting in the way."

The celebrity captions told of exceptional performance, and emphasized distinct style. The display for Joan Benoit Samuelson told of her two world records at the Boston marathon (1979 and 1983) and her Olympic gold medal in 1984. The caption read, "Joanie changed the way the world viewed women runners with her brilliant performances . . . No woman has meant more to running than Joan Benoit-Samuelson."

As I was reading her caption, Tom (Asian, 20s), one of the salespersons, told me that he had met her when she was in town for the Chicago marathon.

Employees exhibited much pride and enthusiasm when talking about the celebrities they had met or when telling me of new athlete endorsers who had been signed. Employees mentioned Oprah, Michael Jordan, Charles Barkley, Deion Sanders, and the Marinos. Endorsers came to the store to pick up merchandise and/or to do special promotions there. John (Black, 20s) noted that when Michael Jordan came in, they closed the store because it was too disruptive, and explained that the company tried to sign the "up and coming" athletes, and had scouts looking for them all the time all over the world. His eyes lit up as he said this about Chet Bergamon: "We just signed him; he's gonna be a star!"

One of the most playful of the celebrity displays featured props from the film *Batman*. Enclosed in a glass display was a black Batboot signed by Michael Keaton. The caption described the work of Nike designer Tinker Hatfield in creating them. In a cross-fertilization of creativity, the lace toggle on the first "batboot" was inspired by the muscular mold of Batman's breastplate and then later incorporated into the next year's Air Jordan Shoe.

Highlighting each display was one or more vivid poster-size photographs of celebrity or amateur athletes in various settings, always wearing Nike gear and engaged in some athletic endeavor (Figure 4.5). Products were displayed in orderly color-coordinated arrangements, typically featuring shoes at the center and flanked by complementary sports attire and accessories. Use of color and arrangement blended ensemble items such as warm-up suits, shorts, T-shirts, socks, caps, and jackets into each other, and distinguished them from other displays nearby. Generally, no more than two inches separated different items, with clothing neatly stacked or hung on racks perpendicular to the wall, which economized on surface space.

My eyes moved from one appealing color combination to the next. John (Black, 20s), an employee, attributed the attractive displays to their corporate merchandiser. Interspersed with the products and celebrity displays were mirrors, which enabled consumers to see themselves trying on the merchandise and positioned their reflections as part of the displays.

Figure 4.5 Steve Prefontaine, legendary University of Oregon runner (at left)

Overall, prices were roughly comparable to those charged for Nike shoes at sporting goods stores. However, distributors were allowed more leeway in competitively pricing the merchandise, as manufacturer's suggested retail prices prevailed here. As some examples, in 1994 Air Max 2 shoes sold for $125; running suits, $95; running bags, $30; hiking boots, $85; cycling shirts, $40; biking shoes, $80; sporty sandals, $60; golf shoes, $115; and golf shirts, $55.

The high prices of the merchandise were mentioned by informants. Jerilyn (Black, 50s) and two other teachers had brought a group of 25 local junior high school students. The students were the traffic monitors, she explained, and they had been brought here as a reward. She estimated that only 10 kids had the shoes at school, and added, "and I know I couldn't afford the sneakers, well, I could afford them, but they're not practical. It's not practical to put $100 in gym shoes." Then she pointed to a display, "I would love to have that red and black pair, though."

Don (White, 30s) had heard about the store from a friend. He was in town from Colorado, with his wife, who was interviewing for a dental residency. "It's cool," he told me, "the prices aren't the greatest, but the layout is cool. Like this stuff," he said, pointing to the display of Air Jordans. "In general, their products are not that much better, but they do such a good job of marketing. It's flashy. They get the top athletes, status symbols."

Nike Town was a promising retail space for study. Its mufti-sensorial displays, the dramatic photographs, the high-tech accoutrements, the various types of music, and the many people moving about combined to create an environment unlike I had experienced before in a store. Many of the celebrity displays were interactive. For example, a mini-basketball court, complete with polished wooden floor, backboard, and piped in sounds of a crowd cheering, permitted potential consumers to try on the basketball shoes and the role of basketball star. Anthony (Latino, 20s), one of the sales personnel, noted that some customers jogged around the store testing the running shoes. Eyes, including my own, were flitting about. I found it difficult to focus on any one item for long. I got lost and ended up going in circles a couple of times. Only later did I realize that I had not touched any of the merchandise on my first visit.

On my second visit, I brought a camera, yet was surprised when I was permitted to use it, having been disciplined against taking photographs in other retail stores and malls. "Take all the pictures you want!" I was told by Robert (White, 30s), the floor manager, as I explained to him my research project and requested permission to take photographs and ask a few questions. I agreed not to interfere with their business. He warned me that employees might not answer my queries: "They're trained not to answer journalists' questions." Nevertheless, all of the employees I spoke with were quite helpful, answering my questions, and volunteering bits of information about the store, the company, and their experiences working there. "This store is the largest," Anthony (Latino, 20s) told me. "It's about 70,000 square feet, our flagship."

Several employees mentioned that *Crain's* magazine, a Chicago business publication, had listed Nike Town as one of the most popular tourist destination in the city, second only to the Art Institute.

There were 140 employees in all. Those I saw in the retail area were almost all young adults, beautiful and healthy in appearance. Their casual wear and friendly demeanor put customers at ease. All sales employees wore Nike attire T-shirts and sweatshirts in the winter, and T-shirts or short-sleeved collared polo shirts in the summer with shorts or warm-up pants, and, of course, Nike shoes. They were quite diverse—men and women, White, Black, Asian, and Latino. Observations of employees were consistent with the information gleaned from the photographs. Of 68 employees coded, 29 (42.6 percent) were White, 24 (35.3 percent) Black, six (8.8 percent) Asian, and 10 (14.7 percent) Latino. Regarding age, 48 (70.5 percent) were in their 20s, 19 (28 percent) were in their 30s, and one (1.5 percent) was in his 40s. Average number of years worked was two.

At least one sales associate was posted in each of the concept rooms, yet the large pavilions had as many as three persons watching people more attentively than museum attendants. David explained to me that it was desirable to work in the big pavilions, since sales associates made more sales and more commissions there. His sales record was $4,400, but anything over $1,000 was noted. According to David, the top sales honors were recorded by a woman, who sold $14,000 worth of merchandise one day. He explained that she had sold a number of claymation Michael Jordan figures costing $750 to Japanese tourists, and added, "It adds up quickly at that rate!" Employees were paid on a straight commission basis of 8 percent of their sales, and were rotated every two hours. In addition, sales personnel were permitted to shop two days a month, with a 40 percent discount and a $150 limit.

Overall, I observed various groups of people at Nike Town—young adults, small groups of men and women, couples with and without children, and a few senior citizens. Many of the groups were comprised of multiple generations, suggesting various family combinations, while others were close in age, suggesting groups of friends or couples. The uniform of choice was casual clothes, namely shorts, jeans and T-shirts, or polo shirts. In fact, of 481 consumers coded from 177 photographs featuring people, only 37 (7.7 percent) were wearing dresses, skirts, or suits.

Consumers' behaviors observed included walking through the site, casually gazing at displays and intently reading them, and looking at and touching products, as well as trying them on and making purchases. Consumers were observed talking to each other, laughing, holding hands, pointing out things to others, taking pictures, and, in a few instances, children were crying or adults arguing.

Consumers used cameras and video equipment to take pictures of the displays, and of each other with the displays. Martha (Asian, 40s) estimated that she had seen as many as 15 people taking pictures in one day, as we watched an Asian man (40s) video the basketball court. "They (the consumers) can't believe it's actually a store," she noted, then added as an afterthought, "and you don't see that at Nieman-Marcos!"

On my way in that day, I had seen a group of four young Black women in their early 20s take pictures of themselves in front of the image of the US women's national basketball team. Later, another Black woman (30s) was teasing her son (8), saying, "Why would I want a picture of you?" to his request for a photo in front of the image of Michael Jordan in the clouds. She took a picture of him there and in front of the display of Dennis Rodman, in which consumers could change the color of his hair by pressing either red, yellow, or green buttons.

Taking pictures was a significant act on the part of consumers. Their photos indicated what consumers designated as memorable, valuable experiences or scenes. As matters of convention, photos and souvenirs are associated with being a tourist and having greater sensitivity to visual elements of the landscape, lingering over a gaze that is visually objectified in the photo (Urry 1995). Martha (Asian, 40s) estimated that half the customers were not from Chicago based on her perusal of the drivers' licenses required on checks and credit cards.

In an attempt to more systematically examine consumers' behaviors, I coded consumers' activities in the photographs that featured people. Of 481 consumers coded in the photographs, 223 (46.4 percent) were interacting with each other, 95 (19.7 percent) were looking at celebrity displays, 93 (19.3 percent) were looking at products, 82 (17 percent) were touching items, 41 (8.5 percent) were interacting with salespeople, and 27 (5.6 percent) were either standing in line to make a purchase or carrying Nike Town shopping bags, indicative of a previous purchase. These groups were not mutually exclusive, as at times a person would be interacting with another group member trying on or closely examining a particular product or display.

The average group size was 1.89 persons, averaged from 97 single shoppers, 140 groups of two persons, 32 groups of three persons, 10 groups of four persons, three groups of five persons, and one group of six. Regarding race/ethnicity, 364 (76 percent) were White, 34 (7 percent) Black, 38 (7.8 percent) Asian, and 45 (9.2 percent) Latino. Regarding age, 63 (13.1 percent) were less than 20 years of age, 176 (36.6 percent) were in their 20s, 146 (30.3 percent) were in their 30s, 49 (10.1 percent) were in their 40s, and 47 (9.8 percent) were in their 50s or older. Estimated average age was 31.5 years, arrived at by multiplying the midpoint of each category by the number of persons in that category.

Consumers' comments partially validated the store's aspirations, as described by Stan (White, 30s), a store manager who had been with the company six years. "It's showcase of Nike apparel," he explained, adding:

> Five years ago, the public had knowledge of our footwear, but not other items. Hopefully, we are inspiring to people who come in, not just as a sport, but as a lifestyle. We aspire to be and perform like some of the athletes who represent our company.

The store succeeded in inspiring informants. Laurie (White, 20s), a local college student, explained, "It's my favorite store, so inspirational, the things on the walls, the sweaters, shirts, hats—I've bought them for myself and my friends." Her favorite room was the poster room. She liked the store because it emphasized health and fitness, and she always wanted to work out after leaving the store. The selection was her other reason: "You go to a department store and there are three kinds of sweaters. Here you pick from tons."

Minette (Black, early teens) described Nike Town as her *dream* store. She had come with the group of 25 local junior high school students as a reward for helping direct traffic at street crossings after school. She and two other students (Latina, Black, early teens) showed me pages torn from a spiral notebook on which they had gotten the autograph of local sportscaster Jim Kelly. She especially liked the basketball area, and one of her companions liked the tennis area the best. I noticed they favored areas featuring the sports they played, just as I had gravitated to the women's basketball and soccer sections.

Other consumers were more critical. Jerilyn (Black, 40s) told me her students talked about the shoes at school:

> They think if you wear his shoes you can be like him, but it's more than the shoes! Jordan was phenomenal—how high he could jump. The kids don't see (the importance of) education. They want it now, quick . . . don't want to do the stair steps to be successful. One percent, that's what the kids see, straight out of high school making 2 million . . . Kids gotta understand, most won't come outta high school and succeed.

She then turned to one of her students (Black, early teens), who was sitting on the next bench, "Didn't you see anything? "Yeah," the girl replied, "but they cost too much for my size."

Maria (Latina, 30s) saw the athletes as *heroes* and role models. She had come to the store with her husband, son, brother, and sister-in-law; the latter two were visiting from Texas. "See the kids gaping," she said, pointing to her son looking up at the *Sports Illustrated* magazine covers, "part of Michael Jordan's success is he's a great man, conscientious . . . but it's important they give some of it back to the community." Her husband Carlos (Latino, 30s) disagreed, emphasizing the athletes' humanness and the business aspects of sports, saying:

> But they're human, they're not perfect . . . The salaries are big business, like when Michael Jordan signed with Nike, that's OK, he has a right to endorse and it allows them to give more devotion to the sport and to underprivileged kids. Or like Jerry Jones, he owns the stadium, signed with Nike and with Pepsi, saying this is my business. You gotta get whatever you can.

Nike Town demonstrates Nike's vision of its past, present, and future. Throughout the store, its architecture, celebrity and merchandise displays, specialty furnishings, and music created a comprehensive, calculated string of sensations and messages that aspired to being a complete, self-contained entity. Self-conscious in its design, Nike Town harkens us back to Barry's (1991b) point that knowledge of how the spectacle was produced was an intrinsic part of its pleasure. The philosophy of the company was most explicitly stated in a brochure:

> NIKE shoes. NIKE clothes. NIKE bags and hats. Posters. Displays. NIKE out the ying yang. No other store sports more cool stuff. A free-form, high-flying, design-inspired assault on the senses. Everything NIKE makes is in this retail laboratory SLASH! museum SLASH! fitness emporium. Part history, part athlete, part village, part cartoon, all NIKE. The past, present and future of sports and fitness around the world. A store only NIKE could build. Nike Town.

Other displays paid tribute to the company, describing its founding and humble beginnings. Displays explained how the idea for Nike shoes first came about as Bill Bowerman put rubber into his wife's waffle iron for Steve Prefontaine. Mild setbacks were mentioned, such as representatives of ASICS in Japan telling co-founder Phil Knight that his new product ideas were crazy. The story featured mystery in that the name Nike came to employee Jeff Johnson in a dream. The display of the blueprints and store model emphasized innovation and recognized the important role of employees in the company, likening it to a team. Its caption read:

> Everything in Nike Town, from the finest detail to the building itself and every shoe, shirt, sock, hat or bag in it, comes from the mind of Nike Design . . . Nike Town is a testament to the possibilities of team thinking. The building, fixtures, displays and products are just the most tangible examples of innovation, none of which would be possible without the effort of every Nike employee.

Throughout Nike Town were clever furnishings that conveyed the harnessing of technology and that brought elements of the sports literally inside the store. Examples include the high-tech clear tube transporters through which merchandise was sent down to sales employees from the warehouse above (Figure 4.6) and the black computer registers. The design, the displays, and even the store itself were carefully designed to fascinate and to communicate. Examples include the plastic air-filled bubble chairs sporting the slogan, "Just Do It," handles on doors and bolts on the guard rails featuring Nike "swooshes," tennis balls painted on the floor in the tennis area, and the wood floor of the mini basketball court.

Figure 4.6 High-tech tube transporter

Music tailored to each concept room further enhanced the spectacle. New age melodies permeated the sports sandals area, swatted tennis balls and cheering crowds enlivened the tennis area, and the high-pitched squeaks of sneakers on wood, the swoosh of a basketball passing through the hoop, and cheering crowds accentuated the basketball area and made me want to get out and play. Others apparently felt the same, as I was approached by two men in their 30s asking for basketballs. In the room for the All Condition Gear (ACG), the calls of birds and crickets, and the sound of setting a climbing rope were audible. Sales associate Anthony (Latino, 20s) told me they were going to remodel it, adding a waterfall and fish to make it more natural.

The various strands of Nike's philosophy were stated on the posters and T-shirts. These, like the products, were artistically displayed in frames and hung on the walls. Captions featured words of humor, intimidation, encouragement, and inspiration. Humorous captions included: "All Natural Fast Food," with a picture of a biker eating flies, and "Talk Dirty to Me; Nike Outdoor," which played on the sexual innuendo of sports activities. Examples of intimidation included Gabrielle Reese about to serve a volleyball with the words, "If looks could kill," and "On the field there are no winners. Only survivors." A third set of meanings encouraged people to get out and be active or take risks: "Explore the World Beneath Your Feet," "There are clubs you can't belong to; neighborhoods you can't live in; schools you can't get into, but the roads are always open. Just Do It," and "Welcome to the Real World." Finally, inspirational captions included, "Heroes are those people who believe they can and do," and "You Gotta Believe."

The video room and displays of souvenirs from Nike Town further spectacularized the store. Souvenirs, including coffee mugs, caps, towels, golf tees, and key chains, marked this as a memorable destination. The video room contained a large screen on which Nike advertisements were continually shown. There were no seats, but people did not stay and watch more than a few ads. In fact, people stood looking at the aquarium longer than the video ads. It was "sensory overload," explained Ben (White, 20s), one of the consumers.

Many aspects of the store were designed to orient consumers, and they did so literally in the store and figuratively in relation to the company. Examples included the complementary maps, the compasses set in the floor, and the scale model. Even the name Nike Town harkens us back to an earlier time, before suburban flight, when the market was the center of town.

Yet, despite the many attempts at orienting consumers, many were disoriented here. Disorientation was demonstrated in the questions consumers frequently asked employees: "Does it cost to come in?" "Can I buy anything?" "Does Michael Jordan own it?" "Who designed it?" Nike Town was not what consumers expected; it was not like other stores, it was more like a museum. There was much reason for the museum comparison. Celebrity memorabilia were collectors' items. Employees were posted in each room like museum attendants. The store was organized into a number of "concept rooms," as the employees referred to the separate but connected rooms for various sports, with separate areas for men, women, and children.

Employees worked to reorient consumers to the store. David (Black, 20s), who had worked there two and a half years, grinned as he told me he thought it was funny when people asked if they could buy stuff here. His response was typically, "Sure, that's why we're here." Yet, reorienting consumers was not the only way in which employees' performance was part of the store experience. Front-stage activities included greeting and conversing with visitors, answering questions, helping try on shoes, ringing up sales, taking payment, and packaging sold products. Backstage activities included discussing schedules and sales figures, rearranging products that had been messed up by consumers, sharing a laugh about the repetitive music, naming the fish in the aquarium, and talking about their dates and about being tired.

Several of the employees mentioned their training. It was similar to the training Disneyland employees undergo, in the sense that Nike Town employees were tour guides, orienting visitors through the site. Robert (White, 30s) explained, "It's a two-week training of company history, product information, and celebrity lore." Employee training used to take place in Portland, but was now conducted on site.

Employees' enthusiasm was only partly the result of their training, however, as their resonance to the meanings conveyed here and the periodic celebrity visits was evident in interviews. Employees enthusiastically tied corporate themes of athletic lifestyle and performance to happenings in their lives. Valeria (Latina, 20s) related to the company theme, performance, as a powerful word that "took her to the next level." She was a dancer and fitness instructor, and was inspired by the store, adding that from the moment she saw it, she knew she had to work there. Cindy (White, 20s) said all her life she had wanted to work for Nike. She had moved from another state to work here, and would soon be transferred to the New York store.

Two years later, I noted many changes. A new line of F.I.T. all-weather clothing replaced the Air Max shoes, and the Air Swoope, named after basketball star Sheryl Swoopes was introduced. There were new sports (e.g., snowboarding and street hockey), and remodeled rooms. Olympic athletes and women were featured prominently (e.g., soccer star Coby Jones and the women's national basketball team). A display had been added containing pictures of local youth athletes that was tied to Nike's national program, Participate in the Lives of America's Youth (PLAY). Many of the displays had been changed or rearranged. The poster room was gone, replaced with collegiate sports team attire. Some of the Michael Jordan displays had been taken out (the golf clubs and claymation figures), while others were now set into the wall (the signed Air Jordans). The Bat Boot had been replaced with a Ninja Turtle Boot from the movie, and the *Sports Illustrated* magazine covers had been relocated. Images of athletes had come and gone as well. Bo Jackson was out as the result of injury, while Dennis Rodman was in, having joined the Chicago Bulls.

Discussion and implications

> The memorable is that which can be dreamed about a place.
>
> (de Certeau 1984: 109)

> It's all about marketing.
>
> (Laurie, Nike customer)

The spectacle at Nike Town was at once like and unlike other spectacles described in the beginning of this paper. As celebrity product showcase, the store incorporated features of contests and festivals in its images and dramatic narratives of unconventional, underdog triumphs, and in the festive nature of the procession through the site, with consumers cast in the roles of explorers and tourists in search of clothing, souvenirs, and meanings. It was linked to athletic contests, such as the Olympics and Super Bowl, through depictions of athletic stars and their accomplishments. Spectacle was consumed both in the store experience itself and as context for additional consumption behavior in the form of purchase behavior; thus, both market and non-market forms were observed.

Spectacular consumer behavior processes

Spectacular consumption processes at Nike Town were fundamentally parti-cipative and communicative. Consumers participated through their movement, sensory response, and in the reasoning processes evident in their comments to their companions and to me, with value assessed as part of the process. Most critically, spectacular consumption behavior was communicative, with the source of its value in the rhetorical qualities of its design and displays. Together, the design and displays produced the raw materials for cultural consumption meanings that consumers drew from and re-inscribed.

Consumers' movement was both physical and figurative. Physical participation consisted of walking through the site, examining its contents, touching them and discussing them with their companions, trying on items, and, for some, buying. Through their movement through the site, consumers placed themselves in key spatial positions relative to its design and displays. Further, one's participation became part of the spectacle for others. Figurative movement consisted of imaginative activities and uses for the products, slogans, and logos (e.g., shooting the hoop, visualizing wearing the products, and saying the slogans), associations to one's past activities or those of others, and the feelings of being transported to another place, an otherworldly site inhabited by super athletes.

Spectacular consumer behavior processes were individual and collective in nature. It was individual in the personal associations, triggered memories and aspirations, and experiences with the personalities and activities expressed by informants, and in the individual images in displays. This sense of being a part of the spectacle via resonance and identification was what consumers were "just doing" more than anything else at Nike Town. By resonance, I mean appreciating and valuing meanings; by identification, I mean establishing one's sense of oneself and connecting with others. The spectacular consumption experience was social in the interactions of informants with others in the groups in which they shopped and with other consumers, as both were part of the experience, and in the depictions of collective endeavors (e.g., images of people working out together, team jerseys, and captions about teamwork). This contrasts with the atomistic characterization of spectacle quoted at the beginning of the paper (Debord 1977).

Design

Nike Town's design featured a plethora of art—the architecture, sculptures, photographs, the design and layout of the products, and the products themselves. The austere concrete facade and block lettering on the storefront provided one of the few cues that this was a major global corporate entity. The architectural design, with its atriums, passageways, and concept rooms, helped siphon consumers through the place, providing multi-sensorial stimulation at every turn, which invited imaginative associations. Large white sculptures of athletes suspended in the air contributed to their celebrity aura, and contrasted with the staidness of traditional mannequins. The photography celebrated the beauty of the male and female body and its athletic abilities.

The sculptures, the glass and wooden cases, the lighting, and the use of the velour ropes and other theatrical props, such as the cables suspending athletes from the ceiling, were quite effective in *invoking a reality somewhat removed from the everyday*. Interactive displays, such as that of Dennis Rodman featuring push button alternative hair colors, put consumers in control of the images. The sensory displays (e.g., Barkley's hand and foot prints, and the sounds of tennis balls being swatted and sneakers squeaking) facilitated consumers in positioning themselves literally in the action.

Positionality (i.e., the interspatial locations of consumers relative to the displays) was a key factor affecting reverential meanings. The high ceilings invited contemplation. Physical paths that placed consumers *below* and *in smaller relative size* to the displays contributed to a spectacular experience by providing an altered perspective for those willing or able to suspend judgment and recalibrate to the dimensions and perspectives of the displays. Such was the case with the suspended mountain bikers, the two-story image of Michael Jordan in the clouds, and the running shoe extending from the wall. The underwater photography shown on the video screens set in the floor gave viewers the sensation of standing on the water. The lighting, consisting of gallery-style small lights focused on the displays, together with the relatively darker areas between the displays, directed the attention and movement of passersby. Other design factors included the perspective, depth, and angle of the photographs in the displays, which brought consumers in close proximity to the celebrity athletes. High-tech accoutrements and furnishings, such as the product locator terminals, the product transport tubes, and the "swooshes" along the railing were suggestive of the future and Nike's attention to detail.

Displays

Displays contained a mix of sculptures and images of celebrity and amateur athletes, human interest stories and slogans, products, and cooperative sports marketing ventures. The heroic symbols of athletes were the most spectacular and the focus of attention. Displays featuring images of winners, gifted professional and amateur athletes always wearing Nike apparel, accompanied by ample lists of their accomplishments, and displayed in glass cases or frames further contributed to their reverential status. The memorabilia were always signed by the athletes, an important testament to their authenticity, and a factor spurring the museum comparison. Significantly, none of the products were used, their immaculate condition further placing the athletes above the spoils of humanity. Celebrity/amateur athlete lore encouraged visitors to identify with these exceptional athletes by emphasizing their human qualities. Examples were the human interest stories of Gale Devers racing the boys home from school and Michael Jordan's superstition in wearing his collegiate shorts under his professional uniform. As significantly, the human interest stories rhetorically shifted attention from the technical aspects of the products to the prowess of potential consumers.

The combinations of products and celebrities in the displays also functioned rhetorically. The glass cases and the proximity of the merchandise to the star athlete images positioned the products as exceptional. Products were billed as celebrities through the same display techniques used with celebrity memorabilia. The inclusion of Nike's specially made boots for the Batman and Ninja Turtles movies further positioned the products within the celebrity world. Products were displayed in color combinations to provide both visual contrast and complementarity, with their display efficiently organized to suggest prospective usage.

Through intertextual juxtapositions of products, celebrities, consumers, and company logos within and outside the store, symbolic associations were effectively bound among each of these separate entities. Narrations regarding the store and company history, together with the celebrity stories and descriptions of the technical aspects of the products, served to anchor the images of athletes to the company and its products in terms of what the athletes had done with these products, and thus what the products could do for consumers. The captions, as in a museum, helped visitors "see" the place in a certain way. They marked the items as valuable, and provided guidelines in interpreting their meanings.

The inclusion of cooperative sports marketers, each of whom played a role in the construction of celebrity athletes, further enhanced perceived meaningful relations among the signs by reinforcing each other's celebrity status. Examples include media, such as *Sports Illustrated*, professional and collegiate sports leagues and teams, such as the National Basketball Association, the National Football League, and Texas A&M University, competitions and awards, such as the Olympics and Wimbledon, and even foods, such as the cereal Wheaties.

Outside, the juxtaposition of Nike Town with other stores in the area produced an opposite meaning function. Nike's casual populism shared with the other concept stores (e.g., Sony, Planet Hollywood, Michael Jordan's Restaurant and Time Warner) contrasted with the social exclusivity of the upscale department stores of the Magnificent Mile, such as Saks and Nieman-Marcos, even as both catered to local residents and tourists. This mixing of an elite clientele with working-class consumers was reminiscent of the early arcades.

Cultural meanings

The meanings conveyed at Nike Town were derived from the data with attention to consumers' testimony, activities, and the images themselves. First, *competition* was a central meaning. At Nike Town, the spirit of competition was conveyed in the images of winners and their stories, and the sounds of crowds cheering in the sports rooms. Competition occurred at a number of levels, both inside and outside the store. Nike competed with other brands for sales of products to consumers and for celebrity athletes' endorsements (e.g., Emmet Smith and Reebok). At other levels, Nike Town competed with other stores along the Magnificent Mile, consumers competed with other consumers athletically and stylistically, and athletes competed in their respective events and for the attention of consumers.

Throughout the store, depictions of winners exalted competition, providing an homage to sports, fitness, and those who engaged in them. Both individual and group sports and fitness activities were depicted in images that drew attention to the pleasures of athletic endeavors, and narratives that described internal and external motivations for the activities. Particular qualities of competition, assertion, aggression, and non-conventionality were featured in the personalities, activities, and styles of such celebrity athletes as Charles Barkley, Andre Agassi, and Dennis Rodman. In addition, words of killer instinct and intimidation appeared consistently in the captions on displays and products, particularly T-shirts and posters.

The second meaning was *peak performance*. The displays signaled achievement and winning in the lists of exceptional performances and awards (e.g., Reggie Miller's eight points in the last nine seconds of a basketball game), depictions of superhuman accomplishments (e.g., athletes depicted in the clouds, above the ground, and otherwise above the rest, all the while wearing Nike shoes), and exhortations inviting consumers to push beyond their limits and excel. Physical and mental ingredients required to achieve were explicitly stated in the celebrity lore (e.g., the descriptions of the training activities and strength of Vin Baker and Mark Allen). Other qualities included dedication, hard work, and the belief in themselves. Significantly, the overlap between athletic performance and bodily libido, which was literally built into the store design and displays in their emphasis on action, and was evident in consumers' enthusiastic and inspired responses, was only alluded to in poster and T-shirt captions.

The third meaning was *style*. The prolific art and aesthetics, the sculptures and photography, the use of lighting and perspective dramatized the athletes' strong, fit, beautiful bodies. The captions on the celebrity displays explained their styles, and how they won with a distinctive flair (e.g., Michael Jordan's unlaced shoes and his University of Carolina game shorts worn underneath his Chicago Bulls uniform, and Agassi wearing denim challenging conventions of tennis whites). Style was a feature of the products themselves, their colors, designs, and their use by consumers. The color-coordinated displays were not only attractive, but also laid out such that pieces of attire were featured together in ensembles. And worn they were. The majority of consumers here wore casual clothes, many of which were Nike.

The final meaning was *recreational activity*. At the same time as competition and exceptional performance were valued at the site, other signs communicated that outdoor activities were fun. Examples include representations of children playing with each other, smiling, and other non-celebrity athletes working out. However, the repeated listings of athletic accomplishments, and the fact that losing was mentioned only in those cases where athletes had experienced setbacks on their way to ultimate victory, served to narrow the range of possible meanings, circling them back to a focus on competing and winning. Even the company slogan, "Just Do It," left unspecified the objective or level of performance. In doing so, it left open whether the challenge is to win or to just try, inviting and enabling identification by the most serious and the most casual athlete alike.

Nike Town was Nike's attempt at constituting consumers' desire. The cultural meanings provided here aided consumers in relating the products to our own lives, even as they positioned us within a "world" construed by Nike. At Nike Town, potentially subversive messages of aggression, intimidation, domination, and nonconformity were cast onto the acceptable realm of sports-wear and sports activities. Thus, cultural meanings were more stylistically transgressive than substantively so in altering any status quo. Meanings were transgressive in the sense of the determined, impetuous, proud, even arrogant personalities of the athletes. Yet, the egalitarian ethic prevailed in messages of hard work and skill that valued the person over the products. Here, sacrosanct American values of competing and doing one's best with stylistic flair and fun reinforced, rather than contradicted, the aspiration-based hero emulation of celebrity displays.

Experiential consumption behavior

The first theoretical contribution of this work is its attention to physical nuances of experiential consumption. Consumers' motor and sensory activities were important parts of spectacle consumption at Nike Town; indeed, they played a formative role in generating cultural meanings. The awesome and inspiring images, the appealing displays of products, the colors and designs visible from one room to the next, the mirrors that placed reflections of its viewers within the center of the displays, and even the other customers in the store *engaged* consumers as they moved through the site. Cultural meanings were produced as an artifact of passage as consumers moved through the design and past the displays, as a function of the trajectory of images consumers produced in their passage through the store.

The physically and imaginatively engaging qualities of the store were its distinguishing characteristics in the production and consumption of cultural meanings. Consumers' experiences of sports and fitness, appreciation of athletes' abilities, and/or identification with sports figures or teams, or the lack thereof, provided the viewing context. For the athletic, being in the store triggered a heightened awareness of moving one's body, and the thrill and satisfaction of physical accomplishment. For the non-athletic sports enthusiast, admiration of others' skills prevailed, typically emphasizing regional loyalties to individual athletes and teams. For those not interested in sports and/or lacking physical abilities, the site was a curiosity they endured for their companions. Importantly, its museum-style displays rendered these otherwise intimidating artifacts of the world of sports accessible and safe, if not valuable. The glass cases and velour ropes not only physically distanced the objects, but did so in hermetically sealed cases.

A blend of experience and cognition

The second theoretical contribution of this research is its attention to the blend of experience and cognition that characterized the spectacular consumer behavior process. It is important to distinguish between narratives about consumer behavior, which would categorize all research in consumer behavior, and the consumption phenomena they represent. Research approaches differ substantially in the aspects of consumer behavior they access. Regarding experiential consumption, judgments capture cognitive processes very well, while observations are important in investigating their kinetic and spatial qualities. Mistrust of the body and of social aspects of consumption, specifically the concern that they will overwhelm or suspend judgment, is a modernist legacy that has maintained an artificial split between mind and body (Joy and Venkatesh 1994). As Gallop (1988) noted, *thinking through the body* raises a distinct set of issues to those approached solely via cognition. For our purposes, the key concern was how the body and mind operated together in consumption behavior.

Consumers' foci of attention were into the displays, with companions, and within themselves. Observations and photographs of consumers were not suggestive of the mindless abeyance to spectacle presaged by Baudrillard (1988) and Debord (1977), although there were noteworthy fantastical and pleasurable elements. Attention to the displays lasted a couple of minutes at the most, more typically a matter of seconds, and then consumers simply moved on. Spectacle consumption was profoundly a physical and imaginative experience, yet it was also informative of product features and styles, and evaluative as consumers engaged in choices and decisions regarding the products. Thus, unlike previous conceptualizations of consumption separating hedonic from informational processing and decision-making (Holbrook and Hirschman 1982), this study of spectacular consumption at Nike Town emphasizes their nexus.

Consumers' participation with store displays served to normalize the otherwise spectacular showings, and was the means through which we interjected ourselves among them. In this sense, the poster caption, "Welcome to the Real World," takes on very literal significance. Nike Town was partial and apart from the real world in many ways, distanced via physical design and philosophy, yet inherently linked and profoundly connected to the social domain via individual cognitive associations and personal experience.

Role of the environment

The third theoretical contribution of this work is its attention to the symbolic communicative properties of the site. Like the hieroglyphs, Nike provided materials for cultural meaning making in the architecture and displays, hence the term "concept store." Significantly, in addition to the role of this physical environment made by Nike as object of consumption in the form of *consumption-stapes*, it played an additional role in producing meaning and enhancing the value of the merchandise displayed for sale.

Thus, the environment was both *consumed directly* and *served as context for further consumption* in the market spectacle. The site, its architecture, and displays were enjoyed by consumers like a museum, just as these features enhanced their appreciation of it as a store. This research reasserts the environment as an important part of consumption behavior, worthy of investigation in its own right, rather than merely an "influence on" other consumption behaviors. Further, this work challenges research conventions imposing a stringent demarcation between consumption phenomena and their context.

Separating context from phenomena limits our understandings of both. In articulating the importance of the study of the environment in social theory, Soja (1989) noted that geographical studies have been severely limited by naive understandings of their degree of social construction. This is evident in our disparate understandings of geography and history. While history is viewed as a human endeavor, geography is naturalized, largely due to its physical characteristics viewed as the result of natural forces. Notably, though, both "natural" environments, such as national parks and beaches, and social spaces, such as malls and stores, have socially constructed aspects and affect forms of subjectivity, as the result of the ways in which they are marketed.

In our case, the study of marketing environments yields important insights regarding their construction and their effects on consumer behavior. Marketing activities in the form of advertisements and media programming are pervasive parts of the contemporary landscape, with a strong influence on consumers' notions of what we believe and our notions of reality (Shrum, Wyer, and O'Guinn 1998). Analogously, marketing-manufactured environments are increasingly pervasive parts of the social landscape that naturalize the interests of participating firms.

The corporate museum as spectacle

Nike Town and other concept stores alter the contours of the marketplace, with important implications regarding relations between marketing institutions and consumers. It was significant that Nike Town was credible as a museum to consumers. Museums house objects of high social value, and, in this sense, are the secular church. Nike Town was ultimately a *house of high value*, and its spectacle lay in its collection of celebrity memorabilia and accompanying beliefs. Using techniques tried and true from the beginning of the department store, Nike and other concept stores are resuscitating the lost art of spectacle in their design and displays. Using celebrity athletes to value and encourage competition, physical performance, fashion, and recreation on a mass scale gives this strategy a postmodern twist.

The most important contribution of this research is its attention to the hybridity of consumption institutions manifest at Nike Town in its combination of qualities of a commercial store with those of a *non*-commercial museum. As mentioned earlier, the museum operates by invoking wonder and resonance as a function of its collections, simultaneously evoking the desire to own and evacuating it by displacing ownership to a reverential manner of looking (Greenblatt 1991). When juxtaposed with the qualities of a museum, the store experience changes from touching and buying/not buying to emphasizing a way of looking and valuing its contents, which further enhances the spectacle. Analogously, when juxtaposed with the qualities of a store, the museum experience blends not touching or owning the objects with being able to do both, hence evoking desire and facilitating its satisfaction by means of an imaginative rumination or purchase.

This research extends schema congruence studies to encompass marketing institutions. Cohen and Basu (1987) demonstrated that consumers used concrete category exemplars to refine categories of stimuli, and that they altered these categories in response to contextual factors, such as marketing activities. Further, Meyers-Levy and Tybout (1989) noted how moderate schema incongruity stimulated processing and product evaluations. Yet, these papers examined product stimuli, with less attention to the malleability of the categories or the effects of incongruent consumption institutions on consumer behavior.

Significantly, both categories of store and museum are renegotiated by consumers in response to increasingly spectacular marketplace sites, such as Nike Town. Here, Nike not only drew from the aura of the sports museum, but also produced and re-inscribed celebrity status to the athletes and the products via a store format through merchandising the celebrity endorsers and displaying their images with inspiring words and products. Museums are typically associated with cultural elites, sacred objects, and public institutions, while stores are more generally associated with mass culture, profane objects, and private companies. In bringing aspects of the store and museum together, Nike is contributing to the dual trends of sacralizing the store and popularizing the museum. Concurrently, museum curators are working to make their collections relevant to a wider public, using marketing techniques and including artifacts with a broader appeal (Karp, Kraemer, and Levine 1992), such as the recent exhibit of electric guitars in the Smithsonian Institution.

More importantly, this incongruent marketplace altered consumers' behavioral processes. At Nike Town, consumers' previous experience in stores and museums contextualized their behavior, yet its moderate schema incongruity in combining elements of store and museum ultimately resembled neither and resulted in disorientation. Notably, sales associates decreased the incongruity by guiding visitors into consumption roles. Yet, their guidance did not negate the effects of museum display in spectacularizing the products. The juxtaposition of store and museum experienced by consumers as they moved through this site produced and conveyed celebratory meanings to the athletes, the products, and the company. Consumers' credibility in the store/museum was further enhanced by the celebrity signatures and techniques of display, particularly the glass cases, velour ropes, absent prices, and attendants posted in each room.

Part of the theoretical significance of Nike Town was tied to the juxtaposition of its persistent categorization as a store by employees with its persistent categorization as a museum by consumers. In its exchange of products for money, Nike Town was commercial to the core. Yet, its most highly valued items, celebrity athletes' clothing and shoes, were museum-quality artifacts. Here, an *increasingly productive cultural role for the corporation* was accomplished via the conjunction of marketers' celebrity-product displays with consumers' activities in sacralizing products via ritual documented in other studies (Rook 1985; Belk, Wallendorf, and Sherry 1989), and imaginative movements through the spectacular store.

The interpenetration of commercial and non-commercial space is one of the characteristics of postmodernity, as is the collapse of metanarratives (Firat and Venkatesh 1995). Yet, these claims have been made on the basis of sparse systematic empirical work. In this paper, historical evidence was provided of the early integration of commercial and non-commercial spaces in the development of the early home stores and arcades. Even non-commercial spaces, such as the church or museum have commercial aspects in their gift shops that set the precedent for the combination store and museum at Nike Town.

It was mentioned previously that collections are a source of legitimization for their sponsoring institutions. At Nike Town, the company's possession and display of the artifacts of highly valued athletes totemically transferred power from the athletes to the corporation and its products. Like the early traders and religious and state leaders, and like the corporate executives who have bought and shown highly valued cultural icons in the US since the turn of the century, the company, Nike, the store, Nike Town, and its owners, the stockholders, derived a marked value and legitimacy from their collection as the result of its ownership and display.

Rather than postmodernists' projected demise of metanarratives, it may be that others are emerging to take their place, which corresponds to these shifts in institutional power. Recall that the museum teaches us a way of seeing, that knowledge is its commodity, and that the symbolism of its design and displays is its mode of communication (Hooper-Greenhill 1992). At Nike Town, marketing strategies featuring museum-quality sports memorabilia and products were accorded high value by consumers, with corresponding effects on the latter's subjectivity.

Spectacle and consumer subjectivity

Consumers' understandings of their circumstances is often considered beyond the scope of our work, yet it is a foundational component of critical consumer research (Murray and Ozanne 1991). In our field, consumers' subjectivity is most directly accessed in terms of what people say, and as such even disguised experimental and survey designs *reproduce it* in *restrictive* forms, although dialogic methods, such as ethnography, are more inclusive.

Bodily experience and imaginative processes of spectacle consumption *were* its most controversial elements, both praised as "the singular most potent space in *Western societies* in which *one* dreams of alternative futures and is released (utopically) from the unthinking reproduction of daily life" (Slater 1993: 207, emphasis added), and denounced as a distraction or beguiling influence (Debord 1977). In teasing out these two disparate views of consumer subjectivity, it is important to juxtapose consumers' behavior at Nike Town with its marketing strategies.

This research approached consumer subjectivity via testimony and self-directed movement in response to the store environment, artifacts, and meanings conveyed by the company. At Nike Town, Nike triggered a tremendous sense of subjectivity on the part of consumers. In experiencing the store design, displays, and products, consumers produced meanings and accomplished the spectacle. A poignant sense of subjectivity was expressed by consumers in their testimonies of their athletic experiences and in their interactions with displays representing the drive, courage, and ambition to surpass one's limitations. The images of the athletes "just doing it," their stories, and the company slogans were quite inspirational and appealing to many consumers who imagine and enact our own forms of "just doing it" each and every day, including, but not limited to, the domain of sports. Consumers' focused attention furthered the heroic status of the celebrity athletes.

Significantly, Nike Town's display of unabashed corporate tribute potentially furthered consumers' consciousness of their relations with the company; at the same time its spectacular presentation emphasized viewing the celebrity athlete memorabilia over consumption, and overwhelmed the company's social relations with employees. Indeed, as noted by Laurie (White, 20s), Nike Town was all about marketing. Don (White, 30s) went so far as to credit the success of the company to the status of its celebrity endorsers. Consumers' pleasure in experiencing the site thus was gleaned partly from their knowledge of its production by the company. Not coincidentally, Nike employed a textbook multisensory approach in providing foundational accounts of the company's history and the development of its spectacle. Like an inside joke, knowing its means of production put consumers inside the perspective of the store, even as they were technically outside it. This dual positioning outside and inside invited reflection, and has been identified as a critical component of consumer consciousness (Scott 1993).

Yet, to grasp the forms of consumer subjectivity associated with spectacle more fully, we must return to its description early in the paper, specifically its limited array of responses. At Nike Town, consumers' involvement centered on exploring, relating to the displays and cultural meanings with references to their lives, taking pictures, socializing, and purchasing or not purchasing, which, for most consumers, was the latter. Considering the level of success of the athletes depicted, which was well out of the reach of most consumers, looking and *buying* made the highly valued celebrities accessible.

Paradoxically, consumers were diminished by the larger-than-life displays even as they were empowered by the meanings and at seeing the artifacts displayed for them. Confronted with the store design and displays and their meanings of competition, performance, style, and recreation, consumers' most frequently asked question to employees was, "Can I buy anything?" This suggests that spectacular consumption constituted alternative subject positions to buying with its bodily experience and imaginings. Highlighted among these alternatives were consumers' faculties in experiencing the site sensorially and imaginatively, like the early strollers in the arcades, as well as contemporary tourists and museum-goers. Yet, unlike the arcades, this was an indoor store, and consumers' freedom in acting out their relations with the company and its products ultimately was channeled by sales associates guiding them back into the more customary subject position of a consumer.

The consumer behavior and market practice dialectic

The final theoretical contribution of this work is its explicit attention to the dialectical relationship between consumer behavior and marketing practice in the marketplace. Bagozzi (1975) noted the fundamental exchange between consumers and marketers, yet we must go further in extending the implications of his research to draw general theoretical relations from spectacular exchanges between consumers and marketers. At Nike Town, significant input from marketing research underscored the entire store design, displays, and the development of new products. In incorporating what they had learned about consumers in their marketing strategies, company representatives imperfectly reproduced and constituted consumers' desire. In this sense, companies such as Nike are not free to use cultural artifacts and other symbols as they see fit, but rather are quite beholden to consumers for legitimization, even as they gain economically and in terms of social power from them.

In turn, consumers took the products, images, and meanings, and used them, incorporating them into our lives to make statements about ourselves to ourselves and others, as has been noted in the literature (Belk 1988). Yet, the meanings conveyed here were not determined solely by consumers any more than consumers determined their own subjectivity. Both cultural meanings and consumer subjectivity are at least partly shaped by the actions of marketers, who anticipate and manifest consumers' value and desire. The dialectical relationship between consumers' behavior and marketing practice was demonstrated in the provision of cultural consumption meanings by Nike and their subsequent reinscription by consumers. Examples were pervasive in the ethnographic account, from the junior high school students wearing the shoes to stand out from their classmates, to the young woman who felt inspired to work out after visiting Nike Town, to my use of the slogan in writing my dissertation.

In their seminal paper on postmodernism, Firat and Venkatesh (1995) suggested that consumer researchers can no longer afford the modernist split of consumption and production. Yet, there is a troubling tendency in postmodern writings to focus predominantly on consumers' production of cultural meanings as the site of effective agency, at the expense of "obsolete" Marxian labor relations. As important as the cultural meanings attached to products by consumers and companies is the latter's exchange of capital with consumers and laborers. While disciplinary conventions measure a company's success in terms of sales dollars, of which Nike garnered $6 billion in revenues in 1996 (Nike 1996), we must broaden our sense of the market exchange to include cultural meanings. As Herrnstein-Smith (1988) noted, separating cultural meanings from economic values limits our understanding of power dynamics in the marketplace.

This research emphasizes the social relations consumption behaviors engender as fundamental parts of the consumption domain. It was previously mentioned that consumption discourse surpassed any hint of the other social relations engendered by the company at Nike Town. Particularly suppressed in the theatrics of Nike Town was its controversial history of relations with laborers and inner-city consumers, yet these relations are legitimate aspects of critical consumer research, as they are made possible by consumption. Media scholar Neil Postman (1985) argued that consumers needed a new way of discerning images, to question them and attend to the social relations they harbor. In this work, it was not clear that consumers needed a new way of discerning images, so much as consumer researchers needed to be attuned to the full realm of consumers' interpretive processes, broadened to include the social relations consumption behaviors engender.

This research is not without limitations. First, it has taken as focus of study the consumption of spectacle at a particular store. Nike Town Chicago was the flagship of the company, located in the city's premier shopping district, and in this sense was more representative of a marketplace spectacle than more generalized market practices. Yet, rather than viewed as an outlier, there is some evidence that Nike Town is exemplary of the emerging market, as spectacular, "concept" marketing techniques are increasingly pervasive (Gantenbeim 1996; Pacelle 1996). The study of spectacular consumption contributes to our understanding of marketer-manufactured environments as agents of cultural meaning.

Second, the methods used in this research were primarily visual. As marketers push elements of the spectacular further, rendering its consumption increasingly experiential, scholars must adapt, using appropriate research methods and approaches. Visual methods were well suited to investigating spectacular consumption behavior, as they directed attention to its experiential qualities and mobile, multi-sensorial manifestations. Supplemented by informant testimony, visual methods provided a valuable perspective on spectacular consumer behavior. Visual methods are well suited to other forms of spectacular consumption as well, such as film, theme parks, and cyberspace, with their blend of manufactured and simulated environments and interactive consumption behaviors. Other methods in the tradition of archaeology push the study of consumption environments further, with attention to comparisons across historical time periods and cultures. Further, projective techniques would allow greater depth exploration of fantastical and imaginative dimensions of spectacle, while longitudinal designs would explore the longer term effects of spectacle on product meanings and values.

Third, this work investigated the institutional configuration of spectacular consumption, noting that social power accrued to marketing institutions as a function of the value they generated. In our field, research has focused more on processes of value generation and consumption than its effects in accruing social power and altering previous institutional relationships between consumers and marketers. Recognizing that corporate interests historically have had a pivotal role in endowing public facilities, and perhaps even constituting our notions of the public itself, only partially abates concerns of the increasing privatization and commercialization of culture. For unlike many of the patrons of the highly valued artifacts that preceded it, Nike is a corporation. It is technically public, yet operates in the interests of such an unrepresentative subset of people as to render the term meaningless. As a configuration of public/private space, Nike Town is part of a long-standing tradition, dating back at least to the arcades, yet it is arguably the most recent and socially significant manifestation of the private ownership of collective cultural icons.

In conclusion, in documenting the interrelationships between economic marketing institutions, such as Nike, and their consumers, this research has taken the first step in investigating the role of commercial institutions in creating and managing collective value. Many questions remain. Further research is called for to study the contours of the generalized belief systems inherent to consumption, in building upon the company specific version provided in this research. As scholars of consumer culture, we must go further in developing our understandings of consumer behavior to include the political potential of consumption, investigating the institutional contexts within which people consume. Significantly, the political democratic impulse has been conflated with economic marketization in the contemporary marketplace. Yet, while these economic and political forces have converged, they are diametrically opposed in many ways. With few exceptions, corporations are not democratic institutions, although all are beholden to consumers. Nevertheless, the market has brought about important democratizing effects in its proliferation of wage labor and mass consumption, even as it has increased divisions between those who have and those who do not.

Finally, further research is also called for that maps out the social hierarchies of emerging forms of consumption, with attention to accumulated consumer products, meanings, and debt. Discussion of replacing the income tax with a consumption task among US Congressional representatives is only the most recent example of increasing attention to the political basis of consumption in this country. Already, there is a sense in which consumer and citizen are used interchangeably. Further work is called for that documents the opportunities and limitations of consumption as an emerging form of social legitimacy and enfranchisement in capitalistic societies.

Acknowledgments

The author gratefully acknowledges the cooperation of the many consumers and employees interviewed. Photographs are reprinted with permission from Nike, Inc.

References

Arnould, Eric J. 1989. "Toward a Broadened Theory of Preference Formation and the Diffusion of Innovations: Cases from Zinder Province, Niger Republic." *Journal of Consumer Research* 16 (September): 239–267.

Bagozzi, Richard. 1975. "Marketing as Exchange." *Journal of Marketing* 39 (October): 32–39.

Barry, Judith. 1991a. "Casual Imagination." *Public Fantasy*. London: Institute of Contemporary Art, 17–41.

Barry, Judith. 1991b. "Pleasure/Leisure and the Ideology of the Corporate Convention Space." *Public Fantasy*. London: Institute of Contemporary Art, 43–49.

Barthes, Roland. 1972. *Mythologies*. New York: Hill & Wang.

Bateson, Gregory, and Margaret Mead. 1942. *Balinese Character: A Photographic Analysis*. New York: New York Academy of Sciences.

Baudrillard, Jean. 1983. *Simulacra and Simulations*, translated by Paul Foss, Paul Patton, and Philip Beitchman. New York: Semiotext(e). Original publication in French, 1981.

Baudrillard, Jean. 1988. *Selected Writings*. Stanford, CA: University of California Press.

Becker, Howard. 1974. "Photography and Sociology." *Studies in the Anthropology of Visual Communication* 1:1: 3–26.

Belk, Russell W. 1975. "Situational Variables and Consumer Behavior." *Journal of Consumer Research* 2 (December): 157–164.

Belk, Russell W. 1988 "Possessions and the Extended Self." *Journal of Consumer Research* 15:2 (September): 139–160.

Belk, Russell W., John F. Sherry, Jr., and Melanie Wallendorf. 1988. "A Naturalistic Inquiry into Buyer and Seller Behavior at a Swap Meet." *Journal of Consumer Research* 14 (March): 449–470.

Belk, Russell W., Melanie Wallendorf, and John F. Sherry, Jr. 1989. "The Sacred and Profane in Consumer Behavior." *Journal of Consumer Research* 16 (June): 1–38.

Benjamin, Walter. 1973. *Charles Baudelaire: A Lyric Poet in the Era of High Capitalism*, translated by Harry Zohn. London: New Left Books.

Campbell, Lily. 1923. *Scenes and Machines on the English Stage During the Renaissance*. Cambridge: Cambridge University Press.

Cohen, Joel, and Kunal Basu. 1987. "Alternative Models of Categorization: Toward a Contingent Processing Framework." *Journal of Consumer Research* 13 (March): 455–472.

Collier, John, Jr., and Malcom Collier. 1986. *Visual Anthropology: Photography as a Research Method*. Albuquerque, NM: University of New Mexico Press.

Crew, Spencer R., and James E. Sims. 1991. "Locating Authenticity: Fragments of a Dialogue." In *Exhibiting Cultures: The Poetics and Politics of Museum Display*, edited by I. Karp and S. Levine. Washington, DC: Smithsonian Institution Press, 159–175.

Dayan, Daniel, and Elihu Katz. 1985. "Electronic Ceremonies: Television Performs a Royal Wedding." In *On Signs*, edited by Marshall Blonsky. Baltimore, MD: Johns Hopkins University Press.

Debord, Guy. 1977. *Society of the Spectacle*. Detroit, MI: Black & Red.

De Certeau, Michel. 1984. "Walking in the City." In *The Practice of Everyday Life*. Berkeley, CA: University of California Press, 91–110.

Deighton, John. 1992. "The Consumption of Performance." *Journal of Consumer Research* 19 (December): 362–372.

Denzin, Norman. 1995. *The Cinematic Society: The Voyeur's Gaze*, London: Sage.

Edell, Julie A., and Richard Staelin. 1983. "The Information Processing of Pictures in Print Advertisements." *Journal of Consumer Research* 10 (June): 45–61.

Enloe, Cynthia. 1995. "The Globetrotting Sneaker." *MS* (March/April): 10–15.

Ewen, Stuart. 1988. *All Consuming Images: The Politics of Style in Contemporary Culture*. New York: Basic Books.

Fırat, A. Fuat, and Alladi Venkatesh. 1995. "Liberatory Postmodernism and the Reenchantment of Consumption." *Journal of Consumer Research* 22:3 (December): 239–267.

Foucault, Michel. 1980. *Power/Knowledge: Selected Interviews and Other Writings 1972–1977*, edited by C. Gordon. Brighton: Harvester Press.

Fox, Stephen J., and J. T. Jackson Lears. 1983. *The Culture of Consumption: Critical Essays in American History*. New York: Pantheon Books.

Gallop, Jane. 1988. *Thinking Through the Body*. New York: Cambridge University Press.

Galvin, Kevin. 1996. "Smithsonian Exhibit Fetes Electric Guitars." *Denver Post*, November 25, 6A.

Gantenbein, Douglas. 1996. "REI: Enjoying the Great Outdoors Indoors." *Wall Street Journal*, October 15, A16.

Giroux, Henry A., ed. 1991. *Postmodernism, Feminism and Cultural Politics: Redrawing Educational Boundaries*, Albany, NY: State University of New York Press.

Greenblatt, Stephen. 1991. "Resonance and Wonder." In *Exhibiting Cultures: The Poetics and Politics of Museum Display*, edited by I. Karp and S. Levine. Washington, DC: Smithsonian Institution Press, 42–57.

Haacke, Hans. 1984. "Museums, Managers of Consciousness." *Art in America* 72 (February): 15.

Harper, Douglas. 1994. "On the Authority of the Image: Visual Methods at the Crossroads." In *Handbook of Qualitative Research*, edited by Norman Denzin and Yvonna Lincoln. Thousand Oaks, CA: Sage, 403–412.

Harris, Neil. 1985. "Designs on Demand: Art and the Modern Corporation." In *Art, Design and the Modern Corporation: The Collection of Container Corporation of America, A Gift to the National Museum of American Art*. Washington, DC: Smithsonian Institution Press, pp. 8–30.

Heisley, Deborah D., and Sidney J. Levy. 1991. "Autodriving: A Photoelicitation Technique." *Journal of Consumer Research* 18 (December): 257–272.

Heisley, Deborah D., Sidney J. Levy, Mary Ann McGrath, and John F. Sherry, Jr. 1991. "To Everything There is a Season: A Photoessay of a Farmers' Market." In *Highways and Buyways: Naturalistic Research from the Consumer Behavior Odyssey*. Provo, UT: Association for Consumer Research, 141–167.

Herrnstein-Smith, Barbara. 1988. *Contingencies of Value: Alternative Perspectives for Critical Theory*. Cambridge, MA: Harvard University Press.

Hinsley, Curtis M. 1991. "The World as Marketplace: Commodification of the Exotic at the World's Columbian Exposition, Chicago, 1893." In *Exhibiting Cultures: The Poetics and Politics of Museum Display*, edited by I. Karp and S. Levine. Washington, DC: Smithsonian Institution Press.

Hirschman, Elizabeth. 1986. "Humanistic Inquiry in Marketing Research: Philosophy, Method and Criteria." *Journal of Marketing Research* 23 (August): 237–249.

Hodder, Ian. 1994. "The Interpretation of Documents and Material Culture." In *Handbook of Qualitative Research*, edited by Norman Denzin and Yvonna Lincoln. Thousand Oaks, CA: Sage, 393–402.

Holbrook, Morris, and Elizabeth Hirschman. 1982. "The Experiential Aspects of Consumption: Consumer Fantasies, Feelings and Fun." *Journal of Consumer Research* 9 (September): 132–140.

Holt, Doug. 1995. "How Consumers Consume: A Typology of Consumption Practices." *Journal of Consumer Research* 22 (June): 1–16.

Hooper-Greenhill, Eilean. 1992. *Museums and the Shaping of Knowledge*. London: Routledge.

Hornik, Jacob. 1992. "Tactile Stimulation and Consumer Response." *Journal of Consumer Research* 19 (December): 449–458.

Joy, Annamma, and Alladi Venkatesh. 1994. "Postmodernism, Feminism and the Body: The Visible and the Invisible in Consumer Research." *International Journal of Research in Marketing* 11 (September): 333–357.

Karp, Ivan. 1991. "Culture and Representation." In *Exhibiting Cultures: The Poetics and Politics of Museum Display*, edited by I. Karp and S. Levine. Washington, DC: Smithsonian Institution Press, 11–24.

Karp, Ivan, and S. Levine, eds. 1991. *Exhibiting Cultures: The Poetics and Politics of Museum Display*. Washington, DC: Smithsonian Institution Press.

Karp, Ivan, Christine Mullen Kraemer, and Steven D. Levine. 1992. *Museums and Communities: The Politics of Public Culture*. Washington, DC: Smithsonian Institution Press.

Kassarjian, Harold H. 1977. "Content Analysis in Consumer Research." *Journal of Consumer Research* 4 (June): 8–18.

Lee, Martyr J. 1993. *Consumer Culture Reborn: The Cultural Politics of Consumption*. London: Routledge.

Lorenz, Christopher. 1990. *The Design Dimension: The New Competitive Weapon for Product Strategy and Global Marketing*. Cambridge, MA: Basil Blackwell.

Lynch, John. 1983. "The Role of External Validity in Theoretical Research." *Journal of Consumer Research* 10 (June): 109–111.

McCracken, Grant. 1986. "Culture and Consumption: A Theoretical Account of the Structure and Movement of the Cultural Meaning of Consumer Goods." *Journal of Consumer Research* 13 (June): 71–84.

McCracken, Grant. 1989. "Who is the Celebrity Endorser? Cultural Foundations of the Endorsement Process." *Journal of Consumer Research* 16:3 (November): 310–321.

McKendrick, Neil, John Brewer, and H. J. Plumb. 1982. *The Birth of a Consumer Society: The Commercialization of Eighteenth Century England*. Bloomington, IN: Indiana University Press.

Marcus, George E. 1994 "What Comes (Just) After Post? The Case of Ethnography." In *Handbook of Qualitative Research*, edited by Norman Denzin and Yvonna Lincoln. Thousand Oaks, CA: Sage, 563–574.

Meyers-Levy, Joan, and Alice M. Tybout. 1989. "Schema Congruity as a Basis for Product Evaluations." *Journal of Consumer Research* 16 (June): 39–54.

Mick, David Glen. 1986. "Consumer Research and Semiotics: Exploring the Morphology of Signs, Symbols and Significance." *Journal of Consumer Research* 13 (September): 196–213.

Mitchell, Andrew A. 1986. "The Effects of Verbal and Visual Components of Advertisements on Brand Attitudes and Attitude Toward the Advertisement." *Journal of Consumer Research* 13 (June): 12–24.

Murray, Jeff, and Julie Ozanne. 1991. "The Critical Imagination: Emancipatory Interests in Consumer Research." *Journal of Consumer Research* 18:2 (September): 129–144.

National Museum of American Art. 1985. *Art, Design and the Modern Corporation: The Collection of Container Corporation of America, A Gift to the National Museum of American Art*. Washington, DC: Smithsonian Institution Press.

Nike. 1996. *Annual Report: It's All About Sports*. Beaverton, OR: Nike, Inc.

Pacelle, Mitchell. 1996. "Razzmatazz Retailers Jolt Chic Shopping Streets." *Wall Street Journal*, October 4, B1.

Paglia, Camille. 1992. *Sex, Art and American Culture*. New York: Vintage.

Palmade, Guy. 1976. *La Epoca de la Burguesia*. Madrid: Closas-Orcoyen, S.L.

Peñaloza, Lisa. 1994. "Atravesando Fronteras/Border Crossings: A Critical Ethnographic Exploration of the Consumer Acculturation of Mexican Immigrants." *Journal of Consumer Research* 21 (June): 32–54.

Postman, Neil. 1985. *Amusing Ourselves to Death*. New York: Viking Penguin.

Redfield, Robert. 1955. *The Little Community: Viewpoints for the Study of a Human Whole*. Chicago, IL: University of Chicago Press.

Rook, Dennis. 1985. "The Ritual Dimension of Consumer Behavior." *Journal of Consumer Research* 12 (December): 251–264.

Rydell, Robert W. 1993. *World of Fairs: The Century of Progress Expositions*. Chicago, IL: University of Chicago Press.

Schiller, Herbert. 1992. *Mass Communications and American Empire*. Boulder, CO: Westview Press.

Schudson, Michael. 1984. *Advertising: The Uneasy Persuasion*. New York: Basic Books.

Scott, Linda. 1993. "Spectacular Vernacular: Literacy and Commercial Culture in the Postmodern Age." *International Journal of Research in Marketing* 10 (Winter): 251–275.

Scott, Linda. 1994. "Images in Advertising: The Need for a Theory of Visual Rhetoric." *Journal of Consumer Research* 21 (September): 252–274.

Sherry, John F., Jr. 1995. *Contemporary Marketing and Consumer Behavior*. Thousand Oaks, CA: Sage.

Shrum, L. J., Robert Wyer, Jr., and Thomas C. O'Guinn. 1998. "The Effects of Television Consumption on Social Perceptions: The Use of Priming Procedures to Investigate Psychological Processes." *Journal of Consumer Research* 24:4 (March): 447–459.

Slater, Don. 1993. "Going Shopping: Markets, Crowds and Consumption." In *Cultural Reproduction*, edited by Chris Jenks. London: Routledge, 188–209.

Soja, Edward W. 1989. *Postmodern Geographies: The Reassertion of Space in Social Theory*. London: Verso.

Sontag, Susan. 1977. *On Photography*. New York: The Noonday Press.

Spradley, James. 1980. *Participant Observation*. New York: Holt, Rinehart & Winston.

Stayman, Douglas M., and Rohit Deshpande. 1989. "Situational Ethnicity and Consumer Behavior." *Journal of Consumer Research* 16 (December): 361–371.

Thompson, Craig, and Elizabeth Hirschman. 1995. "Understanding the Socialized Body: A Poststructuralist Analysis of Consumers' Self-Conceptions of Body Images and Self Care Practices." *Journal of Consumer Research* 22 (September): 139–153.

Urry, John. 1995. *Consuming Places*. London: Routledge.

Wallendorf, Melanie, and Russell Belk. 1987. "Deep Meaning in Possessions: Qualitative Research from the Consumer Behavior Odyssey." Video. Cambridge, MA: Marketing Science Institute.

Wallendorf, Melanie, and Merie Brucks. 1993. "Introspection in Consumer Research: Implementation and Implications." *Journal of Consumer Research* 20:3 (December): 339–359.

Yates, Francis. 1975. "The Entry of Charles IX and His Queen into Paris, 1571." *Astraea*. London: Routledge & Kegan, 127–148.

5 Commentary

The cultural approach to branding

Giana M. Eckhardt

Consumption Markets & Culture has been integral to the development of the cultural approach to understanding the role and influence of brands. The cultural approach to brands highlights the cultural richness of brand meanings (Schroeder and Salzer-Mörling 2006). For example, Holt (2004) demonstrates that successful, iconic brands can tap into cultural shifts in society and provide consumers with a means to adapt to those shifts. As Wu, Borgerson and Schroeder (2013) point out: "In the cultural analysis of brands, brands are treated as symbolic forms enabling companies to compete gainfully, and enabling consumers to achieve optimal identity projection" (Wu, Borgerson and Schroeder 2013: 20). That is, brands are symbols that both tap into and help to create strong cultural currents, which then are used by consumers to produce their own identities. If one takes the view that brands are cultural, ideological and political objects, then brand researchers need to investigate culture, politics and ideology, not just traditional branding topics such as equity, strategy and value (Schroeder and Salzer-Mörling 2006).

Consumption Markets & Culture has been a pioneering outlet in this regard, featuring some of the first and also most in-depth branding studies looking at culture, ideology and politics, many of which are featured in this volume. The three papers featured in this section are certainly illustrative of this trend. In my view, taking a cultural approach to understanding the power of brands is the most potent way to gain insights. My work has tried to illuminate how brands create, as well as reflect, culture. For example, in looking at why the car-sharing brand Zipcar is unable to create a brand community, despite using state-of-the-art techniques to do so, we focus on the nature of access-based consumption, as compared with ownership, and point out the cultural contradictions inherent in the brand. Car ownership has a storied history within the US, and even though there has been a shift toward the share economy, cultural traces still remain, which make consumers embarrassed for others to know they are accessing, rather than own, the car they are driving (Bardhi and Eckhardt 2012).

On a global level, I have also examined how the traditional practice of yoga has been circulated around the world, become a global brand, and had the cultural meanings attached to it change drastically as it is re-appropriated back in its home country. Many of the new cultural meanings associated with the brand are related to the specific history of colonialism and globalization within India, and one cannot grasp the cultural significance of the yoga brand without an immersion into this rich stew (Askegaard and Eckhardt 2012). Similarly, I took a cultural approach to understanding how brands became key in creating a pan-regional sense of identity in Asia (Cayla and Eckhardt 2008). Here, we looked at the cultural codes embedded in brand images and text that were meant to convey a sense of Asian modernity – as compared with Asian tradition – and detailed how those cultural codes were being used by marketers to create an imagined community of Asian consumers. I bring up these examples to illustrate how broad ranging a cultural approach to understanding brands can be, and how key it is to taking a cultural approach to understanding the power of brands.

These three papers in this section approach understanding how brands and culture interact from varied perspectives. Peñaloza's (1998) exploration of how a brand creates a spectacle in a retail environment, and how in turn consumers experience a brand spectacle, was one of the first to look at retailing brands from a cultural perspective. Pettinger (2004), in turn, examines how a brand's culture affects how workers engage in varied workplace practices, again one of the first papers to look at the interaction between brand culture and work. And Kniazeva and Belk (2007) look at food packaging as a literary vehicle in which brand myths can be created and reinforced. While this paper follows in the footsteps of influential scholars who have theorized brands as myth-making devices, it remains one of the only papers to examine packaging specifically – as compared with advertisements – and to parse out how this medium contributes uniquely to the mythologizing of a brand.

In this chapter, I detail how each of these three papers has helped to shape the conversation in those domains, and how more recent research has built upon the pioneering efforts of these papers. Finally, I discuss how we can continue to move our understanding of a cultural approach to brands forward.

Brands, retail spectacles and culture

Peñaloza (1998) details the consumption of a retail spectacle, highlighting the cultural meanings that are implicit and explicit in the flagship Nike Town store in Chicago. As she notes:

> Nike Town is an important site of cultural construction, conveying cultural meanings throughout the store in its design and displays. The . . . space is ideological, in the sense that its design and displays place consumers in particular relations to meaningful symbols and artifacts.
>
> (Peñaloza 1998: 341)

Nike Town is part museum and part store – similar in that way to the Hard Rock Café, for example – in that it displays sports memorabilia, inspiring portraits and larger-than-life displays, in addition to the sportswear it is selling. As Peñaloza (1998) notes, "Nike Town is a . . . private space, with private ownership or copyright of the products, celebrities and images displayed to the public, unlike the public collections of cultural icons at museums" (Peñaloza 1998: 343). Peñaloza (1998) is interested in the significance of Nike as owner and curator of highly valued social icons, in particular Michael Jordan, who is featured heavily in the Nike Town store. This type of curatorial role has typically been held by institutions such as museums in the past.

Peñaloza (1998) uses her investigation of the cultural meanings Nike was able to attach to social space to demonstrate how Nike uses cultural cache and the significance and resonance of particular athletes to build the brand to iconic status. Nike uses spectacle to induce consumers to be in awe of the brand. Nike Town is the temple, Michael Jordan is the God. The Nike Town space allows consumers to try on the role of basketball star; while consumers are trying on sneakers, they can play on the mini basketball court to the sound of a cheering crowd. That is, the space allows consumers to become God, even if only temporarily.

Peñaloza (1998) sums up spectacular consumption behavior as "communicative, with the source of its value in the rhetorical qualities of its design and displays. Together, the design and displays produced the raw materials for cultural consumption meanings which consumers drew from and reinscribed" (Peñaloza 1998: 379). Consumers are a part of the spectacle via resonance and identification. That is, they appreciate and value meanings, as well as establish one's sense of self and connect with others. In sum, the cultural meanings of the brand Nike, as conveyed at Nike Town, are competition, peak performance, style and recreational activity. Peñaloza (1998) notes that potentially subversive messages of aggression and domination are cast into the acceptable arena of sports competition, and thus cultural meanings are stylistically transgressive, rather than altering the status quo. Meanings were transgressive in that the personalities of athletes were impetuous and arrogant. Yet, the egalitarian values of hard work and competing and doing one's best reinforced, rather than contradicted, the aspirational hero emulation. This use of potentially transgressive cultural meanings to reinforce traditional values foreshadows Holt's (2004) later conceptualizations about how iconic brands are created.

Peñaloza (1998) also notes that the cultural meanings within Nike Town are co-created by both the brand and the consumer's interaction with the brand within the retail spectacle. Thus, this paper prefigures the theoretical development of the co-creation of cultural brand meanings (e.g., Pongsakornrungsilp and Schroeder 2011), and provides a blueprint for how this process could happen for later scholars. For example, Peñaloza (1998) points out that Nike is not free to use cultural artifacts and other symbols as it sees fit, but rather is beholden to consumers for legitimization. In sum, this paper was very prescient with regards to conceptualizations that would later become core to our understanding of cultural branding: how a brand can tap into gaps in cultural shifts, à la Holt (2004), and also how there can never be cultural meanings attached to a brand without consumers' co-creation of that meaning, à la Pongsakornrungsilp and Schroeder (2011).

This paper also foreshadows the coming interest in retail spaces and how they uniquely contribute to cultural brand meanings, such as the ESPN zone. Kozinets et al. (2002) highlight the mythical appeal of the narratives created by themed flagship brand stores, as exemplified in the ESPN zone retail space. Similarly, Borghini et al. (2009), in studying the American Girl retail spectacle, point out that successful retailing in these spectacle contexts is highly ideological, and argue for the centrality of retailing in ideological branding. Both of these important cultural branding papers would not have been able to make the contributions that they did without the insights from Peñaloza's (1998) trailblazing study.

Brands, culture and work

Pettinger (2004) examines how brand culture affects working environments for employees. She specifically looks at service work and aesthetic labor in fashion retail, and how they vary from brand to brand. As Pettinger (2004) notes: "Branding is endemic in retail and is currently the dominant strategy around which the market uses cultural means for promotion, and particularly for selling, and hence one way in which the economy is influenced by culture" (Pettinger 2004: 170). In this way, her work echoes that of Peñaloza (1998). What she goes on to do, though, differently from Peñaloza (1998), is highlight how the employees create this retail brand culture via their aesthetic labor. That is, "the work done by sales assistants to present the store involves them in manipulating the branded products, fixtures and fittings of the store in order to produce the branded consumption space" (Pettinger 2004: 173–174). She finds that employees have to engage in higher service levels for higher end brands, which is not surprising. Not only do the service cultures differ between brands, but the way the sales assistants are aestheticized also differs depending on what the brand image and target audience for each brand are, again not surprisingly.

The importance of Pettinger's (2004) work is her focus on the embodied worker. That is, how the cultural meanings associated with a brand are embodied by the employees themselves. In fashion retailing, this happens in the form of beauty and attractiveness. The norms for beauty and attractiveness differ among brands, and she chronicles how employees are embodied differently via clothing, hairstyles and make-up regimes depending on the particular brand culture.

Her contribution to understanding the cultural underpinnings of brands is to point out the contribution made by workers to how the cultural meanings of a brand are presented to consumers, the labor that goes into producing the consumption of branded stores and products. Seeing how an employee wears the clothes along with other elements of his or her dress and style can often play a more important role in terms of solidifying cultural perceptions of a brand compared with more traditional forms of brand building such as advertisements. Just think of going into an Abercrombie and Fitch store, with their uniformly attractive and young staff embodying the lifestyle one hopes to achieve by shopping there. Pettinger (2004) reminds us that the branded environment incorporates the workers themselves, and that workers' bodies are part of how the brand is communicated. We do not have enough scholarship that focuses on the body and its connection to brands; in that sense, this paper is pioneering and will hopefully lead to a renaissance in exploring this angle of branding.

My own work with Susan Fournier hopes to contribute to this understanding (Fournier and Eckhardt, forthcoming). We introduce a theory of corporeal branding, where we focus on how brands are embodied by a person's physical body, as compared with their spirit. We build up this construct in the context of Martha Stewart, where you cannot separate the person from the brand. We describe how aspects of a physical human being, such as mortality, hubris and sociality, are inextricably entwined with the cultural meanings of a brand. While Pettinger (2004) focuses more on the employee aspect of physical human beings, we build upon her insights about cultural meanings of brands being embodied by people, whether it is the brand owners themselves or the employees, or even the consumers.

Brands, culture and myths

Kniazeva and Belk (2007) examine food packaging as stories of cultural production and carriers of mythic content. They demonstrate that packaging uses familiar archetypes and mythical tropes to create narratives, which consumers ultimately co-create along with the brand.

Essentially, the packaging narratives are anti-establishment; they push back against strongly ingrained aspects of today's society. In this case, because the brands Kniazeva and Belk (2007) examined are in the natural food category, they push back against the corporate agro-culture that supplies most of the food in the US, and reassures consumers that they are there to help resist this machine and bring a slice of old-fashioned food back to them. The authors point out that these brands are simply co-opting, appropriating and com-modifying nature, ecology and environmentalism to sell brands. The authors argue that rather than filling a "real" cultural need, such as Volkswagen and Apple have done at various times, these natural food brands are engaging in trendy opportunism. I would argue, though, that the fear of unnatural food is a real cultural fear. Whether these products are actually providing a natural solution is highly debatable – the term natural is not regulated – but they are addressing a real cultural disconnect in society. As Kniazeva and Belk (2007) point out, these mythic narratives do help us to dream of a better world.

The authors argue that these mythic narratives imply that "empowered consumers can temporarily escape imposed world conditions" (Kniazeva and

Belk 2007: 63). That is, the familiar archetypes and tropes lead consumers to think they can escape the agro-industrial complex and get back to a safer time by eating food labeled natural. From a sustainability and ethical standpoint, there has been much debate as to what causes the notorious attitude/behavior gap (Devinney, Auger and Eckhardt 2010). That is, consumers will say things such as they want to eat natural, organic or local foods, yet their buying patterns rarely match up with their stated beliefs and values. Kniazeva and Belk (2007) offer some insight into this issue. If consumers are buying into these mythic narratives, then they feel they can buy a bag of beef jerky labeled natural rather than go to a farmer's market to source something organic or local or healthy. These mythic narratives, in essence, provide justification for consumers to continue their familiar consumption patterns, contributing to the attitude-behavior gap, and also helping to uphold the myth of the ethical consumer. Ultimately, there is no meta-narrative of nature in modern society, so consumers co-create their own version in tandem with branding communications such as packaging to create versions of a myth that suits them.

As a final thought, the authors state that the first stories to appear on packages were in London in the seventeenth century. However, Eckhardt and Bengtsson (2010) trace branding practices in China back to the pre-modern era. In particular, they identify the oldest known "modern" brand – meaning a brand imbued with cultural meaning, not just an identifying mark – to the Song Dynasty (960–1127). It is the White Rabbit brand of sewing needles, and packaging was a key element of how the mythic meaning attached to the brand was communicated and disseminated. The image of and text surrounding the White Rabbit brand was stamped on the wrapping paper – packaging – that accompanied every sewing needle purchase. The key point here is that archetypes and familiar mythic tropes have been used in packaging, in the way Kniazeva and Belk (2007) describe it, for much longer than they, and most branding scholars, acknowledge.

The future of the cultural approach to brands

While investigations into a cultural approach to brands have typically focused on brand campaigns, studying the visuals associated with advertisements, for example, these three papers are unique and important in that they demonstrate that a retail environment, employees and also packaging can have a profound effect on how cultural meanings are embedded in brands, and how consumers are exposed to, interact with and co-create these cultural meanings. While the centrality of retail spaces to brand iconicity has gone on to be well developed in the marketing literature, employees and packaging have not been studied as much. The insights that Pettinger (2004) and Kniazeva and Belk (2007) reveal suggest these might be fascinating areas for researchers to delve into.

I would suggest that in addition to these three components of brands, scholars could also investigate other mediums for disseminating brand culture, such as online spaces (e.g., a company's website or Facebook page, and how it carries and conveys cultural meanings in a unique way). There is also much work to be done as to whether and what global variations on how retail spaces, employees and packaging convey cultural brand meanings. To examine retail spaces, for example, my own work has shown that in China, the nature of the space within a McDonald's is key to understanding the cultural meanings the brand carries, which change based on the nature of the relationships of the consumers using the space at any given time, due to the malleable nature of the self in China (Eckhardt and Houston 2002). Also, in India, a retail space that is perceived as being "foreign" by virtue of what it sells – pizza – cannot get rid of those cultural connotations, no matter how hard they try to position themselves as local via the employees working there, the menu or the products themselves (Eckhardt 2005). That is, the cultural codes are embedded in the space by virtue of it being perceived as foreign, and thus even when the brand managers try to embrace techniques such as those used in Nike Town, they cannot break the codes. These examples suggest that there will be a wide variety of ways retails spaces, employees or packaging can give us insights into culture and branding globally.

Finally, in some of my recent work, I have been exploring the idea that in particular contexts, consumers may look to brands more for their utilitarian value, rather than their symbolic value. For global nomads, for example, who need to stay highly mobile, use value becomes paramount, characterizing what we call their liquid relationship to possessions and brands (Bardhi, Eckhardt and Arnould 2012). Similarly, in access-based consumption, utilitarian meanings trump symbolic ones, as consumers do not create and extend their identities with objects they do not own (Bardhi and Eckhardt 2012). This viewpoint differs significantly from much branding research from the past 50 years, from pioneering brand researcher Sid Levy onwards, which has focused on the symbolic significance of brands (see Rook and Levy 1999).

This viewpoint provides interesting new research questions, though. If consumers are looking to brands to provide them with utilitarian value, and are not trying to connect with brands for identity or community purposes, what does that suggest about the changing nature of culture as embodied in brands? Anthropologist Danny Miller has recently suggested that denim is worn so ubiquitously around the world that it serves to make people fit in rather than stand out (Miller and Woodward 2012). That is, denim allows people to inhabit the ordinary, rather than express their identity in a unique way. Similarly, the advent of trying to look "normal" rather than express one's unique character-istics via clothing is on the rise (Duncan 2014), embracing sameness, rather than striving for difference or authenticity. Inconspicuous brands are also on the rise, where no one can tell which brand you are using (Ledbury Research 2012). That is, brands that used to flaunt their logos, such as Louis Vuitton, have started to drastically shrink or get rid of visible brand markers, and subtle and sophisticated brands, which can only be identified by a very small elite, are on the rise, such as Shang Xia, a joint venture with Hermès that offers high end luxury goods based on the Chinese tea ritual. Finally, Nakassis (2012) documents that for particular lower social class consumers in India, although they want goods with brands on them, it does not matter which brand; all brands are considered equal. The value for them is in the brandedness itself, not in the particular values or meanings an individual brand may hold.

Taken together with our findings, which demonstrate that although consumers love to use the Zipcar service, they are embarrassed of being seen with the brand, and do not want to be engaged in a brand community with other Zipcar consumers (Bardhi and Eckhardt 2012), and that as our world becomes more liquid, people want less permanent relationships with products and brands (Bardhi, Eckhardt and Arnould 2012), a pattern begins to emerge. The symbolic, identity-extending use of brands is on the decline. The use of brand meaning to say something about oneself or to connect with others is not as prominent as it once was.

How can we begin to understand this shift away from the symbolic, identity-enhancing aspects of brands, which has occupied much of the cultural approach to brands' focus for the past 50 years? Will the aesthetics of fashion retail employees matter as much to consumers in the future if consumers are simply trying to look anonymous with their clothing? Will the myths spun on packaging about whether a food is natural or not matter as much if consumers are simply trying to find a utilitarian solution to their hunger? Will the spectacle of a retail space still be able to awe consumers if they are simply interested in the functionality or the "normalness" of sportswear? These are fascinating questions that the cultural approach to brands can take up, and that I look forward to reading about soon.

References

Askegaard, Søren, and Giana Eckhardt. 2012. "Global Yoga: Re-Appropriation in the Indian Consumptionscape." *Marketing Theory* 12 (1): 45–60.

Bardhi, Fleura, and Giana Eckhardt. 2012. "Access Based Consumption: The Case of Car Sharing." *Journal of Consumer Research* 39 (4): 881–898.

Bardhi, Fleura, Giana M. Eckhardt, and Eric J. Arnould. 2012. "Liquid Relationships to Possessions." *Journal of Consumer Research* 13 (2): 133–157.

Borghini, Stefania, Nina Diamond, Robert Kozinets, Mary Ann McGrath, Albert Muñiz, and John Sherry. 2009. "Why are Themed Brandstores so Powerful? Retail Brand Ideology at American Girl Place." *Journal of Retailing* 85 (3): 363–375.

Cayla, Julien, and Giana Eckhardt. 2008. "Asian Brands and the Shaping of a Trans-national Imagined Community." *Journal of Consumer Research* 35 (2): 216–230.

Devinney, Timothy, Pat Auger, and Giana M. Eckhardt. 2010. *The Myth of the Ethical Consumer*. Cambridge: Cambridge University Press.

Duncan, Fiona. 2014. "Normcore: Fashion for Those Who Realize They Are One in Seven Billion." *New York Magazine*, February 24, 66–67.

Eckhardt, Giana M. 2005. "Local Branding in a Foreign Product Category in an Emerging Market." *Journal of International Marketing* 13 (4): 57–79.

Eckhardt, Giana M., and Michael Houston. 2002. "Cultural Paradoxes Reflected in Brands: McDonalds in Shanghai, China." *Journal of International Marketing* 10 (2): 68–82.

Eckhardt, Giana M., and Anders Bengtsson. 2010. "A Brief History of Branding in China." *Journal of Macromarketing* 30 (3): 210–221.

Fournier, Susan, and Giana M. Eckhardt. Forthcoming. "When the Brand is a Person: Understanding and Managing the Corporeal Brands." *Journal of Marketing*.

Holt, Douglas. 2004. *How Brands Become Icons: The Principles of Cultural Branding.* Cambridge, MA: Harvard University Press.

Kniazeva, Maria, and Russell Belk. 2007. "Packaging as a Vehicle for Mythologizing the Brand." *Consumption Markets & Culture* 10 (1): 51–69.

Kozinets, Robert, John Sherry, Benet DeBerry-Spence, Adam Duhache, Krittinee Nuttavuthisit, and Diana Storm. 2002. "Themed Flagship Brand Stores in the New Millennium: Theory, Practice, Prospects." *Journal of Retailing* 78 (1): 17–29.

Ledbury Research. 2012. "Inconspicuous Consumption in the Bag." *Financial Times*, October. Available at: www.ledburyresearch.com/news/archive/inconspicuous-consumption-in-the-bag (accessed 1 September 2014).

Miller, Daniel, and Sophie Woodward. 2012. *Blue Jeans: The Art of the Ordinary.* Berkeley, CA: University of California Press.

Nakassis, Constantine. 2012. "Counterfeiting What? Aesthetics of Brandedness and BRAND in Tamil Nadu, India." *Anthropological Quarterly* 85 (3): 701–722.

Peñaloza, Lisa. 1998. "Just Doing It: A Visual Ethnographic Study of Spectacular Consumption Behavior at Nike Town." *Consumption Markets & Culture* 2 (4): 337–465.

Pettinger, Lynne. 2004. "Brand Culture and Branded Workers: Service Work and Aesthetic Labour in Fashion Retail." *Consumption Markets & Culture* 7 (2): 165–184.

Pongsakornrungsilp, Siwart, and Jonathan E. Schroeder. 2011. "Understanding Value Co-Creation in a Co-Consuming Brand Community." *Marketing Theory* 11 (3): 303–324.

Rook, Dennis W., and Sidney J. Levy. 1999. *Brands, Consumers, Symbols, & Research: Sidney J. Levy on Branding.* Thousand Oaks, CA: Sage.

Schroeder, Jonathan E., and Miriam Salzer-Mörling, eds. 2006. *Brand Culture.* New York: Routledge.

Wu, Zhiyan, Janet Borgerson, and Jonathan Schroeder. 2013. *From Chinese Brand Culture to Global Brands.* New York: Palgrave Macmillan.

Part II
Corporate perspectives

6 Transnational organization and symbolic production

Creating and managing a global brand

John Amis and Michael L. Silk

According to popular and indeed academic rhetoric, our existence in a global age can be characterized by increased interconnectivity, an array of national and supranational bodies operating within common organizing frameworks, and increasing debate as to how to compete across different geographic spaces (e.g., Hardt and Negri 2001; Leung et al. 2005). We contend that within such discussions, culture, and cultural objects, must assume a central role. Indeed, we argue that cultural objects are not just a part of this conjunctural moment; they are both constituent parts, and constitutive of, the economy and everyday life. As Lash and Urry (2007: 4) have argued, "cultural objects are everywhere; as information, as communications, as branded products, as financial services, as media products, as transport and leisure services; cultural entities are no longer the exception, they are the rule." Further, following Askegaaed (2006), with the growing impact of market institutions on almost all aspects of our lives, the branding of cultural objects has emerged as part of an increasingly dominant market economic and commercial ideoscape. This is carried by supranational organizations such as the World Trade Organization, institutionalized in the marketing and management practices of organizational actors, and exemplified by the contemporary sovereign status of the liberal market economy. Coming to terms with the ubiquity of what Lash and Urry (2007) term a *global culture industry* requires academic foci on a variety of areas, including various forms of consumption, social identity, and the flow and transformation of cultural products (e.g., Elliot and Davies 2006; Lash and Urry 2007; Pettinger 2004). As part of garnering understanding on the circulation of global cultural products, our focus lies with making theoretical and practical sense of the operation of organizations and institutions engaged in the concomitant creative production and conceptualization of symbolic products directed toward the exploitation of new and emergent markets.

Of significance for us in this changed spatial landscape are the multinational corporations (MNCs) that have played a defining role in the emergence, operation, and machinations of the global culture industry. The economic, social, and political impacts that such organizations have render an understanding of their management and operation of vital importance to those interested in gaining an holistic understanding of the precursors for and consequences of corporocentric global forces. While much has been written on MNCs, it has become glaringly apparent that our theoretical and practical understanding of top management teams, more often assumed than empirically investigated in the wider organization studies and strategic management literatures, is at a distinctly nascent state when it comes to uncovering the influences on and actions of global corporations (Athanassiou and Nigh 2000; Leung et al. 2005). Against this backdrop, our particular interest here lies in the strategies used by top management teams to reconcile apparently contradictory forces that, on the one hand, point to a growing cultural convergence, but, on the other, require a detailed understanding and embracing of local mores and norms (e.g., recent discussions in Hitt, Franklin, and Zhu 2006; Leung et al. 2005). While clearly central to the management and operation of MNCs, our understanding of the ways in which competing globally and locally oriented cultural pressures intersect is poorly developed (Leung et al. 2005). The corresponding impact on senior managers as they craft strategies to articulate a presence around the world is similarly ill understood.

Consequently, our purpose in this paper is to examine the ways in which the contrasting pressures inherent in the positioning of a global brand, Guinness, are interpreted and acted upon by senior managers. Specifically, our intent is to illuminate the practices and rationales of key decision-makers as they contend with and reconcile changes in the dominant institutional and cultural logics inherent in global competition. While the specific nature of such logics will somewhat vary across different industry sectors and result in variations in the emphases on, for example, global and local positioning, we contend that our findings will resonate across different industries. Most notably perhaps, our focus on the understandings, routines, and practices of actors reveals the sophisticated production of multi-vocal, polysemic discourses that, at one and the same time, negate and engage with the idiosyncrasies of particular markets. We reflect upon the mechanisms by which senior managers must work to reconcile competing, even paradoxical, global, and local values (e.g., de Mooij 1998; Hampden-Turner and Trompenaars 2000; Lewis 2000) in a coherent and compelling manner to point to a need to reconsider how firms compete in divergent global markets.

To this end, the paper is structured in the following way. In the next section, we develop the theoretical background to our ideas. We then move on to detail the methods that we used to collect and analyze the data before presenting and interpreting our findings. The paper is concluded with an assessment of how our work helps to move forward our understanding of the global culture industry.

Transnational corporatism

Given the increase in symbolic regimes of production and consumption that underpin the late capitalist economy (Jameson 1990), the global cultural industries – broadly made up of the media, advertising, popular music, film production, and design – have come to play a key role in (re)constituting the geographic boundaries of markets and in the internationalization of consumer culture (Castells 1996; Hardt and Negri 2001; Lash and Urry 2007; Leslie 1995; Moor 2007; Robins 1997; Thrift 2004). Exacerbated by a neoliberal market economy that has promoted privatization, deregulation, and the removal of trade barriers (Harvey 2007), there has been a concomitant weakening of the nation and associated strengthening of various global processes that have transformed cross-border trade and marketplaces: global economic processes have become characterized by the increasingly prominent role played by MNCs in the establishment of a global culture industry (Frenkel 2001; Lash and Urry 2007).

While the prominent role of MNCs in global trade is widely acknowledged, less understood are the concerted actions of senior managers in response to or in anticipation of the changes to the dominant industry logics. In recent years, we have seen significant alterations in these logics. Far from the "borderless world" (Ohmae 1990) rhetoric heralded by Levitt's (1983: 22) treatise that senior managers should act "as if the entire world (or major regions of it) were a single, largely identical entity" and supply the "same things in the same way everywhere," the logics of a truly global marketplace (Bartlett and Ghoshal 1989) came unstuck when faced by the "warm appeal of national affiliations and attachments" (Robins 1997: 20). Rather than strategic global uniformity, many corporate leaders realized that securing a profitable global presence necessitated negotiating with the local: "and by negotiate I mean it had to incorporate and partly reflect the differences it was trying to overcome" (Hall 1991: 32). Thus, to operate with the language of the local in multiple locations, senior managers co-opted what had been a "radical slogan of an earlier day, 'Think globally, act locally'" (Dirlik 1996: 34) and thereby assimilated the local as part of the modus operandi of transnational corporatism. Attending to the local element within the ranks of transnational corporatism then actively affirmed the continued relevance of national cultures, as firms placed great emphasis on acceding to demands for local differentiation (Robertson 1995; Yoon 2001). That said, the "local" produced under a global system of common difference (Wilk 1995; see also Askegaard 2006) is liable, though not preordained, to be routinely little more than a commercially inspired inflection of what is perceived to be stereotypically representative of local culture. In this sense:

> the recognition of the local in marketing strategy . . . does not mean any serious recognition of the autonomy of the local but is intended to recognize the features of the local so as to incorporate localities into the imperatives of the global.
>
> (Dirlik 1996: 34)

According to this line of thought, the "old structures and boundaries of national states and communities" (Robins 1997: 12) have not been dissolved;

rather, we are ensconced in an historical moment wherein symbolic analysts (Reich 1991) play an ever more significant role in the constitution of contemporary, market-oriented, cartographic boundaries.

More recently, it has been suggested that the "global brand" is making a comeback (Holt, Quelch, and Taylor 2004; Quelch 2003). However, this revised understanding of a global brand is, of course, promulgated in a technological, social, political, and economic context that is very different from when Levitt (1983) was making his observations. Indeed, the global-local logics of the market point to the transnational production of localized spaces, identities, and experiences that facilitate the "continuity of flow" (Harvey 1985: 145) between global production and local consumption. In this regard, and despite the global cosmopolitanizing efforts of many involved in multinational corporatism, "geography still matters" in a very real sense, as local and national specificities continue to shape production and consumption processes in many sectors in different ways (Preston and Kerr 2001; see also Caves 1998).

While we may abstractly theorize the strategic importance of reconciling competing understandings of culturally convergent and divergent spaces and places into managerial practices, related empirical evidence is, at best, mixed. Indeed, if Lash and Urry (2007) are correct in their argument that products no longer circulate as fixed, static, and discrete identities, but instead regularly spin out of the control of producers, transposing, translating, transforming, and transmogrifying as they move through a range of territories, then the management of movements becomes central to the effective circulation of cultural products. This shifts the emphasis of transnational managerial understanding to the practices of global control: the work of producing and reproducing and the organization and management of global economic production systems and marketplaces (Sassen 2000, 2001).

As managers deal with the dynamics of the global marketplace, understanding the ways in which these competing simultaneous pressures for cultural and managerial convergence and divergence are reconciled and enacted has become a topic of significant theoretical and practical import (Hampden-Turner and Trompenaars 2000; Leung et al. 2005). It is clear that narratives of production and consumption do not emerge from nowhere nor exist in a vacuum. They are rather produced, interpreted, and spread by actors who operate in heavily institutionalized contexts (de Cillia, Reisigl, and Wodak 1999). Despite a recent interest in the operations, structure, and practices of the advertising and marketing armatures of organizations, the activities that individuals engage in to negotiate changing institutional requirements and symbolic spaces of production and consumption have received sparse empirical engagement (e.g., Athanssiou and Nigh 2000; Lawrence and Suddaby 2006; Leung et al. 2005; Pettinger 2004). Scholarship that has been conducted in this area has been theoretically driven and focused on a narrow conceptualization of cultural intermediaries, those actors who inhabit the pivotal space between production and consumption, which privileges a small cluster of occupations (Bourdieu 1984; Cronin 2004; Negus 2002).

Scott (1999) proposed that the creativity of workers is mobilized and channeled by the manner in which the apparatus works, including the ways in which specialized but complementary workers come together in the tasks of cultural production. Collaboration among workers in the cultural industries is common. For instance, the producers of commercials depend on an orchestrated collaboration of writers, art directors, actors, set designers, costume designers, photographers, illustrators, typographers, photographers, stylists, models and model makers, musicians, and animators (Soar 2000: 431). In this sense, the creatives' work is reified both in the routines of the agency around them (Soar 2000) and in the cultural field within which they operate. Such cultural fields, like most modern economic systems, almost always take the form of complex intra-firm networks linked together by tightly wrought inter-firm networks of transactions through which many different hands are brought to bear on products, as they go through the process of conception, fabrication, and final embellishment (Scott 1999). Thus, to truly address global symbolic cultural production, following the work of Robins (1997), requires a comprehension of both the worldwide organization of creative production and the exploitation of the new and emergent markets by the "eruption" of significations (Soar 2000) created and conceptualized by symbolic analysts.

This contention closely mirrors Sassen's (2000) call for an examination not only of the communication capacities and the power of transnationals, but also of the infrastructure of facilities and work processes necessary for the implementation of global economic systems. In the balance of this paper, we offer a consideration of the practices, decisions, structures, and strategizing developed within the promotional armatures of transnational corporate entities. For Negus (2002: 504), this conceptualization has afforded a pivotal role to advertising executives, designers, and magazine journalists, a conceptualization that fails to encompass the multitude of other occupational groups that are "crucial to processes of cultural mediation or the linkages which might connect consumption with production." Negus (2002), Pettinger (2004), and Cronin (2004) open up considerations of those occupations that bridge the processes of production and consumption. Negus (2002) importantly proposes that we think about the "ties that bind" creative work to structures of production. This study is one attempt to do just this. As we consider the ways in which senior managers bridge the space between production and consumption within the strictures of dynamic organizational settings, a set of practices emerge that are crucial in understanding the mediations that take place between production and consumption. Just as Pettinger (2004) managed with her research on workers in the fashion retail industry, by addressing the role of actors in the context of the late capitalist organization, we can critically interrogate and demystify the organization, management, and production of advertising and brand images that parade before our eyes in our everyday lives – an area of research that has yet to receive adequate academic consideration (Jhally 1995). In order to reveal and systematically analyze such practices, we present a case study of a group of actors engaged in global management and production practices at Guinness.

Methods

In order to gain the rich data necessary to access the complexities inherent in strategic decision-making processes, we adopted an interpretive approach based on predominantly qualitative data. This allowed us to unveil individuals' understandings of the organizational contexts in which they operate and their rationales for particular courses of action in ways that would not be possible with other approaches (Yin 2003). As Gephart (2004) argues, this approach has great utility in uncovering the human interactions, meanings, and processes that constitute and are constituted by organizational settings. In line with this, our intent was to complement the quantitative data sets that have dominated the international business literatures by providing detailed insight into the rationales for, processes of, and outcomes from the strategies that underpin a global operation.

Typical of case study research, the organization studied was purposively selected based on its theoretical and practical suitability of permitting access to the issues under examination. Guinness, headquartered in London and with brewing operations in more than 50 countries and product sales in over 150, provides an archetypal site from which to address the structure, practices, and management of symbolic production in an MNC. Further, the profitable participation of the firm in the highly competitive global beer industry, an arena characterized by a reliance on and creation of distinctive symbolic production, cemented its appeal. Through a gatekeeper, the Global Brand Director (GBD), who subsequently proved to be an invaluable internal sponsor of the research, access was gained to the key actors in the organization.

While we entered the field with several questions to explore, derived from our interest in the practices of senior managers and their roles in the strategic positioning of the brand, and the use of cultural signifiers to locate it, we were very much open to the emergence of themes that would allow appreciation of the ways in which those at Guinness accommodated various global processes. In this respect, we followed Denis, Lamothe, and Langley (2001) in adopting a partly deductive and partly inductive research design.

Data were collected in a number of ways. Semi-structured interviews were carried out with the individuals responsible for the strategic positioning, articulation, and management of the Guinness brand. Those interviewed consisted of representatives of the Global Brand Executive (GBE) and the three largest Guinness markets, Ireland, Great Britain, and Africa. These markets were selected because they are large enough to warrant significant brand activity and culturally diverse enough to expose the nuances of transnational cultural production practices.[1] Each interview was, with the consent of the participant, taped and fully transcribed to allow a more comprehensive analysis than would have otherwise been possible. Extensive field notes were taken during the interviews, primarily to record linkages between emerging concepts and to highlight potentially useful insights. In this respect, preliminary data analysis began as soon as data collection commenced (Johnson et al. 2004; Miles and Huberman 1994).

The veracity of the interview data was checked by returning the interview transcripts to the interview participants in a process of member checking (Lincoln and Guba 1985). This allowed the opportunity for the identification of any inaccuracies or misinterpretations; no such queries were raised. While the interview data were important, we also gathered extensive amounts of archival data from official Guinness and parent company Diageo publications, internal presentations, employee orientation information, videos of advertising campaigns, consulting reports, and various electronic communications; popular press and academic articles reporting on Guinness' global strategies were also analyzed. This resulted in several hundred pages of very rich data.

Data coding initially involved the assigning of descriptive codes to particular blocks of data to identify the emergence of particular themes. As familiarity with the data increased, so more inferential and interpretive codes were added to identify particular conceptual linkages (Johnson et al. 2004; Miles and Huberman 1994). The consistency of emergent themes across different data sources gave us confidence as to the robust nature of the data set and its utility in allowing us to draw credible conclusions (Amis and Silk 2008). Further, while acknowledging the inevitable partiality of our interpretations, a process of peer debriefing (Lincoln and Guba 1985) and scrutiny of our initial and final interpretations by the GBD supported our belief that we had identified the major themes inherent in the conceptualization, (re)construction and management of the Guinness brand, and also uncovered an inherent logic connecting and underpinning them.

Transnational management and the realization of global markets

The Guinness brand can be traced back to 1759 when Arthur Guinness paid £100 for a 9,000-year lease on St. James's Gate Brewery in Dublin. While originally a brewer of traditional ale, Guinness decided that the future of his company lay with a black beer, porter, imported from England. Consequently, by the end of the eighteenth century, Guinness had turned his back on ale and was brewing only the distinctive "stout" that would make the firm famous. Extensive expansion meant that by 1886, Guinness had become the largest brewery in the world with an annual production of 1.2 million barrels and established overseas markets in North and South America, Africa, the Far East, and Australia (The Brand Map 2001).

The twentieth century saw continued expansion, largely as a result of a series of technical innovations that radically improved product quality and allowed casked, canned, and bottled beer to be sold all over the world. However, despite its evolution into a highly recognizable global brand, Guinness ended the twentieth century with a disjointed approach to brand management and some quite indifferent financial results. A concomitant series of mergers and take-overs ultimately resulted in Guinness becoming a "premium global brand" in the Diageo stable rather than an independent company. The time was thus appropriate to reconsider Guinness' strategic positioning.

At the start of the twenty-first century, the GBD informed us, Guinness was moving from a strategy of "growth, growth, growth" to one that was underpinned by the philosophy that "it's not only about pure growth, it's about how you grow." Central to this was the crafting of a transnational brand strategy in line with a revised consideration of how to engage with the changing logics of the global marketplace. As such, in the following sections, we address the organization and decision-making of those responsible for Guinness, the spatial reach of the brand, and the symbolic production integral to this revised enactment of the global context in which Guinness competes. Clearly, these processes are not discrete; in fact, their coherent integration is seen as a necessary feature of Guinness' transnational strategy.

It is also worth pointing out at this stage that our interest lays firmly in the ways in which various global cultural signifiers have been utilized within circuits of production and consumption. Such a strategy, of course, does not take place in isolation to the broader industry or societies within which Guinness is located. Thus, while the specific components of Guinness' strategy will necessarily be temporally bounded, the underlying theoretical insights that can be gained from studying the use of cultural objects remain applicable. While Guinness has used many of the components that we discuss below for several years, and will no doubt continue to do so, others are more ephemeral. In this respect, whether Guinness sponsors a hurling league, bankrolls a film, supports a rugby competition, or underwrites a music festival is almost irrelevant; the underlying link to and use of cultural objects remains of interest. Similarly, as industry norms ebb and flow, so those involved in symbolic production will emphasize different attributes of the brand. For Guinness, these have included, among others, "Irishness," "Premiumization," irreverence, inner strength, and heritage. Within these varying non-mutually exclusive emphases, cultural symbolism retains a constant presence, even if at different times particular cultural vehicles will be accorded greater or lesser prominence.

In reflecting on these processes, we develop insights into the contemporary development of global brands. More specifically, our work points to the roles that brands play in our cultural and managerial understandings. These force us to go beyond simple, dichotomous global or local theorizing (see also Lewis 2000) to consider the nuanced, polyvocal positions that brands and their cultural signifiers now occupy in our society.

Structural and managerial transformations

Senior managers at Guinness decided that global expansion required a pronounced reorganization of the brand management team. Rather than the decentralized structure that had been in place previously, the appointment of the GBD in 2000 precipitated decision-making becoming highly centralized. A GBE, headed by the GBD, was created to craft and manage the Guinness brand. Reporting to the GBE, a GBT had responsibility for the manifestation of the brand through various promotional strategies and campaigns. Within each of Guinness' key markets, Local Brand Directors articulated the global brand initiatives within their particular locales. This revised structure highlights the shift from what had been a decentralized organization intent on following a devoutly locally oriented strategy to one that encompassed a more coherent global position. It is at this point that we start to see the emergence of a more nuanced global strategy capable of a more sophisticated engagement with different population segments.

Along with increased centralization was recognition of the need for enhanced cultural understanding of the local markets in which Guinness is sold. The GBD informed us that in order to ensure the seamless integration of the brand within the specificities and peculiarities of particular locales reached by the footprints of "Team Guinness," each of Guinness' GBT members had to be informed by a deep knowledge of local cultural mores and norms. As others have suggested, the ability of managers of a MNC to exploit symbolic and other intangible assets is likely to be contingent on the level of local experience upon which they can draw (Delios and Beamish 2001; Lord and Ranft 2000). With respect to those interviewed for this study, the GBD is English and worked out of the Guinness main office in London; however, he traveled extensively to the major markets and, from his comments in our interviews, thus developed a cultural appreciation of many of the markets in which Guinness is sold. This is significant because effective functioning of MNCs is usually dependent upon a leader exhibiting sufficient cultural awareness to anticipate the strains inherent in the operation of transnational teams (Hambrick et al. 1998). Further, all of the African, Irish, and British representatives that we interviewed are citizens of, and predominantly resident in, the regions in which they operate, and thus extremely familiar with local norms, values, and customs.

In order to better understand the intricacies involved in the management and symbolic production of a global brand, Guinness' managers looked to organizations perceived to be successful in negotiating contemporary global economic systems. As the Brand Director for Africa (BD-Africa) explained:

> We looked at brands like Coke, we looked at some of the Proctor [& Gamble] brands and part of the learning was that real, great global brands are managed as a global brand: global benefit, global identity. And I felt one thing, therefore: "was there a potential to run Guinness as a global brand?" Bearing in mind that previously [Guinness] hadn't been run like that, even the product itself, the liquid, differed significantly from one market to the other, [and] a different type of packaging [was used] . . . But the issue was that the brand name is the same and therefore what the brand stands for in the mind of the consumer will be the same thing.

This emphasis on increased homogeneity, superficially at least, takes us back to the mantra of Levitt (1983) and points to a lack of understanding of the variation in cultural consumption that global brands must reconcile. As de Mooij (1998: 5) has pointed out in a pithy, if a little simplistic, differentiation of the desires of consumers and producers, "local markets are people, global markets are products." However, there is evidence that those at Guinness did recognize the need to construct their engagement with consumers around the world in a more sophisticated way.

In addition to drawing on the experiences of peer organizations, Guinness also introduced a formal internal program of structured organizational learning, known as "Share & Spin." This constituted a formal recognition of the need to draw on divergent practices across different global markets in order to capitalize on the repository of cultural understanding that resides within the organization. Managers in each market are, with the assistance of the GBT, expected to draw upon initiatives that have been successfully implemented elsewhere, adapt them as necessary, and introduce them to their local operations. The utility of this strategy partially resides in understanding that the competitive advantage of MNCs is predicated on the ability of subunits to assimilate knowledge from their external environments and effectively transmit it through the organization, particularly through the use of transnational teams (Andersson, Forsgren, and Holm 2001; Lagerström and Andersson 2003). The "Share & Spin" philosophy is realized in a number of ways. First, open communication among individual market representatives, the GBE, and the GBT is demanded of all relevant actors. Second, any ideas with apparent utility beyond a local market are shared via the quarterly Team Guinness newsletter. Third, representatives of different markets are frequently brought together in cross-market teams to work on key initiatives. The management of these devices is seen as crucial in the realization of effective organizational learning.

A further major component of transnational management at Guinness comprises the extensive meetings held between members of the GBT and those in local markets. A member of the GBT will travel from his or her London base to each major market at least once a month with the GBD him or herself traveling to most major markets two or three times a year. According to the GBD, the purpose behind this extensive array of face-to-face meetings is twofold. First, it allows the GBT to act as a conduit of learning, transmitting ideas that have proved useful in other markets. Second, members of the GBT are able to collate an extensive array of information that can be modified and reused elsewhere. While establishing the "direct and intimate social relationships" necessary for the effective transfer of knowledge from one subsidiary to another can be a costly and time-consuming process (Lam 1997: 988), their importance for the competitive positioning of MNCs is difficult to overstate (Athanassiou and Nigh 2000; Hitt, Franklin, and Zhu 2006). Further, such consultative processes ensure that the strategic direction of the organization, while it may be crafted and controlled by senior executives, is directly impacted by culturally embedded workers scattered across disparate markets.

This philosophy is perceived to fit the dictates of operating in a marketplace that is at once global yet heavily accented by local dialects. According to the BD-Africa:

> Somebody has got the key and says this is what this brand is all about and guards that. I mean the brand identity and the brand image has got to be the strongest asset for the brand. And rather than leaving that to be managed at the various levels . . . we maintain the flexibility but we are strong at the centre.

For Guinness, organizational learning has been widely recognized as a mechanism to improve performance across the global markets in which they compete. This reflects the thoughts of those who have noted that the assimilation of knowledge by subsidiaries can be crucial for MNCs (e.g., Andersson, Forsgren, and Holm 2001; Luo 2005). However, some writers have urged caution when attempting to formalize programs of organizational learning across MNCs (e.g., Vermeulen and Barkema 2002). It has been argued that the socially embedded nature of knowledge can impede cross-border transfer (Bhagat et al. 2002; Lam 1997), and, further, that the ascendance of spatial units based around capital accumulation has meant that expansion is subject to time compression diseconomies whereby rates of return are diminished as the complexity of the organization increases (Eisenhardt and Martin 2000). However, these problems are mitigated at Guinness by the ways in which learning initiatives have become imbued into the "administrative heritage" (Bartlett and Ghoshal 1989) of the organization, something frequently overlooked by international management scholars. Initially developed through the transfer of production and distribution techniques and advertising standards (Simmons and Griffiths 2001), Guinness' administrative heritage has facilitated more effective transfer of ideas across the organization than might otherwise have been possible. This has resulted in sustained levels of cooperation across geographically dispersed subunits (Luo 2005). For the community of cultural workers at Guinness, then, their inventiveness and creativity is collectively defined and spatially enabled toward economic ends (see de Cillia, Reisigl, and Wodak 1999), though not always with predictable results. The major outcomes of this strategic organization toward coherent action are discussed below.

Global positioning strategies

As a manifestation of economic production across a global marketplace, key labor processes at Guinness have been organized around three major strategies – the derivation of an overarching "Key Brand Benefit" (KBB), the shift toward a more centralized global marketing strategy, and the development of common advertising for transmission across global markets. Following a "global study" in 2000 and 2001 of all of its major markets, Guinness' management announced that "we have a powerful global consumer insight on which we are building our vision: in a world of increasing speed, disconnection and uncertainty, young men need to draw on their 'innate' inner strength" (Guinness Global Strategy Presentation 2001: 2).

Clearly reinforcing perceived stereotypes of what male beer drinkers value, the gendered narratives that accompany this tag line of inner strength – viewed internally as "the brand's DNA" – are justified by the firm's overt targeting of men aged 18 to 35. In addition to being underpinned by the traditional brand values of power, goodness, and communion, the message of "Guinness reflects my inner strength" was perceived to resonate across global markets in a predictable – if stereotypical – way. The GBD told us that "we know that our brand fulfils this need of inner strength. So whichever market you go into, Africa, the UK, Ireland, 'Guinness [reflects] my inner strength' . . . is a commonly held belief and a very motivating belief."

This resonance is expected to overcome the type of disjuncture that has been noted as problematic when it comes to realizing global processes across local cultures (Bhagat, Steverson, and Segovis 2007; Leung et al. 2005). However, as we note above, the reinforcing of gendered messages is not problematized, or even seemingly considered.

The primacy of the top management team in the creation and articulation of symbolic resources capable of negotiating multiple cultural inferences to proffer a more consistent global position is significant. Central to this revised strategy has been a shift from using seven advertising agencies around the world to just two, BBDO and Saatchi & Saatchi. This, it was anticipated, would lead to a reduction in the brand fragmentation that many senior managers at Guinness saw as inevitable, if the decentralized strategy remained. This was articulated by Guinness' Brand Manager for Great Britain:

> From a parochial point of view, for myself in Great Britain, every time we showed an ad on satellite TV over here, that ad was also shown to everyone in Ireland who was watching satellite TV at the time, which is a fair audience. And when Ireland and ourselves had very different styles of advertising . . . consumers would be watching satellite one minute, see one completely different ad with a different strap line and a different idea behind it to when they switched on to their terrestrial TV. And there are more examples . . . of media starting to cross more countries. Also, the fact that, whether or not it was just consumers in one country or consumers moving around from country to country, they would see a slightly schizophrenic brand because in different countries you would see such a different type of positioning around it. And then thirdly, also an element of cost efficiency by the fact that ultimately we can reach the stage where we can show the same advert in different countries.

Thus, while there is a desire to realize the efficiencies that a global strategy can deliver (Hitt, Hoskisson, and Kim 1997), the decision to develop a common global strategy largely stemmed from the social and technological transformations that have fundamentally altered the industry. This insight demonstrates the need to conceive global strategies that offer broadly consistent value propositions without slipping into a retrenched "one-size-fits-all" position. Interestingly, the identification of media crossing national borders and its subsequent impact on brand consumption has not always been acknowledged (e.g., de Mooij 1998). Our work points to the ways in which the flow of televisual and electronic images, together with the increased flow of people across borders, has radically altered global brand management strategies. The substantially altered institutional context demands a significantly different strategic response from the top management team toward global brand building (Quelch 2003). The McDonald's "I'm lovin' it" campaign, launched in Germany on 2 September 2003, and subsequently rolled out across more than 100 countries, is a similar attempt to address the issues inherent in managing this changed spatiality. At Guinness, the first articulation of this attempt to manifest the KBB within a revised understanding of a convergent global marketplace came with the "Believe" initiative.

Changing spaces: the polysemic logics of "Believe"

"Believe" is a symbolic campaign that constitutes a key pillar in the delivery of the KBB within the new institutional logics that have heavily contoured Guinness' global strategy. As other MNCs (e.g., Anheuser-Busch, Coca-Cola, McDonald's, Nike), Guinness has drawn upon sport in its efforts to instantiate its brand within specific locales (Amis 2003, 2005). The "Believe" campaign embraced the supposed gendered logic of sporting capital in an effort to suture Guinness to the ways in which young men can draw on their inner strength, articulated as self-belief, to achieve challenging objectives. It was an overt attempt to carve out a common global position for Guinness. The first advertisement created for this campaign, "Free In," was launched in Great Britain in February 2002 and subsequently played out across other major global markets. It depicts an unfurling scenario at the end of a hurling match (Guinness 2008):

> Just one minute of injury time left in a knife-edge match and a vicious foul creates a chance. Over the bar and the game is tied, but into the goal and the game is won. Stepping up to take the free as the crowd go wild, our man's mind spins out of control. With a deep breath the player looks down. He sees himself and the coveted silver cup held aloft on the shoulders of exuberant fans, victoriously sipping a well-earned pint of creamy Guinness beer. Inspired by the vision of success he whips the ball up off the ground. If you want it, you've got to believe.

The commercial was seen, particularly by the Irish brand team, as being a natural progression from the sponsorship in Ireland of the "Guinness All-Ireland Hurling Championship," a partnership that has been described by an independent consulting firm as the most effective sport sponsorship in Irish history (Amárach Consulting 2000). The Head of Sponsorship for Guinness in Ireland (HS-Ireland) denoted the close match between the values that underpin the Guinness brand and the sport as being crucial:

> We looked at the DNA of both hurling and Guinness and they are so remarkably similar . . . it's 9.9 out of 10. It's . . . perfect. So when we . . . heard the concept behind the new "Believe" campaign was going to be around hurling, we said "sure, it's so obvious." We've tested it, and it's proven over the last eight years to be a perfect fit.

While the comment above is clearly susceptible to local bias and ex post justification, there is no doubt that hurling holds an iconic association with Ireland in much the same way as Guinness, particularly among the Irish diaspora. Indeed, one essayist has described hurling as a sport "nourished by [Irish] history and culture and the Irish sense of place" (Humphries 2003: 44). In this respect, a local sporting practice has been mobilized as a major cultural signifier of Ireland, one that effectively resonates with the Guinness brand and national sensibilities, identities, and experiences.

It is at this point that we see the movement beyond previous conceptualizations of global and local orientations to a much more nuanced engagement with consumers. Hampden-Turner and Trompenaars (2000) noted the ways in which "value dilemmas," such as emphasizing universalism or particularism, become reconciled across different cultures. We find here that such dichotomous thinking is no longer useful. Rather than attempting to present either a standardized or localized message, hurling was seen as a sport that would operate at multiple levels when "read" by culturally diverse consumers. At one level, the local sporting practice would be surpassed; hurling would thus be coterminous with the key global attributes of the brand. At the same time, however, hurling provided a link to the rich cultural heritage of the Irish nation, a heritage and tradition that Guinness managers could draw upon and employ, however superficially, as part of their global strategizing. As the GBD stated: "In some markets where [an Irish population] exists, like Great Britain, Ireland obviously, the USA, Australia, it tends to be our draught markets [the Irish heritage of the brand is exploited]; in Africa and Asia, it means nothing."

This polyvocal position helps us to move beyond one of the key managerial paradoxes confronting those involved with the presentation and research of global brands, namely the value proposition of global *or* local brand positioning (e.g., de Mooij 1998; Hampden-Turner and Trompenaars 2000; Lewis 2000). Rather, here we point to the ways in which brands can engage different populations in different ways. Given the fragmented nature of consumer groups created by social and economic migrants and the ability of electronic and televisual images to cross national borders, the global brand landscape has changed in ways that render previous "either-or" arguments anachronistic. Thus, we side with Lewis, who argued that managing apparently paradoxical situations (e.g., "think global, act local") requires "rethinking past perceptions and practices," going beyond simple linear and rational problem solving to recognize the tensions and contradictions that can lead to creative solutions of managerial problems. In other words, we can no longer think simply in terms of black or white, we must construct our understandings in shades of gray.

While the "Free In" advertisement employs common imagery that will be differentially interpreted at multiple levels in different places, it is positioned to carry the generic KBB, "Guinness reflects my inner strength," across cultures. However, through an interweaving of simulacra, Guinness also becomes overtly attached to and works to (re)create a heritage as an Irish sporting brand. In this respect, Guinness has created a global campaign that seeks to draw affiliations with particular lifestyles and values, and, at the same time, through a multileveled polysemic text, is located within the tradition and heritage of a national territory. This is an important observation, because a common contention in the international business literature is that managers of MNCs decide on promotional campaigns that have either a local or global emphasis (Melewar and Saunders 1999). In fact, as we uncovered here, such conceptualizations are no longer sufficient. Instead, we must consider the theoretical and practical implications of culturally embedded brands that can simultaneously realize multiple objectives across different markets.

Revised logics of production and consumption: the appropriation and management of culture

Our theorizing above regarding the need to engage with multiple brand interpretations across different markets should not be seen as a call to abandon all local marketing initiatives. In fact, local cultural appropriation retains a significant role in the Guinness brand platform. Notably, in line with the acknowledged potential of sport to reaffirm national cultures within corporate discourse (e.g., Silk and Andrews 2001), Guinness has an established tradition of using sport in various ways across the world. In fact, it has become so important to the global positioning of Guinness, as several other MNCs, that it is worthy of detailed examination. The 1999 Rugby World Cup allowed Guinness to utilize a property in an effective manner across several global markets (Rines 2001). While no other sporting property with such a global reach has since been acquired, local sports initiatives have played a significant role in the delivery of the KBB in different locales. This is important, because advertising assets have traditionally been seen to be less fungible than most organization resources and thus are most in need of local adaptation (Anand and Delios 2002). Consequently, while the "Free In" advertisement may have utility at raising awareness of the KBB, a local component that effectively negotiates national cultural sensibilities has become a necessary feature of Guinness' strategic position. The BD-Africa explained the rationale for this within an African context:

> I am saying the need for self-belief, the need for inner strength is particularly relevant in Africa. The reason for this is that Africans see themselves as coming from a disadvantage. In every way of life, Africa is behind the world. Again, Africans believe, because we are Africans we can overcome all of those obstacles and we can achieve things almost of world standard. It comes through in [soccer] and we've leveraged it, so one good example will be where we begin to say . . . if you believe in yourself and your ability you can overcome your obstacles and your disadvantages and perform at a first world class. We have leveraged that during the [soccer] World Cup with the [soccer] ad, where we have shown Africans training on sub-standard pitches, without sports equipment and saying, "Well, because we are what we are, because we believe in ourselves, we can overcome," and then we lead on from that showing national teams, African national teams, that have played in the World Cup and have performed well. So again, it is tying that need of Africans to believe that in spite of our disadvantages, we can still be reckoned with at the global stage, and tying that to the brand benefit of inner strength, that it reflects your inner strength.

There are three ways in which Guinness has used sport to deliver the KBB in culturally distinctive ways. The first of these is direct sponsorship. In its three biggest markets, Guinness has sponsored several local properties. In Africa, this has mainly centered on soccer. In Great Britain, agreements are in place with both London Irish Rugby Football Club and the professional league in which the team plays, the Guinness Premiership. In Ireland, in addition to golf and horseracing, the most notable sponsorship is the "Guinness All-Ireland Hurling Championship."

The second major way in which sport is utilized is through on-trade promotions tied to televised sporting events. In Ireland, there is a carefully orchestrated series of events that are intended to encourage people to congregate and watch televised hurling games in their local pubs. Quiz nights, musical entertainment, and local talent competitions are all used to promote Guinness while the games are being played (*Not men, but giants* 2001). In England, millions of pounds have been spent on promotions during the soccer World Cup Finals. The resonance of one promotion with the KBB articulated here as self-belief was explained by the BD-GB with reference to England captain David Beckham's goals that first ensured that England qualified for the 2002 World Cup Finals, and second resulted in a decisive win against one of the pre-tournament favorites and long-time rivals, Argentina:

> David Beckham scoring a free kick in the last minute against Greece in the World Cup qualifiers; scoring a penalty against Argentina in the

World Cup. Just look at his face as he goes to take it, and he controls his breathing and he settles himself and it's all about self-belief . . . there are a huge amount of self-belief moments in sport.

Such moments, according to the BD-GB, act as direct articulations of the KBB in a locally specific context that help to reify the managerially prescribed essence of the brand to a local populous.

The final way in which Guinness makes use of sport is as a theme in television advertisements. While the hurling "Believe" advertisement is one transnational example, there are other advertisements that more heavily draw on those sports that play well with local sensibilities and thus constitute a critical part of the strategizing of Guinness' top management team. In Africa, for example, sport has become integrated with advertising campaigns that have featured Michael Power, a fictitious, populist celebrity. In fact, the emergence of Michael Power as a cultural icon in his own right has been attributed to the recent resurgence of the Guinness brand in Africa (Gibbons 2004). The creation of Power is a sophisticated and powerful example of the "thingification" of symbolic representations that Lash and Urry (2007) ascertain is symptomatic of the global culture industry. Imbuing the brand with human characteristics and traits (Aaker 1996; Faurholt Csaba and Bengtsson 2006; Kapferer 2004), as with Beckham and the anonymous "Believe" hurler, Power literally is an embodied purveyor of the Guinness brand DNA: a powerful bio-pedagogical symbolic "thing" capable of embracing the imagined African marketplace.

Power, "the black James Bond who performs a series of death-defying acts in defence of all that's good and honourable" (Koenderman 2002), has appeared in several short "mini-adventures" on radio and television. The character has been developed with the launch of Power's first feature film, "Critical Assignment," a high-budget film, which is rare in that it is filmed entirely in Africa with African actors and African crews (Foster 2003) and is essentially an extended Guinness commercial. Remarkably, the film is often presented as an action thriller with a humanitarian message (ironically, for clean drinking water), but with no acknowledgement of Guinness as funding the film, or of Michael Power as being anything other than an African actor (e.g., African Film Festival 2004; *New York Times* 2005). In effect, Power – and, by association, the Guinness brand – have become institutionalized as taken-for-granted components of an invented African cultural landscape: a corporate-inspired Pan-African cartographic revisionism. This presentation avoids the particularities of specific African markets, offering instead a homogenous cultural, political, and economic climate centered on tourism, panoramic vistas, and a sanitized urban consumerism (for a full-length critique, see Amis, Mower, and Silk 2009). The reinforcement of the KBB is extensive: in addition to portraying situations in which he draws upon his inner strength to succeed, and extensive product placement, Power is known for his on-screen catchphrase, "Guinness brings out the power in you" (Obot and Ibanga 2002).

The impact of the Michael Power campaigns have been attributed to more than doubling product sales by volume between 1999 and 2005 (*Diageo Annual Report* 2005; Gibbons 2004). Indeed, Guinness' perception of the success of Michael Power has resulted in the creation of a very similar symbolic entity, Adam King, to play a corresponding role in Asia (Nathan 2002).

The use of sport and corporately created corporeal vehicles of neoliberal market ideology, the masking of the structural dictates of capital spaces of inequality and the crafted significations of "typical" British, African, and Asian lifestyles and values – all raise questions over corporately defined (and highly gendered) geographic norms. In order to create a seamless integration between the firm's position and the (reified) African, Irish, and British populace, cultural intermediaries at Guinness have developed a multitude of what Harvey (1990) termed "images, simulacra, pastiche" to artificially create a series of "traditions." These traditions are overtly managed to tie Guinness to prominent local sport teams, events, or hyperreal characters in an evocative manner in order to create a manufactured history and thus entrench the KBB as seamlessly as possible within prominent local cultural articulations. In so doing, those at Guinness end up overtly playing to the "masculine republic" (Collins and Vamplew 2002) – the seeming "natural" embeddedness of sport, gendered norms, and alcoholic consumption as part of a regime for the repetitious stylized acts of (nationalized) gendered performance – that further constitutes, if not brews, gender "trouble" (Butler 1990; see also Amis, Mower, and Silk 2009).[2]

Concluding comments

Our intent in this paper has been to provide a case study of the organization and practices of those who are responsible for structuring the spatial dimensions of marketplaces and producing the symbolic images that have become such a prominent feature of our existence. The importance of attaining a detailed understanding of such processes in an age of marked techno-logical and social transformations that have resulted in inherently complex amalgamations of convergent and divergent cultural trends is clear for managers and scholars alike. Furthermore, the financial results achieved by Guinness subsequent to and following the introduction of the strategic approach described here – year on year worldwide sales growth of 3–6 percent between 2001 and 2006 (*Diageo Annual Report* 2002, 2003, 2004, 2005, 2006, 2007) – indicate a notable robustness for a mature and largely stagnant industry. Such results point toward Guinness as an exemplar of effective engagement with the altered institutional logics that managers of MNCs must negotiate. Thus, there are several theoretical and practical insights that emerge from this study that are worth highlighting.

In line with Leung et al.'s (2005) call for theories of international business that better account for simultaneous cultural convergence and divergence, we can point to a revised conceptualization of the institutional logics of the global marketplace. In an age of technologically advanced communications, widespread neoliberal market ideology, and heightened national awareness, it can be meaningless, and even harmful, to create mutually exclusive categorizations of "local" and "global." Rather, effectively straddling the complex and ambiguous logics of the global marketplace involves managing the movement and flow of symbolic products in the global culture industry that, in turn, requires imagining nuanced and sophisticated (re)conceptualizations of place and space. At Guinness, this led to a restructuration of the firm's promotional strategizing, labor processes, managerial structure, and practices. The complexity of such organization is accentuated by the need for tightly centralized control that will permit global coherence. However, to imbue the world's marketplaces with the consciousness of the necessity of special symbolic (and material) attributions to consumer goods (Askegaard 2006) (i.e., to bring even the most disparate places in line with the neoliberal market logics of the global culture industry) requires management structures, processes, and symbolic creations that enable deeper local engagement than ever before.

This push to enhance consumer-brand experiential connections has thus led to attempts to capitalize on the enduring cultural resonance of experiences of belonging within specific imagined "national" markets. Operating under a global system of common difference (Wilk 1995), the senior managers at Guinness recognize the central and prefigurative importance of the local, routinely incorporating difference and particularity within their strategizing (Dirlik 1996; Morley and Robins 1995). Yet, in "achieving a real equidistance, or equipresence, of perspective in relation to the whole world of their audiences and consumers" (Morley and Robins 1995: 113), we point to the capitalization on and redefinition of (national) belongingness in which the locus of control in influencing the manner in which epistemological spaces of identity are represented becomes exteriorized through, and internalized within the cognitive and emotive promotional strategies of MNCs.

For Guinness, necessary integration among spatially disparate subunits was attained primarily through the establishment of highly effective networked and collaborative communication mechanisms. While these embrace electronic, telephonic, and video technologies, senior managers placed great emphasis on face-to-face meetings in order to develop the cultural understanding required for coherent global and multi-local articulation of the brand. Further, the greater the richness of interaction among members of organizational subunits, the greater the likelihood that distal structures and processes will be assimilated across the organization (Andersson, Forsgren, and Holm 2001). In fact, it may well be that the ability to absorb such accumulated expertise will be among the most critical of the capabilities needed for an MNC to prosper (Hambrick et al. 1998; Lagerström and Andersson 2003). This is primarily, it seems from our work, because of the complexities involved in creating an infrastructure capable of facilitating the engagement with consumers at multiple levels across different markets.

This study also highlights the need to understand the multiple ways in which symbolic texts are interpreted in different locales and among different groups. This requires paying close attention not only to the nuances and complexities of producing, organizing, and managing a global cultural product, but to its movement, flow, and modification (see Lash and Urry 2007). This, in turn, necessitates giving attention to corporate efforts to manage movement and the subsequent symbolic and material efforts made to tie products back to the world of production. The likely result will be a greater comprehension of how an array of sophisticated, multilevel texts, and "things" resonate, reflect, revise, and perhaps outright refute the presumed logics of the global culture industry. Of particular interest to us in these dialectical dynamics is how local cultural manifestations, often, it seems, in the form of sporting practices, are proffered as symbolic representations that can operate polysemically to negotiate global markets. At Guinness, sport is used as part of an apparently contradictory, yet mutually reinforcing, strategy to exploit the brand's link with Irish culture, to surpass the constraints of an association with a single nation, and as a locally sensitive practice that could allow for the seamless integration of the brand within specific geographic spaces. While a limitation of our study may be that we draw these conclusions based upon a single organization operating in a single, mature industry, this has allowed us to access the nuances and complexities of global symbolic cultural production in a way that others have often not. However, developing insights from other industries would be helpful in testing the robustness of our ideas.

Furthermore, and inherently intertwined within this debate, the Guinness brand itself also has a currency that varies depending upon the ontological constitution of particular consumer groups. Thus, in Ireland, and among the Irish diaspora, the brand enjoys an iconic status as a symbol of "the homeland." In other areas, "Guinness" is simply another brand of beer. This requires going beyond the global-local debates that describe an apparent paradoxical managerial situation to engage in a much more detailed way with the varied cultural resonance of brands across different, often imagined, consumer groups (Lewis 2000). Practically, the need to develop structures and strategies that allow a brand to engage with global audiences at multiple levels (e.g., through the varying interpretations of the "Free In" hurling advertisement in multiple markets) and also be positioned in locally "sensitive" ways (e.g., the use of locally resonant sports and development of cultural icons such as Michael Power) is of paramount importance. The need, therefore, to account for this multilevel interpretation adds to the inherent complexities and articulations between the structure of organizations within a dynamic global marketplace and processes of symbolic production. This, in turn, must be a central task of any scholarly attempt to make sense of the authorship and practices of those disparate groups that bridge the "enduring distance" between production and consumption (Negus 2002). The relative dearth of studies that have explored the relationships between production and consumption at a global level points to the need for further work in this area.

Acknowledgments

We would like to gratefully acknowledge the insightful comments of editor Jonathan Schroeder, three anonymous reviewers, Rabi Bhagat, Peter Davis, Ben Kedia, and Sheen Levine on earlier drafts of this paper. We are also most appreciative to those at Guinness who were so generous in their provision of time and information.

Notes

1   Each of the three regions examined here does, of course, have varying degrees of cultural diversity within them. Ireland consists of Northern Ireland and the Republic of Ireland; Great Britain has England, Scotland, and Wales; the African region includes Cameroon, Ghana, the Ivory Coast, Kenya, and Nigeria. While there are local initiatives within each region at the country level that reflect local cultural inflections, these initiatives must cohere around the broad strategies in place in each region. Given that senior managers at Guinness consider these three regions as distinct, each with their own brand management teams, we chose to do the same. The cultural diversity among the three regions, the size of the markets, and the well-developed marketing and management strategies in each of them meant that they offered rich bases for comparison.

2   It is beyond the scope of this paper to offer anything more than a cursory treatment of the politics of alcohol advertising. However, we are grateful for a reviewer's commentary on an earlier draft of this paper that directed us to consider this. Despite the key brand benefits that Guinness claim, it would be remiss were we not to point toward literatures that expose alcohol's ability to cause medical, psychological, and social harm through: (1) physical toxicity; (2) intoxication; and (3) dependence. Further, and with specific regard to legislation surrounding alcohol advertising, and despite industry claims that members adhere to codes of responsible advertising, the detrimental influences of marketing practices are not addressed adequately by industry self-regulation (see Babor et al. 2003). It is thus of no surprise that such campaigns, especially those that engage the affective synapses of local sensibilities, through sport or corporeal representative subjectivities such as Michael Power, are deployed by Guinness. This is certainly an area that warrants further investigation.

References

Aaker, David A. 1996. *Building strong brands*. New York: The Free Press.

African Film Festival. 2004. "African events." Available at: www.africanevents.com/AfricanFilmFestival-04.htm.

Amárach Consulting. 2000. *Sponsorship strategies*. Dublin: Amárach Consulting.

Amis, John. 2003. "'Good things come to those who wait': The strategic management of image and reputation at Guinness." *European Sport Management Quarterly* 3: 189–214.

Amis, John. 2005. "Beyond sport: Imaging and re-imaging a global brand." In *Corporate nationalisms: Sport, cultural identity & transnational marketing*, edited by M. Silk, D. Andrews, and C. Cole. Oxford: Berg, 143–65.

Amis, John, Ron L. Mower, and Michael L. Silk. 2009. "(Michael) Power, gendered subjectivities, and filmic representation: Brand strategy and Guinness' Critical

Assignment in Africa." In *Sport, beer, and gender: Promotional culture and contemporary social life*, edited by Laurence A. Wenner and Steven J. Jackson. New York: Peter Lang, 97–117.

Amis, John M., and Michael L. Silk. 2008. "The philosophy and politic of quality in qualitative organizational research." *Organizational Research Methods* 11: 456–80.

Anand, Jaideep, and Andrew Delios. 2002. "Absolute and relative resources as determinants of international acquisitions." *Strategic Management Journal* 23: 119–34.

Andersson, Ulf, Mats Forsgren, and Ulf Holm. 2001. "Subsidiary embeddedness and competence development in MNCs – a multi-level analysis." *Organization Studies* 22: 1013–34.

Askegaard, Soren. 2006. "Brands as a global ideoscape." In *Brand culture*, edited by Jonathan Schroeder and Miriam Salzer-Morling. London: Routledge, 91–102.

Athanassiou, Nicholas, and Douglas Nigh. 2000. "Internationalization, tacit knowledge and the top management teams of MNCs." *Journal of International Business Studies* 31: 471–87.

Babor, Thomas F., Raul Caetano, Sally Casswell, Griffith Edwards, Norman Giesbrecht, Kathryn Graham, Joel Grube, et al. 2003. *Alcohol: No ordinary commodity—research and public policy*. Oxford: Oxford University Press.

Bartlett, Christopher A., and Sumantra Ghoshal. 1989. *Managing across borders: The transnational solution*. Boston, MA: Harvard Business School Press.

Bhagat, Rabi S., Pamela K. Steverson, and James C. Segovis. 2007. "International and cultural variations in Employee Assistance Programmes: Implications for managerial health and effectiveness." *Journal of Management Studies* 44: 229–49.

Bhagat, Rabi S., Ben L. Kedia, Paula Harveston, and Harry C. Triandis. 2002. "Cultural variations in the cross-border transfer of organizational knowledge: An integrative framework." *Academy of Management Review* 27: 204–21.

Bourdieu, Pierre. 1984. *Distinction: A social critique of the judgment of taste*. Translated by Richard Nice. London: Routledge & Kegan Paul.

Butler, Judith. 1990. *Gender trouble: Feminism and the subversion of identity*. London: Routledge.

Castells, Manuel. 1996. *The rise of the network society*. Oxford: Blackwell.

Caves, Richard E. 1998. "Research on international business: Problems and prospects." *Journal of International Business Studies* 29: 5–19.

Collins, Tony, and Wray Vamplew. 2002. *Mud, sweat, and beers: A cultural history of sport and alcohol*. Oxford: Berg.

Cronin, Anne. 2004. "Regimes of mediation: Advertising practitioners as cultural intermediaries?" *Consumption Markets and Culture* 7: 349–69.

de Cillia, Rudolf, Martin Reisigl, and Ruth Wodak. 1999. "The discursive construction of national identities." *Discourse & Society* 10: 149–73.

de Mooij, Marieke. 1998. *Global marketing and advertising: Understanding cultural paradoxes*. Thousand Oaks, CA: Sage.

Delios, Andrew, and Paul W. Beamish. 2001. "Survival and profitability: The roles of experience and intangible assets in foreign subsidiary performance." *Academy of Management Journal* 44: 1028–38.

Denis, Jean-Louise, Lise Lamothe, and Ann Langley. 2001. "The dynamics of collective leadership and strategic change in pluralistic organizations." *Academy of Management Journal* 44: 809–37.

Diageo Annual Report. 2002. London: Diageo.

Diageo Annual Report. 2003. London: Diageo.

Diageo Annual Report. 2004. London: Diageo.

Diageo Annual Report. 2005. London: Diageo.

Diageo Annual Report. 2006. London: Diageo.

Diageo Annual Report. 2007. London: Diageo.

Dirlik, Arif. 1996. "The global in the local." In *Global-local: Cultural production and the transnational imaginary*, edited by R. Wilson and W. Dissanayake. Durham, NC: Duke University Press, 21–45.

Elliot, Richard, and Andrea Davies. 2006. "Symbolic brands and authenticity of identity performance." In *Brand culture*, edited by Jonathan Schroeder and Miriam Salzer-Morling. London: Routledge, 138–52.

Eisenhardt, Kathleen M., and Jeffrey A. Martin. 2000. "Dynamic capabilities: What are they?" *Strategic Management Journal* 21: 1105–22.

Faurholt Csaba, Fabian, and Anders Bengtsson. 2006. "Rethinking identity in brand management." In *Brand culture*, edited by J. Schroeder and M. Salzer-Morling. London: Routledge, 106–21.

Foster, Jo. 2003. "Africa's very own 'James Bond'." BBC News, April 17. Available at: http://news.bbc.co.uk/1/hi/world/africa/2956043.stm.

Frenkel, Stephen J. 2001. "Globalization, athletic footwear commodity chains and employment relations in China." *Organization Studies* 22: 531–62.

Gephart, Robert P. 2004. "From the editors: Qualitative research and the Academy of Management Journal." *Academy of Management Journal* 47: 454–62.

Gibbons, Chris. 2004. "Saatchi & Saatchi: The mark of a loved one." Financial Mail, May 14. Available at: www.adfocus.co.za/adfocus2004/zzzadz.htm.

Guinness. 2008. www.guinness.com/gb_en/ads/Free-In.htm.

Guinness Global Strategy Presentation. 2001. Internal company presentation.

Hall, Stuart. 1991. "The local and the global: Globalization and ethnicity." In *Culture, globalization and the world-system*, edited by Anthony D. King. London: Macmillan, 19–39.

Hambrick, Donald C., Sue C. Davison, Scott A. Snell, and Charles C. Snow. 1998. "When groups consist of multiple nationalities: Towards a new understanding of the implications." *Organization Studies* 19: 181–205.

Hampden-Turner, Charles, and Fons Trompenaars. 2000. *Building cross-cultural competence: How to create wealth from conflicting values*. Chichester: Wiley.

Hardt, Michael, and Antonio Negri. 2001. *Empire*. Cambridge, MA: Harvard University Press.

Harvey, David. 1985. "The geopolitics of capitalism." In *Social relations and social structures*, edited by Derek Gregory and John Urry. London: Macmillan, 128–63.

Harvey, David. 1990. *The condition of postmodernity: An enquiry into the origins of cultural change*. Oxford: Blackwell.

Harvey, David. 2007. *A brief history of neoliberalism*. Oxford: Oxford University Press.

Hitt, Michael A., Victor Franklin, and Hong Zhu. 2006. "Culture, institutions and international strategy." *Journal of International Management* 12: 222–34.

Hitt, Michael A., Robert E. Hoskisson, and Hicheon Kim. 1997. "International diversification: Effects on innovation and firm performance in product-diversified firms." *Academy of Management Journal* 40: 767–98.

Holt, Douglas B., John A. Quelch, and Earl L. Taylor. 2004. "How global brands compete." *Harvard Business Review* 82: 68–75.

Humphries, Tom. 2003. "Sticks and thrones." *The Observer Sport Monthly* 44, October 5, 42–7.

Jameson, Frederic. 1990. *Postmodernism, or, the cultural logic of late capitalism.* London: Verso.

Jhally, Sut. 1995. "Image-based culture: Advertising and popular culture." In *Gender, race and class in media*, edited by Gail Dines and Jean M. Humez. London: Sage, 77–87.

Johnson, Richard, Deborah Chambers, Parvati Raghuram, and Estella Tincknell. 2004. *The practice of cultural studies.* London: Sage.

Kapferer, Jean-Noel. 2004. *The new strategic brand management: Creating and sustaining brand equity long term.* London: Kogan Page.

Koenderman, Tony. 2002. "Power to your elbow." *Financial Mail*, May 24. Available at: http://free.financial-mail. co.za/report/adfocus2002/africa/af2x.htm.

Lagerström, Katarina, and Maria Andersson. 2003. "Creating and sharing knowledge within a transnational team—the development of a global business system." *Journal of World Business* 38: 84–95.

Lam, Alice. 1997. "Embedded firms, embedded knowledge: Problems of collaboration and knowledge transfer in global cooperative ventures." *Organization Studies* 18: 973–96.

Lash, Scott, and Celia Urry. 2007. *Global culture industry: The mediation of things.* Oxford: Polity.

Lawrence, Thomas B., and Roy Suddaby. 2006. "Institutions and institutional work." In *Handbook of organizational studies*, 2nd ed., edited by S. Clegg, C. Hardy, W.W. Nord, and T. Lawrence. Thousand Oaks, CA: Sage, 215–54.

Leung, Kwok, Rabi Bhagat, Nancy R. Buchan, Miriam Erez, and Cristina B. Gibson. 2005. "Culture and international business: Recent advances and their implications for future research." *Journal of International Business Studies* 36: 357–78.

Leslie, Deborah A. 1995. "Global scan: The globalization of advertising agencies, concepts, and campaigns." *Economic Geography* 71 (4): 402–25.

Levitt, Theodore. 1983. "The globalization of markets." *Harvard Business Review* 61: 92–102.

Lewis, Marianne W. 2000. "Exploring paradox: Toward a more comprehensive guide." *Academy of Management Review* 25: 760–76.

Lincoln, Yvonna S., and Egon G. Guba. 1985. *Naturalistic inquiry.* Newbury Park, CA: Sage.

Lord, Michael D., and Annette L. Ranft. 2000. "Organizational learning about new international markets: Exploring the internal transfer of local market knowledge." *Journal of International Business Studies* 31: 573–89.

Luo, Yadong. 2005. "Toward coopetition within a multinational enterprise: A perspective from foreign subsidiaries." *Journal of World Business* 40: 71–90.

Melewar, T. C., and John Saunders. 1999. "International corporate visual identity: Standardization or localization?" *Journal of International Business Studies* 30: 583–98.

Miles, Matthew B., and A. Michael Huberman. 1994. *Qualitative data analysis: An expanded sourcebook.* 2nd ed. Thousand Oaks, CA: Sage.

Moor, Liz. 2007. *The rise of brands.* Oxford: Berg.

Morley, David, and Kevin Robins. 1995. *Spaces of identity: Global media, electronic landscapes and cultural boundaries.* London: Routledge.

Nathan, Darshini M. 2002. "Adam King portrays Guinness values." *The Star*, May 24. Available at: http://biz.thestar.com.my/news/story.asp?file=/2002/7/13/business/dmking&newspagezsearch.

Negus, Keith. 2002. "The work of cultural intermediaries and the enduring distance between production and consumption." *Cultural Studies* 16 (4): 501–15.

New York Times. 2005. "Critical assignment (2003)". Available at: http://movies2.nytimes.com/gst/movies/movie.html?v_id=305860

Not men, but giants. 2001. Internal Guinness promotional video.

Obot, Isidore S., and Akan J. Ibanga. 2002. "Selling booze: Alcohol marketing in Nigeria." In *The Globe: Drinking it in: WHO targets alcohol marketing*, edited by A. McNeill. London: Global Alcohol Policy Alliance, 6–10. Available at: www.ias.org.uk/publications/theglobe/02issue2/globe0202_p6.html.

Ohmae, Kenichi. 1990. *The borderless world*. New York: HarperBusiness.

Pettinger, Lynne. 2004. "Brand culture and branded workers: Service work and aesthetic labour in fashion retail." *Consumption Markets and Culture* 7: 165–84.

Preston, Paschal, and Aphra Kerr. 2001. "Digital media, nation-states and local cultures: The case of multimedia 'content' production." *Media, Culture & Society* 23: 109–31.

Quelch, John. 2003. "The return of the global brand." *Harvard Business Review* 81: 22–3.

Reich, Robert. 1991. *The work of nations: Preparing ourselves for twenty-first-century capitalism*. New York: Knopf.

Rines, Simon. 2001. "Guinness' Rugby World Cup sponsorship: A global platform for meeting business objectives." *International Journal of Sports Marketing & Sponsorship* 3: 449–65.

Robertson, Roland. 1995. "Glocalization: Time-space and homogeneity-heterogeneity." In *Global modernities: From modernism to hypermodernism and beyond*, edited by Mike Featherstone, Scott Lash, and Roland Robertson. London: Sage, 25–44.

Robins, Kevin. 1997. "What in the world's going on?" In *Production of culture/cultures of production*, edited by Paul Du Gay. London: The Open University, 11–66.

Sassen, Saskia. 2000. "Territory and territoriality in the global economy." *International Sociology* 15: 373–93.

Sassen, Saskia. 2001. *The global city: New York, London, Tokyo*. 2nd ed. Princeton, NJ: Princeton University Press.

Scott, Allen. 1999. "The cultural economy: Geography and the creative field." *Media, Culture & Society* 21: 807–17.

Silk, Michael L., and David L. Andrews. 2001. "Beyond a boundary? Sport, transnational advertising, and the reimagining of national culture." *Journal of Sport & Social Issues* 25: 180–201.

Simmons, John, and Mark Griffiths. 2001. *Believe: Six turning points for Guinness that hinged on inner strength*. London: Guinness UDV.

Soar, Matthew. 2000. "Encoding advertisements: Ideology and meaning in advertising production." *Mass Communication and Society* 3: 415–37.

The Brand Map. 2001. Internal Guinness 2-CD-Rom Set.

Thrift, Nigel. 2004. *Knowing capitalism*. London: Sage.

Vermeulen, Freek, and Harry Barkema. 2002. "Pace, rhythm, and scope: Process dependence in building a profitable multinational corporation." *Strategic Management Journal* 23: 637–53.

Wilk, Richard. 1995. "Learning to be local in Belize: Global systems of common difference." In *Worlds apart: Modernity through the prism of the local*, edited by D. Miller. London: Routledge, 110–33.

Yin, Robert K. 2003. *Case study research: Design and methods*. 3rd ed. Thousand Oaks, CA: Sage.

Yoon, Suh-Kyung. 2001. "Working up a thirst to quench Asia." *Far Eastern Economic Review*, 34–6.

7 Retail stores as brands

Performances, theatre and space

Alfons van Marrewijk and Maaike Broos

Introduction

Consumer Culture Theory (CCT) is increasingly focusing on the potential power of spatial settings in terms of communicating fashion brands (e.g. Olins 1989; Crewe and Lowe 1995; Schmitt, Simonsen and Marcus 1995; Miller et al. 1998; Schmitt 1999; Smith 2000; Gregson, Crewe and Brooks 2002a; Turley and Chebat 2002; Kent 2003; Schroeder 2003). CCT studies define branding as the process by which a cultural work is designed and communicated to function as its own advertisement in order to create an audience (Lury 2004). As branding is currently the dominant strategy around which retail competition is structured, retailers use the material environment of retail stores to distinguish themselves from their competitors (Smith 2000; Gregson, Crewe and Brooks 2002b). This is done through the architectural design of shopping malls, retail shops and interior retail spaces (Olins 1989), with fashion houses, clothing stores and shopping centres attracting special attention (Kent 2003). Examples of innovative retail architecture can be found in Prada's flagship stores in New York, designed by Rem Koolhaas, in the fashionable Aoyama district in Tokyo, designed by Jacques Herzog and Pierre de Meuron, and finally in the ESPN Zone. Kozinets et al. (2002) described the architecture of this zone, demonstrating that the building:

> is constructed around a circular theme, such that the gently curving lines on the periphery always return to their originating point. At the centre of the circle is the "production booth" in which the programmer sits, surrounded by monitors, deciding which sports events (and, occasionally, other programmes such as soap operas) will be broadcast on the dozens of embedded screens. With a curved sky-painted dome, a stratospheric cathedral ceiling reminiscent of natural and spiritual realms, a circular staircase and a circular logo-embedded rotunda, the circle is multiply present within ESPN Zone.
>
> (Kozinets et al. 2002: 22)

The symbolic message behind the circularity as expressed in the ESPN Zone is one of human continued attempt to grasp eternity, completion and infinity

(Kozinets et al. 2002). This example typifies how a built environment may use the concept of circularity to create a brand on a physical level. Thus, spatial settings and the aesthetic structuring of a range of expressive artefacts are increasingly pervasive components of the construction and communication of brands (Peñaloza 1998).

Within CCT, servicescape studies generally include environmental dimensions such as ambient conditions (noise, music and aromas) and space (design, layout and furnishing), as well as signs and symbols (style and personal artefacts) (Bitner 1992). In the space dimension, a special emphasis is placed on the impact of spatial design and physical environments on customers and employees (e.g. Bitner 1992; Habraken and Teicher 1998; Peñaloza 1998; Sherry 1998; Sherry et al. 2001; Arnould and Thompson 2005; Rosenbaum 2005). Peñaloza (1998), for example, studied Nike Town and showed how its architectural design with atriums, passageways and concept rooms helped siphon consumers through the place, providing multi-sensorial stimulation at every turn and thus inviting imaginative associations. Other examples include the socially constructed meaning of place in Creigton's (1998) study of the Japanese retail store SEED and Sherry's (1998) study of Nike Town. We learn that the spatial design of retail space not only influences consumers' and shop attendants' behaviour, but also, in return, gives a symbolic meaning to spatial design (Rosenbaum 2005; Schembri and Boyle 2005). In their study of the American Girl brand, Diamond et al. (2009) found that the brand was located within a complex system of sources with connections that are not linear and causal, but rather probabilistic and reciprocal. Retail space is thus "brought into being, orchestrated, performed in interaction and, as negotiated, is accepted, resisted and interpreted by both consumers and shop attendant" (Gregson, Crewe and Brooks 2002b: 1663). If brands represent symphonies of meaning, managers must be viewed as orchestrators and conductors, as well as composers, whose role is not only to coordinate and synchronise, but also to create (Diamond et al. 2009: 131).

Let us now take a closer look at the shop attendants and their interpretation of spatial settings (Turley and Chebat 2002; Pettinger 2004). Recently, organisation and management studies have placed spatial settings for work and their effects on employees centre stage (e.g. Hernes 2004; Kornberger and Clegg 2004; Hernes, Bakken and Olsen 2006; Rafaeli and Pratt 2006; Strati 2006; Yanow 2006; Dale and Burrell 2008; van Marrewijk and Yanow 2010). These studies teach that spatial settings in organisations shape action and interaction by employees and, in turn, are reshaped on the part of these employees. The production and reproduction of space are what Hernes, Bakken and Olsen (2006) called the recursive view on organisational space. In summary, it can be stated that shop attendants form an important factor in the shaping of retail space.

In view of the above, it can be argued that a recursive view on retail space and shop attendants in the construction of retail brands has been understudied, despite a number of earlier investigations (e.g. Olins 1989; Crewe and Lowe

1995; Schmitt, Simonsen and Marcus 1995; Peñaloza 1998; Sherry 1998; Schmitt 1999; Smith 2000; Gregson, Crewe and Brooks 2002b; Pettinger 2004, Diamond et al. 2009). In this paper, we seek to answer the call for empirical studies (Gregson, Crewe and Brooks 2002a; Küpers 2002) on space and spatial arrangement(s) in retail shops as used to construct and to communicate a brand.

This theoretical exploration leads to this paper's research question concerning the way in which a brand is communicated and constructed by management and shop attendants, with a special focus on the spatial settings of the retail store. To answer this question, we investigated the Dutch Oger fashion store, the leading menswear retail company in the Netherlands. We selected Oger because personal service is more extensive in top market segments as stores become more and more exclusive (Pettinger 2004). In addition, clothing stores and shopping centres tend to attract the most design attention (Kent 2003). We were allowed to film the interaction between customers and shop attendants, as well as backstage work processes. The visual recording of events, rituals, physical settings and interviews has proven to be highly useful in consumer research (e.g. Emmison and Smith 2000; Belk and Kozinets 2005). In addition to filming events, this study engaged in qualitative ethnographic research in terms of participant observation, observation and interviewing.

Thus, this paper forms an extension of previous studies of spatial settings in CCT literature. Earlier studies (e.g. Peñaloza 1998; Kozinets et al. 2002) have observed the interplay between design, display and consumption processes in constructing and communicating retail brands. By forging links with organisation studies, our study adds the important role of the staff members in constructing and communicating a retail brand. The findings of our study show how Oger management carefully designed, managed and orchestrated retail space, objects and shop attendants' roles to construct and communicate the Oger brand. Furthermore, this paper introduces "internal design proxemics" as an extra element of Yanow's (2006) analytical concept of spatial settings and is helpful in the analysis of spatial shop design.

The paper is structured as follows. First, a theoretical discussion is presented on the performance of shop attendants in the spatial settings of a retail theatre. The methodological section addresses the question how spatial settings can be studied in retail stores and theorises about the use of film as a research tool. Next, the case of Oger fashion is discussed and findings are presented. Our discussion presents the spatial settings and the socio-material performances that construct the Oger fashion brand. Finally, conclusions are drawn on the production of retail space.

Performances in the retail theatre spatial settings

In developing retail shops, retailers and designers have converted the ordinary experience of consumers into a form of entertainment and hedonistic experience (Miller et al. 1998). The store offers consumers exclusiveness and authenticity by creating factual and spatio-temporal links. In their study on coffee establishments in Sweden and Denmark, for example, Kjeldgaard and Ostberg (2007) found three types of brands, which they called "americana," "culinaria" and "viennesia," referring to places of origin. For example, the "culinaria" establishments mainly refer to Italian names, Italian decor, with baristas from Italy and menus written entirely in Italian to reinforce their Italian identity. In doing this, retail space has become a show stage attracting consumers and allowing retailers to charge a premium price for what may be termed commodity products or services (Kent 2003). Dovey (1999: 15) called this seduction the most subtle and embedded form of spatial power in which people identify themselves with specific spatial settings. Here, one might think of a beautiful upmarket shopping arena, a cool and aesthetically pleasing space that draws one into its folds through the delights of the market that it contains – if only one strolls through and lets oneself go with the unfolding spectacle of beauty, fashion and scents. Gallérie Lafayette in Paris would be such an example. In summary, retailers now frequently use the metaphor of the retail shop as a theatre (Baron, Harris and Harris 2001).

The notion of retail experience as a theatrical experience has been discussed in earlier marketing and consumer literature (e.g. Fisk and Grove 1996; Peñaloza 1998; Sherry 1998; Baron, Harris and Harris 2001; Kozinets et al. 2002; Grandey 2003). These studies frequently refer to theatre concepts such as front-stage, backstage, scripts, roles and settings in the context of service encounters, which originates from Goffman's (1959) dramaturgical perspective on human behaviour in everyday life. This perspective allows us to understand how a theatre removes consumers from everyday life and isolates them in a constructed environment in order to create a unique and aesthetic experience (Fisk and Grove 1996; Gagliardi 2009).

To this end, shop attendants need a mixture of scripted role-playing and improvisation (Sherry et al. 2001: 502). They have to create, clearly visible to all visitors, a drama performance in the spatial settings of a retail theatre (Fisk and Grove 1996). This performance of service is a continual and forced repetition of organisational norms that have the effect of embedding and stabilising cultural practices (Schembri and Boyle 2005). It means that shop attendants need the capacity to perform services as emotional labour (Ashforth and Humphrey 1993). Here, emotional labour is the display of expected emotions by shop attendants during service encounters. It is performed through surface acting, in which emotions are a careful presentation of learned verbal and non-verbal cues, and through deep acting, in which one actually experiences the emotions that one displays (Grandey 2003).

At this point, it has to be noted that employees in the retail industry are generally not used to performing scripted role-playing in retail theatres. Traditionally, they receive low wages, are bored with their work and unmotivated, and they frequently resign from work (Baron, Harris and Harris 2001: 112). Therefore, employees are commonly trained to be actors, to perform corporate acts, to interact with customers and to involve with the store and its products. These roles played by shop attendants in the retail theatre are related to consumer roles.

In this respect, Baron, Harris and Harris (2001) introduced new concepts to denote four different roles that consumers can play in a retail theatre, namely "voyeur," "spect-actor," "sense-ceptor" and "connoisseur." For each of these roles, employees have to act differently. First, in what Baron, Harris and Harris (2001) called the consumer as voyeur, there is minimum employee–consumer interaction, and employees perform backstage roles (supplying products when required and changing environments) or front-stage roles as characters in a scenario. Second, in the case of a consumer as spect-actor, both customers and employees are fully aware of their roles, with employees acting as the primary facilitators of information exchange among customers rather than acting as experts in the field presented. Third, in the case of a consumer as sense-ceptor, employees are backstage, handling merchandise, as well as front-stage, acting as assistants, advisers and facilitators in trials. Finally, with the consumer as connoisseur, employees play front-stage roles as human exhibits, interacting creatively with customers, as well as backstage roles, changing the environment (Baron, Harris and Harris 2001). In summary, for each type of retail theatre, shop attendants need to display distinct roles.

We have now gained insight into the role-playing expected from employees, but how is this related to spatial settings in retail theatres? Diamond et al. (2009: 131) stated that powerful brands are the product of dynamic interaction among multiple sources and, therefore, suggest a more complete and holistic under-standing of sociocultural branding. In line with this view, we feel that a stringent demarcation between consumption phenomena and their context is not possible and not desirable (Peñaloza 1998). On the contrary, it is especially a holistic analysis of spatial settings and social behaviour that results in a better understanding of organisations (O'Toole and Were 2008). Therefore, the social and the material should no longer be seen as distinct and largely independent spheres of organisational life (Latour 1993; Orlikowski 2007). Increasingly, tacit meanings of material forms interact with consumers in retail theatres (Kozinets et al. 2002). Peñaloza (1998), for example, described how sculptures, glass and wooden cases, lighting and the use of velour ropes and other theatrical props, such as cables suspending athletes' portraits from the ceiling, were effective in invoking a new reality for consumers and shop attendants. This socio-material perspective of retail theatres is helpful in studying the material and symbolic stage, as well as the social performance displayed by shop attendants in constructing and communicating the Oger brand.

Methodological reflections on studying organisational spaces

Key methods used in CCT are ethnographic research and qualitative data collection focusing on the experiential and sociocultural dimensions of consumption that are not plainly accessible through experiments, surveys or database modelling (for an overview, see Arnould and Thompson 2005). Similarly, in our study, these methods have played a key role as well. We used ethnographic methods of participative observation, non-participant observation, systematic data collection, recording and filming in a natural setting (Arnould and Wallendorf 1994; Yanow and Schwartz-Shea 2006).

In view of the above, it must be noted here that ethnographic literature emphasises the ways in which the researcher him or herself is the primary research "tool," because the researcher's self is not separable from interpretations and events (Van Maanen 1995). We believe that empathic understanding presupposes an emic perspective: the researcher studies the organisation "from within" and puts him or herself in the employee's shoes (Wallendorf and Belk 1989; Yanow and Schwartz-Shea 2006). Researchers might then gain a "feel" for organisational behaviour within the spatial settings of an organisation (Strati 1999; Warren 2008). In this way, researchers themselves can become valid sources of data through their own experiences, refining their capacity to empathise with others and imagining what it might be like to be them walking through and/or working in these same spaces (Warren 2008: 563).

In this way, initial observations have been made concerning location, atmosphere, in-store design, retail space, clothing, uniforms and customers. Our field research started with a guided tour of the Oger Fashion stores in Amsterdam. Following this introduction, we spent two months observing shop attendants and customers in the Amsterdam-based Oger flagship store and during fashion presentations held by Oger Lusink in The Hague and Amsterdam. Furthermore, desk research was carried out to understand the history, development and vision of the fashion house. We analysed the Oger website, newspaper and magazine articles, and television interviews, as well as two television documentaries on the fashion.

In general, researchers access space through observing spatial vocabularies, with whatever degree of participation, and then through interpreting them (Joy and Sherry 2003; Warren 2008; van Marrewijk 2009). To analyse spatial vocabularies, Yanow's (2006) analytical concept for the study of organisational space is applied here. She proposed a systematic analysis of space and physical arrangements by means of four different categories. First, her "design vocabularies" concern a building's shape, height, width, mass, scale and material and involve a situation-specific comparison of similarities and differences with surrounding buildings. Second, what Yanow called "design gesture" concerns design elements that ignore, contrast or align with surrounding buildings and spaces. Third, her "design proxemics" incorporate the context of culturally specific meaning and involve the social and personal spaces between people that shape human behaviour and interaction. Finally, "décor" includes not only furnishing, furniture, art, chairs, statues and photographs, but also dress codes and hairstyles (Yanow 2006). These four categories were used in our study and amended to include what we term "internal design proxemics" as an extra element in design proxemics.

In our preliminary investigations, we analysed data gathered during the first four weeks on the basis of traditional ethnography, which offered us a framework for filming the Oger theatre. From the first analysis, a series of important topics emerged: street facade, interior design, customer and shop attendant interaction, special boardroom treatment for exclusive clients, backstage control, management philosophy and, finally, the Oger Academy. Visual media were used for further data collection. As was stated in the introduction, filming is an effective and reliable method for the observation of interaction between customers and shop attendants within the spatial settings of a retail store. This enabled us to use camera shots, stills and slow-motion pictures to analyse and to reanalyse, if necessary, behaviour in the greatest possible detail. Film registration allows the researcher to concentrate on different aspects of the image and to recognise diverse and subtle details that would otherwise have been missed (El Guindi 2004; Belk and Kozinets 2005). Our film shoot was taken during two full weeks by a cameraman – a student of the School of Arts working on his examination project – and a freelance sound technician. Scenes to be filmed were based upon the topics discussed earlier. Similar techniques have been used by Collier (1967), Barbash and Taylor (1997), Ruby (2000) and Belk and Kozinets (2005).

Still, in view of the above, it must be stated that the presence of audiovisual media may hinder the interaction between researcher and field of study (Pink 2007). In our case, however, this phenomenon proved to be of little influence because the people we filmed (many of them were media and soccer stars) had a wide experience with public exposure. We had permission to openly film customers in the shop but were not allowed to interview them, as they wanted to go about their business undisturbed. Customers were always asked permission before filming. It took shop attendants approximately three days to become used to the camera presences in the store.

In-depth interviewing is generally viewed as an important part of market-oriented ethnography (Arnould and Wallendorf 1994). During the shoots, in-depth interviews were held – and filmed – with founder Oger Lusink, his two sons, two management team members and five shop attendants. We chose not to be filmed ourselves when conducting research as our main focus lay on the interaction between shop attendants and consumers. Film shoots started at 8.15 a.m. and lasted until 9.00 p.m., resulting in 22 tapes with a total of 17 hours of film.

It is a well-known fact that the analysis of visual data is time consuming (Pink 2007; Rose 2007); it took us roughly 80 hours. First, all 17 hours of film were watched in their entirety as we made notes on the topics of interest mentioned earlier. A second viewing of the film data focused on the interaction of spatial settings, materiality and the performance demonstrated by shop attendants. Next, the selected scenes were viewed again and transcribed. This could result in the translation of (Dutch) interview data or a description of an interaction between shop attendants and customers. These findings were compared with the results from data gathered earlier.

Spatial design of the Oger theatre

The Oger flagship store in Amsterdam is located in the middle of one of the most expensive and prestigious Dutch shopping streets. Customers of the Oger flagship store first enter the Pieter Cornelis (PC) Hooftstraat – named after a sixteenth-century Dutch poet. Many flagship stores and luxury shops are established in this exclusive shopping street, with the flagship stores of Louis Vuitton, Lyppen Diamonds and Ralph Lauren neighbouring the Oger flagship store. However, Oger is the largest of all and occupies the street numbers 75, 77, 79 and 81. The shopping street attracts rich and wealthy consumers, as well as consumers looking for a special shopping experience. On a daily basis, international media stars, soccer players and other celebrities drive their luxury cars in the street to go shopping. The Dutch language even has a special name to denote these massive cars: "PC tractors." On many occasions, we observed Oger customers parking their cars in the loading area in front of the shop where they were not allowed to park. In summertime, the shopping street itself has the decor of a large "catwalk," visited by numerous Dutch celebrities and thereby attracting media attention. The location of the Oger flagship store in the PC Hooftstraat, what Yanow (2006) called the "design gesture," attracts rich and wealthy consumers and simultaneously excludes consumers who are intimidated by the spatial settings (Dovey 1999). Customers approaching the Oger flagship store notice that:

> Two flags with the Dutch national colours are flying above 25-metre-wide shop windows. On these windows, the first name of the founder can be found in five different places, printed in large gold letters. Wim, a 26-year-old shop attendant, is impeccably dressed in his Corneliani suit, cleaning the lower part of the window with a white cloth. It is his job to do this every morning as the entrance has to be perfectly clean. Two consumers passing by can now clearly observe the menswear and the shop interior through the windows and are given a red-carpet welcome at the open entrance.
>
> (Film observations)

Oger Fashion is regarded as one of the top menswear business enterprises in the Dutch fashion industry (Van Dijk 2008). Together with his brothers Martin and Rob, Oger Lusink started the company in 1989. It was his first of seven stores, located in the most prestigious PC Hooftstraat in Amsterdam. Later, the company expanded to Haarlem, Rotterdam, Den Haag, Enschede and, in early 2009, to Antwerp, Belgium. Furthermore, Oger Lusink runs franchise stores of the Italian label Ermenegildo Zegna, of women's designer Erny van Reijmersdal, and he runs the Donna Oger shop for ladies wear. The company's headquarters, based in Purmerend, coordinates the purchase of Italian menswear brands such as Corneliani, Borelli Cucinelli, Brioni and Canarelli, and they also outsource the tailoring production of two house labels to Italy. Oger Fashion is a family business with both Oger's sons, a number of nephews and nieces and more than 130 employees.

The front-stage of the Oger flagship store in Amsterdam is designed to host three different spatial areas, each on a distinct split-level floor. The areas, connected by stairs, have numerous spaces, settings and corners for shop attendants to interact with their clients. In each area, a different range of products is presented, with casual clothing in the Informal area, business suits in the Dressed4Success area and the self-selected made-to-measure wardrobe in the Atelier Italia area. The three areas are designed according to the Dutch cliché values of an "Italian fashion atelier": quality, style, warmth, chaos and passion. "Our stores have to reflect the hectic atmosphere of an Italian atelier," the store manager explained. Although Oger management frequently visit Italian ateliers to buy fabrics and suits, the shop attendants are Dutch and have never visited an Italian atelier.

The "Italian design" is combined with the spatial setting of an English gentlemen's club. Oger Lusink's earlier work experience in London formed the source of inspiration for the club idea. Management and employees associate "English" with warmth, intelligence, respect and trust:

> It may be chaotic, but it has the warmth of an English gentlemen's club. On our desk lies a book of the most beautiful libraries in the world and that's important to us. For Oger, a library implies the knowledge of generations and that's quite powerful; to browse and indulge in the book in a peaceful atmosphere. It provides the employees with a feeling of security.
>
> (Interview with store manager)

The front-stage of the theatre serves as the platform for the social interaction between customers and shop attendants. Although its design has a clear philosophy, the question is whether the shop attendants actually experience any security from the spatial settings (Figure 7.1).

Socio-material performances in the Oger theatre

The Oger flagship store is decorated with a large number of theatrical probes, such as golden handles and banisters. In the shop, large mirrors measuring 2×1 and 2×2 metres, with golden antique-looking frames, are located in front of a round table with two leather Chesterfields. The mirrors reflect chandeliers and wooden parquet, which is polished every morning. In addition, a huge basket full of apples is placed upon a long table at the entrance. Next to the basket stands a three-layered fountain pouring out hot chocolate. Other objects stem from the shop's range of menswear accessories: ties, watches, cuffs, aftershave lotions and shoes are presented in luxury compartments. There is even a special cabinet with different coloured braces. Finally, objects can be found with shop attendants wearing tape measures around their necks, while

Figure 7.1 Split-level floor (still of film "Getting acquaintance with Oger" © Broos)

others carry them in their suit pockets. All shop attendants are dressed in suits – which have to be purchased from the store – making them human exhibits.

In this setting of theatrical probes, customers are served coffee under the soft tones of lounge and jazz music. At the same time, the customer listens to the shop attendant who discusses different kinds of fabric. The shop attendant thus constructs a performance using a mirror, table, coffee and suits in racks (Figure 7.2):

> Peter, a 24-year-old shop attendant, is busy with a customer. He has four different suits hanging on the wall, while the customer fits a jacket and moves towards a man-size mirror. Customer to Peter: "It is too tight, especially on the shoulders it does not fit very well, but I very much like this fabric. If the fit were slightly more natural, that would be fine." Peter: "Shall we start with selecting the fabric? Would you like to have another cup of coffee?" While the customer sits down in the Chesterfield chair at a wooden table to drink his coffee, Peter brings in his colleague, Taco. Taco shakes hands with the client. Peter to client: "Together, we will customise your suit."
>
> (Film observation)

In the example given above, we see a discussion between the customer and the shop attendant about suit details and fabric. Here, the shop attendant plays the role of an adviser with his colleague acting as the assistant specialised in "measuring." In the above performance, it is not so much the actual presence of shop attendants, but rather the number of attendants that symbolises luxury (Csaba 2008). Other artefacts – such as ladders – are part of the script. To collect the items of clothing required, employees have to use a small ladder to reach the upper parts of the cupboards that go up to the ceiling, while the customer is watching and drinking his coffee. According to the shop attendants interviewed, this symbolises the level of service: "we do everything for the client."

The performance continues after the customer's measurements have been taken:

> The customer is drinking his coffee while Vincent brings two books with fabric samples. While the customer remains seated, Vincent bows down to show his client different fabrics, forcing himself into an uncomfortable position. The customer feels the different fabrics, takes a smell and then makes his decision: "I like this one, but I can't really see the colours well

Figure 7.2 Theatrical probes in Oger shop (still of film "Getting acquaintance with Oger" © Broos)

in this light." Vincent: "OK, shall we walk outside?" Both Vincent and the customer descend the staircase, go outside and study the fabrics in daylight. The customer again touches and feels the fabrics and finally says, "This one." "OK," says Vincent. They return, walk up the stairs, and the customer sits down to finish his coffee.

(Film observation)

Here, we see that the shopping street itself also forms part of the Oger theatre. Walking outside to see fabrics in daylight, to feel the material – and even to smell it – is all part of the socio-material performance.

The Italian atelier

Central to the concept of the "Italian atelier" design are long wooden counters and tables that are used to tailor clothes. Given the size of the room, some tables are small and long, others are square or round. Tables with flower bouquets are situated everywhere in the shop. Most of these occupy a central position in the various shop spaces, with customers and attendants intermingling. It was frequently observed that attendants measure suits and fold them on these tables, that coffee cups are put on the tables and that social small talk between shop attendants and customers takes place at the edge of a table:

> Simon rests one of his hands on the table while responding to his international client who is standing at the other side of the table; "Everything is going well now with the family. It is such a joy, ours is just three now. Have I shown you the pictures? Don't children grow fast?" Client nods and takes a sip of his coffee.
>
> (Film observation in shop)

The tables are also used by craftsmen demonstrating their knowledge and craftsmanship to customers during special "Italian weekends." During these weekends, the atmosphere of an "Italian atelier" is imitated. One man in a leather apron polishes shoes at one of the tables while customers are watching him. A tailor shows his craftsmanship in the shop window by displaying how to stitch a hand-made suit. Other references to Italy can be found in many artefacts, such as the Italian Maserati cars that are parked in front of the store. An "Italian" smell is created by bowls filled with potpourri positioned in different places in the shop. In the interviews, employees and management frequently mention Italian-style elements, fashion brands, passion and Italian atmospheres in relation to Oger's Italian atelier concept. Oger Lusink even connects the organisation's family structure with successful Italian family brands:

> Thanks to the interest of my nieces, nephews and sons . . . we've built up a sense of family, because they all want to join (the company). Look at

Italy, you see the Benettons, the Zegnas, the Agnellis. The most successful companies in Italy are family-run.

(Interview with Oger Lusink)

Like an Italian "patron," the owner regularly acts as host and is physically present in the store: he walks around, exchanges kisses, makes jokes and shakes hands with customers as well as employees. He performs the role of a celebrity among other celebrities on Saturdays.

On Saturdays, when he's in the store, he's really the centre of it all. He talks to people, they talk to him. He's really good at that.

(Interview with shop attendant)

The "sacred" boardroom

The characteristics of the English gentlemen's club are best observed in the exclusive boardroom. This spacious room is located separately from the rest of the shop, on the highest floor. It is only open to members of the Dutch Royal family, business leaders and celebrities and, at the request of these customers, outside regular shopping hours. The room's limited access and its location are in line with the patterns selected for most executive's offices – on the top floors (Betts 2006). Indeed, the interior of Oger's boardroom with its large open fire, a library half filled with books, a large wooden table with a cigar box on top, four large silver candles, designer furniture, a chandelier full of small crystals, leather chairs and a wooden floor most resembles artefacts and spatial design associated with boardrooms as discussed by Betts (2006). She studied boardrooms in different organisations and stated that "the board room signifies that the organisation is important enough to have a separate space dedicated to holding particular, usually quite expensive, furniture" (Betts 2006: 162). The spatial layout and the special opening hours of Oger's boardroom provide an exclusive floor for the highest level of service: in total privacy and discretion, men can select clothing from the walk-in wardrobe.

Boardroom objects act in very particular contextualised ways to create and signify power (Betts 2006: 165). The boardroom in the Oger theatre, with its oak table, chandelier, elegant Chesterfields and a portrait of the Dutch Royal family, is meant to let each shop attendant think that:

I'm surrounded by the most beautiful things in the world. Nothing can go wrong. What we've got here is to be found nowhere else.

(Interview with store manager)

However, not all employees feel secure enough to offer the high level of service needed in the boardroom. For some of the shop attendants, the performance required is too difficult:

I feel that it's not my cup of tea. You have to spend a lot of time talking to the customer and know a lot about big boats and expensive cars and watches. Well, that's too much for me.

(Interview with shop attendant of Dressed4Success)

For others, the theatre is a pleasant stage for performing. During our presence, we observed how John, a good-looking shop attendant, is, in our perception, flirting with a client to break the ice:

Clearly, she [the wife/girlfriend] is making the decision on buying. While the man she is accompanying waits for her decision in a corner of the room, she interacts with John. They laugh, while John moves his hair behind his ears as she does. They step towards each other, and for a moment the two touch, while laughing and drinking coffee. In the corner, the man is still waiting with his new outfit.

(Film observations)

We interpreted John's behaviour in this scene as "deep acting" (Grandey 2003).

Backstage control

In terms of control, it can be stated that the Oger management orchestrates the drama performances demonstrated by shop attendants backstage, invisible to the consumers. These performances have to be absolutely perfect and in line with the company's management philosophy:

Perfection is the slogan I live by. I love perfection; I love it when things are organised perfectly, when they're clean. When the lights all work, the van looks good, the store windows look fantastic, my employees look good. When the atmosphere is nice.

(Interview with Oger Lusink)

To reach this type of perfection, the company's philosophy is transferred to new employees through training. Training takes place outside regular working hours – which is not paid extra – and the programme consists of four modules: (1) expert knowledge; (2) technology; (3) sales skills; and (4) media training and team building. Every new employee is offered a temporary contract and is informed about the tasks and roles of a personal adviser (Van Dijk 2008). After a successful initial period of six months, the new employee obtains a contract for another six months. Then, he or she starts the second module in which technology and expertise are taught. In a third module, sales skills are taught. After successfully passing the tests, employees finally obtain a fixed contract. The training programme frequently uses the metaphor of the theatre. In "module 1," interactions between customers and personal advisers are discussed by the commercial manager:

Seven new shop attendants are grouped around the darkly polished wooden table boasting two silver candles. The commercial manager explains that the personal relationship between customer and shop attendants includes personal emotions and passion. The commercial manager: "We offer a drama set, and you are to have a leading role in the play. I use this metaphor often, for I see people who do in fact have the right qualities don't always pay attention and may even disappear into the background, ending up with only a minor role."

(Film observations)

As we saw in the example above, much attention is paid to drama, passion and roles. Nevertheless, we also observed a gap between managerial rhetoric and daily practices in the shop. Management rhetoric emphasised the moving away of the company's transactional history, where it was important how much one sold, towards a 'culture where we talk about how many customers we serve' (interview with commercial manager). In daily practice, however, we observed the undiminished importance of turnover and sales:

Saturday afternoon after closing time, all 18 shop attendants gathered in a circle to listen to the commercial manager who complimented Vanessa, a shop attendant, on her "mega" sales that week. Commercial manager: "Friday, Vanessa called a number of people in her personal network to offer some new menswear and she sold for more than 10,000 euros that afternoon. A mega sale. Very well done, Vanessa." Vanessa responded by saying: "I didn't do this on my own."

(Film observation)

Such pressure is demanding for employees. Moreover, the high level of service, the need for perfection, the social interaction with customers and the drama involved all require an employee's total commitment. For some employees, these demands are too much:

Recently we had a young man of 26 who became heavily overworked. This may have had various causes, but one of them could be that his inner feelings and his outside performance didn't complement each other. (When this happens) one can become exhausted.

(Interview with commercial manager)

The spatial settings of the Oger theatre makes it hard for shop attendants to "hide." They are, in fact, together with the customer, performing front-stage. To perform the role needed in the Oger theatre, shop attendants choose to wear a mask and select a strategy to deal with tensions related to the job:

If you go to the PC Hooftstraat in the morning, you put on your mask and you change completely, so to speak. And if you go home in the evening, you take the mask off. It's the mask of something you really are not; what you have to do is keep it on all day to manoeuvre between all sorts of clients. With a lot of clients you normally wouldn't socialise, but you have to in business.

(Interview with shop attendant)

The backstage control of the shop attendants' acculturation, commitment and role performance appeared to be important themes in the orchestration of the Oger brand.

Discussion

This paper explored how the Oger brand is communicated and constructed by management and shop attendants within the spatial settings of the flagship store. As with other branded servicescapes (e.g. Diamond et al. 2009), the Oger flagship store serves as a repository of objects and experiences gathered from outside sources. The Oger management has carefully designed, composed and orchestrated the Italian atelier, the English gentlemen's club and the boardroom in which customers have their momentary glimpses of identification with fame and glory. The symbolic message behind the spatial design of the Oger flagship store is that of human's quest for wealth and fame. These spatial settings together construct the Oger theatre (Table 7.1).

The spatial settings of this Oger retail theatre make up the stage for shop attendants to perform and play their roles. They follow a script in which they approach customers as celebrities, engage in a personal conversation on family, lifestyle and glamour and serve drinks and salmon bites. Shop attendants then passionately show new fabrics and suits to the customers using different theatrical props such as tables, books and chairs. When customers are interested, a second shop attendant will join the performance to measure the suit. Here, mirrors and tape measures play an important role. Then, the shop attendant invites customers to study the fabrics in daylight, outside the shop, before making the decision to buy the suit. This performance is what Baron, Harris and Harris (2001) called a "consumer as connoisseur" retail performance. Socio-material performances in the spatial settings of the Oger flagship, such as discussed above, together construct and communicate the Oger brand (Table 7.2).

An important element in the socio-material performance is the "internal design proxemics." This incorporates the context of culturally specific meaning and involves the social and personal spaces between consumers and shop attendants that shape their behaviour and interaction in the shop. In the Oger case, we have observed how objects and spatial settings such as mirrors and tables stimulate personal performances between shop attendants and customers and how the boardroom adds culturally specific meaning to the social interaction between shop attendants and consumers. This "*in*ternal design proxemics" is an extension of Yanow's (2006) spatial categories which, among others, focus on the design proxemics of a building's *ex*terior.

Table 7.1 The spatial settings of the "Oger theatre"

Spatial categories	Oger fashion theatre
Design vocabularies	Width of the facade indicates status Three distinct spatial areas represent different "theatres" (Informal, Dressed4Success and Atelier Italia) Each theatre is situated at a distinct split-level floor Four neighbouring sites in the centre of the most expensive shopping street indicating its prestige
Design gesture	Shop facade with its large golden letters resembles that of other shops in the street Twenty-five-metre-wide shop windows clearly distinguish the shop from other (smaller) shops
Internal design proxemics	Position of mirrors, tables, leather chairs, cups of coffee and suits stimulates and enhances personal performances involving shop attendants and customers Design set-up mimicking an Italian atelier with customers and shop attendants intermingling Corporate design is found in the boardroom
Decor	Decor features traditional theatre de cor elements consisting of dark red colours combined with golden artefacts, mirrors and chandeliers Pictures of the Dutch Royal family Shop attendants wear special Oger "uniforms" Red-carpet welcome is organised at an open entrance with "Italian" Maserati and Porsche cars parked in the street

Table 7.2 Socio-material performances as demonstrated by shop attendants in the Oger theatre

Socio-material performances

Spatial location of the shop attracts rich and wealthy consumers while simultaneously excluding others

Mirrors, tables, leather chairs, cups of coffee and suits combined with the social interaction between shop attendants and customers play a vital role

Corporate spatial settings and exclusive opening hours of the boardroom breathe the ambience of a royal lodge restricted to special customers only

Scripted enactment of intimacy

The showing, smelling and testing of fabrics inside as well as outside the shop

Shop attendants socially interact with customers in numerous spaces, settings and shop corners

The owner plays the role of an "Italian patron" on Saturdays

Demonstration of personal and emotional involvement with customers as well as the mingling of shop attendants and customers around tables

Extra attendants are called in for measurements

Critical to the success of controlling brand experiences are the processes of socialisation and aestheticisation demonstrated by shop attendants. In the current case, we have seen that shop attendants are selected and trained to perform the emotional labour needed. And it is not only shop attendants who carry out this type of labour; the Oger management, too, play a role as "patrons" or "family members" imitating an Italian fashion family. The spatial design of the Italian atelier, the English gentlemen's club and the boardroom stress the performative character of the job. Unsurprisingly, all the employees regard their work as a demanding performance. Some of them are uneasy about the drama and emotions that are needed to perform and perceive their performance as "putting up a mask," while others find it hard to show empathy and to interact creatively with customers. These are examples of private identities conflicting with the brand (Pettinger 2004).

Conclusions

This paper explored, with a special focus on the spatial settings, how management and shop attendants of Dutch menswear fashion house Oger communicate and construct the Oger brand. The study makes a valuable contribution in the quest for empirical studies on space and spatial arrangements in retail shops (Gregson, Crewe and Brooks 2002a; Küpers 2002). The Oger case shows how management carefully designed, managed and orchestrated retail space, objects and shop attendants' roles in an "Oger theatre" to construct and communicate the brand. This theatre gives both customers and shop attendants a context for the performance of services and tells them about the nature of goods and services to be found in that specific store (Pettinger 2004). The shop attendants performed their "authentic" roles and interacted with the (not so) rich and famous to support the consumers' hedonistic experience of exclusiveness and authenticity. The store offers consumers exclusiveness and authenticity by creating a factual and spatiotemporal link with Italian fashion ateliers and English corporate boardrooms. Such a linkage was also found by Kjeldgaard and Ostberg (2007) in their study on coffee establishments in Sweden and Denmark. In both cases, we observe the interconnection between economic and aesthetic realms in selling products through "authentic" performances in theatres (Pettinger 2004; Schroeder and Salzer-Mörling 2006).

In these performances, we observed the importance of management and shop attendants in constructing and communicating the Oger brand. Earlier studies (e.g. Peñaloza 1998; Kozinets et al. 2002) have observed the interplay between design, display and consumption processes in constructing and communicating retail brands, but undervalued the roles of staff members. Their roles in the construction of retail brands could be explored by connecting organisation and management studies to consumer culture studies. This connection resulted in a deeper understanding of how selection, acculturation, training, control and management of shop attendants are critical in the construction and maintenance of the "Oger brand." In this construction and maintenance, retail spaces shape action and interaction by staff members and in turn are reshaped on part of these staff members, as indicated by Hernes (2004).

Literature on organisation culture and identity can be helpful to consumer culture scientists to better understand how brands are communicated through different communication channels and how espoused organisational values (Martin 2002), values that corporations want to present themselves to consumers, are aligned with enacted values, values that staff members and consumers experience in retail shops, and with practices of shop attendants. The case study of Benetton is such an example of connecting the concepts of corporate identity and brand (Borgerson et al. 2009). In the same line, the connection of organisation and management studies with consumer studies increases our understanding of the production and reproduction of spatial settings in constructing brands (Gregson, Crewe and Brooks 2002a; Diamond et al. 2009). We suggest that the literature of organisation studies may be useful for further research on consumer, markets and culture.

Acknowledgements

I thank the participants of the stream *Making brands come alive: How organisations, stakeholders and customers mobilise their identity* of the 25th EGOS Colloquium held in Barcelona, 2–4 July 2009, for their insightful suggestions and comments. I also thank the three anonymous reviewers of CMC and Dvora Yanow for their valuable comments.

References

Arnould, Eric, and Craig Thompson. 2005. "Consumer Culture Theory (CCT): Twenty years of research." *Journal of Consumer Research* 31 (4): 868–82.

Arnould, Eric, and Melanie Wallendorf. 1994. "Market-oriented ethnography: Interpretation building and marketing strategy formulation." *Journal of Marketing Research* 31 (4): 484–504.

Ashforth, Blake, and Ronald Humphrey. 1993. "Emotional labor in service roles: The influence of identity." *The Academy of Management Review* 18 (1): 88–115.

Barbash, Ilisa, and Lucien Taylor. 1997. *Cross-cultural filmmaking. A handbook for making documentary and ethnographic films and videos.* Berkeley, CA: University of California Press.

Baron, Steve, Kim Harris, and Richard Harris. 2001. "Retail theatre: The 'intended effect' of the performance." *Journal of Service Research* 4 (2): 102–17.

Belk, Russell, and Robert Kozinets. 2005. "Videography in marketing and consumer research." *Qualitative Market Research: An International Journal* 8 (2): 128–41.

Betts, Jan. 2006. "Framing power: The case of the boardroom." *Consumption Markets & Culture* 9 (2): 157–67.

Bitner, Mary Jo. 1992. "Servicescape: The impact of physical surroundings on customers and employees." *Journal of Marketing* 56 (2): 57–71.

Borgerson, Janet L., Jonathan E. Schroeder, Martin Escudero Magnusson, and Frank Magnussonn. 2009. "Corporate communication, ethics, and operational identity: A case study of Benetton." *Business Ethics: A European Review* 18 (3): 209–23.

Collier, John, Jr. 1967. *Visual anthropology: Photography as a research method.* Albuquerque, NM: University of New Mexico Press.

Creigton, Millie. 1998. "The SEED of creative lifestyle shopping." In *Servicescapes: The concept of place in contemporary markets*, edited by John Sherry. Chicago, IL: NTC Books, 199–228.

Crewe, Louise, and Michelle Lowe. 1995. "Gap on the map? Towards a geography of consumption and identity." *Environment and Planning A* 27 (12): 1877–98.

Csaba, Fabian. 2008. *Redefining luxury: A review essay. Creativity at Work.* Copenhagen: Copenhagen Business School.

Dale, Karen, and Gibson Burrell. 2008. *The spaces of organisation & the organisation of space. Power identity & materiality at work.* Hampshire: Palgrave MacMillan.

Diamond, Nina, John Sherry, Jr., Albert Muñiz, Jr., Mary Ann McGrath, Robert Kozinets, and Stefania Borghini. 2009. "American Girl and the brand gestalt: Closing the loop on sociocultural branding research." *Journal of Marketing* 73 (2): 118–34.

Dovey, Kim. 1999. *Framing places: Mediating power in built form.* London: Routledge.

El Guindi, Fadwa. 2004. *Visual anthropology, essential method and theory.* Walnut Creek, CA: Alta Mira Press.

Emmison, Michael, and Philip Smith. 2000. *Researching the visual. Series: Introducing qualitative methods*, London: Sage.

Fisk, Raymond, and Stephen Grove. 1996. "Applications of impression management and the drama metaphor in marketing: An introduction." *European Journal of Marketing* 30 (9): 6–12.

Gagliardi, Pasqual. 2009. "Organisations as designed islands." *Island Studies Journal* 1 (4): 43–52.

Goffman, Erving. 1959. *The presentation of self in everyday life.* New York: Doubleday.

Grandey, Alicia. 2003. "When 'the show must go on': Surface acting and deep acting as determinants of emotional exhaustion and peer related service delivery." *The Academy of Management Journal* 46 (1): 86–96.

Gregson, Nicky, Louise Crewe, and Kate Brooks. 2002a. "Shopping, space, and practice." *Environment and Planning D: Society and Space* 20 (5): 597–617.

Gregson, Nicky, Louise Crewe, and Kate Brooks. 2002b. "Discourse, displacement, and retail practice: Some pointers from the charity retail project." *Environment and Planning A* 34 (9): 1661–83.

Habraken, John, and Jonathan Teicher, eds. 1998. *The structure of the ordinary: Form and control in the built environment.* Cambridge, MA: MIT Press.

Hernes, Tor. 2004. *The spatial construction of organisation.* Amsterdam: John Benjamins.

Hernes, Tor, Tore Bakken, and Per Ingvar Olsen. 2006. "Spaces as process: Developing a recursive perspective on organisational space." In *Space, organizations and management theory*, edited by Stewart Clegg and Martin Kornberger. Copenhagen: Liber and Copenhagen Business School Press, 33–63.

Joy, Annamma, and John F. Sherry. 2003. "Speaking of art as embodied imagination: A multi-sensory approach to understanding aesthetic experience." *Journal of Consumer Research* 30 (2): 259–82.

Kent, Tony. 2003. "2D23D: Management and design perspectives on retail branding international." *Journal of Retail & Distribution Management* 31 (3): 131–42.

Kjeldgaard, Dannie, and Jacob Ostberg. 2007. "Coffee grounds and the global cup: Glocal consumer culture in Scandinavia." *Consumption Markets & Culture* 10 (2): 175–87.

Kornberger, Martin, and Stewart Clegg. 2004. "Bringing space back in: Organizing the generative building." *Organization Studies* 25 (7): 1095–114.

Kozinets, Robert, John Sherry, Jr., Bernett DeBerry-Spence, Adam Duhachek, Krittinee Nuttavuthisit, and Diana Storm. 2002. "Themed flagship brand stores in the new millennium: Theory, practice, prospects." *Journal of Retailing* 78 (1): 17–29.

Küpers, Wendelin. 2002. "Phenomenology of aesthetic organising ways. Towards aesthetically responsive organizations." *Consumption Markets & Culture* 5 (1): 21–46.

Latour, Bruno. 1993. *We have never been modern*. London: Harvester Wheatsheaf.

Lury, Cecilia. 2004. *Brands. The logos of the global economy*. London: Routledge.

Maanen, John van. 1995. *Representation in ethnography*. Thousand Oaks, CA: Sage.

Marrewijk, Alfons van. 2009. "Corporate headquarters as physical embodiments of organisational change." *Journal of Organization Change Management* 22 (3): 290–306.

Marrewijk, Alfons van, and Dvora Yanow, eds. 2010. *Organisational spaces. Rematerializing the workaday world*. Northampton, MA: Edward Elgar.

Martin, Joanne. 2002. *Exploring organizational culture*. London: Sage.

Miller, Daniel, Peter Jackson, Nigel Thrift, Beverly Holbrook, and Michael Rowland. 1998. *Shopping place and identity*. London: Routledge.

Olins, Wally. 1989. *Corporate identity: Making business strategy visible through design*. Boston, MA: Harvard Business School Press.

Orlikowski, Wanda J. 2007. "Sociomaterial practices: Exploring technology at work." *Organization Studies* 28 (9): 1435–48.

O'Toole, Paddy, and Prisca Were. 2008. "Observing places: Using space and material culture in qualitative research." *Qualitative Research* 8 (5): 616–34.

Peñaloza, Lisa. 1998. "Just doing it: A visual ethnographic study of spectacular consumption at Niketown." *Consumption Markets & Culture* 2 (4): 337–400.

Pettinger, Lynne. 2004. "Brand culture and branded workers: Service work and aesthetic labour in fashion retail." *Consumption Markets & Culture* 7 (2): 165–84.

Pink, Sarah. 2007. *Doing visual ethnography: Images, media and representation in research*. London: Sage.

Rafaeli, Anat, and Michael Pratt. 2006. *Artifacts and organizations. Beyond mere symbolism*. Mahwah, NJ: Lawrence Erlbaum Associates.

Rose, Gillian. 2007. *Visual methodologies: An introduction to the interpretation of visual materials*. London: Sage.

Rosenbaum, Mark. 2005. "The symbolic servicescape: Your kind is welcomed here." *Journal of Consumer Behaviour* 4 (4): 257–67.

Ruby, Jay. 2000. *Picturing culture, explorations of film & anthropology*. Chicago, IL: The University of Chicago Press.

Schembri, Sharon, and Maree Boyle. 2005. "Sociospatiality, place and the consumption experience." Paper presented at 11th Asian Pacific Regional Studies, 3–7 December, Melbourne, Australia.

Schmitt, Bernd. 1999. *Experiential marketing: How to get customers to sense, feel, think, act, and relate to your company and brands*. New York: The Free Press.

Schmitt, Bernd, Alex Simonsen, and Joshua Marcus. 1995. "Managing corporate image and identity." *Long Range Planning* 28 (5): 82–92.

Schroeder, Jonathan. 2003. "Building brands: Architectural expression in the electronic age." In *Persuasive imagery: A consumer response perspective*, edited by Linda Scott and Rajeev Batra. Mahwah, NJ: Lawrence Erlbaum, 349–82.

Schroeder, Jonathan, and Miriam Salzer-Mörling. 2006. *Brand culture*. London: Routledge.

Sherry, John F. 1998. "The soul of the company store: Niketown Chicago and the emplaced brandscape." In *Servicescapes: The concept of place in contemporary markets*, edited by John Sherry, Jr. Lincolnwood, IL: Niketown Chicago Business Books, 109–50.

Sherry, John, Jr., Diana Robert Kozinets, Adam Storm, Krittinee Duhachek, Benét Nuttavuthisit, and DeBerry-Spence. 2001. "Being in the zone, staging retail theatre in the ESPN Zone Chicago." *Journal of Contemporary Ethnography* 30 (4): 465–510.

Smith, Barton. 2000. "The store as a brand." *DSN Retailing Today* 39 (23): 19–20.

Strati, Antonio. 1999. *Organization and aesthetics*. London: Sage.

Strati, Antonio. 2006. "Organisational artifacts and the aesthetic approach." In *Artifacts and organizations*, edited by Anat Rafaeli and Michael Pratt. Mahwah, NJ: Lawrence Erlbaum Associates, 23–41.

Turley, Lou W., and Jean-Charles Chebat. 2002. "Linking retain strategy, atmospheric design and shopping behaviour." *Journal of Marketing Management* 18 (1–2): 125–44.

Van Dijk, Cees. 2008. "Het fashion-statement van Oger." Available at: www.elsevierretail.nl/1068226/Fashion/Fashion-artikel/HetFashion-statementVanOger.htm (accessed 25 November 2009).

Wallendorf, Melanie, and Russell Belk. 1989. "Assessing trustworthiness in naturalistic consumer research." In *Interpretive consumer research*, edited by Elizabeth Hirschmann. Provo, UT: Association for Consumer Research, 69–84.

Warren, Susan. 2008. "Empirical challenges in organizational aesthetics research: Towards a sensual methodology." *Organization Studies* 29 (4): 559–80.

Yanow, Dvora. 2006. "Studying physical artifacts: An interpretive approach." In *Artifacts and organizations*, edited by Anat Rafaeli and Michael Pratt. Mahwah, NJ: Lawrence Erlbaum Associates.

Yanow, Dvora, and Peregrine Schwartz-Shea, eds. 2006. *Interpretation and method: Empirical research methods and the interpretative turn*. New York: M. E. Sharpe.

8 Learning to say g'day to the world

The development of Australia's marketable image in the 1980s

Robert Crawford

In 2006, Tourism Australia launched its ill-fated "Where the Bloody Hell Are You?" campaign. With its crude tagline and focus on the bikini-clad Lara Bingle, the campaign sought to appeal to the "everyman" audience that had been the target of Australia's most successful tourism campaign – the Paul Hogan "Say G'day to Australia" campaign of the 1980s. Tourism Australia hoped that the new twist on this old formula would yield similar results. Such hopes were dashed. While the campaign generated significant public attention, it failed to attract a sufficient number of tourists to Australia. Its image of Australia was pilloried at home and abroad, and it was unceremoniously dumped in 2008. Although a new agency was appointed to handle the account and to reinvigorate "Brand Australia," the development of an entire new strategy would take time. In the interim, a stopgap measure would be needed in order to halt the "Where the Bloody Hell Are You?"-led demise.

The solution to this problem was to approach Hollywood director Baz Luhrmann, who was in the country filming *Australia*, to develop an interim campaign. Both Tourism Australia and Luhrmann were well aware of the unique synergies and cross-promotional opportunities between the two projects. As Tourism Australia's introductory brochure for the campaign reveals, both parties shared significant synergies: "The buzz created by the Twentieth Century Fox marketing campaign and the movie offer Tourism Australia an exciting opportunity to make Australia 'the' must see destination" (Tourism Australia 2008: 1).

Launched with great fanfare in October 2008, Luhrmann's "Walkabout" series of advertisements inevitably attracted significant attention. At the time of writing, it was still unclear whether the campaign was a success. Government spokespeople have claimed that the campaign is working (Lee 2009: 5). However, the previous Tourism Minister had made similar claims about the "Where the Bloody Hell Are You?" campaign months after its launch (Marszalek 2007). Observers were more critical. Some felt that it had gone too far in the opposite way to its predecessor, labelling it "too white collar" (Lee 2008: 3). Paul Hogan was equally dismissive, telling advertising website Brand Republic that it failed to focus on Australia's friendly and laid-back image: "The new ads should focus on Australia's friendly and laid-back people: 'If I go to your house for a visit and I want to come back, it's because I enjoyed your company, not your furniture'" (Sandison 2008).

Industry commentators on the Australian Broadcasting Corporation (ABC) programme the *Gruen Transfer* also agreed. "It's a great ad for having a holiday but not a great ad for Australia," observed Dan Gregory, creative director at SMART. Comparing it to the "Say G'day to Australia" campaign, he went on to explain that "you look at that ad [Say G'day] and it's not you need a holiday, it's I need a bit of Australia" (*Gruen Transfer* 2009).

The perceived failure of the "Where the Bloody Hell Are You?" campaign and, indeed, the solution provide a unique opportunity to re-examine the campaign against which they have inevitably been measured. As the Brand Republic report and the *Gruen Transfer* discussion neatly illustrate, the Hogan campaign of the 1980s and the results stemming from it remain the benchmark for all Australian tourism campaigns. The logic behind such comparisons has been simple: if we did it back then, we can do it again. But can the results of a campaign that is over 20 years old still be relevant? It will be argued that the logic underpinning such comparisons is flawed – a point that is neatly highlighted by the "Where the Bloody Hell Are You?" campaign. As the creators of the campaign and the image it conveyed, Tourism Australia and M&C Saatchi were both responsible for looking to the past without grasping the real reasons why Hogan had been so successful. In short, they had assumed that Hogan's success could be replicated by updating the old formula. Their lack of insight would only become apparent when the number of tourists heading for Australia fell.

The astounding success that Brand Australia enjoyed in the 1980s cannot be understood without reference to the broader social and cultural conditions that precipitated it. This article therefore examines the ways in which commercial interests have intersected and interacted with broader cultural and social changes. In his survey of Australian nationalism and popular culture in the 1980s, Graeme Turner's *Making it National* examined the ways in which business interests purported to be speaking for the nation (Turner 1994: 13–14). Interestingly, the advertising industry and its role in cultivating this three-way relationship between commercial interests, nation and popular culture are not directly examined. Taking up from where Turner leaves off, this article follows the advertising industry and its construction of Australian images (both on and behind the television screen) from the 1960s through the early 1990s. By examining the activities of Paul Hogan and the Mojo advertising agency in relation to the broader social and cultural context, this article will suggest that of the tourism campaign of the 1980s represented a high point of Australian advertising – one that occurred at the cusp of the global age. Moreover, this study will also demonstrate the commercial dangers of nostalgic interpretations of the past.

Finding a voice

The arrival of commercial television in Australia in 1956 signalled the beginnings of a new age for Australia's advertising industry. The advent of commercial television was eagerly awaited by local admen. Combining both sight and sound, television advertising promised to be the greatest ever advertising medium (Crawford 2007: 107–10). Moreover, Australians were enjoying an enormous economic boom. Australian consumers were not only in a position to view these commercials in their suburban lounge rooms, they were also in a position to act on the advertisers' exhortations to "buy, buy, buy!" Such conditions did not go unnoticed by transnational advertisers and advertising agencies. Australia's booming economy and commercial television stations soon encouraged them to spread their operations down under.

The arrival of McCann-Erickson in 1959 signalled the arrival of a new era in Australian advertising. Having bought out the local agency Hansen-Rubensohn, the American agency quickly set about modernising its latest acquirement. This process was replicated by other international agencies over the course of the 1960s. While some bought out local agencies, others opted to start a new branch from scratch (Crawford 2008: 137–8). By the mid-1960s, questions were being asked about the new arrivals and their impact on Australia's advertising industry. Industry newspaper *B&T: Broadcasting and Television* thus opined:

> If American concepts and attitudes, primarily devised and produced to be aimed at Americans, are going to smother the robust typically-local and successful concepts Australian advertising has built over many years, as it looks, somebody will be the poorer for it.
>
> (B&T 1964: 5)

Such questions were not unwarranted. As in other countries, the local Australian staff working in these multinationals were required to follow the directives, formulas and strategies devised by their American bosses (Mattelart 1991: 31–3). While these directives certainly improved the agencies' day-to-day operations (particularly those that had been overtaken), their impact on the agencies' output was perhaps more ambiguous. As agencies obediently followed the imported blueprints, their advertising became more conservative and progressively blander. The "mid-Atlantic" accent utilised by spokespeople in so many advertisements appeared to reflect this dull conformity. However, a small number of admen and adwomen were beginning to find these conditions altogether unbearable. It would only be a matter of time before they acted on their frustrations.

In 1968, John Singleton co-founded the SPASM advertising agency. Singleton had cut his teeth at the J. Walter Thompson agency before taking up the role of creative director at Berry-Currie, a smaller local agency. Both experiences had provided him with the skills and knowledge for starting up his own agency. Known for his anti-authoritarian, larrikin[1] demeanour and shrewd acumen, it seemed inevitable that Singleton would branch out on his own and begin to produce innovative yet highly idiosyncratic advertisements. His most successful campaign was for David Holdings wholesale grocery and liquor distributor. Created in 1974, the commercials simply outlined the cost of the retailer's wares before asking viewers loudly and repetitively, "Where do you get it?" (Stone 2002: 60–1). Singleton's loud, brash and distinctively Australian-sounding advertisements were derided by critics for being ocker.[2] This uniquely Australian form of advertising divided the advertising industry. Defending ocker advertisements from the critics, *Advertising News* argued that it was an important part of Australia's coming of age:

> We can't see why the broad Australian accent and colloquialisms should come in for all the criticism they do . . . Critics blame the exponent of all-that's-earthy-in-Australian-English John Singleton and claim it is setting school children a bad example . . . Ockerism is a manifestation of Australia growing up. It is our own language and not imported. It would be a pity if our 1976 culture couldn't take it in its stride.
>
> (Parsons 1976: 2)

Like Singleton, *Advertising News* was well aware that such appeals struck a chord with the consuming public. Others in the industry would also cotton on to the drawing power of an Australian appeal.

A tale of two agencies

The exodus of creative talent from the transnational agencies that had begun as a small trickle in the late 1960s would grow into a steady stream over the course of the 1970s. By placing creativity ahead of conformity, these "boutique" agencies or "hot shops" were producing a distinctively Australian form of advertising. While Armand Mattelart observes a similar development occurring in Europe, the experience in Australia was also linked to local cultural conditions.

One of the first, and arguably the most influential, advertisements using this distinctive brand of appeal was the campaign for Winfield cigarettes devised in 1972 by Sydney hot shop Hertz-Walpole. One of the creative minds working on the project was Allan "Jo" Johnston, another creative adman who had been disenchanted by working for a large transnational agency. Jo had only recently joined the agency before taking up the Winfield account. He would later recall how Hertz-Walpole selected the campaign and its spokesman:

> At that stage Jim Walpole said "you should see this fellow on *A Current Affair*, this Paul Hogan. He's a sort of ocker sort of bloke, they have a three minute segment, he's very interesting you know." We were already heading in an Australian direction anyway, as an agency we were tired

of being pro-American. We were trying to find our own way and we'd started to work on the launch of the commercial and decided we'd go the full Australian way with Hogan.[3]

As Jo notes, the first advertisement featured a young Paul Hogan. Wearing a tuxedo and standing before an orchestra, the visual image outwardly displayed the air of sophistication that had become a hallmark of cigarette advertising on Australian television. However, once Hogan commenced speaking in his broad Australian accent (concluding with the famous tag line "Let 'er rip, Boris"), it became clear that this was a parody – a piss-take that no Australian could miss. The campaign instantly struck a rapport with the audience. Hogan's celebrity status across the nation soared, as too did Winfield's sales, which skyrocketed from nowhere to become the leading brand on the market.

Viewing Hogan's broad accent as the key to Winfield's success, other advertisers desperately cast any ocker with a broad Australian accent and bad grammar as the spokesman for their campaigns. While some ocker advertisements worked, the majority did not. As their volume increased, the novelty of the ocker advertisements began to wear thin – Australian audiences could only take so much mangled speech. Significantly, those responsible for these failed campaigns had altogether misunderstood the nature of Hogan's appeal (Crawford 2007: 7). His accent and delivery were only one part of the campaign's success, albeit an important one. Hogan himself suggested as much when he told the Sydney Advertising Club that the industry had "bastardised" the "ocker approach." Criticising the grammar used in these advertisements, an exasperated Hogan declared, "I don't know how some advertising people can sleep at night" (*Advertising News* 1976: 32). The point that Hogan was making was later taken up by Jo, who explained:

> Hogan was . . . classed as an ocker, but we never considered ourselves as ocker in style of advertising. We used Hogan for tourism [in the 1980s] and he was very Australian, but I didn't consider him ocker; he was just more your Digger . . . whilst he was very working-class, he was a very shrewd operator, very quick, which I think Australians are proud of, they're working class, but they're as sharp as the next bloke and they're street wise and they're . . . very quick-witted and ironic in their humour and that's hard to catch.[4]

As Jo reveals, the real key to Hogan's appeal lay in his distinctive wit and his ability to use it to make audiences feel better about themselves and, indeed, the advertised product. The accent only served to reinforce the relationship between Hogan and the viewers watching from their suburban homes.

By 1975, Jo had left Hertz-Walpole to work freelance. Sharing an office with another creative freelancer, Alan "Mo" Morris, Jo and his officemate found that they worked well together, and they decided to join forces to form another hot shop (*AdNews* 1998: 76). Their Mojo agency made an immediate impact on the local advertising scene. Deftly combining creative ideas, catchy jingles and an innate feel for the type of appeal that spoke to the "average" Australian, Mojo's advertising struck a direct chord with its audience. Their brand of advertising emulated the successful components of Hogan's appeal and applied it to an even wider market. They also deliberately avoided the use of ocker appeals. "Unlike John Singleton, we never chose to offend or to outrage," Morris would later explain. "We did mostly feel good advertising . . . they [viewers] turn on the television to be entertained and we chose to entertain them."[5] Their advertisements for the fledgling World Series Cricket competition, for example, did exactly this. In addition to selling the new competition, the "C'mon, Aussie, C'mon" jingle was taken up by Australians as a de facto anthem that was often sung with greater gusto than "God Save the Queen" or "Advance Australia Fair." In Sydney, the Tooheys brewery became a market leader on the back of Mojo's "I Feel Like a Tooheys or Two" campaign, while mums across the nation were told that they "oughtta be congratulated" for providing a good meal and, of course, for adding a dollop of Meadow Lea margarine on to it. In the space of four years, Mojo's string of catchy commercials saw it mature from a small creative hot shop to a fully fledged agency offering clients a complete service that went from creative idea to the purchase of timeslots.

In Melbourne, the emerging Australian appeal took on a different tone to what had been created in Sydney. More conservative than their northern neighbours, Melbourne audiences did not take to the loud and brash form of advertising pioneered by Singleton. It was said that Melbourne was the city in which "ockers feared to tread" (Wynne 1976: 12). Significantly, Mojo's more benign brand of Australian appeal did not encounter the same resistance. The largest locally owned agency in Melbourne was Monahan Dayman Adams (MDA), which began to develop its creative credentials when Philip Adams joined in 1968. Within seven years, MDA was the largest Australian-owned agency, boasting various blue-chip accounts. However, it was the agency's social advertising or "community service announcements" that earned it kudos from the Australian audiences and advertising colleagues. Created in 1975 for the Victorian government and adopted by other state governments, the long-running "Life. Be in It" campaign encouraged Australians to live more active lives. It focused on Norm, a character whose preference for sport (as an observer rather than a participant) and a beer or two suggested that he was something of an ocker. The "Slip, Slop, Slap" advertisements for the Anti-Cancer Council similarly urged Australians to take greater care of themselves when enjoying the outdoors. The signifiers of Australian-ness in these advertisements were more subtle than those created by Sydney agencies. However, Australian audiences identified with their look, sound and message. In complementing the Mojo style, MDA's advertising contributed to audiences' growing sense of pride in being Australian.

MDA's contribution to Australia's growing sense of national pride was not limited to its social advertisements. By the 1980s, the gap between locally owned agencies and their transnational counterparts had been further exacerbated by the growing trend among the latter to raise extra capital by becoming public companies. In 1984, MDA announced that it would be the first Australian agency to subject itself to the mercy of the stock exchange. Its aim was to sell off 30 per cent of its capital in order to raise $3.44 million. MDA's principals used their prospectus to explain that the decision had not been solely driven by commercial interests:

> By selling part of the company to the Australian public, we can not only stay Australian, but it is the first step towards us becoming a much larger company and one that can compete on a more equal footing with the multinationals.

> (Parsons 1984: 8)

The result was conclusive. Oversubscription revealed that Australian investors had faith in the local agency and its output, not to mention the buoyancy of the advertising industry MDA hoped to use its newly acquired funds to expand abroad, and within days it was fulfilling its ambitions. Its first buyout was the Hong Kong agency CitiAd. A succession of purchases, mergers and newly established branches followed, as MDA now set about introducing the world to a new image of Australia (*AdNews* 1984: 62). Such expansionist dreams demonstrated that Australians possessed the confidence to take on the world.

Selling Australia to the world

The ocker Australian image that had been cultivated and celebrated in the 1970s was first introduced to the world through the success of the 1972 film *The Adventures of Barry McKenzie*. Written by Barry Humphries, directed by Bruce Beresford and produced by MDA's Adams, the film received mixed responses. The image of the Australian innocent abroad using uniquely ocker colloquialisms to express bemusement at his new surroundings was celebrated as much as it was scorned. His passion for Foster's lager likewise divided audiences. The critics of his bacchanalian ways initially included the manufacturer of the very product he so gleefully imbibed. Carlton and United Breweries, the company behind the Foster's brand, was reluctant to be associated with the ocker image. However, an about-turn occurred when the brewer realised that this unique product placement opportunity would be offered to competing brands. As John Sinclair notes, the company would later recognise the integral role performed by this film in establishing the Foster's brand name in the British market (Sinclair 2007: 21–2). This inroad would prove to be worth its weight in gold when the brewery embarked on its global marketing campaign in the 1980s.

Rather than using a crude Barry McKenzie character to sell Foster's to British drinkers, the British agency Boase Massimi Pollitt opted for a more benign figure – Paul Hogan – who had ironically been rejected by Humphries from being in the film (Macnab 2003). Although Hogan was well known in Australia, he was still unknown in the UK. The first Foster's advertisements featuring Hogan appeared in the autumn of 1982. The Hoges persona that had been used to such great effect for Winfield was now being used by a British agency to woo the British consumer. However, Hogan deemed that the scripts prepared by the British copywriters required revision. Feeling that the original scripts presented an embarrassing view of the ocker abroad, Hogan himself undertook the revisions (Oram 1987: 127). The first advertisement in the series was an immediate success. Standing before a group of British journalists, Hoges explained:

> G'day. They've asked me over from Oz to introduce youse all to Foster's Draught, here it is. Cripes! I'd better start with the basics. It's a light, golden fluid, like, except for the white bit on top, the head, and it's brewed from malt, yeast and hops. Technical term is lager . . . But everyone calls it Foster's. Aah, ripper. Tastes like an angel cryin' on yer tongue.
>
> ("Fosters")

Describing the campaign as "a classic marketing success," the *Times*' Torin Douglas noted that the £3 million advertising campaign had produced "distinctive commercials that have caught the imagination of the public" (Douglas 1982: 19). Just months later, the campaign would receive a further boost when episodes of *The Paul Hogan Show* were broadcast on British television's Channel 4. Imitations also appeared. Following in Foster's wake was XXXX, another Australian beer trying to break into the British market. Its "black ocker" campaign was created by another non-Australian agency, Saatchi and Saatchi, and featured the tagline "Australians wouldn't give a XXXX for anything else" (Housham 1987: 28), a tagline that was still being used in the British market some 20 years later. Such advertisements indicate that the Australian image had now become readily transferable.

Hogan's spectacular success in the British market did not go unnoticed at home. Recognising the success that the Australian image was now enjoying abroad, Australians set about capitalising on it and its uniqueness. Hogan's unique ability to sell Foster's, as well as his homeland, to British consumers, was identified by the Australian Tourism Commission when it was preparing to target consumers in the US. There was now only one spokesman to be had. Launched on American television in January 1984, the "Come and Say G'day" campaign featuring Paul Hogan was devised by Mojo and the American agency N. W. Ayer. While Mojo brought Hogan to the campaign, the Americans made him throw another "shrimp" on the barbie rather than the Australian prawn. Reflecting on the campaign that they had helped market some 20 years earlier, Bill Baker and Penny Bendell, the campaign's American contributors, highlighted the campaign's appeals: "It used friendliness, the Australian accent, a cheeky sense of humor, and a sunny invitation at a time when Americans were concerned by terrorism abroad . . . and the need to feel welcome when they travelled" (Baker and Bendel 2005). Within months, it was apparent that Hogan had scored yet another hit. Australia and Australian symbols were now on the minds of American tourists and, indeed, Madison Avenue's advertising executives (Roberts 1984: 6). Seeing Hogan's rapport with consumers on the American side of the Atlantic Ocean, Foster's employed him as their spokesman there in 1985. At home, it was becoming apparent that Hogan's Midas touch was symbolic of something greater: "Even the original ocker, Paul Hogan, seems to have outlived all the negatives associated with ockerisms. He has developed into a folk hero, and reflects Australia's confidence and class" (Cross 1984: 16). By attributing the success of such campaigns to Australian creativity, such comments have tended to obscure the novelty impact of this unique campaign.

Hogan's international success and belief in his own abilities encouraged him to think about other ways of entertaining his audiences. He reasoned that film could provide a unique vehicle for his comedic writing and acting talents. Moreover, the medium also provided another way to tap into his newfound international audience. His idea, entitled *Crocodile Dundee* (1986), would revolve around the adventures of an Australian bushman who goes to New York. The protagonist, Mick Dundee, would redeploy the persona that had been used to such great effect in the Winfield, Foster's and Australian Tourist Commission campaigns. The image of Australia in the film would simultaneously feed into and out of the imagery that he had successfully forged in the advertising realm. However, as Tom O'Regan notes, the odds initially appeared to be stacked against the project. Neither the director nor the writer had any cinematic experience, while the innocent abroad storyline "was also out of step with prevalent international cinematic norms, relying neither on special effects nor on spectacle" (O'Regan 1988: 157). Its avowed Australianness was similarly out of step with the ways that Australians had been representing their country abroad. Nevertheless, the film secured the financial support from some 600 backers, including Australian media magnate (and noted gambler) Kerry Packer and cricketers Greg Chappell and Dennis Lillee (O'Regan 1988: 161). Given the important role that they had played in launching his career, one could reasonably expect that Hogan's advertising mates, such as Mo and Jo, also backed the film. Advertising's presence was also evident in the decision to allocate an extensive proportion of the funding to publicity purposes (O'Regan 1988: 158–60). The combination of self-confidence, market awareness and astute business sense resulted in *Crocodile Dundee* and its immediate successor becoming international box office hits.

Underscoring the intimate connections between *Crocodile Dundee* and the advertising world was the boost enjoyed by the advertisers that had employed Hogan in the wake of the film. The Australian Tourist Commission's campaign, for example, was given another lease on life as the advertisements were now "celebrity endorsement ads ... They now had a different impact on the audience" (Baker and Bendel 2005). The tourism and beer industries were not the only ones to benefit from the global interest in Brand Australia. Australia's advertising industry was also enjoying its time in the sun courtesy of the *Crocodile Dundee* factor. The international spotlight on Australia had alerted some American agencies to the lower costs of producing an advertisement Down Under (Brock 1987: 40). Others, however, were drawn by the quality of productions coming out of Australia. The success of the Australian-made advertisements for Energizer batteries (featuring the eccentric ex-Australian Rules footballer Mark "Jacko" Jackson) prompted its advertiser, Union Carbide, to import the campaign to the US. While it met with "mixed reactions," the creators happily noted, "At least we know they're watching ... It's flattering that a local concept like this has been picked up in the US" (*B&T* 1987: 48). Looking at the broader picture, the *Times* in London noted that Hogan's film and commercial work, coupled with other Australian successes, were all headed in one direction:

> Thanks to the success of Hogan, the affable, tinny-clutching, unsophis-ticated chauvinist Australian bloke is now an international folk hero. The successes of the yachting-crazy businessman, Alan Bond, and this year's Wimbledon winner, Pat Cash, have fed the patriotic fever that will peak in next year's celebrations of Australia's bicentenary.
>
> (*B&T* 1987: 28)

With Australians and the Australian image taking the world by storm, the imminent bicentennial celebrations could not have arrived at a more opportune moment.

Celebration of a nation

In 1986, Mojo and MDA, the two advertising agencies that had been respons-ible for popularising the Australian image to audiences in Australia and abroad, moved to join forces. It was initiated by the opportunity to secure the $10.5 million Australian Bicentennial Authority (ABA) account to advertise the nation's bicentennial celebrations in 1988. Rather than going head to head, the two agencies opted to join forces temporarily in order to outmuscle their larger challengers – specifically those that were either multinational agencies or affiliated with multinational agencies. The stratagem worked. In addition to combining the impressive track records of two agencies, the move also performed a political function. "The decision will certainly go down well in Canberra where politicians have been better known to twitch when attention is drawn to Government contracts that have gone to overseas companies," commented advertising industry journal *B&T*. The journal also drew atten-tion to the contribution that multinational agencies had made to the local advertising industry and noted that Australia's international advertising success would not have occurred without it (*B&T* 1986b: 16). Such comments suggest that Australia's advertising industry may have matured, but this growth had not occurred in isolation.

Plans to celebrate the bicentenary of the European settlement of Australia had commenced in the late 1970s. The ABA had been established to coordinate and promote these celebrations. Its early years, however, were dogged by political squabbling, confusing ambivalence and general sense of apathy. The event's initial motto, "Living Together," was symptomatic of these flaws. Designed to include all Australians and to bridge their differences – most notably those between Aboriginal Australians and those whose forebears had arrived since 1788 – the motto failed to resonate among Australians. Moreover, it tended to make a mockery of the much-publicised in-fighting within the ABA. The hefty $10.5 million publicity budget therefore sought nothing less than a complete turnaround of fortunes. Such a sum inevitably attracted the interest of the advertising industry, and the ABA was heartened by the positive response to its call (O'Brien 1991: 293).

As the bicentenary consisted of thousands of events at national, state and community levels, it was a difficult task to project the event in any precise or factual form, let alone the philosophical ideas underpinning it. As Denis O'Brien notes, Mojo/MDA's brief was consequently boiled to down to the very basics:

> Of necessity, the main television campaign was unable to convey anything of the mass of projects making up the national program. What it did was create a climate of imminent celebration. Anything deep, meaningful or heavyweight would have to be handled in another way.
>
> (O'Brien 1991: 294)

"Celebration of a Nation," the bicentenary's new slogan, certainly conformed to this brief. Devoid of any deep significance, it simply told Australians that they should be preparing themselves for a big party.

The centrepiece of the giant public relations campaign was the 90-second television commercial. It featured 60 Australians in front of Uluru cheerily singing the jingle "Celebration of a Nation." Echoes of the "Living Together" slogan were still evident in the selection of location and the on-screen talent. Both would prove problematic. As Leanne White notes, Uluru might have been selected as a sign of respect to Indigenous Australians, but it could just as easily be seen "as another action of European dominance and obvious disregard for a sacred Aboriginal site" (White 2004: 33). The attempt to make the singers representative of the broader community was restricted by the brief and the medium's limitations. Celebrities from the arts, entertainment and sporting arenas therefore dominated, as the advertisement sought to generate public excitement about the size and scope of the impending celebrations. The sound of the didgeridoo in the opening scenes, together with prominent positioning of the single visibly Aboriginal singer, inferred somewhat incredulously that all Australians would be celebrating the bicentenary. In New South Wales, the ABA advertisement was also supported by a state advertising campaign. Capitalising on its central place in the historical event being commemorated, the advertisements created for the New South Wales state government also fed into the ABA campaign. Its shortrun jingle thus sang:

> It's our Bicentenary
> And we're all about to see
> That you helped to make this State great
> So join the celebration
> It's the best place in the nation
> Yes you helped to make this State great
> Now it's been two hundred years
> Since the nation started here.
>
> (Ashton 1989: 16)

While this jingle similarly identified at the bicentenary as a party, it nevertheless recognised that the bicentenary was also an anniversary of a historical event.

While the content of the ABA's television advertising campaign had its obvious deficiencies, the same could not be said of its reach. By late 1987, market research had revealed that 99.3 per cent of Australians were aware of the bicentenary and the imminent celebrations (O'Brien 1991: 125). Awareness of the event was stimulated by other public relations initiatives. The bicentenary's logo, for example, raised awareness of the event while generating much-needed income. Like so many aspects of the bicentenary, its beginnings were rocky. A ribbon shaped in the outline of the Australian landmass, the yellow and blue logo had initially come under fire for excluding Victoria and Tasmania (White 2004: 32). Redesigned to include these southern states and to feature the nation's green and gold sporting colours, the new logo was displayed prominently throughout the lead-up to the bicentenary and, indeed, throughout bicentennial year. Licences to use the logo were contracted out to 216 companies, netting the ABA a healthy $2.6 million. In order to safeguard its source of funding, legislation prevented the commercial use of such terms as "Bicentenary," "200 years" and "1988." Speaking to the *Sydney Morning Herald*, the ABA's licensing manager defended the decision to deny other commercial organisations from using these terms: "All we're trying to do is prohibit the use of these words because it can become quite confusing when they are attached to commercial products not vetted by the ABA" (Pakula 1988: 3). While such measures made financial sense, they tended to give the impression that the ABA was more interested in protecting profits than promoting the nation. This perspective came to the fore in May 1988. Having been denied the right to sell T-shirts drawing attention to the Aboriginal viewpoint of the bicentenary ("200 Years of Suppression and Depression"),

Sydney Aboriginal artist Louis Davis challenged the validity of the ABA's ban in the High Court. The judges ruled in his favour, stating that legislation granted "protection which is grossly disproportionate to the need to protect the commemoration and the authority" (Hewett and Blunden 1988: 8). Although the timing meant that it was ultimately a pyrrhic victory (the decision was handed just days before the bicentenary drew to a close), it nevertheless underscored the way in which commercial interests informed and interacted with the idea of nationhood.

In terms of size, scale and symbolic meaning, few of the events staged during the bicentenary compared with the sight of the "tall ships" sailing Sydney Harbour on 26 January 1988. This spectacle was, in fact, two separate events – the first was the First Fleet Re-enactment while the second was the Tall Ships event. The two differed in significant ways. The former was a commercial initiative that involved eighteenth-century-styled ships re-enacting the journey from England to Australia taken by the First Fleet. In contrast, the latter was an official ABA-sponsored event that used the larger and visually more impressive ships from the late nineteenth century to celebrate Australia's maritime history. The trials and tribulations of the First Fleet Reenactment provide a more illuminating insight into the ways in which commercial interests intersected with the national image.

The project organiser, Jonathan King, had first called for a re-enactment of the First Fleet in the 1970s. Over the following decade, he was involved in a constant battle with the ABA to secure funding for his dream. The ABA's reluctance to sponsor the event ultimately reflected the fundamental issue that plagued the entire bicentenary – this was a celebration of the arrival of Europeans who were responsible for the decimation of the Aboriginal way of life. Not surprisingly, the official celebrations were firmly focused on the Australia of the present – "Celebrate 88" – over the past. Despite King's claims that the First Fleet re-enactment would promote Australia and generate tourism, it fell foul of the state orthodoxy, although it did secure some funding from the New South Wales Bicentenary Council (King 1989: 3). King consequently embraced commercial initiatives. Berths on board the ships were sold for each leg of the journey while books, videos and other souvenirs were similarly sold to raise much-needed revenue. However, the income was insufficient, and the First Fleet Reenactment Committee (which had registered its name prior to the ABA's protective legislation) looked to commercial sponsors. Coming on board just as the First Fleet re-enactment was in danger of running aground, the commercial sponsors made their presence felt when the First Fleet re-enactment finally reached Sydney Harbour. As the First Fleet re-enactment sailed into view of the television cameras, the logos of Coca-Cola and Australia Post were unfurled from the ships' masts for all the world to see. "[I]n the absence of sufficient government funds Coke had turned out to be 'the real thing'," King would later muse (King 1989: 301). The sponsors' banners, however, did not dim the overwhelming response he received:

"Congratulations – here's a tinny for ya!" a bare-chested helmsman yelled, throwing a can of Fosters beer. "Welcome to Australia!" called a smartly dressed yachtie.

"They said you'd never make it. But we knew you would. You showed 'em, you beauty."

Here, again, the advertising industry's impact on the expression and understanding of conceptualisations of Australian identity is unmistakeable. The can of Foster's symbolises Australia, while the "They said you'd never make it" comment (repeated throughout King's account as something of a mantra) is taken from a popular beer commercial – one that was created by Mojo for Allan Bond's Swan brewery. Such identification reveals the degree to which the advertising industry's images and jingles had clearly penetrated the national psyche.

Triumph and collapse

Working together on the "Celebration of a Nation" campaign encouraged the heads of Mojo and MDA to consider a more permanent association. This occurred some five months after the announcement that they had secured the ABA account. The decision reflected the realities of working in an increasingly globalised industry. While both agencies were strong in the domestic market, neither possessed the critical mass to become a key player on the international scene. MDA had already made forays into the international market but was struggling to make any real inroads. For Mojo, the merger delivered the infrastructure through which it could realise its international ambitions. While *B&T* felt that "on paper it's a good fit," it nevertheless wondered "how much of the Mojo ethos survives MDA's expansionary adventures." "One thing's for certain," it added, "there'll be one less good agency" (*B&T* 1986c: 22). Others were less sure about the merger or, indeed, its plans for world domination. Singleton likened the move to a marriage between The Beatles and the Post Office, while Geoffrey Cousins, the CEO of the largest agency in Australia, George Patterson, claimed, "their plans for the US are pie-in-the-sky stuff . . . It's simply too large a step" (*B&T* 1986c: 3). Undaunted by such criticisms, Mojo MDA wasted little time in embarking on in its inter-national expansion. Within months of the merger, the new agency had acquired the Qantas account in the US by buying out the agency Allen and Dorward (*B&T* 1986a: 1). By cutting out the foreign middleman, the new agency unambiguously demonstrated its desire to establish itself as *the* Australian agency and to reclaim the Australian image.

B&T's concerns about the degree to which Mojo's ethos would survive the merger would prove to be unfounded, as Mo and Jo quickly established themselves as the new agency's prime movers. MDA's heads had already anticipated that the two admen would assume control over the agency's creative output – Adams had made it clear that his interests now lay outside advertising. However, MDA's managing director Malcolm Spry had not envisaged that Mo and Jo would also be calling the shots on the agency's international expansion: "I suppose we thought they'd be happy running the agency and would let us get on with the other side of things. But, quite naturally, they are concerned about their investment" (Coombs 1990: 94). Mojo's tough, uncompromising and avowedly Australian approach to the business side of advertising was illustrated in the exchange between Don Morris (Mo's brother and Mojo's third principal) and Spry about the best way to break into the London market:

> "We give them plenty of sizzle but no steak," Don snorted. "And we should try to get into *Campaign* magazine. It doesn't matter if what they say turns out to be wrong. As they say, any publicity is good publicity."

> "The thing is not to be chauvinistic in the way we go about it . . .," Malcolm was interrupted by Don, loudly: "We *will* be bloody creative chauvinists. None of your cultured bullshit!" he said, good-naturedly, to Malcolm.

> Malcolm grimaced. "Okay, but we don't want to put people off-side. We have to be very careful because we would hate it if the Brits started talking about 'those bloody Australians.'"

> "Yeah, but look at Bondy and Stokes," Don said, "the way they've broken into other markets. You've got to be a rule-breaker. The same applies to us in London."

> "For sure, but wouldn't it be better for us to wait until we've got something to show before we start being brash?"
>
> (Coombs 1990: 76)

Spry's final question was ignored. It seems that modesty did not register in the Mojo ethos. As Mo explained in an interview, the agency saw itself as the "the little Aussie battler" who was determined to take on the world (*B&T* 1988: 19). The Mojo outlook was simple: there was no point in taking a half step if a full one could be made.

Mojo MDA's entry into the London market was just as Don Morris had envisaged. The battler agency's arrival attracted coverage from Britain's advertising industry and mainstream press outlets. The "rugged" Wayne Kingston, the London branch's CEO, thus told the *Times* that the agency would be introducing a unique brand of advertising:

> There hasn't been a new style of advertising brought here for some time. British advertising can be the best in the world. But it also has one of the highest proportions of people copying each other. There is not nearly enough down-to-earth advertising to the person.
>
> (Bidwood 1987: 28)

Marketing Week was slightly more sceptical, wondering how they would translate their homely Australian colloquialisms for British audiences (Bidwood 1987: 19). Despite its condescending tone, the British publication nevertheless raised valid questions. Was Mojo MDA a one-trick pony? Could it really export its distinctly Australian ethos and attitude?

The agency had expected that its London branch would be staffed by "Australian expats who know the London scene" as they had an innate understanding of the agency's "style of advertising" (Coombs 1990: 117). However, it publicly announced that it would be employing locals as well as Australians – a strategy that owed as much to public relations as it did to the agency's long-term goal of securing British accounts (in addition to the Australian accounts that were held by British agencies). "We're here for the long-haul," Kingston explained. "The move [Mojo MDA's entry into UK] is part of the long-term development of an international agency, not just because Australia is flavour of the month" (Bidwood 1987: 19). Of course, being flavour of the month did no harm to the agency's operations. Such pragmatism also indicated that patriotic pride could only go so far – global expansion required a global attitude.

A similar strategy had also been adopted for the agency's entry into the toughest market of them all – the US. Having taken over Allen and Dorward, Mojo MDA now moved to export its advertising ethos. "There's a disarming honesty about our work that will make the Americans take notice . . . I think there is a certain ballsiness about our advertising which is lacking in the US," explained Scott Whybin in the agency's typically cocksure style (Parsons 1987: 40). Mojo MDA's self-belief, however, could also be a weakness – a point that was highlighted by the principal of the American agency that they had acquired. Don Dorward, the chief executive of Mojo San Francisco, thus warned the agency's Australian principals that there was a fine line between self-confidence and conceited arrogance:

> I'd always seen the Pacific basin as an area to be reckoned with. And American companies weren't doing a good job. They were doing what American companies always try to do; they try to Americanise everyone else. That's somewhat similar to you Australians, by the way, and that's something these people are going to have to watch. American industry is not ready to be restructured by some upstarts from Australia. Mojo shouldn't think that they are going to take over the world: it won't happen. But that's the way they think.
>
> (Coombs 1990: 272)

As Dorward's comments reveal, Mojo MDA's brash self-confidence was not far removed from the conceited arrogance that they had initially rejected.

It was not long before Dorward's prophecy was realised. As the bicentenary celebrations were drawing to a close, Mojo MDA's dreams of world domination were also showing signs that they too were nearing an end. It would be economics, rather than arrogance, that ultimately finished the agency's international assault. A weakening economy had hit the advertising industry hard. However, Mo felt that the agency was still well placed to meet the challenge: "None of our clients could be said to be gloomy . . . Then again they are in recession proof industries such as beer, gambling, food" (Browne 1988: 19). However, the agency was no longer an island and it too began to feel the pinch – especially in its overseas offices.

Although the agency's group billings were $350 million, its resources had been stretched to the maximum. The American venture had proven to be particularly costly. As a publicly listed company, it needed to expand or risk ruin. The situation meant that the principals of Mojo MDA were confronted with two choices – either merge again or sell out completely. In January 1989, the dream, like the celebration of a nation, came to an end with a whimper, rather than a bang. After talks with various agencies, Mojo MDA announced that it would be selling to Chiat/Day (Burbury and Mitchell 1989: 1). Selling out for $77 million, Mojo's principals were now reduced to significant minority shareholders in the new Chiat/Day/Mojo agency.

Although some admen echoed Cousins' claim that the agency had bitten off more than it could chew, Australia's advertising community was generally saddened by news of Mojo's demise. The takeover had dramatically revealed what many had known but hoped to be untrue – Australia was simply too small and lacked a sufficient number of Australian-based global advertisers to sustain an international advertising agency. National pride was also damaged: "Psychologically, local agencies will feel disappointment . . . to the minority of wholly-owned local agencies . . . Mojo burst out of this frustrating bubble and emerged, as we say, a hero, an exemplar of the Australian fighting-against-the-odds ethos" (Ruwald and Skinner 1989: 29). The more dramatic fall from grace experienced by fellow international high-flyers, such as "Bondy" and "Skasey,"[6] not to mention Paul Hogan's inability to move beyond his Mick Dundee persona, similarly signalled that Australia's 15 minutes of fame were over.

Concluding remarks

The Australian image that took the world by storm in the 1980s represents a seminal moment in Australian cultural history. Growing out of the frustrations with the foreign images that had been foisted on Australian audiences since the 1960s, the ocker image was used to speak to Australians in their own voice before going on to introduce Australia to the world. The image proved to be a spectacular success, attracting waves of tourists to Australia. It also provided Mojo MDA with an opportunity to embark on an ambitious attempt to establish itself as Australia's own multinational agency. However, the agency's fall is as revealing as its rise. While it had succeeded in selling the distinctive Australian ethos to audiences and clients across the globe, it also struggled to make it on the international stage – the emerging multinational networks had already become too large. Increased globalisation has since made it almost impossible for another Australian agency to harbour similar aspirations, let alone act on them like Mojo MDA. To this end, Australia's advertising industry and Australian audiences have been right to highlight the success of Mojo MDA and its Australian image. However, this success should not be overestimated.

The rise and fall of the Australian image in the international limelight during the 1980s also provides an important insight into the reasons why certain images are marketable and why others are not. As the Winfield campaign revealed, this marketable image of Australia did not emerge suddenly or within a vacuum. Cleansed of its crudity, the ocker of the 1980s acquired a transferability that enabled it to enter other markets. While the bicentenary raised fundamental questions about the state of the nation being celebrated, the "Celebration of a Nation" campaign and its reception nevertheless illustrated the degree to which the commercial interests were interacting with the ways that Australians expressed their sense of identity. The rise and fall of Mojo MDA and the dreams of international recognition that went with them similarly underscored this relationship.

Each of the examples discussed in this article cannot be understood without a consideration of their broader social and cultural contexts. As they occurred at a unique point in time, the likelihood that the same conditions will recur any time soon is highly unlikely. Tourism Australia's great expectations based on the success of the Hogan campaign of the 1980s are therefore flawed in a fundamental way. To expect Australia to resume its 15 minutes of fame is as reasonable as expecting a fourth instalment of the Crocodile Dundee films to be the next box office smash. Times have changed; audiences have moved on. Perhaps the most perceptive comment on this situation was uttered by the Undersecretary for International Protocol character in the "Bart vs. Australia" episode of television cartoon sitcom *The Simpsons*: "As I'm sure you remember, in the late 1980s the US experienced a short-lived infatuation with Australian culture," he explained. "For some bizarre reason, the Aussies thought this would be a permanent thing. Of course, it wasn't" (1995). Ongoing references to Hoges and the "Say G'day" campaign unfortunately suggest that many in Australia still cling to these nostalgic hopes.

Acknowledgements

The research undertaken in this article was made possible by way of a visiting fellowship to the National Museum of Australia. The author would like to thank the staff at the NMA's Historical Research Centre for their support.

Notes

1   The *Macquarie Dictionary* defines a larrikin as an "uncultivated, rowdy, but good-hearted person."
2   The *Macquarie Dictionary* defines an ocker as "a boorish, uncouth, chauvinistic Australian."

3   Personal interview conducted with Allan Johnston, 4 June 2004, Sydney.
4   Personal interview conducted with Allan Johnston, 4 June 2004, Sydney.
5   Personal interview conducted with Alan Morris, 29 April 2004, Sydney.
6   Alan Bond and Christopher Skase were entrepreneurs whose media empires grew rapidly during the 1980s. By the end of the decade, their respective empires had collapsed in dramatic circumstances.

References

AdNews. 1984. "MDA – on the road to becoming a regional force." 14 December.

AdNews. 1998. "Jo's fingers are hurtin' again." 30 October.

Adventures of Barry McKenzie. Film. Directed by Bruce Beresford. Sydney: Longford Productions, 1972.

Advertising News. 1976. "Hogan tells you why you can't sleep at night." 30 April.

Ashton, Paul. 1989. *Waving the waratah: Bicentenary New South Wales*. Sydney: NSW Bicentenary Council.

B&T: Broadcasting and Television. 1986a. "Mojo connects with Qantas in US." 14 November.

B&T: Broadcasting and Television. 1986b. "Mojo/MDA: A wise choice by the ABA." 28 March.

B&T: Broadcasting and Television. 1986c. "One less good Aussie agency." 1 August.

B&T: Broadcasting and Television. 1987. "Jacko's juggernaut confuses in the US." 11 September.

B&T: Broadcasting and Television. 1988. "Struth our ads are dinky di bonzer." 29 April.

Baker, Bill, and Peggy Bendel. 2005. "Come and say g'day! Travel Marketing Decisions, Summer." Available at: www.atme.org/pubs/archives/77_1898_11926. cfm.

Bidwood, John. 1987. "How Wayne Kingston is swinging it in London." *B&T: Broadcasting and Television*, 6 November.

Broadcasting and Television. 1964. Editorial. 19 March.

Brock, Frank. 1987. "The Yanks are coming." *B&T: Broadcasting and Television*, 4 September.

Browne, David. 1988. "Who's the most creative in the land?" *B&T: Broadcasting and Television*, 12 February.

Burbury, Rochelle, and Mark Miller. 1989. "CDP my partner Chiat/Day/Mojo." *B&T: Broadcasting and Television*, 13 January.

Coombs, Anne. 1990. *Adland: A true story of corporate drama*. Melbourne: William Heinemann.

Crawford, Robert. 2007. "'Anyhow . . . where d'yer get it?': Ockerdom in adland Australia." *JAS* 90: 1–15.

Crawford, Robert. 2008. *But wait there's more. . .: A history of Australian advertising, 1900–2000*. Melbourne: Melbourne University Press.

Crocodile Dundee. Film. Directed by Peter Faiman. Sydney: Rimfire Productions, 1986.

Cross, Stefanie. 1984. "Different strokes." *B&T: Broadcasting and Television*, 7 September.

Douglas, Torin. 1982. "How Paul Hogan sold lager and himself to the British." *Times*, 25 September.

Gruen Transfer. 2009. Television programme. Season 2, Episode 1. Australia: Australian Broadcasting Corporation (ABC), 2004.

Hewett, Tony, and Verge Blunden. 1988. "T-shirt artist wins war of words." *Sydney Morning Herald*, 7 December.

Housham, David. 1987. "An ocker invasion." *Times*, 26 August.

King, Jonathan. 1989. *Battle for the bicentenary*. Sydney: Hutchinson Australia.

Lee, Julian. 2008. "Tourism ads too 'white collar'." *Sydney Morning Herald*, 13 October.

Lee, Julian. 2009. "Tough times, but campaign working." *Sydney Morning Herald*, 13 March.

Macnab, Geoffrey. 2003. "A fistful of Fosters." *Guardian*, 8 January.

Marszalek, Jessica. 2007. "Tourism numbers increase despite strong Aussie dollar." *Australian Associated Press Financial News Wire*, 5 November.

Mattelart, Armand. 1991. *Advertising international: The privatisation of public space*. London: Routledge.

O'Brien, Denis. 1991. *The bicentennial affair: The inside story of Australia's "birthday bash"*. Sydney: ABC Enterprises.

O'Regan, Tom. 1988. "'Fair dinkum fillums': The *Crocodile Dundee* phenomenon." In *The imaginary industry: Australian film in the late '80s*, edited by Elizabeth Jacka and Susan Dermody. Sydney: Australian, Film Television and Radio School, 155–75.

Oram, James. 1987. *Hogan: The story of the son of Oz*. London: Columbus Books.

Pakula, Karen. 1988. "ABA doesn't mince words over banned 88 jargon." *Sydney Morning Herald*, 22 April.

Parsons, Barrie. 1976. "Knocking the ocker-mocker." *Advertising News*, 30 April.

Parsons, Barrie. 1984. "MDA has done the whole industry a service." *AdNews*, 2 November.

Parsons, Barrie. 1987. "Mojo MDA 'Ozketeers' on creative crusade." *B&T: Broadcasting and Television*, 13 February.

Roberts, Paul. 1984. "The explosion down under." *B&T: Broadcasting and Television*, 26 October.

Ruwald, John, and Darrell Skinner. 1989. "Back in the time of heroes." *B&T: Broadcasting and Television*, 17 March.

Sandison, Nikki. 2008. "Australia film panned by critics as cliched tourism ad." *Brand Republic News*, 19 November. Available at: www.brandrepublic.com/News/863311/Australia-film-panned-critics-cliched-tourism-ad/?DCMP=ILC-SEARCH.

Sinclair, John. 2007. "Agents of 'Americanisation': Individual entrepreneurship and the genesis of consumer industries." *JAS* 90: 17–33.

Stone, Gerald. 2002. *Singo: Mates, wives, triumphs, disasters*. Sydney: HarperCollins.

The Simpsons. 1995. "Bart vs. Australia." Television programme. Episode 2F13. US: Gracie Films, Twentieth Century Fox Television, 1995.

Tourism Australia. 2008. "Tourism Australia's destination campaign by Baz Lurhmann." October. Available at: www.tourism.australia.com/content/Destination%20Campaign/Transformation/Bazstrategybrochure.pdf.

Turner, Graeme. 1994. *Making it national: Nationalism and Australian popular culture*. Sydney: Allen & Unwin.

White, Leanne. 2004. "The bicentenary of Australia: Celebration of a nation." In *National days/national ways: Historical, political and religious celebrations around the world*, edited by Linda K Fuller. Westport, CT: Praeger Publishers, 25–39.

Wynne, Alan. 1976. "Advertisers: Many pluses." *Advertising News*, 20 August.

9   The technology of branding

Sidney J. Levy

An olio is a collection of diverse materials, whether of food, art, or literature. A curator has the responsibility for the care of an olio. That responsibility includes interpreting and organizing the presentation of the olio. I will present this collection of three articles about branding from *Consumption Markets & Culture* by first summarizing the history of ideas about branding that is the environment and the context for the fruition of their research. I will then interpret the significance of these studies for understanding the current nature of what we may term the situation of branding.

The concept of branding

The concept of branding has grown from its original meaning that was focused in ancient times on marking, signifying, and identifying ownership of property such as cattle, prisoners, and slaves. Other forms of branding include tattooing by South Seas groups to signal personal, familial, and social statuses and conditions. Also, in an informative paper titled "Prehistories of Commodity Branding," David Wengrow (2008) describes objects that served branding purposes found in a 3000 BCE Nile Valley royal tomb. Hieroglyphics boast of the "finest oil of Tjehenu" interred with the ruler as one element of the scope and grandeur of his life, thereby branding both the ruler and the commodity with this association.

Over the centuries, the idea of branding endured primarily as a reference to the branding of cattle. However, as trade developed in modern times, the marketing of commodities became identified with their purveyors and packaged in small units with names on their labels and promotion of these names. I wrote about the importance of this fact in "The product and the brand" (Gardner and Levy 1955) and helped create awareness of the "brand image" and the more active and deliberate concern with branding that is vividly apparent in the three articles I will discuss.

Curating the olio

Chapter 6 by John Amis and Michael Silk, "Transnational organization and symbolic production: creating and managing a global brand," focuses on the branding activities of products from the Guinness beverage company. This is a case study of a core issue of widespread concern to corporations in the globalization economy, viz. whether, and/or to what extent, to adapt branding activities to local cultures. Some adjustment may always be necessary, if only in the use of a foreign language and currency, but companies differ considerably in their sensitivity to local cultures and in the use and development of local personnel. In this respect, managers are like anthropologists who either seek out the curiosities of exotic places or who orient to their aspects of common humanity. The authors convey a lively sense of the struggle between the competing aims of negating the local culture and accommodating it.

The next chapter (Chapter 7), by Alfons van Marrewijk and Maaike Broos, "Retail stores as brands: performances, theatre and space," gives further emphasis to the role of branding in all spheres, including the environment provided by retail stores, by specifying the ways they achieve their distinctions. When model and designer Ines de la Fressange worked to revive the brand image of Roger Vivier, the French fashion designer who created the stiletto heel and fashioned shoes for rich and famous women such as Queen Elizabeth and actress Ava Gardner, she said:

> I choose the flowers and I interview and hire all the saleswomen. I wanted every Vivier store to smell the same way, so I created an amber-scented candle that's in all of them. Basically, everything that leaves Vivier passes before my eyes. There are very few recipes for great brands, but one of them is to be vigilant about every single detail.
>
> (Levine 2010)

Marrewijk and Broos remind us that this recipe applies to all establishments by showing its application to notable retail stores.

Chapter 8 "Learning to say g'day to the world: the development of Australia's marketable image in the 1980s," by Robert Crawford, also includes the wooing of foreign audiences. It is an engaging case study that illuminates many elements of the branding situation. He gives a detailed and insightful explanation of the way various factors—many participating individuals, agencies, and audiences in different countries—acted and responded to create images of Australia as a source of products and as an attractive destination for tourists. He shows the way these different components contended and their consequences in success and failure. He dramatizes the emergence of Australia in the international consciousness, its prosperous period in the sun, and its subsidence.

Crawford's story is interesting in itself as a history of economic international relations and, as he says, "The rise and fall of the Australian image in the international limelight during the 1980s also provides an important insight into the reasons why certain images are marketable and why others are not." Using the Australian situation demonstrates in a matter-of-fact way that branding is not limited to specific products, but serves countries (and all other entities) as well.

These three chapters are valuable in the way they illustrate and highlight the variety of inputs that are available from the retail setting with its minutiae and ambiance of the immediate setting that may draw consumers to enter, to the branding by countries distributing their products and enticing travelers to visit them. We may also go further by saying that "certain images are marketable and others are not." Fundamentally, all images are marketable to someone, depending on one's goal, and there is no one formula for success; what works for one time may not for another. For example, Australia is a complex entity with many possibilities, and what suits one retail store is unlike another. A dimly lit Walmart neighborhood store seems suitably drab for its economical theme while a major competitor, Target, is a bold red and white, brilliantly lit.

The triumph of Paul Hogan as *Crocodile Dundee* peaked and faded with his ongoing tax problems but other facets of Aussie life are available to appeal to diverse audiences, not necessarily some optimal biggest one. Australian culture plays with the paradoxes of its convict history, its aborigines, its outback, and its Great Barrier Reef joined with a high degree of civilized culture. When we visited Australia, we saw universities, attended the ballet, and heard Joan Sutherland sing in *Il Trovatore* at the iconic Sydney Opera House. We also rode with a guide to the outback, encountered a wild beast on the road, and on a cloth by a river were served a lunch that included caviar hors d'oeuvres and wine.

The technology of branding

The numerous issues touched on by the three case studies testify to the richness inherent in the concept of branding. To explicate this potential and the striving for ideal or optimal branding shown in the olio above, I will use a device called the Ideal Brand Pyramid (IBP) (Figure 9.1). This pyramid follows the triad of *ethos, pathos*, and *logos* that Aristotle used in his *Rhetoric* and also the triangle that inspired the work of semiotician Charles Peirce (1931–1938), who pointed out relationships among the object (icon), its representations (index), and its meanings (symbolism). I translate those concepts into the IBP triad of function, people, and aesthetics of branding.

The technology of branding starts with the object being branded, no matter what it is, and is concerned with what it is and what it does. It may be a product, a service, an idea, a person, anything of interest that is being put forward. This corner of the triangle refers to all the facts about the object being promoted. These constitute the rich arsenal of possible references, including descriptions and claims, features, functions, benefits, results, pricing, and how the object is distributed and made available. Its *ethos* is the evaluation of its truth and integrity.

The appeals are interwoven. The presence or absence of credibility arouses emotions. *Pathos* (Greek for "suffering" or "experience") refers to our emotional reactions. Does the brand arouse excitement, surprise, happiness, desire, or, conversely, fear, anxiety, anger, indifference? What are the

Figure 9.1 The Ideal Brand Pyramid

psychosocial qualities of the offering, who are the people involved—managers, professional personnel, customers, celebrities, persons in everyday life, etc.—and what are their relevant thoughts and feelings?

Logos (logo, logic) refers to how the presentation is made, the aesthetics of its appeal to the rationality (the word) of its meaning: sense, nonsense? Is the offering satisfying, pleasant to see, to hear it, touch it, smell it, and taste it? Is it beautiful, ugly, hard, utilitarian, ethereal, grand, or trivial? Aesthetic visualizations are especially encapsulated in logos that act powerfully to bring the brand and its distinction to mind. It is interesting that many countries have logos that can stand for their brands, such as the US Stars and Stripes, the Canadian Maple Leaf, and the Japanese Rising Sun. But when I asked a convenient sample about Australia, no such formal image came to mind, although there were relevant reminders such as kangaroos and the Sydney Opera House that could be formalized to serve the purpose. Crawford's study did not address this form of visualization, but it is especially valuable in illuminating the interactions that went on among the participants in determining what to show and say in presenting Australia as a brand.

Inputs from the three corners of what the brand is, those engaged in the exchange, and how it is presented are interwoven like a helix to create what comes to mind for thought, feeling, and action, when we consider browsing an Apple or a Macy's store, downing a Guinness or a Budweiser, and taking a trip to Australia or Helsinki.

Summary comments

It is worth noting that these case studies are excellent examples of qualitative research. They do not focus on a single explanatory variable, but each uses an olio of its own—a diversity of data—to gain insight into their respective branding situations. To refresh our awareness and appreciation of this traditional behavioral science approach, I have recently referred to it as "olio and intègraphy as method" (Levy 2014). Curating the three papers shows that case studies are a useful method, demonstrating that while case studies may be unique and individualistic narratives by their nature, they also teach about everyday issues of branding and management.

My theme here is the contemporary richness of the branding concept demonstrated above by the curated olio. Each branded object—that is, any entity, person, object, organization—is branded by creating an identity with a name and characteristics up for exchange. This nature, these qualities, attributes, features, whatever, form a "cloud of associations" from which branding—selective perception and reputation—is drawn by the self and by others.

That image is not a single thing; it forms the reputation expressed in marketplace exchanges, whether these are about a product such as Guinness, a local environment such as a retail store, or a huge environment such as Australia. Adding to the product and the people is the most recent emphasis on aesthetics—the awareness of the importance of visual imagery, design, and response of the senses. Guinness found its distinctive appeal in uniting the strength of its product with the psychological strength of its drinkers. Australia rose to global glory for a time embodied in the charisma of Paul Hogan. And we were shown what it takes to make a retail house a home.

The product and its distribution dominated the early days of modern branding, and what it is and what it does remain essential to gain the regard of its audiences. The "Consumer Revolution" of the 1950s brought forth an added concentration on how those audiences think and feel about the brand, highlighting its "image" and the importance of market segments. It also enlarged the role of brand management people with their philosophies, researchers, engineers, designers, media, and so forth, in the creation of imagery.

Taken together, the three cases work to show the large character of the concept of branding. They illustrate how managers aspire toward creating and effectuating their versions of the Ideal Brand and how their choices lead to their differential results by drawing upon, mingling, and emphasizing content from many elements.

References

Gardner, Burleigh B., and Sidney J. Levy. 1955. "The Product and the Brand." *Harvard Business Review* March–April: 33–39.

Levine, Joshua. 2010. "French Twist." *Wall Street Journal Magazine*, September. Available at: http://magazine.wsj.com/hunter/second-chapter/french-twist (accessed September 10, 2014).

Levy, Sidney J. 2014. "Olio and Intègraphy as Method and the Consumption of Death." *Consumption Markets & Culture*. In press.

Peirce, Charles Sanders. 1931–1938. *Collected Papers*. Cambridge, MA: Harvard University Press.

Wengrow, David. 2008. "Prehistories of Commodity Branding." *Current Anthropology* 49: 7–34.

Part III

Consumer perspectives

10 Consumer-brand assemblages in advertising

An analysis of skin, identity, and tattoos in ads

Sofie Møller Bjerrisgaard, Dannie Kjeldgaard and Anders Bengtsson

Brands have taken center stage in contemporary consumer culture, furnishing consumers with cultural materials with which they can construct experiences, social relations, and identities (Arvidsson 2006). Although the concept of brands has traditionally been closely related to products (Strasser 1989), brands clearly are emerging as vehicles of meaning that not only offer consumers a lens through which to experience the world (Holt 2002), but also provide firms with a central focus for organizing business (Kornberger 2010).

In this context, the marketer's task of building strong brands develops foremost into an exercise of meaning management (Brown, Kozinets, and Sherry 2003). Marketers and advertisers become professionals of entanglement in an ongoing attempt to assign products a set of cultural meanings that position these products as if they were already part of consumers' lifeworlds. This perspective, prevalent in interpretive consumer research, often assumes a certain relationship between brands and consumers, in which brands foster identity formation and social orientation by establishing emotional ties between the consumer and the brand (Fournier 1998). Scholars have recently criticized this understanding of the consumer-brand relationship as being overtly consumer-centric and as naturalizing the divide between human agency and the natural/technical/material world in which such agency unfolds (Giesler and Venkatesh 2005; Campell, O'Driscoll, and Saren 2010).

This paper examines how marketers leverage institutionalized consumer-brand relations and include the human body in the assemblage of brand meaning. In particular, we analyze how marketers use a specific body practice – tattooing – to shape brand meanings and hereby (re)produce a variety of imageries of consumer-brand relationships (O'Reilly 2006). Marketing communication has a long tradition for brands of all kinds to use the human body to communicate cultural values (Schroeder and Borgerson 1998), and research in consumer culture theory (Arnould and Thompson 2005) has demonstrated that brands and marketing communication play an important role in constructing the body in consumer culture (Scott 1994; Patterson and Elliott 2002; Schroeder and Zwick 2004; Thompson 2004). The human skin is particularly central to understanding the dynamics of identity formation in consumer culture, because it "reflects the dynamic relationship between inside and outside, self and society, between personal identity projects and marketplace cultures [and] represents a meeting place of structure and agency" (Patterson and Schroeder 2010: 256).

The aim of this study is to demonstrate how advertising circulates a variety of imageries of consumer-brand relationships that are assembled through the use of tattoos in ads. By stressing advertising as a significant realm for the (re)production of institutionalized consumer-brand relations, the article examines how the use of tattoos in market communication is part of three different consumer-brand assemblages contained in the field of interpretive consumer research. We argue that existing theorizations of consumer-brand relationships significantly perpetuate a dualistic understanding of consumers and brands in which the agentic potential resides solely on the side of the consumer and the brand merely serves as a cultural resource consumers mobilize in their search for identity and social orientation. We further argue that such depiction is widely circulated and reproduced in advertising.

Additionally, we argue that, in our understanding of consumer-brand relationships, the depiction of brand tattoos in advertising can be read as a circumvention of dominant consumer-centrism. We take this position because the use of brands as a tattoo motif relocates agency from the consumer to the brand and indicates a relationship in which the brand extends onto the body, mobilizing consumers' bodies as a means of commercial expression. We argue that such consumer-brand assemblages parallel recent attempts in consumer research to move beyond a consumer-centric understanding of consumption and consumers to a networked understanding in which the assemblage of subjects and objects into socio-technical agencements offers a fruitful course for analyzing contemporary sociality (Latour 2005).

To this end, we conduct a visual analysis of tattoo imagery in advertising. We develop a categorization of the assemblages of consumers and brands in contemporary marketing communication featuring tattooed models and provide a close reading of a selection of ads representing these categories.

Advertising and professionals of entanglement

Conceptualizations of advertising as a central institution that mediates the commercial realm of the market and the cultural realm of everyday life are relatively widespread (e.g., Slater 2002) and are encapsulated in the notion of cultural economy (du Gay and Pryke 2002). Recent attempts to address the significance of advertising for understanding the particularities of contemporary consumer culture have been criticized as being ahistorical and thus overemphasizing both the impact of advertising and the difference from earlier times (McFall 2002). Slater (2002) argues that, despite these criticisms, micro-level analysis of advertising practices is particularly pertinent to the study of the simultaneous cultural and economic character of market actions. Further, micro-level analysis demonstrates how economic actions are always culturally informed and how cultural knowledge is leveraged instrumentally in the name of profitability. Thus, the culture-economic interplay becomes particularly visible within advertising, where advertising practitioners figure as key professionals of entanglement.

Entanglement refers to the interlinked process through which products are simultaneously positioned meaningfully vis-à-vis consumers and their imagined lifeworlds but also in relation to substitutable products in a competitive marketplace (Slater 2002). This simultaneous positioning means that advertising practitioners are engaged in calculations that are both economic and cultural. A related view is that practices of entanglement take place within an "economy of qualities," in which products' qualities and characteristics undergo constant negotiation of meaning. In this dynamic condition, the cultural calculations and entanglements that advertising and other market agents conduct constitute the core practices through which the functioning and organization of markets are performed (Callon, Méadel, and Rabeharisoa 2002).

At the core of advertising practitioners, cultural calculations is not only the entanglement of products, but also the production of consumer subjectivities (Cochoy 2005; Miller and Rose 2008; Zwick and Cayla 2010). As advertising practitioners, like everybody else, have no direct access to any objective and complete understanding of consumers, the envisioning of a particular version of the consumer figures as one of the core elements of cultural calculation and a prerequisite for product entanglement. Cochoy (2005: 37) ascribes the "invention" of the consumer at the end of the nineteenth century to the need to stabilize spatially expanding and fluctuating market demands. In the same vein, Miller and Rose (2008) demonstrate how advertising and market research practitioners mobilize the consumer as a complex psychological being. They argue that only empirical research can move our understanding of contemporary markets beyond general claims about the logic of capitalism and into the complex ways in which assemblages of people, commodities, habits, and technologies constitute market systems (Miller and Rose 2008: 140f). A recent anthology of marketing practices and practitioners compiled through a perspective of governmentality explicitly focusses on the multiple ways in which the consumer subject is brought to life in the course of marketing (Zwick and Cayla 2010).

The purpose of the present study was to align the perspective of cultural calculation and entanglement of products with the idea of marketing as the governing of consumer subjectivities. Hence, we seek to attend to the (re)production of consumer-brand relationships, as these are assembled in market communication. These consumer-brand relationships are not evoked arbitrarily by advertising practitioners, but are steeped in institutionalized axioms that serve to naturalize certain kinds of relationships between consumers and brands.

The institutionalized depictions of consumer-brand relationships as implicitly or explicitly assumed in the marketing literature have been discussed by Holt (2002). Invoking the notion of institutional isomorphism (Powell and DiMaggio 1983), he argues that branding as a particular practice of product entanglement has developed a dialectic relationship with consumer culture. That is, social actors tend to share a set of institutionalized conventions that are gradually granted legitimacy and normative influence through mimetic behavior. Holt outlines a historical institutional analysis of branding practices that delineates three paradigmatic forms of branding, each carrying implicit assumptions about consumers' relationships to brands. These paradigmatic forms also appear in the literature on advertising.

Modern branding, according to Holt, is characterized by the axiom of cultural engineering, which denotes the ability of advertisers and brand managers to associate specific cultural meanings and moral ideals with brands. In such a perspective, consumer desire and taste is channeled without difficulty from marketers to consumers. Consumers appear passive and easily contained within well-defined social groups, where brands serve as markers of group identity and affiliation. In advertising research, this perspective materializes in Ewen's (1976) notion of advertising practitioners as "captains of consciousness," which portrays the consumer as the unknowing victim of corporate manipulation of the subconscious. Williamson (1978) argues that advertising operates in accordance with a semiotic system by which the meaning of the ad is given – independently from the reader. Through a dialectic movement, Holt argues for the development of a postmodern branding paradigm emerging from consumers' increasing awareness and criticism of the manipulative techniques of modern cultural engineering principles that contrast sharply with modern ideals of individualism and freedom of choice. The postmodern branding paradigm portrays an active, participative consumer engaged in the creation of brand meanings and celebrates the imagery of the emancipated sovereign consumer, who mobilizes brands as cultural resources and uses these as building blocks in the formation of personal biographies and identity narratives (Fırat and Venkatesh 1995). In advertising research, this representation of consumer subjectivity was initially advanced by Scott (1994), who draws on reader-response theory for the analysis of consumers' active interpretation of market communication.

Along similar historical lines, Arvidsson (2004) argues that market research techniques have developed from being strategies of containing consumer identities within predefined categories to strategies that exploit consumer creativity in the process of value creation. That is, the subjectivity of the consumer converts from passive to active and from stable to dynamic. In an emerging post-postmodern branding paradigm, the urge for brand authenticity and relevance as an identity resource is challenged by the anti-branding movement, in which brands are no longer undisputedly accepted as a pool of cultural resources. Instead, brands are critically examined and embedded in an ethical agenda for organizational behavior that reaches beyond formal organizational boundaries and requires transparency and consistency in all organizational matters.

Within this post-postmodern branding paradigm, the relationship between brands and consumers does not depend on the cultural engineering of producers or the creative efforts of sovereign consumers, but on brands that "act like a local merchant, as a stalwart citizen of the community" and demonstrate civic responsibilities (Holt 2002: 88). This view suggests a different role for the brand in society and implies agency. Such an outline of the institutional development of branding practices accentuates the dialectic relationship between the wider consumer culture and marketers' practices of entanglement. With respect to the use of tattoo imagery in advertising, this dialectic relationship means that advertising practitioners can employ tattoos in their cultural calculations, because tattoos signify a set of consumption and identity-creating practices in the economy of qualities. Hence, advertising agencies use tattoos and tattoo practices in marketing communication in concordance with the axiomatic conventions of branding. In turn, advertising provides the economy of qualities with institutionally isomorphic depictions of brand-consumer relationships. From this perspective, the expressions of brand images in advertisements are not creative revelations, but are pieces of text or visual representations rooted in a specific cultural context. Advertising therefore constitutes a "cultural system" (Sherry 1987; McQuarrie et al. 2005), within which a variety of brand-consumer relationships are assembled within different brand cultures.

Clearly, the assemblage of consumer-brand relationships in marketing communication is neither trivial nor neutral. Through the analysis of print advertisements and TV commercials deploying tattoo imageries, we identify three different consumer-brand relations that reproduce more widely shared depictions of consumer-brand relationships within the marketing literature and amplify more recent understandings of these relationships.

The Body Inc.

The use of the body, in general, and tattoos, in particular, in marketing communication constitutes a particularly fertile area for the exploration of institutionalized consumer-brand assemblages in branding and advertising. Consumer researchers generally agree that the body has increasingly become a malleable object that consumers use in constructing identity (Schouten 1991; Thompson and Hirschman 1995; Askegaard, Gertsen, and Langer 2002). The malleable body becomes part of the constant creation and re-creation of coherent autobiographical narratives of the self (Giddens 1991). In such a context, the body becomes a feasible site for consumption that can be changed and improved to meet or oppose socially desirable ideals. Contemporary consumers employ a variety of techniques, products, and services, such as body building, tanning, anti-wrinkle creams, steroids, dieting, fat farms, plastic surgery, and tattoos, to either change or keep the body intact in order to be able to present a body that corresponds to perceived socially desirable ideals

(Jensen 1999). Changing the shape and appearance of one's body to conform to cultural standards of beauty has a long history (Schouten 1991). Practices such as tattooing have been performed for at least 5,000 years, and foot-binding of Chinese women – creating the "lotus foot" – can be traced back to the Sung Dynasty (AD 960–1280).

In Western societies, however, the role of the body has changed (Turner 1996). The emergence of a consumer culture has produced a shift, by which "the labouring body has become a desiring body" (Turner 1996: 2). The body's job in society has moved from that of being a resource for capitalist production and for military power, where bodily desires had to be kept under control, to that of being a consuming body in consumer cultural capitalism. Another shift in the cultural meaning of the body is the collapse of Cartesian mind–body dualism (Fırat and Venkatesh 1995). This breakdown has meant that in late-modern consumer culture, the body has become a site for self-reflexive identity articulation, a malleable object that not only can, but should, be worked on (Shilling 2003).

These shifts in the meaning of the body signify that body modifications formerly associated with marginal or subcultural milieus have become part of the general consumer culture and part of the fashion system that draws on the cultural resources available for meaning transfer purposes (McCracken 1986). Previous research on tattooing has debated whether contemporary tattoos are simply body adornment or something more significant. Turner (2000: 40) contends that body marks such as tattoos are narcissistic and thus playful signs of the self and posits that "tattoos have become a regular aspect of consumer culture, where they add cultural capital to the body's surface."

Consequently, in a society of individualization, the modern tattoo becomes simply another sign to be read within consumer culture. Thus, Turner's position is that tattooing today, in postmodern neo-tribalism, is characterized by voluntary membership, so that marking of the body is optional. Neverthe-less, the socio-historically established cultural meaning of tattoos associated with deviance and subcultural formations remains, and manifests the diverg-ence of tattooing from other bodily self-care practices: "In this way, tattoos reiterate within cultural and strategic arenas as emblems of consumer identity, agency, and, often, deviancy, informed by cultural histories of skin, sexuality, and resistance" (Patterson and Schroeder 2010: 263).

To be recognized as meaningful, a brand has to draw on existing cultural resources and structures of cognition. But following the market logic, an advertisement must also differentiate itself. Working along the continuum of recognition and differentiation, advertising agencies draw on cultural resources. In this space between recognition and uniqueness, the tattoo appears to be a meaningful symbol that, over time, has gained broad acceptance as a way of expressing mainstream identity, and has become a resource for mass cultural expression. Simultaneously, the tattoo has kept its momentum of transgression because of its permanence and irreversibility, which separate it from other modes of identity expression and communicative signs and symbols

(Sanders 1989). Although tattoos have increased in popularity, the practice of changing the body permanently in this way is still associated with uniqueness, for consumers as well as for the advertising industry that seeks to associate these meanings with a certain brand image.

Some scholars hold that not only the socio-historic meanings of tattooing lend it communicative potency and analytical strength (Patterson and Schroeder 2010). These characteristics also arise from the mediating nature of human skin between individual agency and social structure and the ability to debate the naturalized understanding of the sealed individual self. Discussion of the borders between individuality and sociality is relevant to the variety of consumer-brand assemblages produced in advertising through tattoo imagery.

Method

The study of consumer culture includes the study of the stuff that surrounds us and makes up the material world in which we live. Miller (2010: 5) has recently argued for a more serious treatment of "stuff" as the pathway to a more insightful understanding of subject-object relations. As much as humans make stuff, stuff makes us; not necessarily in the sense that stuff represents who we are, but that it offers a way of understanding the complex relationships between people and things. Actor-network theory takes a similar stance in that it assigns agency not only to human actors, but also to things, technologies, and devices (Latour 2005).

We take this dialectic between subject and object as a starting point for the study of how marketing communication materializes consumer-brand relationships through various strategies of representation. To demonstrate how marketers are engaged in the assemblage of specific consumer-brand relationships, we examine a convenience sample of print advertisements and TV commercials originating from numerous countries. To collect the empirical material, we employed both online and offline searches. Ads were collected from Adforum (www.adforum.com) and the gay, lesbian, bisexual, and transgender ad critic organization, the Commercial Closet (www.commercial closet.org). Further data were gathered from two websites specializing in tattooing (www.tattoo-passion.com and www.tattoo-net.de). We also searched for print ads in five volumes (2000–2005) of the US editions of the men's magazine *GQ* and the women's magazine *Cosmopolitan*. These data-collection efforts generated a convenience sample of over 150 print ads and broadcast commercials.

The data were analyzed using critical visual analysis (Schroeder 2006) and include visual genealogical perspectives emerging from the historic develop-ment of tattoo culture to show how advertising draws on historically embedded visual histories (Schroeder and Zwick 2004). Visual research approaches consider ads to be both aesthetic objects and socio-cultural artifacts – that is, they are symbolic forms of culture and they are also situated on wider systems of representation (Schroeder and Zwick 2004; McQuarrie et al. 2005). Ads hence constitute "ethnographic material," the analysis and interpretation of which can provide insights into cultural categories and their dynamics just as other ethnographic materials do, such as documents, consumer interviews, literature, and the like. As part of our investigation, we use a semiotic analysis (Mick 1986) to interpret the relationships between the brand, the body, and the tattoo, and hence the kinds of possible assemblages of consumers and brands at stake.

Representation of tattoos in ads

The following section offers a categorization of advertisements based on different genres of tattoo imageries. The categories reflect the preceding theoretical position and have emerged through an iterative process of theoretical reflection and empirical examination of the collected material. Our analysis begins with an interpretation of the types of cultural discourse of body modification the ad draws upon, which in turn assembles different kinds of consumer-brand relations. The use of Peirce's semiotic taxonomy – *symbol, index,* and *icon* (Mick 1986) – enables us to distinguish between assemblages of consumer-brand-tattoo that represent institutionalized and emergent consumer-brand relations. A symbolic relationship between tattoo and brand emerges through conventional association, which generally implies reproduction of existing cultural meanings and categories. In other cases, the relationship between the brand and the tattoo is either one of resemblance or of shared attributes. Such an indexical relationship between tattoo and brand visually depicts an affinity between the characteristic of tattooing/tattoos and the brand. Finally, the iconographic relationship is characterized by physical resemblance between the tattoo and the brand – either the product itself or the brand logo.

From previous research on tattoo culture among mainstream and subcultural producers and consumers, as well as readings of the cultural history of tattoo practices primarily in Western cultures, we identified three forms of tattoo-brand-consumer assemblage, each implying and reproducing a specific consumer-brand relation: the body as canvas, fashion expression, and the brand extended. While we explicate all three genres, we analyze the brand-extended category more extensively since it represents a different form of consumer-brand assemblages, and in the practices of entanglement it draws on the other two genres.

The body as canvas

The first category, the body as canvas, represents a genre of tattoo consumption that is closely related to the body modification subculture (Goulding and Follet 2002) and socio-historically established cultural meanings associated with tattooing more widely. This category represent parts of tattoo culture that consider tattoos an essential part of the body and as collectible items (Vail

1999). The body as canvas draws on discourses rooted in "traditional" body modification subcultural expressions, including traditional tattoo imagery (such as Maori tribal tattoos), tattoo practices associated with biker and sailor subcultures, and the body modification subculture in general. The body modification discourse refers extensively to the irreversible and transgressive nature of tattooing and represents the body as a project of malleability in accordance with the institutional prescriptions in the diverse subcultural settings (Sanders 1989). Tattoos falling into the body as canvas category are generally constituted as being either marginal or in opposition to mainstream culture. In our sample of ads with tattoo imagery, we find examples of body as canvas advertisements that portray stereotypical images of tattoos, suggesting a relationship between tattoos, low cultural capital, and, for example, criminal activities.

The decisive commonality between this set of different tattoo imageries and related practices is the explicit association of the tattoos with distinctive and recognizable social groups. This association means that the body as canvas category is reproductive of a consumer imagery that presupposes consumer subjectivity as easily contained within confined limits of social groups, of which the tattoo serves as a recognizable marker. This presupposition, in turn, assumes the responsiveness of consumers to marketers' manipulative meaning management. In this way, the tattoo indicates, along with other semiotic signifiers of the ad, the potential meanings ascribed to the consumers of the brand in question. The specific entanglement of imageries of tattoo practices with particular social groups expresses a cultural calculation that assumes the potential ad reader finds resonance with the cultural world depicted.

In Figure 10.1, which is a business-to-business ad for a telecom company, a lawyer and his client appear in front of a well-known Danish prison. The tattoo on the arm of the client reinforces (intentionally or not) the classic stereotypical relationship between social groups and tattoo culture. Again, the relationship between the tattoo and the brand is, at best, conventional. In the assemblage of the ad, the tattoo serves merely as a prop that draws on the socio-historically established meanings of tattoo culture.

In an ad for Adidas's sponsorship of the New Zealand rugby team, the All Blacks, the use of a tattoo plays a fundamentally different role in relation to the brand. A picture of a traditional Maori face tattoo is printed in black and white with the logo of Adidas and the All Blacks in the top-left and right-hand corners, respectively (we have not been able to obtain copyright permission to reprint the ad, but the image is used to sell the All Blacks merchandise T-shirt, see www.thewoolpress.com/shop/mates-rates.all-blacks/all-blacks-face-t-shirt/for illustration). This ad represents the body as canvas category by entangling the cultural history of tattooing (a traditional Maori tattoo), the rugby team, and the brand to construct a culturally resonant representation. The ad seeks to establish a positive brand image through a symbolic constellation with Maori warriors and probably project a certain fearlessness, rather than fashionableness.

Without determining in any concrete manner the potential readings by consumers or advertiser intentions of these examples, we suggest that advertising practitioners, through their conventional uses of tattoo symbolism, evoke a consumer-brand relationship that assumes resonance with consumers by way of a cultural calculation of knowledge of social identity stereotypes.

Figure 10.1 TDC Mobil print advertisement (published with permission from TDC)

Fashion expression

Fashion expression reflects a genre that, in many ways, stands opposite to the body as canvas. This category represents the use of a single or a few tattoos as a fashionable way to adorn the body in accordance with contemporary mainstream fashion discourse (Kjeldgaard and Bengtsson 2004). Fashion expression as a category draws on a fashion discourse that increasingly embraces certain kinds of tattoos along with other body modifications, accentuating existing mainstream bodily ideals. A fashion tattoo can be distinguished by being an "innocent" expression that does not cause any major objections in mainstream culture. Fashion expression tattoos often play peripheral roles in ads and are often only one cultural element in specific entanglements to represent a certain contemporary style in the ads. This peripheral role means that the tattoo could be exchanged for another fashionable element holding similar cultural meaning (cf. McCracken 1986). In a print ad from a famous Dove campaign, "Real Beauty," featuring supposedly ordinary women, one model displays a tattoo, which is inserted into a discourse of normality as yet another mode of (in this case female) adornment (see www.brandchannel.com/features_effect.asp?pf_id=259 or a number of other sites, as we could not get copyright permission to reprint the advertisement). The tattoo is one element of a practice of entanglement to form a brand identity that encompasses a multitude of female consumers who are considered to be "normal"/mainstream. It hence draws on contemporary fashionableness of consumer tattoo practices to evoke "the ordinary woman."

Several ads for clothes and jewellery brands use tattooed models for fashion expression. The role of the tattoo is symbolic in these ads as they are often used as an additional element of ornamentation in establishing a certain aesthetic of the ad. To establish such an aesthetic, the tattoo could be replaced by other sign elements. Most ads from our sample that are categorized as fashion expression incorporate tattoos that are entirely symbolic, thereby seeking to establish a link between the brand and the tattoo by convention.

Unlike the body as canvas tattoos, the assemblages in the fashion expression category do not allude to the potentially transgressive and deviant meaning of tattooing. Instead, this type integrates the logic of fashion and body malleability associated with postmodern consumer society. Even though this category of tattoo imagery relates to the brand through symbolic convention, it draws on a distinctively different set of cultural meanings. These meanings lend themselves to the articulation of consumer-brand relationships in which the consumer extends their selves through commercial and fashion resources (McCracken 1986; Belk 1988; Arnould and Thompson 2005).

The brand extended

The tattoo imagery in the two former categories holds no explicit references to branding per se, whereas the category labeled "the brand extended" represents tattoos of brand symbols (Bengtsson, Östberg, and Kjeldgaard 2005).

This category draws equally on the discourses of fashion and body modification, but the goal of the particular entanglements is to suggest an unusual constellation representing an emergent consumer-brand assemblage.

In Figure 10.2, the naked woman is about to get the logo of Mary Read tattooed on her shoulder, illustrating the brand extended category. Because the tattoo displays the logo of the brand, the relationship between the tattoo and the brand is iconic (Mick 1986). Our interpretation is that the specific form of entanglement is one of resonance with the potential reader in the

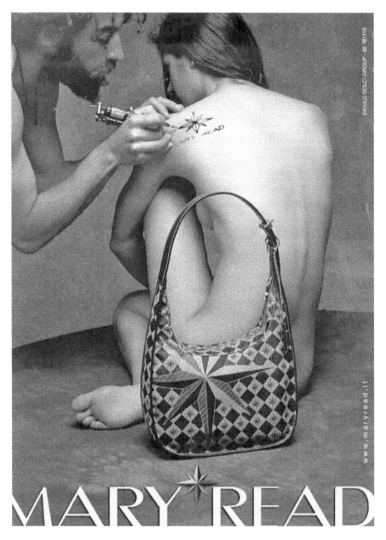

Figure 10.2 Print advertisement for Mary Read (published with permission from R3 Communicazione)

representation of the act of acquiring the tattoo, and one of transgression in that the image being tattooed is a brand.

Another example of the brand extended category appears in an Eastpak ad. The ad portrays a young man in the process of getting a full size tattoo of the image of an Eastpak backpack on his back. In addition to the backpack, several other tattoos cover the back as if they were painted on a canvas. This exemplifies a brand extended advertisement that draws on the body as canvas. The backpack tattoo is iconic because it depicts a visual representation of the product. It is indexical because the ad message draws on the permanence and durability of tattoos and seeks to transfer those characteristics to the brand, explicated by the slogan in the upper right-hand corner: "built to resist." Unfortunately, we were not able to obtain copyright permission to print the ad.

The ad for Perrier Jouët in Figure 10.3 illustrates another example of the brand extended. The tattoo is an example of a fashion expression with both iconic and indexical relationship with the brand. The flower tattoo is an iconic representation of the brand because the same flower appears on the bottle. Tattoos are often associated with uniqueness and therefore are considered unforgettable. Given that the ad seeks to link the brand with this meaning through the ad copy, which states "Unforgettable," the relationship between the brand and the tattoo can also be considered indexical.

As in the Mary Read ad in Figure 10.2, the specific form of entanglement in the Eastpak ad mentioned above and in Figure 10.3 resonates with the cultural practice of tattoo acquisition combined with a transgression that destabilizes conventional ideas of consumer subjectivity. In this case, the merging of the aesthetics and qualities of the brand with those of the tattoo, materialized and embodied on the consumer skin, suggests a consumer subjectivity that diffuses agency among brand, tattoo, and consumer. The consumer subject is decentralized and becomes one part of an assemblage that constitutes agency.

The advertisements in the brand extended category go beyond drawing on existing cultural material. They suggest that the assemblage of fashion, body modification, and consumer-brand relationships expressed in iconic or indexical relationships are unusual. We are here not necessarily interested in the possibility of reading the ads as reflecting a perhaps small existing cultural practice, nor as an encouragement for consumers to emulate this kind of consumption practice. Also, we do not interpret the ads as expressions of consumer identity projects realized through intimate brand relations, as the prevailing lens of a consumer culture theory perspective would (cf. Fournier 1998). Instead, we argue that by using tattoos, the materialization of marketing practices assembles yet another imagery of brand-consumer relationships that reaches beyond the consumer subjectivity of a creative and emancipated individual. By inscribing commercial symbolism onto the body, marketing practitioners render the double-sidedness of the human skin as both the boundary of the individual body and interface with social structure visible (Patterson and Schroeder 2010).

Figure 10.3 Ad for Perrier Jouët (published with permission from Champagnes GH
         Mumm & Perrier Jouët, Pernod Ricard; the advertisment has not been
         used by Perrier Jouët after 2005)

Discussion

In the brand extended category, we show how two wider contemporary
cultural discourses inflect the advertisements analyzed, namely the body
modification discourse and the fashion discourse. Both discourses treat the body
as malleable. One is rooted in marginal, subcultural traditions of Western
societies that are used by "modern primitives" (Velliquette and Murray 1999)
to explore the possibilities of bodily articulation. The other is rooted in the

modern fashion system's logic of innovation and planned obsolescence. The discourses and their manifestation in the ad categories explored above stand in a dialectical relationship, since the fashion discourse will draw on the body modification discourse for inspiration and the body modification culture will change its practices to maintain its oppositional relationship to mainstream culture.

Prior consumer research has suggested that tattooing has become part of mainstream culture (Goulding et al. 2004). Our sample of marketing communication featuring tattoo imagery in mainstream media vehicles provides further support for this idea. However, the cultural meaning associated with tattooing suggests that this type of body art is far from acquiring equal status with other mainstream body adornment practices. We find examples of advertisements that play on classification of certain social groups, advertisements that depict the practice of tattooing as something undesirable, and advertisements in which tattooing is used to give persons depicted in the ads a rebellious, transgressive persona.

The practice of tattooing is, then, situated in the wider cultural history of this practice rather than having gained a "value-neutral" status as a free-floating commodity sign. In this sense, the ads reproduce existing, historically constituted meanings of the tattoos and the bodies they adorn. We have argued that the symbolic relationship between the tattoo and the brand to which it is supposed to lend meaning implies a reproductive use of conventional cultural meanings surrounding the body and tattoo practices. As we have demonstrated, this use applies to tattoo imagery within both the fashion and the body as canvas categories.

However, these two categories evoke different consumer subjectivities and assemble different relationships between the consumer and the brand. The body as canvas category is steeped in the production of stereotypical consumer classifications and combines the tattoo with the brand to form a marker for group identification.

Thereby, this category evokes an image of the consumer as being easily contained within predefined segments and a passive recipient of marketing practitioners' production of ready-to-wear cultural resources. In opposition, the fashion category assembles an emancipated, mobile, and creative consumer whose relationship to brands does not depend on the authoritative narration of marketing practitioners. Instead, the consumer–brand relationship assumed by the fashion category resembles Holt's descriptions of the postmodern branding paradigm. Given that tattooing has become a widespread practice, one might conclude that marketing communication is no more than a mirror of society, and as such we can expect tattoos to appear in the communication of brands. While marketing communication reinforces myths in that it stereotypes which consumer types engage in tattooing, it also circulates the practice more widely in consumer culture. Hence, the practice itself becomes demystified by its increasing presence in mass media and by being drawn into the mass-market commercial sphere. As we saw in a range of ads, tattoos are used in a distinctly positive manner (because of the transgressive qualities discussed above) and tattooing specifically and body modification more generally are inserted into the range of signs that potentially are available for style and identity construction.

Kornberger (2010: xii) expresses the crucial role of brands in the following terms: "They (brands) are so mashed up with our social world that they have become a powerful life-shaping force." Instead of understanding brand tattoos as the extension of individual identities through brands, we propose a networked understanding of consumer-brand relationships in which brands extend onto the bodies of consumers and acquire agency. Such an understanding of brands as a cultural form entangled in socio-technical agencements disputes the consumer-centric nature of consumer research by questioning the imagery of the consumer as a sealed individual vis-à-vis the social world.

Conclusion

Our discussion of the production of consumer-brand assemblages through the use of tattoos in marketing communication seeks to contribute to an emerging body of literature concerning the multitude of brand cultures (Schroeder 2006). In this area, others have stressed the importance of understanding brand cultures as historically and contextually rooted and argued for a more reflexive understanding of branding and brands (Cayla and Arnould 2008; Schau, Muñiz, and Arnould 2009). In addition to these important contributions to the understanding of brands as central cultural forms in contemporary society, we wish to allude to the variety of consumer-brand relationships circulating among academic expert systems, marketing practice systems, and wider communications theories (Ringberg and Reihlen 2008).

The assemblages of consumer-brand relations identified here through the semiotic analysis of tattoos in advertising are embedded in Western advanced capitalist contexts dominated by assumed individualized subjectivities and as such exemplifies how advertising practitioners, as central cultural producers, assemble possible consumer-brand relations through practices of entanglement and cultural calculation. We argue that a more reflexive concern for the mobilization of various consumer-brand relations inform the understanding of how brands operate and may potentially serve to circumvent the consumer-centric understanding of contemporary consumer research and move it toward an understanding of identities as multiple, networked, and emerging (Epp and Price 2010). The assemblage of subjects and objects into socio-technical agencements offers a fruitful course for analyzing the contemporary brand culture. The study presented in this article does so in a relatively narrow empirical scope, focusing on commercial representations. However, an assemblage perspective could fruitfully be applied in more complex social contexts, such as identity performance in a Goth context (Goulding and Saren 2009), to analyze the emergence of consumer-object relations beyond a mere contextual or consumer-centric analysis. Furthermore, applying a networked perspective on brand cultures would facilitate analyses that include multiple actors, practices, cultural discourses, material objects, and cultural representations. This would move the study of brand culture beyond but including consumer life worlds, producerly practices, or historical accounts. Future research is needed that continues recent attempts (Holt and Cameron 2010) at an integrated, networked perspective on brand culture.

Thus, to unfold the nature of the brand as a cultural form, future research could focus on other brand culture contexts undergoing a transformation toward marketization. In such contexts, the processes of entanglement in the branding process may stand out more clearly and potentially provide insights into other cultural calculations of the relationships between consumers and brands.

Acknowledgments

The authors thank Fleura Bardhi, Northeastern University and Matthias Bode, University of Southern Denmark for comments and suggestions on earlier versions of this article. We would also like to thank Emma Gregg, Freelance Picture Editor, UK, for her research on copyright permissions for the visuals in this article. Finally, thanks to TDC, R3 Communicazione, VF Corporation, and Pernod-Ricard for granting permission to publish their advertisements.

References

Arnould, Eric J., and Craig J. Thompson. 2005. "Consumer culture theory (CCT): Twenty years of research." *Journal of Consumer Research* 31 (4): 868–82.

Arvidsson, Adam. 2004. "On the pre-history of the panoptic sort: Mobility in market research." *Surveillance and Society* 1 (4): 456–74.

Arvidsson, Adam. 2006. *Brands: Meaning and value in media culture.* London: Routledge.

Askegaard, Søren, Martine C. Gertsen, and Roy Langer. 2002. "The body consumed: Reflexivity and cosmetic surgery." *Psychology and Marketing* 19 (10): 793–812.

Belk, Russel W. 1988. "Posessions and the extended self." *Journal of Consumer Research* 15 (September): 139–68.

Bengtsson, Anders, Jacob Östberg, and Dannie Kjeldgaard. 2005. "Prisoners in paradise: Subcultural resistance to the marketization of tattooing." *Consumption, Markets and Culture* 8 (3): 261–74.

Brown, Stephen, Robert V. Kozinets, and John F. Sherry Jr. 2003. "Teaching old brands new tricks: Retro branding and the revival of brand meaning." *Journal of Marketing* 67 (July): 19–33.

Callon, Michèl, Cécile Méadel, and Vololona Rabeharisoa. 2002. "The economy of qualities." *Economy and Society* 31 (May): 194–217.

Campell, Norah, Adrian O'Driscoll, and Michael Saren. 2010. "The posthuman: The end and the beginning of the human." *Journal of Consumer Behavior* 9 (March): 86–101.

Cayla, Julien, and Eric J. Arnould. 2008. "A cultural approach to branding in the global marketplace." *Journal of International Marketing* 16 (4): 86–112.

Cochoy, Frank. 2005. "A brief history of the 'customer' or the gradual standardization of markets and organizations." *Sociologie du Travail* 47 (5): 36–56.

du Gay, Paul, and Mike Pryke. 2002. *Cultural economy*. London: Sage.

Epp, Amber M., and Linda L. Price. 2010. "The storied life of singularized objects: Forces of agency and network transformation." *Journal of Consumer Research* 36 (5): 820–37.

Ewen, Stuart. 1976. *Captains of consciousness: Advertising and the social roots of the consumer culture*. New York: McGraw Hill.

Fırat, Fuat A., and Alladi Venkatesh. 1995. "Liberatory postmodernism and the reenchantment of consumption." *Journal of Consumer Research* 22 (December): 239–67.

Fournier, Susan. 1998. "Consumers and their brands: Developing relationship theory in consumer research." *Journal of Consumer Research* 24 (March): 343–73.

Giddens, Anthony. 1991. *Modernity and self-identity: Self and society in the late modern age*. Palo Alto, CA: Stanford University Press.

Giesler, Markus, and Alladi Venkatesh. 2005. "Reframing the embodied consumer as cyborg: A posthumanist epistemology of consumption." In *Advances in consumer research*, Vol. 32, edited by M. Geeta and A.R. Rao. Provo, UT: Association for Consumer Research, 661–9.

Goulding, Christina, and John Follet. 2002. "Sub-cultures, women and tattoos: An exploratory study." In *Gender, marketing and consumer behavior*, Vol. 6, edited by Barbara Kahn and Mary Frances Luce. Valdosta, GA: Association for Consumer Research, 37–45.

Goulding, Christina, and Michael Saren. 2009. "Performing identity: An analysis of gender expressions at the Whitby goth festival." *Consumption Markets & Culture* 12 (1): 27–46.

Goulding, Christina, John Follet, Michael Saren, and Pauline McLaren. 2004. "Process and meaning in getting a tattoo." In *Advances in consumer research*, Vol. 31, edited by B. E. Kahn and M. F. Luce. Valdosta, GA: Association for Consumer Research, 279–85.

Holt, Douglas B. 2002. "Why do brands cause trouble? A dialectical theory of consumer culture and branding." *Journal of Consumer Research* 29 (1): 70–90.

Holt, Douglas B., and Douglas Cameron. 2010. *Cultural strategy: Using innovative ideologies to build breakthrough brands*. New York: Oxford University Press.

Jensen, Anne F. 1999. *Acknowledging and consuming fashion in the era after "good taste": From the beautiful to "the hideous"*. Odense: University Press of Southern Denmark.

Kjeldgaard, Dannie, and Anders Bengtsson. 2004. "Consuming the fashion tattoo." In *Advances in consumer research*, Vol. 31, edited by G. Menon and A. R. Rao. Valdosta, GA: Association for Consumer Research, 172–7.

Kornberger, Martin. 2010. *Brand society: How brands transform management and lifestyle*. New York: Cambridge University Press.

Latour, Bruno. 2005. *Reassembling the social: An introduction to actor-network theory*. Oxford: Oxford University Press.

McCracken, Grant. 1986. "Culture and consumption: A theoretical account of the structure and movement of the cultural meaning of consumer goods." *Journal of Consumer Research* 13 (June): 71–84.

McFall, Liz. 2002. "Advertising, persuasion, and the culture/economy dualism." In *Cultural economy*, edited by P. du Gay and M. Pryke. London: Sage, 148–65.

McQuarrie, Edward F., Linda Scott, John F. Sherry, Jr., and Melanie Wallendorf. 2005. "Roundtable on advertising as a cultural form." *Advertising and Society Review* 6 (4): doi: 10.1353/asr.2006.0009.

Mick, David G. 1986. "Consumer research and semiotics: Exploring the morphology of signs, symbols, and significance." *Journal of Consumer Research* 13 (September): 196–213.

Miller, Daniel. 2010. *Stuff.* Cambridge: Polity.

Miller, Peter, and Nicholas Rose. 2008. *Governing the present.* Cambridge: Polity.

O'Reilly, Daragh. 2006. "Commentary: Branding ideology." *Marketing Theory* 6 (2): 263–71.

Patterson, Maurice, and Richard Elliott. 2002. "Negotiating masculinities: Advertising and the inversion of the male gaze." *Consumption Markets & Culture* 5 (3): 231–46.

Patterson, Maurice, and Jonathan Schroeder. 2010. "Borderlines: Skin, tattoos and consumer culture theory." *Marketing Theory* 10 (September): 253–67.

Powell, Walter W., and Paul J. DiMaggio. 1983. "The iron cage revisited: Institutional isomorphism and collective rationality in organizational fields." *American Sociological Review* 48 (April): 147–60.

Ringberg, Torsten, and Markus Reihlen. 2008. "Communication assumptions in consumer research: An alternative sociocognitive approach." Consumption Markets & Culture 11 (3): 173–89.

Sanders, Clinton R. 1989. *Customizing the body: The art and culture of tattooing.* Philadelphia, PA: Temple University Press.

Schau, Hope J., Albert Muñiz, and Eric J. Arnould. 2009. "How brand community practices create value." *Journal of Marketing* 73 (September): 30–51.

Schouten, John W. 1991. "Selves in transition: Symbolic consumption in personal rites of passage and identity reconstruction." *Journal of Consumer Research* 17 (March): 412–25.

Schroeder, Jonathan E. 2006. "Critical visual analysis." In *Handbook of qualitative research methods in marketing*, edited by R. W. Belk. Northampton, MA: Edward Elgar, 303–21.

Schroeder, Jonathan E., and Janet L. Borgerson. 1998. "Marketing images of gender: A visual analysis." *Consumption Markets & Culture* 2 (2): 161–201.

Schroeder, Jonathan E., and Detlev Zwick. 2004. "Mirrors of masculinity: Representation and identity in advertising images." *Consumption Markets & Culture* 7 (1): 21–52.

Scott, Linda M. 1994. "Images in advertising: The need for a theory of visual rhetoric." *Journal of Consumer Research* 21 (September): 252–73.

Sherry, John F. 1987. "Advertising as a cultural system." In *Marketing and semiotics: New directions in the study of signs for sale*, edited by J. Umiker-Sebeok. Berlin: Mouton de Gruyter, 441–61.

Shilling, Chris. 2003. *The body and social theory.* 2nd ed. London: Sage.

Slater, Don. 2002. "Capturing markets from the economists." In *Cultural economy*, edited by Paul du Gay and Mike Pryke. London: Sage, 59–77.

Strasser, Susan. 1989. *Satisfaction guaranteed: The making of the American mass market.* New York: Pantheon Books.

Thompson, Craig J. 2004. "Marketplace mythology and discourses of power." *Journal of Consumer Research* 31 (June): 162–80.

Thompson, Craig J., and Elizabeth C. Hirschman. 1995. "Understanding the socialized body: A poststructuralist analysis of consumers' self-conceptions, body images, and self-care practices." *Journal of Consumer Research* 22 (September): 139–53.

Turner, Bryan S. 1996. *The body and society*. 2nd ed. London: Sage.

Turner, Bryan S. 2000. "The possibility of primitiveness: Towards a sociology of body marks in cool society." In *Body modification*, edited by M. Featherstone. London: Sage, 39–50.

Vail, Angus D. 1999. "Tattoos are like potato chips . . . you can't have just one: The process of becoming and being a collector." *Deviant Behavior: An Interdisciplinary Journal* 20 (3): 253–73.

Velliquette, Anne M., and Jeff B. Murray. 1999. "The new tattoo subculture." In *Mapping the social landscape: Readings in sociology*, edited by S. Ferguson. Mountain View, CA: Mayfield, 56–68.

Williamson, Judith. 1978. *Decoding advertising – ideology and meaning in advertising*. London: Marion Boyers.

Zwick, Detlev, and Julien Cayla, eds. 2010. *Inside marketing: Practices, ideologies and devices*. New York: Oxford University Press.

11 Consumer multiculturation

Consequences of multicultural identification for brand knowledge

Eva Kipnis, Amanda J. Broderick and Catherine Demangeot

Introduction

Brand meaning formation is a dynamic process in which consumers and brand managers draw from extant sociocultural discourses "to give meaning to the products they consume or sell" (Varman and Costa 2013). Consequently, there is a growing need for frameworks that integrate the sociocultural processes shaping the "outside-in" perspective of brand meanings formation (brand image perceived by consumers) with the "inside-out" perspective (brand identity as intended to be communicated by the company) (Schroeder 2009). This paper is concerned with advancing our understanding of how the complex cultural identity discourses in diversifying sociocultural contexts affect interpretation of brand meanings by locally born consumers (we refer to these consumers as "mainstream" throughout the paper).

The culture-based meanings of brands embody the visible evidence of self-image and cultural group membership (Elliott and Wattanasuwan 1998). As identities evolve in response to contextual changes, individuals use brands to (re)discover, preserve, (re)construct and dispose of a part of identity (Kleine and Kleine 2000). Extant research identifies complex identity transitions experienced by ethnic migrants that result from interaction with multiple systems of cultural meanings, those of co-residing cultural groups as well as those introduced through media and advertising (Askegaard, Arnould and Kjeldgaard 2005). In postmodern reality, migrants, even those of the same ethnic origin, can form identities that differ significantly by strength of identification with cultures and subcultures they interact with. Some develop multicultural identities (i.e. internalize two or more cultures as equally significant and accessible systems of being in a marketplace); the identities of others are uni-cultural (i.e. internalizing one culture as a core system that guides being). The diversification of cultural identity dispositions has a differential effect on the interpretation of consumption experiences and the evaluation and subsequent adoption or rejection of certain practices and products. Multicultural ethnic consumers differ from uni-cultural ones in how they process advertising claims (Luna and Peracchio 2005), respond to persuasion appeals (Lau-Gesk 2003) and accept or reject brand values (Sekhon and Szmigin 2009).

However, there is a growing recognition that the migrant-centric approach produces a single-sided view of identity transformations among the individuals who are exposed to multiple cultural influences (Luedicke 2011). Indeed, international marketing theory generally is concerned with wider consumer audiences than a particular ethnic segment in a given marketplace. Yet, prior studies largely reduced the considerations of how mainstream consumers (the non-migrants "born into" the local majority of that marketplace) make sense of and negotiate between multiple cultural meanings, to the "global-local" perspective (Kjedlaard and Askergaard 2006). Conceptions of brand country-of-origin (COO), the key informant of managerial practices for culture-based brand meaning formation, evolved in a similar vein (Varman and Costa 2013). A gap in the literature exists whereby the role of foreign culture (FC), a construct that according to early COO studies (Alden, Steenkamp and Batra 1999) can encapsulate meanings distinctly different from those assigned as global meanings, has been mostly omitted from conceptualizations of cultural identity discourses of mainstream consumers.

In this paper, we argue that complex identity evolution through multiple cultural experiences is a phenomenon that is equally relevant to mainstream and migrant consumer spheres if these experiences are lived by both groups in a same (given) multicultural marketplace. While not disputing the notion of global culture (GC), we contest the reduction of the effects of globalization on mainstream populations to a local-global dichotomy since it: (1) negates the plurality of cultural meanings that mainstream consumers are exposed to through globalization channels; and (2) leaves out the possibility that FCs as distinct ideologies may have a powerful impact on the identity and consumption of mainstream populations. For example, a native Swede married to a Chinese and living in a Swedish city hosting sizeable groups from different cultures may see their identity negotiations evolve to include particular FCs that they are in continuous contact with other than (but not excluding) LC (Swedish) and GC. We propose that composite identities developed by mainstream consumers subsequently elicit the formation of complex culture-informed consumption attitudes, behaviors and brand meanings that cannot be captured solely by the current global-local paradigm.

This paper contributes to culture-based consumer behavior and marketing literature by providing a coherent, integrative framework that unpacks the effects of multiple cultural forces in a multicultural marketplace on the identity development of mainstream consumers and on their brand knowledge. We consider brand knowledge as the focal construct representative of the brands' cultural meanings formation process (Keller 1993). We conceptualize a multicultural marketplace as a multidimensional environment, where multiple cultural forces (local, global and foreign) converge at one point of concurrent interaction with mainstream and migrant consumers alike. We also posit that, in a multicultural marketplace, mainstream consumers' identities may evolve over time to internalize multiple diverse cultures. In terms of the organization of the paper, we first integrate several strands of ethnic and international marketing literature dealing with the impact of different types of cultures on identity development and consumption. In light of this synthesis, we clarify the definitions of the key types of cultural influences that may affect individual cultural identity negotiations. We then extend acculturation theory (Berry 1980) beyond immigrant groups, and develop the construct of consumer multiculturation, which demonstrates how consumers may develop affiliations with one, two or multiple cultures, resulting in various types of cultural identities. Applying social identity – brand image congruence theory (Reed 2002) – to consumer multiculturation, we show that existing culture-based consumer behavior theories cannot satisfactorily explain all mainstream consumers' behavioral responses to the cultural meanings of brands that can emerge in a multicultural marketplace. Finally, we consider implications for future research on cultural identity and culture-based consumption behaviors in international marketing.

Theoretical background

Exploring the disconnects between existing conceptions of culture-based brand meanings created through positioning and cultural processes in the environment

Culture is fundamental to identity construal as it provides individuals with "the sense of the self derived from formal or informal membership in groups that impart knowledge, beliefs, values, attitudes, traditions, and ways of life" (Jameson 2007: 200). As such, culture constitutes a coherent ideology that is: (1) "man-made" (i.e. constructed and shared by identifiable collectives of individuals as a striving for distinctiveness from other collectives); and (2) used by individuals as frames of self-identification references to delineate acceptable and non-acceptable ideas and behaviors in this collective (Parsons 1951). Brands have emerged as objects that materialize political, cultural and social ideologies in the environment and contribute to these ideologies' transformation (Schroeder 2009). People use brands as referents to retain, discover, try out, reject, adopt or adapt existing and new cultural aspects of identity (Askegaard 2006). Consumer response to brand meanings stems from brand knowledge, defined as cognitive and abstract brand-related information held by consumers (Keller 2003). The overall attitudinal disposition to a particular culture influences the order of information processing and thus affects brand awareness. For example, Supphellen and Gronhaug (2003) show that ethnocentric consumers tend to process brand information from top to bottom (i.e. starting by identifying whether the brand is local or non-local), whereas non-ethnocentric consumers process brand information from bottom to top, starting by evaluating the attributes of a specific brand. Cultural cues or primes present in brand communications can activate cultural identity and affect the interpretation of communication appeals (such as linguistic, visual, value, etc.) and subsequent perceptions of brand image (Roth and Diamantopoulos 2009).

International marketing studies of culture-based consumer brand knowledge (CBK) are underpinned by COO research (Balabanis and Diamantopoulos 2008; Pecotich and Ward 2007). While early conceptions of COO stem from known or presumed brands' "made in" associations (i.e. associations of brands' physical origin in a country or region), more recent conceptions delineate product-country-images (PCI); brand-origin or culture-of-brand-origin (COBO); country-of-manufacture (COM); country-of-assembly (COA) and country-of-design (COD) dimensions of the COO construct (see Pharr 2005 for a review). We base our conceptualization on the concept of COBO. Following Lim and O'Cass (2001), we define COBO as the culture to which a brand is perceived to belong, and view COBO as the focal concept for the study of culture-based CBK. The notion of COBO does not restrict brands' cultural associations to the "made in (a particular country)" associations and therefore accounts for more intricate and subtle cultural associations evoked by brand names (Ristorante pizza of German manufacturer Dr Oetker), visual images (Alpine scenery in Milka's packaging design and adverts), and linguistic appeals ("Quadratisch. Praktisch. Gut" strapline of Ritter Sport) (Mikhailitchenko et al. 2009; Verlegh 1999). In addition, COBO has been demonstrated to be more acutely and correctly denoted by consumers than other COO dimensions (Srinivasan, Jain and Sikland 2004). While cognitive COBO associations are based on the practices of a culture that affect products' functional attributes, such as quality or taste, conative and affective COBO associations are rooted in social identity-brand image congruence theory (Reed 2002) since consumers view possessions as tangible evidence of their self-identity.

Understanding how cultural identity dispositions form and evolve is crucial for studying culture-based CBK. According to Kleine and Kleine (2000: 279), identities are projects that "continually evolve overtime," whereby people may attempt to change their identities entirely or modify them by contracting other aspects of identity. By consuming brands, one may enact a deployment or derogation of an ideology, norms and practices associated with a particular culture as part of current identity reinforcement or of identity evolution (Batra et al. 2000). However, while depicting a materialization of diverse (local, global and foreign) cultural ideologies within a given marketplace through branding, extant frameworks only partly unpack the evolutionary effects of these ideologies on the cultural identity formation of mainstream consumers. Table 11.1 presents a brief summary of the four conceptions of COBO brand meanings (global, local, glocal and foreign) currently prevailing in the international marketing literature. The table indicates three main disconnects between culture-based branding theory and the sociocultural transformations occurring in marketplaces.

First, Table 11.1 highlights that while the studies of culture-based CBK recognize the transformational impact of GC and the effects of local contexts on consumer readings of the meanings of global brands as symbols of the global world, studies focusing on the effects of FCs' biases on consumption and brand perceptions have surprisingly evolved as a stand-alone stream within the international marketing literature and are not fully integrated in cultural identity discourse. Such a conceptual division is startling given an increasing recognition of the need to explore the role of cultures and subcultures other than global and local in the identity transitions of mainstream consumer groups (Craig and Douglas 2006). It is important to clearly distinguish between global and specific foreign cultural dispositions when studying cultural identity formation as they have markedly differential effects on consumer behavior and brand knowledge. Consumers regard brand globalness as a symbol of participation in the GC that unites people across national borders and creates an "imagined global identity that they share with likeminded people" (Özsomer and Altaras 2008: 9). Conversely, brand associations with a particular FC symbolize deployment of a specific authentic identity. Distinct foreign meanings, practices, ideas, lifestyles and goods can become widely accepted, adopted and/or transformed (if compatible) in local cultural contexts (Eckhardt and Mahi 2004).

Second, it is important to take a holistic view as to whether and how the interplay between global, foreign and local cultural influences affects the identity formation of mainstream consumers. The emergence of new cultural identities within mainstream consumer groups that integrate multiple cultures going beyond the global-local paradigm may have implications for culture-based consumption theory. Some studies have uncovered novel culture-based branding approaches that have not been coherently integrated with the previous body of culture-based CBK research. For example, Cayla and Eckhardt (2008) find that managers developing contemporary Asian brands deploy multiple and diverse cultural meanings and use a collage of multiple-cultural referents that "goes beyond globalization models" (Cayla and Eckhardt 2008: 226). Yet, we still know very little about how the identities of mainstream consumers diversify beyond local/global/glocal alternatives, what processes contribute to such diversity and how these diverse identities affect expectations and responses to culture-based brand meanings. Third, and finally, the summary provided in Table 11.1 indicates that current conceptions root the notions of "local" and "foreign" in notions of culture at the level of nation states (countries). However, several studies note that the notion of national culture alone does not fully reflect the complexities of sociocultural transformations occurring within and between contemporary national marketplaces (Bauman 2000; Craig and Douglas 2006).

It is necessary to bridge the gap between the evolved conceptions of culture and cultural identity and the conceptions of culture-based branding. With this in mind, we develop a conceptual framework that: (1) clarifies definitions of local, global and FCs as integrated elements that are simultaneously present

Table 11.1 Summary overview of cultural contexts in the global marketplace, their impact on COBO-based brand meanings created through positioning and consumer response to these meanings

Type of consumption culture	Definition	Findings on culture-based brand meanings created through positioning and consumer response	Literature references
Global culture (GC)	Common models of social order and lifestyle authoritative in many different settings. The spread of these models across the world through multiple channels (i.e. technology, international trade, media and marketing) led to homogenous global marketplace, globally shared consumption meanings, images, narratives and behavior.	Consumption of brands positioned to create perceived "globalness" is regarded by consumers as representation of global village membership, or a "passport to global citizenship." Perceived brand globalness positively affects perceived quality, prestige and thus purchase likelihood (Steenkamp, Batra and Alden 2003; Strizhakova et al. 2008).	Alden, Steenkamp and Batra (1999, 2006), Steenkamp, Batra and Alden (2003) and Strizhakova et al. (2008)
Local culture (LC)	Unique models of social order and lifestyle; authority of one's home country national/ cultural norms, meanings and images.	Consumption of brands positioned to create strong association with LC by using local appeals in communications builds memorable and positively valued brand experiences. Local appeals evoke local cultural values are perceived by consumers as "down to earth."	Steenkamp and De Jong (2010), Wilk (1995) and Zhang and Schmitt (2001)
Glocal culture (GLC)	Integration of the global and the local (i.e. a hybrid blend of GC and local cultural norms, values and images). Global meanings are interpreted and transferred into local meanings unique for the focal LC.	Integrating global appeals with local specifications enhances positivity of consumer readings of the meaning of brands positioned as international/global and make them more relevant to consumers' cultural context.	Eckhardt and Mahi (2004), Hsieh and Lindridge (2005), Kjeldgaard and Askergaard (2006) and Kjeldgaard and Ostberg (2007)
Foreign culture (FC)	Models of social order, culture and lifestyle of a foreign country that result in unique consumption meanings associated with this country.	Associating advertising appeals (aesthetic, spokesperson and thematic signs) with a specific foreign country that has a positive image among consumers enhances positivity of consumer readings of the meanings of the brand.	Alden, Steenkamp and Batra (1999) and Leclerc, Schmitt and Dube (1994)

in a multicultural marketplace and can be deployed, albeit differentially, in individual identity negotiations; and (2) considers how local, global and foreign cultural meanings engaged in identity processes of the mainstream consumers affect their expectations and response to brand meanings.

Conceptual framework

Evolution of culture and cultural identity conceptions: consequences for consumption

Culture evolves responding to environmental changes (Nakata 2003). Recent literature asserts that the emergence of transnationally homogenous "global culture" ideology is one, yet by far not the only one, of globalization's cultural consequences (Robinson 2001). Rather, globalization has led to the emergence of an "interactional meeting place" (Hermans and Kempen 1998: 1118) for a dynamic inter-group exchange of cultural information that results in complex transformations of cultures and of the ways they are deployed for identity construal. Along with homogenization, simultaneous processes of cultural localization, delocalization and hybridization occur (see Table 11.2 for full definitions).

It is clear that, while the construct of culture remains focused on the notion of a coherent ideology developed and maintained by a human collective, the sociology of cultures' development and deployment by individuals in a locale can neither be defined exclusively within the boundaries of national or ethnic groups, nor as national cultures' convergence into a transnationally universal (global) culture (Wimmer and Glick Schiller 2002). The mobility of cultures facilitates the emergence of identity discourses whereby individuals can simultaneously integrate composite identity links with several cultures that become interwoven within a given locale (Hannerz 1996). Since people use goods to extract "contingent identities derived from the [cultural] differences" (Askegaard, Arnould and Kjeldgaard 2005: 2) and to "create and survive social change" (McCracken 1990: 11), such complex identity discourses differentially affect consumption.

Research investigating the evolving complexities of cultural identities and their impact on consumption followed two avenues. The first focuses on the types of cultural identities formed by individuals migrating physically from one locale to another. These individuals may differ in their motivation to migrate, ways of developing or maintaining identity links with the cultures of locales they emigrate from and immigrate to, and use of possessions as symbolic facilitators of these identity negotiations. Global nomads or expressive expatriates often migrate for non-utilitarian reasons and retain the cultural capital of their previous locale (D'Andrea 2007). They use possessions and consumption rituals to re-territorialize (i.e. socially adjust themselves to the culture of a new locale), and turn to different practices and possessions if migrating again (Bardhi, Eckhardt and Arnould 2012). Conversely, those who migrate to and settle in a different locale for economic or political reasons are concerned with learning to live in a new locale whilst retaining cultural heritage, such as kinship or rituals, of their putative locale of origin, often without an assumed need to return to it (Appadurai 1996). They develop deterritorialized identities and use possessions and consumption practices to anchor themselves to their heritage (Oswald 1999). Identity negotiations of migrating individuals have therefore been predominantly considered to evolve between the local (national) culture of their new residence and their culture-of-origin. The second stream of research focuses on types of identities and expectations/perceptions of symbolic attributes of material objects formed by mainstream individuals (i.e. the non-migrant persons "born into" and remaining in a locale). Identity negotiations of these individuals have been considered to evolve between local (national) and global (or transnational) systems of cultural meanings (Kjeldgaard and Askegaard 2006). However, recent work points to more complex cultural identity transitions that result in composite identities integrating two or more types of cultures. While current evidence mostly emerges from the studies focusing on "physically migrating" groups (Askegaard, Arnould and Kjeldgaard 2005; Wamwara-Mbugua, Cornwell and Boller 2008), a handful of studies identify similar complexities among mainstream populations (Holliday 2010; Jamal 2003), thus suggesting that greater intricacies in consumption behaviors are possible. The next section shows that these complexities can be explicated by the sociological evolution of how cultures are perceived and deployed in deterritorialized, localized and hybrid identity discourses, and offers revised definitions of the local, foreign and global cultures' concepts that account for these changes.

Table 11.2 Summary definitions of cultural transformations facilitated by globalization

Cultural transformation process	Definition
Homogenization (or translocalization)	A new type of culture emerges as a translocally universal ideology that is not linked to a particular territory or territories, but rather is viewed as an ideology of global unity.
Localization	The uniqueness of a culture as ideology is exclusively defined through its links to a particular geographic territory by people residing in this territory.
Delocalization	A culture linked to a particular territory emerges as a distinct ideology in multiple locales and therefore is no longer exclusively defined through links to a particular geographic territory.
Hybridization	Two or more elements from different cultures integrate to form a new cultural element.

Source: Craig and Douglas (2006), Bauman (2000) and Beck (2000).

Mainstream populations interacting with emerged multicultural environments: key contributing forces and types of cultural influences

Growth in the number of ethnic minority populations, and the continuing efforts of policymakers to promote equality have led to a greater integration of ethnic minorities with mainstream populations. For example, projections for the USA and UK indicate considerable predicted growth of ethnic minority groups, with currently dominant populations of these countries remaining constant in size (Haub 2008; Wohland et al. 2010). According to the same projections, ethnic minority groups will be significantly less segregated from the majority populations and significantly more affluent than at present. The integration of migrant minorities with mainstream populations also results in a significant rise in mixed ethnic or mixed race families (see Frey 2009; Waters 2008 for reports on USA and UK; similar evidence is reported for many other countries, such as Canada, the Netherlands, Finland, etc.). Individuals of mixed ethnic/racial populations have been shown to consider several ethnic components of their identity to be of equal importance (Aspinall 2003). Echoing this shift in the cultural composition of societies, studies from anthropology and sociology assert that the increasing coexistence of many cultures and subcultures within a given locale calls for further scholarly research into the meaning of "local" in cultural discourse (Korff 2003; Roudometof 2005). Indeed, if a number of subcultural groups co-reside and mix in a given country, which culture would be considered as local to them? Therefore, we define *local culture (LC) as the ideology of one's current place of residence (i.e. an ideology existing in a given locale), which is regarded by those residing in this locale as ways of life and systems of values, beliefs, material objects (products) and symbols that originate in the locale and uniquely distinguish this locale from other locales* (e.g. in the USA – American culture; in France – French culture, etc.).

Intensified inter-group contact and integration also lead to the development of identities that cannot be captured solely through one's ancestral and national links. While uncovering identity links with multiple cultures and subcultures such as culture of origin, national culture of residence, GC and subcultures of other co-resident groups, ethnic migrant studies reviewed above (Askegaard, Arnould and Kjeldgaard 2005; Wamwara-Mbugua, Cornwell and Boller 2008) do not consider how the identity processes of mainstream consumers are affected by the diversifying composition of societies. That is, although literature claims that the cultural lifestyles and consumption practices of mainstream consumers can change as lifestyles and behaviors of subcultural migrant groups become integrated with those of host societies (Jamal 2003), it is unclear whether and how cultural practices and norms adopted by mainstream individuals from (sometimes multiple) migrant populations contribute to changes in the sense of self and identity among mainstream consumer groups. According to Jiménez (2010: 1756), "ideological, institutional and demographic changes" facilitate the increasing elasticity of the link between ancestry and identity resulting in the formation of affiliative ethnic identities, defined as individual identities "rooted in knowledge, regular consumption and deploy-ment of an ethnic culture that is unconnected to an individual's ethnic ancestry until that individual regards herself, and may be regarded by others, as an affiliate of a particular ethnic group" (Jiménez 2010: 1756).

Furthermore, affiliative identities cannot be restricted to inter-group ethnic links within a locale, nor to links with GC only (Arnett 2002). Research into cultural affinity suggests that people can develop a "feeling of liking, sympathy and even attachment" (Oberecker, Riefler and Diamantopoulos 2008: 26) towards a particular FC both through experiences with bodily (people) and non-bodily (scenery, media and brands) representatives of this culture(s), and could consider the latter a part of their in-group. That is, accessibility of multiple cultural ideologies through global technoscapes, consumption-scapes and ideoscapes (Appadurai 1996) allows persons to connect to several cultural realities through imagination and develop/maintain multicultural identities. Eloquent in its simplicity is Appadurai's (1996) metaphor of "hyphenated identities" (i.e. Italian-American, Asian-American-Japanese, Native-American-Seneca). While Appadurai's metaphor mainly refers to the global spread of diasporic identities as "a delocalized transnation, which retains a special ideological link to putative place of origin" (Appadurai 1996: 172), affiliative ethnic identity and cultural affinity studies (Jiménez 2010; Oberecker, Riefler and Diamantopoulos 2008) demonstrate that identity hyphenation also pertains to non-diasporic (i.e. non-ancestral) links. However, while the literature generally accepts that individuals' understanding of "foreign" and "global" differs (Alden, Steenkamp and Batra 1999), conceptual distinction between the two meanings and their impact on culture-based consumption requires clarification.

GC has been defined by researchers as transnationally shared symbols, images, models of lifestyle and consumption that originated from the West (predominantly the USA). At times, the meanings of Western and "global" culture are interpreted as interchangeable. In our view, such a conception is unhelpful for at least two reasons. First, the definition of GC as a constellation of "Western imaginary" (Cayla and Arnould 2008: 88) emerged at the time of political, economic and cultural dominance of the West European countries and the USA. The rapid advancement of such emerging countries as India, China and Brazil has caused a change in the power balance of global society and greater penetration by these countries in the global marketplace. Brands, such as Acer (Taiwan), Lenovo (China) and Lukoil (Russia), are emerging that integrate the meaning of "globalness" into their communications similarly to established Western brands (Guzman and Paswan 2009). Therefore, while in essence "global" culture remains an integration of transnationally shared symbols, cultural and consumption norms, its original Western-inspired cultural context may be diffused as more countries see themselves as not merely participants, but also contributors to the global society (Iwabuchi 2002). It appears more plausible to base definitions of GC in the contemporary world on symbols, images, models of lifestyle and consumption that are "developed in different parts of the world and shared transnationally," rather than are "Western and shared by the rest of the world."

Second, although Western countries may have been initial contributors to the emergence of GC, they each carry specific cultural stereotypes, such as warmth, competence, work ethics, leisure, etc. (Chattalas, Kramer and Takada 2008). These stereotypes are widely used by some Western brands to position themselves with reference to a specific culture; for example, Saab is positioned as "so Swedish"; Levi's is "powerfully associated . . . with American style" (Cayla and Arnould 2008: 96). These brands, while globally available to consumers and associated with Western cultures, communicate culture-specific meanings. Contrast this with other brands that eliminate culture-specific associations from their communications to create the meaning of "globalness"; for example, Dutch Frito-Lay changed the name of the "leading potato chip brand from Smiths to Lay's" (Steenkamp, Batra and Alden 2003: 53). It appears that the meaning of "global" evolved to carry a distinctly different set of cultural stereotypes than a meaning of "foreign" and can no longer be used interchangeably with "Western" or "American." Hence, we define *global culture (GC) as an ideology that is regarded by consumers as a set of translocally universal values, beliefs, lifestyle, material objects (products) and symbols that are developed through contributions from knowledge and practices in different parts of the world, are present, practiced and used across the world in essentially similar manner and symbolize an ideological connectedness with the world regardless of residence or heritage.*

Our definition of FC(s) aims to characterize the cultures other than GC and LC present in multicultural societies. These other cultures may not be originating from, yet still be present, in a given locale through the migration of multiple ethnic groups or through the "import" of these cultures via global channels. The adjective "foreign" is defined as "dealing with or relating to other countries; or coming or introduced from outside" (Oxford Dictionaries 2010). While GC is perceived to be present and similar around the world thus "shared" by all cultural groups, the meaning of "foreign" remains powerfully associated with a culture regarded as originating from a particular locale different from the locale of residence, and introduced through cultural experiences from outside of the LC. Therefore, we define *foreign culture (FC) as an ideology that is regarded by those residing in a given locale as a system of values, beliefs, lifestyle, material objects (products) and symbols originating from and represented by an identifiable cultural source(s) (a country, group of people) that is different from LC (or ideology of residence) and is known to individuals either as culture-of-origin, diasporic culture of ethnic ancestry or an aspired-to FC with no ancestral links.* In culturally diverse societies, individuals may be strongly influenced by more than one FC: the identity of an individual of Italian descent in the USA may be influenced, along with Italian and American cultures (ancestry/heritage and residence links), by French culture if he holds an affective bias toward France and by an African culture if he is in a relationship with someone of African origin (affiliative links).

This example illustrates why rooting the study of composite cultural identities in nationality/ethnicity and migrant/non-migrant classifications may be problematic in multicultural marketplaces. Under past definitions, this individual's LC would be identified as American, and could not account for Italian and African cultural influences. If considered within frameworks of national and ethnic identity (Keillor and Hult 1999; Phinney 2005) this individual would be identified as Italian-American, but the affiliative identities that this individual may develop (with African-American subculture through direct interactions with spouse and other members of his or her subcultural group, and with French culture through global channels) would not be captured. Instead, the definitions of LC and FC just proposed overcome the restrictiveness of past conceptualizations by enabling to distinguish and capture the ancestral and affiliative cultural influences on this individual's identity formation: American culture is the LC and other cultures making up his identity (Italian, African and French cultures) are FCs represented in the locale.

The wide diversity of co-residing groups and the elasticizing link between cultural ancestry, nationality and identity suggests a growing need for scholarly focus to shift toward considering migrant *and* mainstream individuals as "marketplace beings." The cultural identity processes of both groups should be studied *within the multiple cultures* represented in a given marketplace, whether these representations are materialized by members of co-resident cultural groups and/or by brands, media and other non-bodily marketplace actors (Arzubiaga et al. 2008). Therefore, as a parsimonious conceptualization of the contemporary cultural landscape, we propose the concept of "multiple-cultural environment" (Figure 11.1), which integrates the key types of cultures (local, global and foreign) that individuals interact with in a multicultural marketplace.

Figure 11.1 illustrates that the interplay of multiple-cultural forces converging at one point of interaction with the individuals in a given marketplace must be thought of and analyzed as a whole and concurrently. Through this concomitant interaction with all elements of the multiple-cultural environment, individuals may deduce unique *multicultural* meanings. Studies on glocal culture demonstrate that through interactions with global and local cultural forces in a marketplace new types of cultures can emerge (Kjeldgaard and Ostberg 2007). However, it is also important to consider whether other "hybrid" cultures and hyphenated identities emerge since in a multiplecultural environment individuals interact with FCs as well as GC and LC.

Effects of diversified cultural identity processes on brand knowledge: from consumer acculturation to consumer multiculturation

The concept of a multiple-cultural environment is useful to understand the multicultural interactions of individuals in a multicultural marketplace. However, the interactions with multiple cultures do not de facto transform

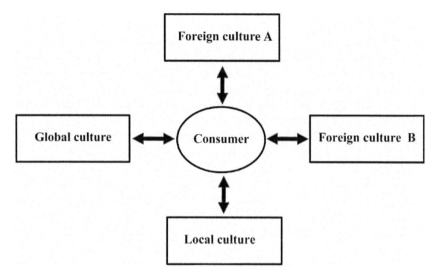

Figure 11.1 Multiple-cultural environment

consumers into multiculturals: rather, they generate multicultural awareness. Cultures can be embraced by some individuals and yet be strongly opposed by others (Witkowski 2005). In marketing terms, the evaluation of and response to culture-based brand meanings by consumers internalizing multiple cultures will be significantly more elaborate than the response of those consumers opposing any given cultural force(s) in the multiple-cultural environment.

A theory that successfully lends itself to the analysis of consumer behavior transformed by multicultural contacts is the theory of acculturation, defined as "changes that happen over time when two or more cultures come into continuous contact" (Redfield, Linton and Herskovits 1936 in Berry 1980: 9). Even though this definition is broader, until recently acculturation has been predominantly utilized to explicate divergent behaviors of *immigrant* persons as an outcome of these persons (re)evaluating and (re)negotiating their identities in the new sociocultural contexts of the host countries. The bi-dimensional construct of acculturation (Berry 1980) distinguishes four acculturation strategies (also called modes) that migrant individuals select as a form of being and living in a new host culture. *Assimilation* entails individuals abandoning their home cultural values and beliefs systems and adopting the systems of the host society, or dominant culture. Individuals in a *separation* mode reject cultural norms and values of the host society and maintain the identity of cultural origin. *Integration* encompasses individuals amalgamating newly learnt and acquired cultural values, beliefs and norms of the host society with their own identity of cultural origin. *Marginalization* refers to one's divergence from both the culture of origin and the host culture and possibly developing a third, hybrid culture. Consumer acculturation theory evolved as a specific area of enquiry into social motives and skills for consumption resulting from the diverse identity negotiations of immigrant individuals of the same origin (Peñaloza 1989). The willingness of immigrant consumers to engage with some brands has been shown to depend on whether they deploy single or multiple cultures as referent frames to perform an identity. Uni-cultural individuals enact their identity by avoiding brands whose meaning does not communicate association with the single culture they have internalized (Josiassen 2011); multicultural individuals positively respond to brands whose meanings enable them to enact their identification with internalized cultures (Luna and Peracchio 2005).

An acculturation theory approach may provide international marketing scholars with the required explanation of how and why mainstream consumers within a locale might develop differing perceptions of and attitudes toward cultural meanings of brands. Indeed, the original definitions of acculturation encompass the confluence of two or more cultures (Redfield, Linton and Herskovits 1936 in Berry 1980) and do not limit acculturation processes to cultural transitions of immigrants (Peñaloza 1989). Similarly to responses of migrant consumers to cultural meanings of brands observed by prior studies, if a brand is not perceived to accurately depict one's evolved identity dispositions, culture-based CBK may develop into a sense of "misfit" (i.e. "not me" or "not me any more") and result in neutral or even negative response among uni-cultural or multicultural mainstream consumer groups (Kleine and Kleine 2000). A handful of international marketing studies have pioneered the application of acculturation theory to analyze the differential effect of GC upon the consumption behaviors of mainstream consumers. Cleveland and Laroche (2007) and Alden, Steenkamp and Batra (2006) follow Berry's bi-dimensional model (Berry 1980) and consider diversified identity strategies adopted by mainstream consumers as a result of negotiating between local and global consumption cultures. Other studies (Leung et al. 2005; Steenkamp and De Jong 2010) identify similar outcomes (subtractive multiculturalism versus additive multiculturalism), albeit without the foundation of the acculturation theory.

Although presenting an important step forward in understanding the cultural and consumption transformations of mainstream consumers, these studies neglect FCs as the third important element identified in the concept of a multiple-cultural environment. We propose that for an acculturation approach to be utilized more fruitfully, it needs to include the "foreign culture(s)" dimension. As we demonstrate, our definition of "foreign culture(s)" accounts for the affiliative and ancestral elements of cultural identities of mainstream individuals that may not be captured in the global-local dichotomy. Hence, we extend the dimensionality of the traditional bi-dimensional acculturation model (Berry 1980) to account for multiple-cultural dimensions of mainstream consumers' contexts. We define consumer multiculturation as *a process of changes in the cultural identification and consumption behaviors of individuals that happen when the individual, social group and/or society as a whole come into continuous contact with multiple cultures.* Through the process of consumer multiculturation, identities are negotiated over time between LC, GC and one or more FCs. Through these negotiations, one develops positive or negative identity associations with each of these cultures, which results in different types of cultural identities that integrate one, two or more cultures, whether cultures of national and ethnic cultural ancestry only or other cultures that represent affiliative aspects of one's self.

Conceptual model

Based on the theorizing above, we posit eight cultural identity orientations that one may develop through multiple-cultural experiences. In line with Berry (1980), the consumer multicultural identity orientations (CMIO) matrix (Figure 11.2) maintains that the cultural identification of an individual changes as a result of interactions with multiple cultures when one regards developing or maintaining relationships with particular cultures as being of value. However, using Appadurai's (1996) metaphor of hyphenated identities, the CMIO matrix captures a broader range of identity hyphenation that may occur in a multiple-cultural environment than conceptualized previously.

Individuals may internalize: (1) multiple types of cultures, developing forms of multicultural (multi-hyphenated) identities (e.g. global-local-foreign-full adaptation; two or more foreign-local-foreign adaptation); (2) two types of cultures, developing forms of bi-cultural (hyphenated) identities (e.g. global-local-global adaptation; local-one foreign-foreign adaptation; foreign-global-imported cultures orientation); or (3) one type of culture while rejecting other types, developing or maintaining forms of uni-cultural identities (e.g. local – LC orientation, global – GC orientation or foreign – FCs orientation). The eighth orientation, alienation, is based on the conceptualization of Alden, Steenkamp and Batra (2006) and encompasses the rejection of material cultural symbols and disengagement from a materialistic lifestyle. Building on social identity-brand image congruence theory (Reed 2002), Figure 11.2 also posits consumption consequences specific to each type of orientation. Clearly, prior conceptions of global, local and glocal identity dispositions can explain culture-based CBK development when target mainstream consumers engage primarily with LC and GC. However, other dimensions of consumer multi-culturalism than glocalism (Kjeldgaard and Ostberg 2007) identified in the CMIO matrix indicate that consumer behavior theory requires a fuller appreciation of how the foreign meanings integrating with other cultural meanings in the locale may influence consumption attitudes and culture-based CBK.

Through encounters with multiple cultures (represented by people, media, brands, organizations and travel), one may become multicultural and develop identity links with LC and FC(s), yet not necessarily engage with GC; integrate positive identity dispositions towards all three forms of cultures; or select FC(s) as the focal self-referent frame for identity construal while rejecting LC

	GC	FC	LC	Consumer Multiculturation Strategy	Definition	Consumption consequence	Expectations to COBO-based brand meanings*	Linkages with culture-based COO/COBO consumer behavior theories
Is it of value to maintain or develop relationships with multiple cultural systems?	Yes	Yes	Yes	**Full adaptation**	Positive disposition towards local cultural in-group, specific foreign out-groups and global community – a hybrid blend of local, global, and particular foreign culture(s).	Willingness to consume a wide variety of brands that blend the meanings of local, global and aspired-to foreign culture(s).	GC, LC and specific FC(s)	'Thin' and 'thick' cosmopolitanism, world-mindedness, internationalism, patriotism
	No	Yes	Yes	**Foreign adaptation**	Positive disposition towards local cultural in-group and specific foreign out-group(s) combined with derogation of 'other' out-groups and global community – a hybrid blend of local and particular foreign culture(s).	Preference for brands perceived as local and originating from aspired-to culture(s).	LC and specific FC(s)	'Thick' cosmopolitanism, patriotism, ethnocentrism, nationalism
	Yes	No	Yes	**Global adaptation (globalized identity)**	Positive disposition towards local cultural in-group and global out-group. A hybrid blend of local and global cultures, with no identification with particular foreign culture(s).	Willingness to consume a wide variety of brands that blend global and local cultures' meanings.	GC and LC	'Thin' cosmopolitanism, world-mindedness, internationalism, patriotism
	Yes	Yes	No	**Imported cultures orientation**	Negative disposition toward local cultural in-group combined with strong aspiration to global community and particular foreign culture(s).	Derogation of one's own country products and preference for global brands and brands perceived origin from particular foreign cultures.	GC and specific FC(s)	Xenocentrism, 'thin' cosmopolitanism
	Yes	No	No	**Global culture orientation**	Negative disposition toward local cultural in-group and aspiration toward homogenous global culture.	Preference for 'truly global' (transnational) brands and global-perceived brands.	GC	'Thin' cosmopolitanism
	No	Yes	No	**Foreign culture orientation**	Negative disposition toward local cultural in-group combined with strong aspiration toward particular foreign out-group(s).	Selective preference of brands perceived origin from aspired-to culture(s).	Specific FC(s)	Xenocentrism
	No	No	Yes	**Local culture orientation**	Positive disposition towards local cultural in-group combined with negative attitude towards all out-groups.	Favoritism of local-perceived brands.	LC	Ethnocentrism, rationalism, patriotism
	No	No	No	**Alienation**	Rejection or lack of interest in material symbols of all cultures.	Product evaluations are based on their functional characteristics (i.e. price, etc.) or on 'no-brand' cues.	No COBO-based brand meanings	

Figure 11.2 CMIO matrix

and GC. Diversifying identity dispositions will elicit a diversification of the culture-based CBK formation process as mainstream consumers of different cultural identity orientations will manifest their dispositions through a willingness to consume brands perceived to materialize culturally congruent meanings. That is, since cultural identity dispositions influence consumer elaboration of the consideration set, association of a given brand with a culture(s) rejected through identity negotiation in a multiple-cultural environment may result in consumers having no willingness to elaborate on specific characteristics of brand image and therefore having low levels of awareness or specific knowledge about the attributes of the brand. Similarly, if consumers reject material symbols of cultures (Alienation CMIO), they will respond negatively to brands perceived to symbolize cultural belonging or ideologies and have no willingness to elaborate on other attributes. Conversely, some consumers may be more responsive to brands perceived to represent explicit foreign meanings either instead of or in addition to global and/or local meanings.

Finally, an analysis of culture-based CBK formation within the CMIO framework also highlights a major disconnect that challenges the explanatory power of the theories of COO stereotyping (Batra et al. 2000) and out-group orientations (Sampson and Smith 1957) in multiple-cultural environments. Linking national/ethnic identification or out-group cultural biases to consumption, these theories distinguish notably differing COBO-based attitudes, from: (1) favoritism of home country/culture and its produce and rejection of all non-local (i.e. global and foreign) cultures and products (Han 1988; Shimp and Sharma 1987) or particular FCs and products (Klein, Ettenson and Morris 1998); to (2) aspiration of non-local and/or particular FCs and preference of foreign-perceived products (Cannon and Yaprak 2002; Mueller, Broderick and Kipnis 2009). Table 11.3 summarizes key definitions.

Figure 11.2 details the implicit linkages between CMIO and COBO-based consumer behavior theories summarized in Table 11.3. These linkages highlight that each of the individual COBO-based theories captures only one of the many potential cultural choices guiding consumption in multicultural marketplaces, failing to produce an integrative picture that explains the attitudes of culturally diverse consumer base. The theories summarized in Table 11.3 explored consumer behaviors and attitudes toward local and non-local products in isolation from one another and offer explanations of consumers' culture-informed attitudes and behaviors that may be perceived as mutually exclusive. However, establishing that consumers are not ethnocentric (Shimp and Sharma 1987) does not explain whether consumers are xenocentric (Kent and Burnight 1951) or cosmopolitan (Cannon and Yaprak 2002). Similarly, the theory of consumer xenocentrism (Mueller, Broderick and Kipnis 2009) establishes consumers' general preference for foreign products and derogation of one's own country products, but it does not explain whether this favoritism is general or culture-specific.

Further, analysis of culture-based CBK formation within the CMIO framework offers some explanation to the emerged variances and complex

Table 11.3 Summary definitions of COO/COBO-based consumer behavior theories

Construct	Definition	Consumption implications	Literature references
Cosmopolitanism	"Willingness to engage with the other" (Hannerz 1992: 252); readiness to engage with diverse cultural experiences (i.e. world citizenship); aspiration to dynamic cultivation of cultural capital and commitment to being non-judgemental and objective when processing cultural experiences	Tendency to consume a wide variety of products associated with different countries/cultures, product evaluations are not based on local/national traditions	Cannon and Yaprak (2002) and Hannerz (1992)
World-mindedness	Acceptance and adaptability to ideas and cultural norms of other countries/cultures. Concern for social and environmental issues in context of the world	Openness to, interest in and adoption of consumption norms and products of foreign countries/cultures	Hannerz (1992)
Cultural openness	Acceptance or no hostility toward FCs	General openness and lack of negative attitude to products of foreign countries/cultures	Sharma, Shimp and Jeongshin (1995)
Xenocentrism	Favorable attitudes toward out-groups combined with ingroup derogation	Aspiration toward and preference of foreign products	Kent and Burnight (1951) and Mueller, Broderick and Kipnis (2009)
Internationalism	Positive feelings for other nations and their people, concern for welfare of people in other countries	Favoritism of foreign products to support other countries/cultures	Kosterman and Feshbach (1989)
Ethnocentrism	Favorable attitude toward the in-group combined with an unfavorable attitude toward out-groups	A belief about inappropriateness of buying foreign products	Shimp and Sharma (1987)
Patriotism	Strong emotional attachment to own country	A belief of duty to purchase domestic products	Druckman (1994) and Han (1988)
Nationalism	Emotional belief in own country's superiority combined with hostility toward the others	Favoritism of domestic products fueled by belief and willingness for own country's economic superiority, combined with boycott of foreign products	Druckman (1994) and Frank (1999)

relationships between individual culture-based attitudes and behaviors identified by a number of extant studies. Cannon and Yaprak (2002) establish that individuals harboring cosmopolitan values may differ in their attachment to their LC. Current sociological research identifies that cosmopolitan values can be either directed toward particular cultures/countries/regions (i.e. "rooted" or "thick" cosmopolitanism), or indicate openness to and acceptance of diverse cultural norms on a global scale (i.e. "thin" cosmopolitanism) (Roudometof 2005). Shankarmahesh (2006) challenges the accepted view of attributing the concepts of cultural openness (Sharma, Shimp and Jeongshin 1995) and worldmindedness (Hannerz 1992) exclusively to consumers' willingness to engage with non-local cultural experiences and products. Shankarmahesh's (2006) study draws antecedent socio-psychological links between cultural openness and world-mindedness and in-group cultural identification and domestic consumption and posits that culturally open individuals may become ethnocentric through judgment of other cultures at the point of self-identification. It would be reasonable to presume that in multiple-cultural environments where consumer interaction with several cultures is virtually inevitable, multicultural consumer identification influences consumption attitudes and behaviors such that consumers may integrate varying, at times contradictory, responses and attitudes to domestic, foreign and GCs. For example, consumers internalizing LC and specific FC(s) (foreign adaptation) will harbor culture-based attitudes differing from the attitudes harbored by the consumers internalizing the global and LCs (global adaptation). The former may be willing to engage with experiences from specific FCs but not with the experiences from all over the world ("thick" cosmopolitanism) and at the same time harbor ethnocentric, patriotic and nationalistic attitudes toward their LC and FC(s) they identify with. The latter would harbor positive attitudes toward other nations and their representatives and be willing to engage with diverse cultural experiences on a global scale ("thin" cosmopolitanism, world-mindedness and internationalism), and remain patriotic toward their LC.

We do not question the validity of fundamental constructs such as ethnocentrism or cosmopolitanism as in some cases they may indeed enable a better explanation of culture-based behaviors. Rather, we build on these individual theories to: (1) outline a research agenda for consumer behavior research by highlighting some of the limitations arising when using these theories to explain the complexities in culture-based attitudes and behaviors of consumers in multicultural marketplaces; and (2) develop an integrated framework that caters for these limitations. Individual theories may be reducing the complexity of culture-informed consumption in multicultural marketplaces as they focus on a particular behavioral phenomenon in response to particular COO/COBO cues. Conversely, the CMIO matrix places emphasis on the analysis of identity negotiations at the point of contact with each type of culture. As localization, delocalization, translocalization and hybridization transform marketplaces into locales where multiple cultural meanings become interwoven, foreign and global meanings may be rejected, accepted for niche consumption (i.e.

certain populations or certain circumstances), widely adopted as distinct global or foreign ideologies, or internalized and adapted as new, hybrid cultural meanings made relevant to the specifics of local ideologies within a given marketplace (Eckhardt and Mahi 2004). Capturing these responses simultaneously through the CMIO matrix, rather than through the application of individual COBO-based theories, allows a better grounded study of culture-based CBK formation in multicultural marketplaces that takes account of the intricacies of cultural identity discourse affecting consumers in their locale.

Conclusions and further research

This paper proposed the concept of consumer multiculturation to advance understanding of diverse identity transitions and their impact on consumption and CBK of mainstream consumer groups in multicultural marketplaces. By integrating the literature on the multicultural consumption of ethnic migrant groups with the stream of existing knowledge on consumer responses to GC, LC and FC(s), we have shown that multiculturalism is not limited to migrant groups and that studies of mainstream consumers' cultural identity processes should be extended from the usual global-local dichotomy to include other FC(s) dimensions. We developed a conceptual framework that considers the contemporary cultural landscape as a complex multiple-cultural environment where people interact with multiple types of cultures concomitantly. It conceptualizes the process of mainstream consumer cultural identity formation as consumer multiculturation and considers varying types of identities that emerge depending on whether mainstream individuals develop positive or negative affiliations with one, two or more cultures. A comprehensive range of eight possible identity orientations results, and we consider the implications of CMIO for CBK. Finally, we show how these CMIO may relate to the theories of country- or culture-of-origin-based consumption behaviors.

Overall, consumer multiculturation offers the promise, for international marketing researchers, of a parsimonious framework within which diverse consumer behaviors such as ethnocentrism, xenocentrism and cosmopolitanism can be analyzed and accounted for. The CMIO framework enhances the predictive power of COBO-based consumer behaviors and eliminates the "noise" and confusion of multiple theories on FC/LC bias. It opens up several avenues for further research. First, research should focus on exploring and confirming the dimensionality of the proposed construct of consumer multiculturation. Of particular interest would be multicultural identity orientations (i.e. full adaptation, foreign adaptation and imported cultures orientation) and alienation, as knowledge about these orientations in mainstream populations is scarce. Further research can shed light on the psychosocial antecedents of these behaviors.

Second, further research would benefit from exploring the dimensions of consumer multiculturation empirically and testing them in various cross-cultural settings. For example, acculturation literature boasts a wealth of immigrant-specific scales (Cuellar, Arnold and Maldonado 1995; Lerman, Maldonado and Luna 2009). These scales, however, do not account for multiple dimensions of cultural identity and they are not directly transferrable to research on mainstream consumers. Appropriate measures would enable the empirical testing of the conceptualized linkages between consumer multiculturation orientation and individual theories of consumer response to foreign/domestic perceived brands. Finally, the diversification of cultural contexts within marketplaces may require that, in addition to glocal branding, novel approaches to multicultural brand positioning, such as multicultural collaging (i.e. the use of multiple diverse cultural referents uncovered by Cayla and Eckhardt (2008: 223)), should be developed more prominently to support the creation of brand meanings that are more congruent with the multicultural identity dispositions of some consumer groups. Previous research investigating the use of multiple-cultural cues in branding has been predominantly focused on how differing combinations of COBO cues with COM, COA and COD cues influence consumer evaluations of the functional attributes of the brand such as quality and safety (Chao 2001; Insch and McBride 2004). Less is known about whether use of multiple-cultural cues may evoke strong emotional responses from consumers if the symbolic meanings of the communicated cues appeal to consumers' bi- and multi-cultural identifications.

We acknowledge that our conceptualization is not without its limitations. The focus of this paper is to consider the effects of consumers' cultural encounters within a multicultural environment on cultural identity development. Space limitations precluded us from elaborating on other factors such as social class, age, gender, economic and cultural capital identified by prior research as factors playing a significant role in the formation of cultural identity dispositions (Peñaloza 1989; Vida and Fairhurst 1999). The effects of these factors' interplay with consumer multiculturation on consumption responses to cultural experiences would be another important avenue to explore.

Although this paper focuses on the multicultural identity processes of mainstream consumers, the attractiveness of the consumer multiculturation construct is that it may offer an inclusive analysis of cultural identification within a diverse consumer base that incorporates both home nationals and multiple ethnic immigrant groups alike. While more work is needed to advance consumer multiculturation to cater for both mainstream and migrant groups, it allows a more sophisticated comprehension of identities negotiated between multiple cultures, while overcoming the weaknesses of the dichotomous "globalization versus localization" or "culture-of-origin versus new host culture" approaches. By analyzing consumers' identity orientations within a CMIO matrix, diverse positive and negative attitudes toward cultures and their products can be captured and explained. Such an approach has both theoretical and practical relevance since it addresses calls to draw from the full spectrum of diverse cultural contexts evolved through globalization, to accurately explain identity transitions and understand consumer expectations and perceptions of brand meanings (Yaprak 2008). In fact, the relevance of such an approach could not have been better summarized by anyone but Berry himself (Berry 2006: 732): "I believe that there is no longer any justification for looking at only one side of the intercultural coin in isolation from the other. To continue to do so would produce research that is both invalid and ethnocentric." The time has come for marketers to turn the intercultural coin.

Acknowledgments

The authors thank Jan-Benedict Steenkamp and Hans Baumgartner for their insightful comments on the framework. We also would like to thank the editor, Jonathan Schroeder, and three anonymous reviewers for their very helpful recommendations on the earlier versions of this paper.

References

Alden, Dana L., Jan-Benedict E. M. Steenkamp, and Rajeev Batra. 1999. "Brand Positioning Through Advertising in Asia, North America, and Europe: The Role of Global Consumer Culture." *Journal of Marketing* 63 (1): 75–87.

Alden, Dana L., Jan-Benedict E. M. Steenkamp, and Rajeev Batra. 2006. "Consumer Attitudes Toward Marketplace Globalization: Structure, Antecedents and Consequences." *International Journal of Research in Marketing* 23 (3): 227–239.

Appadurai, Arjun. 1996. *Modernity at Large: Cultural Dimensions of Globalization.* Minneapolis, MN: University of Minnesota Press.

Arnett, Jeffrey J. 2002. "The Psychology of Globalization." *American Psychologist* 57 (10): 774–783.

Arzubiaga, Angela E., Alfredo J. Artiles, Kathleen A. King, and Nancy Harris-Murri. 2008. "Beyond Research on Cultural Minorities: Challenges and Implications of Research as Situated Cultural Practice." *Exceptional Children* 74 (3): 309–327.

Askegaard, Soren. 2006. "Brands as Global Ideoscape." In *Brand Culture*, edited by Jonathan E. Schroeder and Miriam Salzer-Mörling. London: Routledge, 81–92.

Askegaard, Soren, Eric J. Arnould, and Dannie Kjeldgaard. 2005. "Postassimilationist Ethnic Consumer Research: Qualifications and Extensions." *Journal of Consumer Research* 32 (1): 160–170.

Aspinall, Peter J. 2003. "The Conceptualisation and Categorisation of Mixed Race/Ethnicity in Britain and North America: Identity Options and the Role of the State." *International Journal of Intercultural Relations* 27 (3): 269–296.

Balabanis, George, and Adamantios Diamantopoulos. 2008. "Brand Origin Identification by Consumers: A Classification Perspective." *Journal of International Marketing* 16 (1): 39–71.

Bardhi, Fleura, Giana M. Eckhardt, and Eric J. Arnould. 2012. "Liquid Relationships to Possessions." *Journal of Consumer Research* 13 (2): 133–157. doi:10.1086/664037.

Batra, Rajeev, Venkatram Ramaswamy, Dana L. Alden, Jan-Benedict E. M. Steenkamp, and S. Ramachander. 2000. "Effects of Brand Local and Nonlocal Origin on Consumer Attitudes in Developing Countries." *Journal of Consumer Psychology* 9 (2): 83–95.

Bauman, Zygmunt. 2000. *Liquid Modernity.* Cambridge: Polity Press.

Beck, Ulrich. 2000. *What Is Globalization?* Cambridge: Polity Press.

Berry, John W. 1980. "Acculturation as Varieties of Adaptation." In *Acculturation: Theory Models and Some New Findings*, edited by Amado M. Padilla. Boulder, CO: Westview, 9–25.

Berry, John W. 2006. "Mutual Attitudes Among Immigrants and Ethnocultural Groups in Canada." *International Journal of Intercultural Relations* 30 (6): 719–734.

Cannon, Hugh M., and Attila Yaprak. 2002. "Will the Real-World Citizen Please Stand Up! The Many Faces of Cosmopolitan Consumer Behavior." *Journal of International Marketing* 10 (4): 30–52.

Cayla, Julien, and Eric J. Arnould. 2008. "A Cultural Approach to Branding in the Global Marketplace." *Journal of International Marketing* 16 (4): 86–112.

Cayla, Julien, and Giana M. Eckhardt. 2008. "Asian Brands and the Shaping of a Transnational Imagined Community." *Journal of Consumer Research* 35 (2): 216–230.

Chao, Paul. 2001. "The Moderating Effects of Country of Assembly, Country of Parts, and Country of Design on Hybrid Product Evaluations." *Journal of Advertising* 30 (4): 67–81.

Chattalas, Michael, Thomas Kramer, and Hirokazu Takada. 2008. "The Impact of National Stereotypes on the Country of Origin Effect." *International Marketing Review* 25 (1): 54–74.

Cleveland, Mark, and Michel Laroche. 2007. "Acculturation to the Global Consumer Culture: Scale Development and Research Paradigm." *Journal of Business Research* 60 (3): 249–259.

Craig, Samuel C., and Susan P. Douglas. 2006. "Beyond National Culture: Implications of Cultural Dynamics for Consumer Research." *International Marketing Review* 23 (3): 322–342.

Cuellar, Israel, Bill Arnold, and Roberto Maldonado. 1995. "Acculturation Rating Scale for Mexican Americans-II: A Revision of the Original ARSMA Scale." *Hispanic Journal of Behavioral Sciences* 17 (3): 275–304.

D'Andrea, Anthony. 2007. *Global Nomads. Techno and New Age as Transnational Countercultures in Ibiza and Goa*. London: Routledge.

Druckman, Daniel. 1994. "Nationalism, Patriotism, and Group Loyalty: A Social Psychological Perspective." *International Studies Quarterly* 38 (2): 43–68.

Eckhardt, Giana M., and Humaira Mahi. 2004. "The Role of Consumer Agency in the Globalization Process in Emerging Markets." *Journal of Macromarketing* 24 (2): 136–146.

Elliott, Richard, and Kritsadarat Wattanasuwan. 1998. "Brands as Symbolic Resources for the Construction of Identity." *International Journal of Advertising* 17 (2): 131–144.

Frank, Dana. 1999. *Buy American: The Untold Story of Economic Nationalism*. Boston, MA: Beacon Press.

Frey, William H. 2009. "Mixed Race Marriages." *The Milken Institute Review*, Second Quarter (April 2009): 5–7.

Guzman, Francisco, and Audhesh K. Paswan. 2009. "Cultural Brands from Emerging Markets: Brand Image Across Host and Home Countries." *Journal of International Marketing* 17 (3): 71–86.

Han, C. Min. 1988. "The Role of Consumer Patriotism in the Choice of Domestic Versus Foreign Products." *Journal of Advertising Research* 28 (3): 25–31.

Hannerz, Ulf. 1992. *Cultural Complexity: Studies in the Social Organization of Meaning*. New York: Columbia University Press.

Hannerz, Ulf. 1996. *Transnational Connections. Culture, People, Places*. London: Routledge.

Haub, Carl. 2008. "U.S. Population Could Reach 438 Million by 2050, and Immigration Is Key." Available at: www.prb.org/Articles/2008/pewprojections.aspx.

Hermans, Huber J. M., and Harry J. G. Kempen. 1998. "Moving Cultures: The Perilous Problems of Cultural Dichotomies in a Globalizing Society." *American Psychologist* 53 (10): 1111–1120.

Holliday, Adrian. 2010. "Complexity in Cultural Identity." *Language & Intercultural Communication* 10 (2): 165–177.

Hsieh, Ming-Huei, and Andrew Lindridge. 2005. "Universal Appeals with Local Specifications." *Journal of Product & Brand Management* 14 (1): 14–28.

Insch, Gary S., and J. Brad McBride. 2004. "The Impact of Country-of-Origin Cues on Consumer Perceptions of Product Quality: A Binational Test of the Decomposed Country-of-Origin Construct." *Journal of Business Research* 57 (3): 256–265.

Iwabuchi, Koichi. 2002. "From Western Gaze to Global Gaze." In *Global Culture: Media, Arts, Policy and Globalization*, edited by Diane Crane, Nobuko Kawashima, and Kenichi I. Kawasaki. London: Routledge, 256–270.

Jamal, Ahmad. 2003. "Marketing in a Multicultural World: The Interplay of Marketing, Ethnicity and Consumption." *European Journal of Marketing* 37 (11/12): 1599–1620.

Jameson, Daphne A. 2007. "Reconceptualizing Cultural Identity and Its Role in Intercultural Business Communication." *Journal of Business Communication* 44 (3): 199–235.

Jiménez, Tomas R. 2010. "Affiliative Ethnic Identity: A More Elastic Link Between Ethnic Ancestry and Culture." *Ethnic and Racial Studies* 33 (10): 1756–1775.

Josiassen, Alexander. 2011. "Consumer Disidentification and Its Effects on Domestic Product Purchases: An Empirical Investigation in The Netherlands." *Journal of Marketing* 75 (2): 124–140.

Keillor, Bruce D., and G. Thomas M. Hult. 1999. "A Five-Country Study of National Identity: Implications for International Marketing Research and Practice." *International Marketing Review* 16 (1): 65–84.

Keller, Kevin L. 1993. "Conceptualizing, Measuring, Managing Customer-Based Brand Equity." *Journal of Marketing* 57 (1): 1–22.

Keller, Kevin L. 2003. "Brand Synthesis: The Multidimensionality of Brand Knowledge." *Journal of Consumer Research* 29 (4): 595–600.

Kent, Donald P., and Robert G. Burnight. 1951. "Group Centrism in Complex Societies." *American Journal of Sociology* 57 (3): 256–259.

Kjeldgaard, Dannie, and Soren Askegaard. 2006. "The Glocalization of Youth Culture: The Global Youth Segment as Structures of Common Difference." *Journal of Consumer Research* 33 (2): 231–247.

Kjeldgaard, Dannie, and Jacob Ostberg. 2007. "Coffee Grounds and the Global Cup: Glocal Consumer Culture in Scandinavia." *Consumption Markets & Culture* 10 (2): 175–187.

Klein, Jill G., Richard Ettenson, and Marlene D. Morris. 1998. "The Animosity Model of Foreign Product Purchase: An Empirical Test in the People's Republic of China." *Journal of Marketing* 62 (1): 89–100.

Kleine, Robert E., III, and Susane S. Kleine. 2000. "Consumption and Self-Schema Changes Throughout the Identity Project Life Cycle." *Advances in Consumer Research* 27 (1): 279–285.

Korff, Ruediger. 2003. "Local Enclosures of Globalization. The Power of Locality." *Dialectical Anthropology* 27 (1): 1–18.

Kosterman, Rick, and Seymour Feshbach. 1989. "Toward a Measure of Patriotic and Nationalistic Attitudes." *Political Psychology* 10 (2): 257–274.

Lau-Gesk, Loraine G. 2003. "Activating Culture Through Persuasion Appeals: An Examination of the Bicultural Consumer." *Journal of Consumer Psychology* 13 (3): 301.

Leclerc, France, Bernd H. Schmitt, and Laurett Dube. 1994. "Foreign Branding and Its Effects on Product Perceptions and Attitudes." *Journal of Marketing Research* 31 (2): 263–270.

Lerman, Dawn, Rachel Maldonado, and David Luna. 2009. "A Theory-Based Measure of Acculturation: The Shortened Cultural Life Style Inventory." *Journal of Business Research* 62 (4): 399–406.

Leung, Kwok, Rabi S. Bhagat, Nancy R. Buchan, Miriam Erez, and Cristina B. Gibson. 2005. "Culture and International Business: Recent Advances and Their Implications for Future Research." *Journal of International Business Studies* 36 (4): 357–378.

Lim, Kerry, and Aron O'Cass. 2001. "Consumer Brand Classifications: An Assessment of Culture-of-Origin Versus Country-of-Origin." *Journal of Product & Brand Management* 10 (2): 120–137.

Luedicke, Marius K. 2011. "Consumer Acculturation Theory: (Crossing) Conceptual Boundaries." *Consumption Markets & Culture* 14 (3): 223–244.

Luna, David, and Laura A. Peracchio. 2005. "Advertising to Bilingual Consumers: The Impact of Code-Switching on Persuasion." *Journal of Consumer Research* 31 (4): 760–765.

McCracken, Grant. 1990. *Culture and Consumption: New Approaches to the Symbolic Character of Consumer Goods and Activities.* Bloomington, IN: Indiana University Press.

Mikhailitchenko, Andrey, Rajshekhar G. Javalgi, Galina Mikhailitchenko, and Michel Laroche. 2009. "Cross-Cultural Advertising Communication: Visual Imagery, Brand Familiarity, and Brand Recall." *Journal of Business Research* 62 (10): 931–938.

Mueller, Rene D., Amanda J. Broderick, and Eva Kipnis. 2009. *Consumer Xenocentrism: An Alternative Explanation for Foreign Product Bias.* Charleston, SC: College and University of Charleston. Unpublished Working Paper.

Nakata, Cheryl C. 2003. "Culture Theory in International Marketing: An Ontological and Epistemological Examination." In *Handbook of Research in International Marketing,* edited by Subhash C. Jain. Cheltenham: Edward Edgar, 428–469.

Oberecker, Eva M., Petra Riefler, and Adamantios Diamantopoulos. 2008. "The Consumer Affinity Construct: Conceptualization, Qualitative Investigation, and Research Agenda." *Journal of International Marketing* 16 (3): 23–56.

Oswald, Laura R. 1999. "Culture Swapping: Consumption and the Ethnogenesis of Middle-Class Haitian Immigrants." *Journal of Consumer Research* 25 (4): 303–318.

Oxford Dictionaries. 2010. "Oxford University Press." Available at: http://oxford dictionaries.com/view/entry/m_en_gb0309920.

Özsomer, Aysegul, and Selin Altaras. 2008. "Global Brand Purchase Likelihood: A Critical Synthesis and an Integrated Conceptual Framework." *Journal of International Marketing* 16 (4): 1–28.

Parsons, Talcott. 1951. *The Social System.* London: Routledge.

Pecotich, Anthony, and Steven Ward. 2007. "Global Branding, Country of Origin and Expertise." *International Marketing Review* 24 (3): 271–296.

Peñaloza, Lisa N. 1989. "Immigrant Consumer Acculturation." *Advances in Consumer Research* 16 (1): 110–118.

Pharr, Julie M. 2005. "Synthesizing Country-of-Origin Research from the Last Decade: Is the Concept Still Salient in an Era of Global Brands?" *Journal of Marketing Theory & Practice* 13 (4): 34–45.

Phinney, Jean S. 2005. "Ethnic Identity in Late Modern Times: A Response to Rattansi and Phoenix." *Identity* 5 (2): 187–194.

Redfield, Robert, Ralph Linton, and Melville J. Herskovits. 1936. "Memorandum for the Study of Acculturation." *American Anthropologist* 38 (1): 149–152.

Reed, Americus, II. 2002. "Social Identity as a Useful Perspective for Self-Concept-Based Consumer Research." *Psychology & Marketing* 19 (3): 235–266.

Robinson, William I. 2001. "Social Theory and Globalization: The Rise of a Transnational State." *Theory and Society* 30 (2): 157–200.

Roth, Katharina P., and Adamantios Diamantopoulos. 2009. "Advancing the Country Image Construct." *Journal of Business Research* 62 (7): 726–740.

Roudometof, Victor. 2005. "Transnationalism, Cosmopolitanism and Glocalization." *Current Sociology* 53 (1): 113–135.

Sampson, Donald L., and Howard P. Smith. 1957. "A Scale to Measure World-Minded Attitudes." *Journal of Social Psychology; Political, Racial and Differential Psychology* 45: 99–106.

Schroeder, Jonathan E. 2009. "The Cultural Codes of Branding." *Marketing Theory* 9 (1): 123–126.

Sekhon, Yasmin K., and Isabelle Szmigin. 2009. "The Bicultural Value System." *International Journal of Market Research* 51 (6): 751–771.

Shankarmahesh, Mahesh N. 2006. "Consumer Ethnocentrism: An Integrative Review of Its Antecedents and Consequences." *International Marketing Review* 23 (2): 146–172.

Sharma, Subhash, Terence A. Shimp, and Shin Jeongshin. 1995. "Consumer Ethnocentrism: A Test of Antecedents and Moderators." *Journal of the Academy of Marketing Science* 23 (1): 26–37.

Shimp, Terence A., and Subhash Sharma. 1987. "Consumer Ethnocentrism: Construction and Validation of the CETSCALE." *Journal of Marketing Research* 24 (3): 280–289.

Srinivasan, Narasimhan, Subhash C. Jain, and Kiranjit Sikand. 2004. "An Experimental Study of Two Dimensions of Country-of-Origin (Manufacturing Country and Branding Country) Using Intrinsic and Extrinsic Cues." *International Business Review* 13 (1): 65–82.

Steenkamp, Jan-Benedict E. M., Rajeev Batra, and Dana L. Alden. 2003. "How Perceived Brand Globalness Creates Brand Value." *Journal of International Business Studies* 34 (1): 53–65.

Steenkamp, Jan-Benedict E. M., and Martin G. De Jong. 2010. "A Global Investigation Constellation of Consumer Attitudes Toward Global and Local Products." *Journal of Marketing* 74 (6): 18–40.

Strizhakova, Yuliya, Robin A. Coulter, and Linda L. Price. 2008. "Branded Products as a Passport to Global Citizenship: Perspectives from Developed and Developing Countries." *Journal of International Marketing* 16 (4): 57–85.

Supphellen, Magne, and Kjell Gronhaug. 2003. "Building Foreign Brand Personalities in Russia: The Moderating Effect of Consumer Ethnocentrism." *International Journal of Advertising* 22 (2): 203–226.

Varman, Rohit, and Janeen A. Costa. 2013. "Underdeveloped Other in Country-of-Origin Theory and Practices." *Consumption Markets & Culture.* doi:10.1080/10253866.2012.668366.

Verlegh, Peeter W. J. 1999. "Ingroups, Outgroups and Stereotyping: Consumer Behavior and Social Identity Theory." *Advances in Consumer Research* 26 (1): 162–164.

Vida, Irena, and Ann Fairhurst. 1999. "Factors Underlying the Phenomenon of Consumer Ethnocentricity: Evidence from Four Central European Countries." *International Review of Retail, Distribution & Consumer Research* 9 (4): 321–337.

Wamwara-Mbugua, L. Waikiuru, T. Bettina Cornwell, and Gregory Boller. 2008. "Triple Acculturation: The Role of African Americans in the Consumer Acculturation of Kenyan Immigrants." *Journal of Business Research* 61 (2): 83–90.

Waters, Mary C. 2008. *Comparing Immigrant Integration in Britain and the US.* Cambridge, MA: Harvard University. Paper prepared for the Harvard Manchester Initiative on Social Change.

Wilk, Richard R. 1995. "Learning to be Local in Belize: Global Systems of Common Difference." In *Worlds Apart: Modernity Through the Prism of the Local*, edited by Daniel Miller. London: Routledge, 110–133.

Wimmer, Andrea, and Nina Glick Schiller. 2002. "Methodological Nationalism and Beyond: Nation State Building, Migration and the Social Sciences." *Global Networks* 2 (4): 301.

Witkowski, Terrence H. 2005. "Antiglobal Challenges to Marketing in Developing Countries: Exploring the Ideological Divide." *Journal of Public Policy & Marketing* 24 (1): 7–23.

Wohland, Pia, Phil Rees, Paul Norman, Peter Boden, and Martyna Jasinska. 2010. "Ethnic Population Projections for the UK and Local Areas 2001–2051." Working Paper 10/02. University of Leeds. Available at: www.geog.leeds.ac.uk/fileadmin/downloads/school/research/projects/migrants/WP_ETH_POP_PROJECTIONS.pdf (accessed December 3, 2010).

Yaprak, Attila. 2008. "Culture Study in International Marketing: A Critical Review and Suggestions for Future Research." *International Marketing Review* 25 (2): 215–229.

Zhang, Shi, and Bernd H. Schmitt. 2001. "Creating Local Brands in Multilingual International Markets." *Journal of Marketing Research* 38 (3): 313–325.

12 The role of commodified celebrities in children's moral development

The case of David Beckham

Patricia Gayá Wicks, Agnes Nairn and Christine Griffin

Introduction

The moral dimension of marketing to children is a hotly debated subject as witnessed by a recent flurry of best-selling titles such as *Toxic Childhood* (Palmer 2006), *The Commercialisation of Childhood* (Compass 2006) and *Born to Buy* (Schor 2004). In line with a rich academic literature on the consumer socialisation of children (see Roedder John 1999 for a 25-year review), the "moral" focus of such work tends to be on the ethical implications of engaging with children as a specific market segment. In contrast, this article explores the more subtle and complex roles that consumption culture may play in the moral development of children themselves, an area that has received far less attention. We take as our point of departure Cook's (2004: 148) observation that the "conceptual and analytical import" of children's consumer culture has tended to be overshadowed by (the quite justifiable) moral solicitude focused on fighting against aggressive marketing to children. We build specifically on his view that "children's involvement with the materials, media, images and meanings that arise from, refer to and are entangled with the world of commerce figures centrally in the making of persons and of moral positions in contemporary life" (Cook 2004: 149).

In advancing our arguments, we concentrate on the role of commodified celebrities in children's understanding of moral questions, taking English soccer hero David Beckham as an example. Celebrities have become a pivotal part of our consumer culture and their importance can usefully be understood through Kellner's (2006) critique of media culture and the triumph of the spectacle. Kellner borrows from French theorist Guy Debord's ([1967] 1977) concept of the *society of the spectacle*, which "describes a media and consumer society organized around the production and consumption of images, commodities, and staged events" (Kellner 2006: 2). Kellner expands on this by arguing that "Media spectacles are those phenomena of media culture which embody contemporary society's basic values, serve to enculturate individuals into its way of life, and dramatize its controversies and struggles, as well as its modes of conflict resolution" (Kellner 2006: 2). Celebrity figures are themselves manufactured and managed components of the media spectacle, and as Kellner (2006: 5) explains, they "provide dominant role models." We suggest that Beckham's embodiment and reinforcement of particular values, norms and behaviours (whether intentional or not) occurs under conditions of high visibility and close scrutiny and thus make him a relevant locus of attention for understanding aspects of children's moral development in the context of consumer culture.

Morality, celebrity and children's moral development

The objective of this paper is thus to consider some of the ways in which the culture of celebrity and spectacle contribute to the construction of role models and cultural icons, and the ways in which children might draw on such constructions in developing their own moral discourses. The paper is structured around three key questions. First, how do children draw on the central cultural and social resources furnished by celebrities to inform the relational processes that shape their understanding of moral issues? Second, what kind of morality is likely to emerge when iconic celebrities become a site in which children's relationship to moral issues is developed? Third, what does this mean for children's understanding of a global media culture, which revolves around a culture of spectacle and commodified celebrity?

We begin by examining the role model position occupied by celebrities in contemporary culture and the specific and special place occupied by David Beckham in an English context. From here, we briefly consider the traditional view of children's moral development and consumer socialisation and we question the applicability of such views when the site of moral development is celebrities. Next, we present findings from a qualitative study of 150 junior school children on the role of branded commodities in their everyday lives. We concentrate on children's discourse around Beckham and analyse the nature of the morality that spontaneously emerges from their intense debate and negotiation. We conclude by discussing the implications for those interested in childhood moral development in a society of the spectacular, including marketing practitioners and researchers, teachers, parents and policymakers.

Celebrity role models

Children's active engagement with celebrities can be understood as a healthy, generative dynamic, at least in part. For example, White and O'Brien contend that:

> Playing out hero themes is one way in which children come to understand their society, their role within that society, and their potential for positive

impact on it. Since heroes are individuals, they offer young students something specific and concrete to study.

(White and O'Brien 1999: 83)

That celebrities influence how young people understand themselves and the world around them is supported by Biskup and Pfister (1999), who focus on the social construction of gender and body identities and consider the extent to which athletes serve as role models for boys and girls. They summarise the appeal of celebrity role models thus:

> [Role-models and idols] offer essential help and orientation, for children and adolescents in particular. This is especially true in the case of stars and idols who, constantly produced and presented by the mass media, take on the functions of role-models . . . [and] . . . bring sparkle and glamour into the workaday routine.

(Biskup and Pfister 1999: 99)

That role models and idols are *produced* and *presented* by the mass media is an important point. Children of today have, throughout their lifetimes, been exposed to the heightened consumer and media culture increasingly associated with sports in general and, in the UK, with soccer specifically (Swain 2000). Indeed, in recent years, much attention has been given to celebrity endorsement (often in the shape of successful sportspeople) as a marketing strategy by both marketing researchers and practitioners. But Biskup and Pfister (1999) argue that celebrities and role models do more than add a dash of excitement to young people's lives or the products they endorse: they also generally represent and *reinforce* prevailing values and norms.

David Beckham: a celebrity *par excellence*

David Beckham is one of the most iconic sportspersons of recent times. An English soccer player, he has achieved fame and recognition worldwide both on and off the pitch. From 1995 to 2002, Beckham played for Manchester United, one of the most successful clubs in England. In 2002, he transferred to the Spanish club Real Madrid.

In January 2007, Beckham announced that he had signed a new multi-million dollar contract with the US soccer team LA Galaxy, which he is due to join at the end of the present season. Beckham captained the English national team from November 2000 until the end of England's campaign in the 2006 World Cup. He became a household name both in the UK and abroad not only because of his performance as a midfielder and his famous "crosses" and "free kicks," but also because of his relationship with wife Victoria, formerly a member of the pop music girl-band Spice Girls. The couple—commonly known as "Posh and Becks"—have regularly occupied the media limelight since the start of their relationship in 1997. In these various spheres—as a soccer legend, half of a celebrity couple and a fashion icon—Beckham has attracted hype and vilification in equal measures.

Significantly, Beckham's celebrity is also highly commodified: he is involved in many lucrative marketing initiatives and sponsorship deals, as part of a phenomenon that is widely referred to as "Brand Beckham." In some respects, then, Beckham may be understood as a branded commodity with global reach, and available for consumption through the commercialisation of football, celebrity magazines, his own branded clothing range for younger children, and the various brands and products he endorses. Soon after his contract with LA Galaxy was announced, the club's president, Alexi Lalas, went on the record as saying that David Beckham is "worth every penny [of his five-year deal worth $250 million]; since we announced the deal we've sold thousands of tickets and shirts . . . He will help revolutionise Major League Soccer economically and from a football point of view." Lalas continues: "He has given the club a lot although he hasn't even played yet. If you want something great, you have to pay for it" (*BBC News Online* 2007). It is hardly surprising, then, that significant interest has been shown by the academic community in David Beckham as a contemporary cultural and consumer icon and commodified celebrity who is a brand in his own right (see Ireson 2001; Cashmore and Parker 2003; Giardina 2003; Parker and Steinberg 2004; Kellner 2006).

In making further sense of David Beckham's iconicity, we draw on Holt's (2003) proposition that brands or individuals become icons when they forge a deep connection with the culture, and when they speak to important and contested aspects of the national ideology. Such myths and/or icons "provide ideals to live by, and they work to resolve life's most vexing questions" (Holt 2003: 44). On the one hand, Beckham's iconicity could be understood to speak to the national conversation around such aspects of modern life as celebrity; style; success; performance and wealth. But just as Beckham's iconicity fuels the celebration and hype around these aspects of modern markets and culture, so it could be understood as a concentrated site for the problematisation of the same. Our interest in this paper is in how children draw on Beckham as a cultural and social resource through which to engage with complex moral dilemmas as part of the process of their moral development in the context of their relational social worlds.

Approaches to children's consumer socialisation and moral reasoning

Until recently, the dominant approach to understanding *both* the moral development *and* the consumer socialisation of the child rested on a general acceptance of Jean Piaget's (1960, 1967) age-stage model of childhood cognitive and social development, sometimes termed "developmentalism." In developmentalism, the child's mental and interactive capacities evolve in a linear fashion through a set of biologically predetermined stages. In line with this understanding of the child, much of the focus of consumer research has been on the effects of age on the emergence and use of brand meanings (see Belk, Bahn and Meyer 1982; Belk, Mayer and Driscoll 1984; Valkenburg and Cantor 2001; Achereiner and Roedder John 2003). Correspondingly, those concerned with enhancing children's ability to act as educated consumers have focused on identifying ways to improve their knowledge-acquisition skills (see Peracchio 1992); and, indeed, recent research published in this journal provides a useful critique of discursive representations which construct children and advertising in relation to one another in the increasingly popular field of media literacy education (see O'Sullivan 2007). Tellingly, in her landmark review of 25 years of research into consumer socialisation of children, the organising conceptual framework appropriated by Roedder John (1999) centres on successive stages of development, "with each stage characterizing children's thinking, reasoning, and processing at particular ages" (Roedder John 1999: 184). More recently, Chaplin and Roedder John (2005) have explored the extent to which children, like adults, draw on brands to create and communicate their self-concepts, but the focus remains on age-related differences and developmental factors affecting such self-brand connections. Thus, much of the research in this field has been underpinned by the implicit view of children as "beings in the making who will become 'complete' persons at some point in the future" (Cook 2004: 148).

Of course, we acknowledge that "maturational influences" (Tappan 2006: 14) are important, and it is worth noting that in the study presented in this paper, 10 and 11 year olds were generally found to be more articulate and able to engage in more complex discussions of moral issues than 7 and 8 year olds. Nevertheless, we argue that over-reliance on the "developmentalist approach" may provide a somewhat limited view (see also Nairn and Griffin 2007; Nairn, Griffin and Gayá 2008). First, such an approach focuses almost exclusively on biological age, thus privileging nature over nurture in what it means to be a child, and overlooking other non-age-related factors, such as gender, ethnicity, cultural context and social class. Furthermore, the developmentalist approach adopts a predominantly cognitive perspective, and largely underplays the social dynamics of interpretation, peer-group interaction and emotion. Finally, the cognitive psychology approach seems to suggest that what it means to be a child is both timeless and universal, and does not take into account changes in the sociocultural context in which children exist.

In an effort to circumvent the above shortcomings, the framework upon which we have drawn in our study is that of Consumer Culture Theory (CCT), a term coined by Arnould and Thompson (2005: 868) to refer to "a family of theoretical perspectives that address the dynamic relationships between consumer actions, the marketplace, and cultural meanings." This framework focuses on the ways in which groups of people select, interpret, use and assign meaning to marketplace offerings "in the myriad messy contexts of everyday life" (Arnould and Thompson 2005: 875). Ritson and Elliot's (1999) study of teenagers' social uses of advertising is one example of a study situated within a CCT framework; our own study has parallels with Ritson and Elliot's (1999) study in that it seeks to understand how the research participants themselves— in this case, children between the ages of 7 and 8, and 10 and 11—adopt, adapt and assign meanings to aspects of consumer culture—in our case, commodified celebrities.

Just as the cognitive-developmentalist paradigm has dominated—and arguably restricted—the study of children's consumer socialisation, so too has it traditionally framed mainstream conversations—both theoretical and practical—around the development of moral reasoning. Sometimes referred to as "the Kohlberg legacy" (Bergman 2004), such an approach argues that the capacity for moral reasoning develops through a number of identifiable developmental stages (Kohlberg 1976; 1981), roughly corresponding to the stages of cognitive development identified by Piaget. Kantian-inspired educational psychologist Lawrence Kohlberg (1976) maintains that the highest level of moral development occurs when adults use their capacity for abstract reasoning to make decisions based on universal ethical principles, such as those related to *justice*.

That generalisable and abstractive/prescriptive moral judgements are considered to be the "hallmark of morality" (Lourenço 2003: 44) is both implicit and explicit in the work of many other moral theorists (see Turiel 1983; Colby and Kohlberg 1987; Turiel, Killen and Helwig 1987) and, indeed, is backed by a long tradition of moral philosophy, from Plato to Kant (Haynes 1998). Alternative, postmodern traditions, including those of feminist ethics (Gilligan 1982; Noddings 1984; Mullet 1988; Jaggar 1992), and critical race theory (Bell 1997, 2002; Delgado 1999; Delgado and Stefancic 2000; Barber 2001), as well as the re-emergence of virtue ethics (MacIntyre 1985; Carr and Steutel 1999), have succeeded in challenging this paradigm. Hekman (1995), for example, recognises that discourses that relegate morality to the realm of abstract principles are hegemonic in Western societies, and responsible for silencing not only the "different" moral voice (Gilligan 1982), but also the ways in which we *think* and *talk* about morality, and our understanding of ourselves as moral persons engaged in moral discourse and moral action in the messy contexts of our everyday lives.

Along similar lines, moral theorist Mark Tappan (2006: 9) poses a signifi-cant challenge to narrow definitions of moral functioning as "thinking and reasoning" about abstract principles, instead arguing that we give form and substance to our moral voices (and to our moral action) through the use and mastery of "socio-cultural tools." These tools, or "moral mediational means," include words, language and forms of discourse that originate, and are often hegemonic, in one's particular socio-historical context. Thus, Tappan (2006: 4) warns against "[limiting] our focus to individual mental functioning, on the one hand, or to the social/cultural/historical setting, on the other." Following Wertsch (1998), he proposes the notion of mediated action as a useful way to "live in the middle," since this involves focusing "on both the agent and agency, on both 'what person or kind of person performed the act' in question, and 'what means or instruments she used' (Wertsch 1998: 24)" (Tappan 2006: 4). As our interest is to consider the intersections between contemporary consumption culture and children's evolving understanding of moral ambiguities and complexities, the notion of "mediated action" or "agents-acting-with-mediational means" provides a particularly useful framework, to which we return in the discussion of our findings.

Perspectives conceptualising both morality and consumption in ways which recognise the place of the concrete human person, situated in a specific time and place and connected to other thinking-feeling persons in complex processes of meaning making, therefore form the conceptual framework for our empirical work, to which we now turn.

Method

The findings reported here emerged from a larger empirical study that posed the following question: *How do children mobilise, interpret and assign social meaning to the brand symbols made available to them?* In 28 group discussions with children from two junior schools in England, we sought to explore children's engagement with brands and consumption culture from a contextual perspective, as a social interpretive phenomenon and as something that is a product of, as well as actively productive of, a specific historical period peopled with specific actors. Methodological decisions were taken with the following overarching purpose in mind: we wished to discover how children themselves adopt, adapt and assign meanings to consumption objects and commercial influences in their everyday lives. Specifically, in line with our intention to capture a child's view, rather than an adult's view, we wanted to ensure that the consumption objects included in our study were those that children saw as meaningful to them. This is an important departure from previous studies on children's consumer socialisation, where the subject matter for discussion is suggested by adults (Belk, Bahn and Mayer 1982; Belk, Mayer and Driscoll 1984). Indeed, more broadly, recent research published in this journal argues that "an important unrealised possibility for solving the 'problem' of advertising to children would be to refocus the research agenda on children's, rather than adults', perspectives" (O'Sullivan 2007: 309). Our aim was also to move away from conventional Piagetian-centred approaches that emphasise cognitive development as a key factor determining how children relate to consumption. Arguably, such approaches focus on ascertaining the extent to which children of different ages can correctly interpret the adult world, as if adult understandings are the ideal or objective standard by which human behaviour should be understood. Instead, our focus was on the nature of the discourses and processes through which children collectively responded to the consumption objects that they identified as particularly relevant and/or interesting.

In fulfilling the above objectives, our study was divided into two phases. The first phase was designed to identify the consumption objects for discussion in the second phase. In an effort to speak to children from a range of social and economic backgrounds, we approached one private school and one state school in a small English city. We obtained permission from the schools, parents and the children themselves to hold group discussions with 72 children (12 groups of six children), drawn in equal numbers from Year 3 (ages 7 and 8) and Year 6 (ages 10 and 11). In order to gain access to a range of social situations in which meanings could be explored, we arranged the groups so that in each school a third were girls only, a third boys only and a third mixed.

In each group, we asked the children to collectively list "the things kids in your class are into at the moment." Two researchers independently analysed the interview scripts and the lists and flip charts created during the group discussions and together selected the 14 brands mentioned most consistently across groups and that generated most excitement, interest and debate (although not necessarily consensus). These were used as the stimuli for the second part of the study (see Table 12.1). The brand list notably included a range of sports stars, pop stars and TV shows as the children clearly regarded these as symbolic commodities in the same way as toys and games.

The empirical basis for this paper lies in the findings from the second phase of the study, which took place six months after phase one (in the summer of 2005), and which consisted of facilitated in-depth discussions with a further 56 children (16 groups of three or four children) in the same year groups of the same schools. In line with our commitment to understand children's negotiations from their own point of view, rather than that of an adult, we drew our methodology for phase two from within the existential-phenomenology paradigm as applied to consumer research by Thompson, Locander and Pollio (1989). Drawing on the work of Giorgi (1983), Thompson, Locander and Pollio (1989: 133) propose that blending existential philosophy and phenomenological methodology results in a "contextually based, holistic psychology that views human beings in non-dualistic terms and seeks to attain a firstperson description of experience." In line with suggestions for this sort of research by Kvale (1983), it was important for the children as interview subjects to feel empowered to share their experiences, particularly as they were in a school setting where adults are usually in control. It was made clear from the outset that brands for discussion had been suggested by other children, not by adults, and there were no right or wrong answers, just a real interest in their own views. The researcher simply presented each group with a picture of each of the 14 brands in turn and asked, "What do you think of . . . ?"

Our dataset consisted of 390 double-spaced A4 pages of verbatim transcript and over eight hours of video footage of the children's discussions. The researcher's contribution to the discussion was less than 5 per cent (about 10 double-spaced pages out of 390) and consisted mainly of the introduction of each picture or invitations to particular children to contribute. Analysis of the body language in the videos and a word count of the contribution made by each child convinced us that none of the groups had been hijacked by a

Table 12.1 The 14 brands selected for discussion in phase two

Busted	A boy band marketed at children that split up in 2005
McFly	Another boy band marketed at children, launched after Busted and still going
Britney Spears	Twenty-something singer, popular with children
David Beckham	Celebrity captain of the England soccer team at the time of the study
The Simpsons	Popular American cartoon TV show
Barbie	Fashion doll that has been marketed to girls for over 40 years
Bratz	New series of fashion dolls marketed specifically at female "tweens"
Action Man	Action figure that has been marketed to boys for several decades
Beyblades	Small spinning tops used to fight against other children's tops
Pokemon	Japanese trading card game
PlayStation, Xbox, GameCube	Three competing brands of video games console
Yu-Gi-Oh	Japanese trading card game, produced after Pokemon

dominant child. Moreover, as we conducted 16 groups (a large number for most qualitative research purposes), the effects of one or two dominant individuals in the whole text was minimised. We thus felt we had achieved the goals of the phenomenological interview process in a group setting: attaining children's own views of their experience of brands.

Of course, the findings presented in this paper are limited in a number of ways. The research was restricted to discussions with children in two schools, both located in the same city in the South West of England. Future studies should work with a more diverse sample of children from different socio-economic and ethnic backgrounds. Furthermore, our analysis concentrated on one celebrity from the field of sport. Future work could usefully explore how children's moral discourses unfold around TV shows such as *Friends* or *The Simpsons* (the latter of which formed a further locus of attention for the children in our study), and around popular bands, particularly "manufactured" groups such as NSYNC. Indeed, for the children in our study, the question of perceived "authenticity" formed a key basis for judgemental comparison between the boy bands McFly and Busted, and future papers could look at this issue in greater detail. Along similar lines, future papers could also usefully expand on the expression of ambiguity, uncertainty and discomfort in relation to other brands that attract media vilification for their ethical credentials such as Nike and McDonald's.

Analytic procedure

Three researchers separately conducted a qualitative thematic discourse analysis of the 390 pages of transcript, using video footage for clarification of tone of voice. In line with our interpretive framework, we used an emic approach where the interpretation in the first instance relies on the respondents' own terms and category systems rather than the researchers' (Kvale 1983 cited in Thompson, Locander and Pollio 1989). The researchers met in order to challenge each other's reading of the text in an attempt to minimise interpretations not strictly emic in nature. The next stage of analysis was based on the hermeneutic circle (Bleicher 1980), which involves an iterative, part-to-whole reading strategy by which researchers develop a holistic understanding of each individual group discussion transcript, while noting similarities and differences across age groups, gender and schools.

Having been asked by the interviewer, "What do you think of David Beckham?" the children went on, unprompted, to focus on Beckham's participation in commercial spheres. Their talk about Beckham was characterised by its vehemence, high emotional tone, intensity of disputes and sharp differences of opinion regarding Beckham's sporting ability, physical appearance, family life and his involvement in commodified celebrity culture. The group discussions were also notable for the wide range of moral issues addressed by the children in their talk about Beckham and the dilemmatic quality of their discourse in this respect.

In the following sections, we present our interpretation of data that illustrates children's experience of adult narratives that constitute David Beckham as a role model in addition to their own debates and discussions around "showing off," "trying too hard" and "just reward." The data show how children were able to grapple with complexities and hold moral ambiguities around Beckham's increasingly intensified engagement in commercial spheres. We present relevant interview extracts, accompanied by our qualitative interpretation of the data.

Findings and interpretations

Perseverance, hard work and courage: children's responses to adults' narratives about Beckham

Children's accounts reflected their exposure to pervasive narratives about Beckham that circulate in popular culture or as recounted by parents and significant adults. A number of children told the story of Beckham being sent off during the 1998 World Cup, and expressed admiration for the way in which he became a stronger player following this low point in his career. In an 11-year-old boy's words:

> I think he's quite uh, hard inside because sort of things we got told about the 1998 World Cup when he missed a penalty—when he fouled, yes.

But he was sent off and everyone in England blamed it on him and most people would've just left England and deserted to another country . . . So he's quite tough . . . I admire that he, like, didn't just run away from it all. He faced up to it, and played the best football that he could.

(Boy, single-sex Year 6 group, private school)

This boy seems to be articulating, with a certain degree of clarity and sophistication, a particular set of attributes and/or behaviours that are to be applauded: in this case, "facing up to" difficulties, doing one's "best" and being "tough" and "hard inside." Interestingly, the children we interviewed would have been babies and toddlers in 1998, and indeed it appears that accounts of Beckham are, in part, shaped by the stories they themselves have been told by adults or encountered in the media. On occasion, children recounted instances in which such stories were shared with the intention to instil "perseverance," "hard work" and "courage in the face of adversity" as positive qualities to strive towards, as the following extract suggests:

Boy 1:   Um, yeah, David Beckham, he's good at football, and, um, coz Mr Rover was saying at Assembly the other day about the abuse he was suffering from, um, coz of a match against Argentina a while ago, not sure when, when he kicked someone coz he was a bit annoyed. Coz he was on the floor coz he just—

Boy 2:   That guy dived!

Boy 1:   Yeah, I know.

Interviewer: OK, so . . .

Boy 1:   And he was being abused by everybody.

Girl 1:   Yeah, he got sent off.

Boy 1:   And then in the match, or two years later, or in the next season, he was doing just amazing. He did, he gave 200 per cent, as Mr Rover says.

Interviewer: So why do you think that Mr Rover was telling you this story?

Boy 1:   Err, because he didn't give up when a lot of players probably would have, and he had the courage to face all the people who were abusing him.

(Mixed Year 6 group, private school)

Thus, we see that, in part, discourses that present Beckham as a role model seem to be *constructed* in interactions among children and significant adults. In the example presented above, it seems evident that the head-teacher perceived that the story of David Beckham's "fall from grace" and his eventual "redemption" would be an engaging and valuable lesson for children.

That such narratives are co-constructed is indicated by a 10-year-old girl's reflections on David Beckham's own account of his life, as represented, mediated and *spectacularised* in his autobiography:

> He's had like, goods and bads in his life and when he writes his autobiography so you actually know what he's been through and everything, so I think you should give him a bit of respect for what he does and everything, but sometimes he just takes it over the top.
>
> (Mixed Year 6 group, private school)

"Trying too hard": children's ambivalence towards Beckham's commodification and self-promotion

The latter sentiment (going "over the top") is a common theme in discussions around Beckham. The 10-year-old girl quoted above expresses empathy in relation to "the goods and bads in his life" and "what he's been through," as well as "respect for what he does." Thus, she seems to be differentiating between what she understands as the *actuality* of his life, which she is able to view with respect and appreciation, and what she understands as a tendency by David Beckham to want to stretch this further somehow, or "take it over the top."

So what does "taking it over the top" mean in this context? The accusation would seem to refer to several dimensions of Beckham's conduct and children's value judgements around these. In part, Beckham's perceived tendency to "overdo" things seems to be closely associated with the care and attention that he gives to his appearance, and is evidently off-putting to some children. For example, a 10-year-old boy explains:

> I don't know, I just sort of feel, I dunno like, he just tries to look, like handsome ... But he ends up being, looking like he wants to look handsome. Like he's trying too hard.
>
> (Mixed Year 6 group, state school)

The discomfort expressed by the boy above is likely to be rooted, at least in part, in hegemonic understandings of gender identity and traditional masculinity, which Beckham's behaviour might be understood to challenge to some degree (see Parker and Steinberg 2004). Additionally, we contend that the above quote says something about children's perceptions around *(in)authenticity* and the process of *spectacularisation*. The children are able to appreciate Beckham's perseverance, determination and hard work in relation to his sporting career as positive virtues. However, "trying too hard" to present himself as handsome and "looking like he wants to look handsome" is constructed as problematic by at least some of the children. We suggest that what they find troubling is the sense that he draws too much attention to himself and to his intentional, self-conscious project of commodification, and that a more subtle, low-key approach would be preferred. This is further evidenced by the following point made by an 8-year-old girl:

> I quite like him, the only thing I don't like about him is [that] he thinks too much about himself and his hairstyles, he sometimes, every match, he sometimes he just has his hair in a different place.
>
> (Mixed Year 3 group, private school)

It is significant that the child quoted above explains that what she finds disquieting is that "he thinks *too much* about himself." This suggests that he is seen as somewhat self-obsessed, and, moreover, as *consciously* and *deliberately* constructing himself to an excessive degree. This intentional self-construction is seemingly embodied through his choice of hairstyle, but, more importantly, through the perception that he is *continually* changing styles, and doing so in the public eye (in "every match").

A 10-year-old boy from a different group also expresses distaste in relation to Beckham's fashion choices and constantly changing appearance:

> Well, I'm, I'm, I don't particularly like him because he's a bit of a—he's always trying, I dunno, diamond earrings on which are worth 2 million pounds, which is actually pointless . . . And he's, kind of always shows off and like getting new hairstyles every week isn't—it's very odd . . .
>
> (Single-sex Year 6 group, private school)

The boy's assertion that Beckham is "always *trying* . . . *on*" diamond earrings, that he "always *shows off*" and that he "*[gets]* new hairstyles every week" could be saying something about David Beckham's *active* and *unceasing* involvement in presenting and calling attention to himself, in other words, in his spectacularisation. "Showing off" seems to refer to several types of behaviour, including conspicuous, wanton and spectacular consumption: consider, for example, the boy's reference to the "pointless[ness]" of the £2 million diamond earrings.

In a related vein, and as will be demonstrated hereafter, "showing off" seems also to refer to: (1) actively courting high visibility in the press; and (2) flaunting one's wealth, status and other assets (including, in the case of the male person, conventionally attractive physical appearance)—and doing so in the prospect of additional material gain. Hence, children's discourse around the appro-priateness of "showing off" seems to revolve around what it is that is being rendered too *visible* or *obvious*. In this case, Beckham's actions would seem to be making the *planned* and *conscious* element of his branded image too obvious, highlighting the fact that the commodified image of Beckham that is available for public consumption is not authentically him, but something that is purposefully *styled* and *staged*. (For a recent exploration of the dynamics of artists' (manufactured) authenticity and audiences' responses and interpreta-tions of [in]authenticity around this, as well as implications for the practice of leadership and followership, see Ladkin and Taylor 2007).

"Showing off" seems also to encompass the act of receiving too much money in exchange for insufficient work/effort. This led the children to engage with questions around just and proportionate monetary reward, to which we now turn.

The commercialisation of sport and the question of proportionate reward

While the children seemed to represent Beckham's *sporting* achievements as worthy of respect and celebration, the levels of *material* success he has attained seem to be viewed as somewhat unsettling, and give rise to questions about proportionate and just reward. In the interview extract presented below, the children appear to draw—whether consciously or unconsciously—on the opportunities offered by the present dialogical interchange to affirm their own evolving understanding of what proportionate and just reward would mean in this context. At the same time, engagement in such a dialogical space allows children to practice navigating the subtleties and uncertainties that arise. The differences of opinion gave rise to some interesting tensions, especially for some of these children who are on the edge of puberty, relating to how they make sense of others' viewpoints and how these impact on aspects of their own self-concepts.[1]

Girl 1: I hate David Beckham, he's horrible, he just shows off, every magazine I read, he's in there, he just shows off.

Girl 2: Do you know why, cause he's actually fit and no one else is fitter than him and that's why he's always in the magazines and adverts—

Boy 1: For one advert he must get about 5 million pounds!

Girl 2: That's cause he's mega fit.

Boy 1: Stop saying that, it's scary!

Girl 2: I'm trying to get round to you that he is F-I-T, that does spell "fit"!

(Mixed Year 6 group, state school)

The above exchange demonstrates that while some children expressed disbelief and discomfort at the material wealth and high visibility commanded by Beckham, others viewed his fame and fortune as the just reward for the qualities he embodies, in particular his physical attributes. While the boy and the first girl seem to be of the opinion that Beckham cannot possibly be worthy of such intense media attention and admiration, nor of such substantial financial remuneration, the second girl argues that it is his authentic and absolute claim to fitness or sexual attraction ("he's actually fit and no one else is fitter than him"), which explains and justifies this state of affairs. Hence, we see tensions experienced in interpreting the extent to which the hype around David Beckham could be seen as (dis)proportionate and/or (un)justified.

Of course, the question with which the children grapple, regarding whether the immense material rewards reaped by celebrity sportspeople are appropriate, is one that reflects undercurrents of discontent in a society in which increasingly extensive gaps in material wealth are experienced (see MacDonald and Marsh 2005).

The extract below provides further evidence that common discourses around rightness and wrongness are socially mediated and situated within specific socio-historical contexts:

> Boy 1:   I think he's a bit of a show off.
> Interviewer: A bit of a show off. Do you hear much about him? Like on TV . . .
> Boy 1:   Yeah, in the paper, that's where I've got that thing from, that he gets like loads of money, and my dad was reading it, and then, coz he doesn't like him either, I think. And then he says, "Blimey, he gets lots of money, for just sort of sitting around, doing nothing."
>
>   (Single-sex Year 6 group, state school)

Indeed, the many references to Beckham's participation in adverts and the speculation as to the large sums he receives in exchange may be interpreted as a critique of the increasing commercialisation of soccer players. This is again a trend that has elicited its share of condemnation from spectators of many walks of life. Such condemnation forms part of a situated, common discourse upon which children draw.

Grappling with complexity: the dilemmatic nature of children's moral development

We would argue that an important quality of children's discussions around David Beckham is their apparent appreciation of some of the subtleties, complexities and uncertainties that are inherent in making sense of and passing judgement on others' actions and the negotiated and dilemmatic quality of their discourses. Shortly after the (somewhat heated) "F-I-T" debate in reply to one of the boys' accusation that "All he thinks about is adverts," the second girl again defends Beckham, saying: ". . . he does, like, think about his family, because he has actually just had, what's the baby called, Cruz, that's it, and I think Brooklyn's a lot like him . . ." In their debates around David Beckham, the children grapple with the paradox of a man who epitomises the increasingly commercialised world *par excellence* and who can, at the same time, be construed as an active and engaged father and husband, a male pin-up, and, furthermore, as a role model in relation to sporting achievement, perseverance and hard work, and as an ambassador of England and long-term captain of the national team in what is popularly construed as the national sport.

Children come face to face with the many ambiguities and complexities involved in making sense of what David Beckham's persistent and intensified participation in commercial spheres means for his positioning as a successful sportsman, team captain, a would-be role model and even a committed family man. The 8-year-old girl quoted below, for example, attempts to articulate her sense that fame and performance do not necessarily go hand in hand. If anything, the child seems to be pointing to a causal link between "thinking too much of himself" and what she sees as his flagging performance as a soccer player:

> Yeah I like [David Beckham] . . . I just think he plays very well . . . but he's starting to think too much of himself and he's not getting so good anymore, coz he's thinking too much of himself . . . I just think that it's best when he's not famous.
>
> (Mixed Year 3 group, private school)

We therefore contend that while at times the children seemed able to articulate their perspectives quite clearly—for example, their apparent dislike of Beckham's cashing in on adverts—their discussions were also characterised by an awareness of the various different perspectives available from which to view Beckham and his status as a soccer player, style icon, commodified celebrity and so on. In the tail end of a discussion in which the children express their disapproval of the media attention allegedly coveted by David and Victoria Beckham, the children are also able to engage in a complex debate concerning the difficult relationship between highly visible celebrities such as "Posh and Becks" and an insatiable media industry:

Boy 1:	I think it's wrong how the press can manipulate people, I think they should be, they should have to get permission from the person who they are writing the story on to publish the story.
Interviewer:	Uh-huh.
Boy 1:	I reckon they should be able to fine people for, newspapers for writing, discriminating . . .
Boy 2:	Yeah saying like he's with (inaudible).
Interviewer:	OK, so you think that the press manipulate him in a way?
Boy 1:	Like naming the new child like on the radio before they've even got out for, you know—
Boy 2:	It's like before they left the hospital told the press, and then they like, I reckon they should've asked them for permission coz they told the hospital that they didn't want anyone to know and they told the press that . . .
Interviewer:	OK, so you don't really like the way the press does that then?
Boy 1:	No.

Boy 2:   No, I think it's wrong.

Boy 1:   Even though like not many people like him and lots of people would like him to get out of football and like be a normal person, I think it's still quite wrong that he should just get blamed for all those things.

(Single-sex Year 6 group, state school)

What is particularly notable about the above extract is that this discussion reflects a fairly sophisticated discussion of moral issues, including an appreciation of the tensions between an individual's right to privacy and the freedom of the press, and of the notion of shared accountability and culpability. Hence, although aspects of the children's discussions seem to suggest that they hold David Beckham himself responsible for the choices made in positioning himself as something other than "a normal person," some children are also able to appreciate the role of the popular media and of the public gaze in contributing to such constructions.

By and large, the moral perspectives evidenced in the children's conversations seemed less to do with abstracting, intellectualising or achieving a final clarity around a static set of moral convictions. Rather, an important aspect of these conversations seemed to be that of appreciating and navigating the tensions and contradictions encountered when making sense of David Beckham as a complex cultural icon. An 11-year-old girl appreciates the intensity of feeling with which conversations around Beckham are sometimes imbued, and is able to acknowledge that she finds herself both drawn and conflicted by such strength of feeling:

I don't know what I think about him because he is, he's been in so much, because my cousin was a huge fan of him and Man United, but then he absolutely hated him and cut up all his shirts because he moved to Real Madrid. And he thought that he betrayed Man United, but many people don't like actually know what happened behind all the football and stuff, so, I don't know what to think of him, but I think he's a bit of a show-off and I do take the mick out of him sometimes.

(Mixed Year 6 group, private school)

Following on from two boys' comments: ". . . he doesn't need to do other stuff like modelling" and "Yeah, he just wastes his time, I mean he's got so much money, I mean, what can you spend it all on?" she continues to put forward an alternative perspective that complicates and clouds the matter, and highlights the more facile and off-hand nature of the boys' comments:

He might be in debt though, that's the only problem coz many people, you think they're amazingly rich but they show their house and everything and you wonder why they make so much exposure to their family and everything, then you think, oh my gosh, they're in so much debt they have to do this.

Thus, the girl quoted above problematises others' certainty around David Beckham: earlier, she had made reference to her cousin's intense allegiance to Beckham, and the sense of betrayal that said cousin suffered following Beckham's move to Real Madrid. And yet, she does not ally herself with either of these extremes; instead, she senses that there may be something unknown (and knowable) "behind all the football and stuff." Above, she wonders whether Beckham's iconic celebrity façade might hide a secret—his debt—which would explain his otherwise incomprehensible engagement in celebrity culture and the commodification of his and his family's lives/selves.

Discussion

We now turn to a discussion of the three central questions posed by this paper: How do children draw on the central cultural and social resources furnished by celebrities to inform the relational processes that shape their understanding of moral issues? What kind of morality is likely to emerge when iconic celebrities become a site in which children's relationship to moral issues is developed? What does this mean for children's understanding of a global media culture, which revolves around a culture of spectacle and commodified celebrity?

1   How do children draw on the central cultural and social resources furnished by celebrities to inform the relational processes that shape their understanding of moral issues?

The children in our study drew on Beckham as a cultural and social resource through which to engage with complex moral dilemmas in the context of their relational worlds. Specifically, Beckham was seen as a concentrated site for the discussion and problematisation of such aspects of modern life as celebrity, style, success, performance and wealth.

At least some of the "mediational means" and "socio-cultural tools" (Tappan 2006) upon which children drew in our study emerged from, were entangled with, and/or responded to, specific aspects of consumption culture. These included hegemonic understandings of masculinity, evolving understandings of the commercialisation of sport, the cult of the celebrity and the role of the media glare, as well as of the nature of paid employment, wealth distribution, consumption and debt. Additional mediational means included the language of individual rights, responsibility and culpability, and such commonly accepted virtues as perseverance, hard work, modesty and loyalty to one's country/team. Thus, we suggest that the children drew on the multiple cultural and social resources available to them in order to make sense of David Beckham's iconicity, and that, in doing so, they became involved in articulating, affirming and reinforcing their understandings of what is considered good in their social context(s).

Furthermore, it would appear that adult narratives that frame David Beckham as a role model are underpinned by this intention. For example, the narrative around Beckham's "fall from grace" following the match with Argentina in the 1998 World Cup, and his eventual "redemption," could be understood in Tappan's terms as a socio-cultural tool that children and adults appropriate in order to "make sense of a particular social situation, and thus to construct a response to the [moral] question[s]" (Tappan 2006: 10). In this case, the relevant moral questions, if explicitly framed, might have been along the lines of: *How might we make amends for past mistakes? What is the appropriate way to respond to criticism and adversity?* Understood in this way, engagement with the seemingly remote but very public foibles of figures such as David Beckham allows children to tease out responses to moral questions that are directly relevant and significant to them, even at a relatively young age.

2   What kind of morality is likely to emerge when iconic celebrities become a site in which children's relationship to moral issues is developed?

We propose that children's understanding of morality does not necessarily involve their internalisation of an apparently universal set of moral values that identify "good" and "bad" actions. The kind of morality that emerged in our study when celebrities such as Beckham become the site in which children's understanding of morality developed can be characterised as *ambivalent, contested, negotiated, located* and *mediated. Ambivalent,* because of the general absence of clear-cut distinctions and certainties around what constitutes "right" and "wrong," "good" or "bad." As we have seen, engagement with a concrete, controversial figure muddies understandings and brings into relief some of the complexity associated with making value judgements (for example, at what point does perseverance cross the line into "trying too hard?"). Because of this, such a morality is likely to be *contested.* Indeed, children's dialogue around David Beckham allows them to critically engage with such grey areas as consumerism, self-promotion, celebrity status, material wealth and media representation, and to form their own (socially and culturally mediated) perspectives on the extent to which these dynamics are (un)desirable and (un)commendable. Inherent to this, of course, is the ever-present possibility for disagreement, debate and doubt.

Furthermore, such a morality could be described as *negotiated,* since—as shown by the children's conversations—values and perspectives are established in relationship with others, and are revisited and refined in discursive spaces in ongoing ways. Thus, we see that, in their current discussions, children draw on previous conversations and existing narratives around David Beckham, and on significant others' interpretations of him. We therefore arrive at a morality that is quite distinct from that advocated by the cognitive-developmentalist paradigm that has traditionally dominated (Hekman 1995; Bergman 2004) understandings of moral reasoning and moral functioning. Such a morality is not based on abstract, universal principles, nor on cognitive-rational internal monologues divorced from social influences, but is instead *located* within specific cultural and historical contexts. It is also *mediated* since it is framed within, shaped by and in constant dialogue with specific "socio-cultural tools" and "mediational means," which in this case include participation within, and discourses around, the cults of the celebrity, of the spectacle and of global media culture.

Our study suggests that children's experiences of an increasingly commercialised world, and their active participation in common discourses around celebrity, media and commodification, meaningfully contributes to their understanding of moral issues. It does so by making space for engaged and located sense making, for the holding of ambiguity and contention, and for the appropriation of, and negotiation around, specific moral discourses.

3   What does this mean for children's understanding of a global media culture, which revolves around a culture of spectacle and commodified celebrity?

Children's discourses around David Beckham provide them with a means of articulating, debating and negotiating some of the moral ambiguities and complexities of contemporary consumer culture. Specifically, the children focused on Beckham's production (by himself and others) as a spectacular celebrity, and expressed ambivalence and discomfort around the commodified self, spectacular consumption, the commercialisation of sport and an insatiable media. However, we do not suggest that our findings point to an utter rejection of or resistance to these aspects of consumption culture on the part of children. Indeed, the findings presented here could be interpreted as evidence that children themselves are caught up in the cult of the spectacle. In responding to our open-ended question "What are kids in your class into at the moment?" the children's accounts reflected the influence of media culture on what was important to them, since much of what they chose to talk about could be described as spectacularised and *mediated*. But the children in our study were not just passive recipients of these productions and representations. In saying this, we again align ourselves with Kellner (2006), who rejects the notion that political spectacles are all-powerful and overwhelming, and instead points to the unpredictability of the politics of the spectacle, to the uncertainty of a spectacle's success, and to the possibility of it backfiring.

The children engaged with the subject of David Beckham in ways that were *both* framed within, and bounded by, global media culture and the cult of the celebrity *and that also* allowed them to proactively identify, construct and experiment with moral dilemmas and ambiguities in terms that were meaningful to them and are relevant in the context of their increasingly commercialised childhoods. Indeed, we see children's expression of ambiguity, discomfort and uncertainty as part and parcel of their moral unfolding in the context of a culture where issues of markets and consumption necessarily intersect with questions around the pursuit of a "good" life, and where children and adults engage with questions of ethics and morality *as an inherent part of* their engagement with objects and acts of consumption.

Implications

If we are to help children navigate their increasingly commercialised lives, we need to advance thinking on both children's moral development and consumer socialisation beyond the cognitive-rational, developmentalist view. This raises some important implications for marketing researchers and practitioners, which we now outline, before turning to the implications for parents, teachers and policymakers.

Implications for marketing researchers and practitioners

As marketing practitioners and researchers seeking to better understand children's consumer socialisation, we need to go beyond simply ascertaining whether children understand the persuasive intent of marketing directed towards them, and develop a much richer understanding of the complex social roles that brands and celebrities play in children's everyday lives. In this, we align ourselves with Schroeder and Borgerson's (2005: 581) suggestion that "there is relatively little education about marketing communication's social, cultural and pedagogical roles," and also with their argument (following Scott and Batra 2003) that rather than restrict ourselves to "an information-based model of marketing communication as persuasion," we need to "fully [acknow-ledge] how marketing also acts as a representational system that produces meaning outside the realm of the promoted product or service" (Schroeder and Borgerson 2005: 579).

In this vein, we have offered support to alternative understandings of children's relationship to moral issues, which emphasise the situated, con-textual, dialogic and constructed nature of the moral domain. Such an understanding would enable us to see that the cult of the spectacle and the celebrity—and its embodiment through David Beckham—*produces* meaning, becomes a *site* for children's unfolding moral discourses, *and also* becomes a *subject* for children's exploration. Thus, the relationship we outline between particular aspects of consumption culture and moral development is a com-plicated one, emphasising *both* the role of consumption culture as a framework *within which* moral unfolding happens, *and* children's ability to construct morally engaged positions that hold complexity and ambivalence around the "rightness" and/or "wrongness" of specific aspects of consumption culture.

Our findings therefore support the view that those of us concerned with children's participation in consumption need to go beyond the polarised debate, which alternatively portrays children in terms of vulnerability or autonomy (O'Sullivan 2007), as *either* innocent, gullible victims of the marketing machine *or* as savvy social agents able to creatively appropriate consumer culture. Cook (2004: 149) argues for a third position:

one that rejects the either/or structure of the problem, [and] understands that the battles waged over and around children's consumer culture are no less than battles over the nature of the person and the scope of personhood in the context of the ever-expanding reach of commerce.

Through engagement with processes and acts of commodification, children can come to form and articulate their own (albeit culturally and socially mediated) judgements regarding the extent to which they can see *value* in such commodification. This in itself should be of interest to marketing practitioners and researchers, as they reflect on how children make sense of and respond to an increasingly commercialised world, in the multiple roles that they occupy, not only as active consumers, but as spectators, commentators, opinion leaders and influencers vis-à-vis consumer culture.

Implications for teachers, parents and policymakers

Beyond implications for the study of children's consumer socialisation, an understanding of children as moral actors in the messy contexts of their everyday lives has important implications for teachers, parents and policy-makers concerned with children's moral education and with the ethical implications of their participation in increasingly commercialised contexts. First, our findings suggest that through engaging with concrete figures and specific situations of interest to them, children are able to make space for individual and collaborative sense making and debate around what they experience as the relevant ambiguities and issues of tension and contention. Thus, we advocate that any effort to engage children in formal education around morality and values would do well to: (1) privilege those subjects of study and discussion that the children themselves identify as being of relevance and interest to them; (2) attend to the common discourses on which children draw, and recognise that moral choices and moral voices are inherent and implicit within these; and (3) begin from the specific moral ambiguities, uncertainties and tensions that children choose to get "stuck into."

Second, and following on from point (3), those concerned with children's moral education would do well to recognise children's emerging ability to hold tensions and to appreciate some of the complexity and uncertainty involved in making value judgements, even around such complex and pervasive influences as that of the cult of the celebrity and the spectacular. Arguably, many stories for children rely on simplistic representations of "good" versus "evil" and on versions of "hero" and "villain" archetypes. The implication is that, alongside proposing particular role models and specific moral values and/or frameworks (around "democracy" and "Britishness," for example), teachers, parents and policymakers need to consider how children's moral education could be constituted so as to facilitate debate and the development of critical reflexiveness around the complex social patterns and dynamics of which they are a part. Importantly, this may include critical reflection on the assumptions held around the nature and feasibility of "moral education," children's or adults', within the particular discourses we occupy and appropriate. We would thus privilege those approaches that incorporate informal conversation, debate and criticality, and that acknowledge and reflect on the tensions and contradictions often felt by people when attempting to make sense of the human condition and of their lived experience. We argue that such approaches are likely to be experienced as more meaningful and effective than those grounded in the assumption that complex human dynamics such as "Britishness" can be packaged and "taught" in straightforward, unilateral ways.

Third, and following on from all of the above, an understanding of ourselves—both children and adults—as implicitly moral persons engaged in moral discourse and moral action in the messy contexts of our everyday lives signifies an explicit shift in the ways in which we might talk about ethical decision-making and value judgements with one another. We may help children to see that they will continually be faced with choices regarding how they interpret morality and themselves and others as moral persons, and that claims of uncertainty and confusion ("*I don't know what to think*") may represent not moral immaturity, but a moral self in the thick of critical engagement with complex questions and with opportunities for morality-in-the-making.

Conclusion

In conclusion, we suggest that the children in our study were—implicitly if not explicitly—engaging in discussion around moral action and expressing moral voices. Moral discourses emerged not in self-conscious, forced or abstractive ways, but naturally, in the ebbs and flows of conversation, as children drew on discourses around celebrities, consumption, commodification and the spectacular. Having given support to understandings of moral development that emphasise its contextual and situated nature, future research designs could create opportunities for children to explore the moral dilemmas that are immediately relevant to them in their own lives and could pursue the role of both adults and children in co-constructing, reinforcing and resisting particular moral discourses. We suggest that these kinds of conversations need to be seen not only as the domain of philosophers and students of meta-ethics, but as legitimate questions to ask in relation to content-, context- and person-specific ethical dilemmas, including those raised by processes and acts of commodification in contemporary consumption culture.

Acknowledgements

We would like to express our gratitude to the schools and the children for their participation in this research. We are also indebted to the anonymous reviewers and our colleagues Professor Jonathan Schroeder, Dr Donna Ladkin,

Richard Bolden and Dr Inmaculada Adarves-Yorno for their helpful comments on earlier drafts of this article.

Note

1 It should be noted that in current British parlance, "fit" relates to sexual attractiveness rather than athletic condition.

References

Achereiner, Gwen Bachmann, and Deborah Roedder John. 2003. "The meaning of brand names to children: A developmental investigation." *Journal of Consumer Psychology* 13 (3): 205–19.

Arnould, Eric J., and Craig J. Thompson. 2005. "Consumer culture theory (CCT): Twenty years of research." *Journal of Consumer Research* 31 (March): 868–82.

Barber, Michael D. 2001. "Sartre, phenomenology and the subjective approach to race and ethnicity in Black Orpheus." *Philosophy and Social Criticism* 27 (3): 91–103.

BBC News Online. 2007. "LA Galaxy say Beckham worth money." 29 January. Available at: http://news.bbc.co.uk/sport1/hi/football/6310305.stm (accessed 4 February 2007).

Belk, Russell, Kenneth Bahn, and Robert Mayer. 1982. "Developmental recognition of consumption symbolism." *Journal of Consumer Research* 7 (June): 4–17.

Belk, Russell, Robert Mayer, and Amy Driscoll. 1984. "Children's recognition of consumption symbolism in children's products." *Journal of Consumer Research* 10 (March): 386–97.

Bell, Derrick. 1997. *Constitutional conflicts.* New York: Anderson Press.

Bell, Derrick. 2002. *Ethical ambition: Living a life of meaning and worth.* New York: Bloomsbury.

Bergman, Roger. 2004. "Caring for the ethical ideal: Nel Noddings on moral education." *Journal of Moral Education* 33 (2): 149–62.

Biskup, Claudia, and Gertrud Pfister. 1999. "I would like to be like her/him: Are athletes role-models for boys and girls?" *European Physical Education Review* 5 (3): 199–218.

Bleicher, Josef. 1980. *Contemporary hermeneutics.* London: Routledge & Kogan Paul.

Carr, David, and Jan Steutel, eds. 1999. Virtue ethics and moral education. New York: Routledge.

Cashmore, Ellis, and Andrew Parker. 2003. "One David Beckham? Celebrity, masculinity, and the soccerati." *Sociology of Sport Journal* 20 (3): 214–31.

Chaplin, Lan Nguyen, and Deborah Roedder John. 2005. "The development of self-brand connections in children and adolescents." *Journal of Consumer Research* 32 (June): 119–25.

Colby, Anne, and Lawrence Kohlberg. 1987. *The measurement of moral judgment.* Cambridge: Cambridge University Press.

Compass. 2006. "'The Commercialisation of Childhood'. Compass: Direction for the Democratic Left." Available at: http://clients.squareeye.com/uploads/compass/documents/thecommercialisationofchildhood.pdf (accessed 27 May 2007).

Cook, Daniel T. 2004. "Beyond either/or." *Journal of Consumer Culture* 4 (2): 147–53.

Debord, Guy. [1967] 1977. *The society of the spectacle*. Translated from French by Fredy Perlman and John Supak. Detroit, MI: Black & Red.

Delgado, Richard. 1999. *When equality ends: Stories of race and resistance*. Boulder, CO: Westview.

Delgado, Richard, and Jean Stefancic. 2000. "Critical race theory: The cutting edge." 2nd ed. Philadelphia, PA: Temple University Press.

Giardina, Michael D. 2003. "'Bending it like Beckham' in the global popular: Stylish hybridity, performativity, and the politics of representation." *Journal of Sport and Social Issues* 27 (1): 65–82.

Gilligan, Carol. 1982. *In a different voice*. Cambridge, MA: Harvard University Press.

Giorgi, Amedeo. 1983. "A phenomenological approach to the problem of meaning and serial learning." In *Duquesne studies in phenomenology*, Vol. 1, edited by Amedeo Giorgi, C. T. Fischer, and E. L. Murray. Pittsburgh, PA: Dusquesne University Press.

Haynes, Felicity. 1998. *The ethical school*. London: Routledge.

Hekman, Susan. 1995. *Moral voices, moral selves: Carol Gilligan and feminist moral theory*. Cambridge, MA: Polity Press.

Holt, Douglas. 2003. "What becomes an icon most?" *Harvard Business Review* March: 43–9.

Ireson, Gren. 2001. "Beckham as physicist?" *Physics Education* 36 (1): 10–13.

Jaggar, Alison M. 1992. "Feminist ethics." In *Encyclopedia of ethics*, edited by Lawrence C. Becker and Charlotte B. Becker. New York: Garland Press.

Kellner, Douglas. 2006. "Media culture and the triumph of the spectacle." Available at: www.gseis.ucla.edu/faculty/kellner/papers/medculturespectacle.html (accessed 25 May 2007).

Kohlberg, Lawrence. 1976. "Moral stages and moralization: The cognitive-developmental approach." In *Moral development and behavior: Theory, research, and social issues*, edited by Thomas Lickona with Gilbert Geis and Lawrence Kohlberg. New York: Holt, Rinehart & Winston.

Kohlberg, Lawrence. 1981. *The philosophy of moral development*. San Francisco, CA: Harper & Row.

Kvale, Steinar. 1983. "The qualitative research interview: A phenomenological and a hermeneutical mode of understanding." *Journal of Phenomenological Psychology* 14 (Fall): 171–96.

Ladkin, Donna, and Steven Taylor. 2007. "Constructing authenticity: Arts-based methods as a means of developing the authentic leadership self." Unpublished paper.

Lourenço, Orlando. 2003. "Making sense of Turiel's dispute with Kohlberg: The case of the child's moral competence." *New Ideas in Psychology* 21: 43–68.

MacDonald, Robert, and Jane Marsh. 2005. *Disconnected youth? Growing up in Britain's poor neighbourhoods*. London: Palgrave Macmillan.

MacIntyre, Alisdair. 1985. *After virtue*. London: Duckworth.

Mullet, Sheila. 1988. "Shifting perspectives: A new approach to ethics." In *Feminist perspectives: Philosophical essays on method and morals*, edited by Lorraine Code, Sheila Mullet, and Christine Overall. Toronto: University of Toronto Press.

Nairn, Agnes, and Christine Griffin. 2007. "'Busted rocks but Barbie's a minger': The role of brands in the everyday lives of junior school children." *Nordicom*. Forthcoming.

Nairn, Agnes, Christine Griffin, and Patricia Gayá Wicks. 2008. "Children's use of brand symbolism: A consumer culture theory approach." *European Journal of Marketing*. Forthcoming.

Noddings, Nel. 1984. *Caring, a feminine approach to ethics and moral education.* Berkeley, CA: University of California.

O'Sullivan, Terry. 2007." Get MediaSmart®: A critical discourse analysis of controversy around advertising to children in the UK." *Consumption Markets & Culture* 10 (3): 293–314.

Palmer, Sue. 2006. *Toxic childhood: How the modern world is damaging our children and what we can do about it.* London: Orion.

Parker, Andrew, and Deborah Steinberg. 2004. "The transfigural and the totemic: David Beckham, sexuality and popular culture." Paper presented at Pleasure and Danger Revisited: Sexualities in the 21st Century, Cardiff University, July 2004.

Peracchio, Laura A. 1992. "How do young children learn to be consumers? A script-processing approach." *Journal of Consumer Research* 18 (4): 425–40.

Piaget, Jean. 1960. "General problems of the psychological development of the child." In *Discussions on child development: Proceedings of the World Health Organisation study group on psychological development of the child,* IV, edited by J. Taner and B. Elders. New York: International Universities Press.

Piaget, Jean. 1967. *Six psychological studies.* New York: Random House.

Ritson, Mark, and Richard Elliott. 1999. "The social uses of advertising: An ethnographic study of adolescent advertising audiences." *Journal of Consumer Research* 26 (3): 260–77.

Roedder John, Deborah. 1999. "Consumer socialization of children: A retrospective look at twenty-five years of research." *Journal of Consumer Research* 26 (December): 183–213.

Schor, Juliet. 2004. *Born to buy: The commercialised child and the new consumer culture.* New York: Scribner.

Schroeder, Jonathan E., and Janet L. Borgerson. 2005. "An ethics of representation for international marketing communication." *International Marketing Review* 22 (5): 578–600.

Scott, Linda, and Rajeev Batra, eds. 2003. *Persuasive imagery: A consumer response perspective.* Mahwah, NJ: Lawrence Erlbaum Associates.

Swain, Jon. 2000. "'The money's good, the fame's good, the girls are good': The role of playground football in the construction of young boys' masculinity in a junior school." *British Journal of Sociology of Education* 21 (1): 95–109.

Tappan, Mark B. 2006. "Moral functioning as mediated action." *Journal of Moral Education* 35 (1): 1–18.

Thompson, Craig, William Locander, and Howard Pollio. 1989. "Putting consumer experience back into consumer research: The philosophy and method of existential-phenomenology." *Journal of Consumer Research* 16 (September): 133–46.

Turiel, Elliot. 1983. *The development of social knowledge: Morality and convention.* Cambridge: Cambridge University Press.

Turiel, Elliot, Melanie Killen, and Charles Helwig. 1987. "Morality: Its structure, functions, and vagaries." In *The emergence of morality in young children,* edited by Jerome Kagan and Sharon Lamb. Chicago, IL: The University of Chicago Press.

Valkenburg, Patti M., and Joanne Cantor. 2001. "The development of a child into a consumer." *Journal of Applied Developmental Psychology* 22 (1): 61–72.

Wertsch, James. 1998. *Mind as action.* New York: Oxford University Press.

White, Stephen, and Joseph O'Brien. 1999. "What is a hero? An exploratory study of students' conceptions of heroes." *Journal of Moral Education* 28 (1): 81–95.

13 Limits of the McDonaldization thesis

eBayization and ascendant trends in post-industrial consumer culture

Aaron Ahuvia and Elif Izberk-Bilgin

The way a people provide for themselves will always be a central aspect of daily life, hence an important source of metaphors for the nature of society as a whole. Not surprisingly, then, throughout American history, certain businesses or industries have functioned as icons for the prevailing cultural zeitgeist, even if they directly represented only a small slice of reality. The cowboy is a striking example of this; while this profession was only a tiny percentage of the population, the cowboy signified a cultural ethos on an epic scale. Later, Henry Ford's assembly line would represent rationalized work within a culture where science, rationality, and centrally controlled large-scale organizations typified the emerging dominant zeitgeist.[1] Ritzer's (1983) McDonaldization thesis elaborately illustrates this highly scientific-rational spirit of the modern society. In "The McDonaldization of Society," Ritzer (1983) argued that McDonald's, with its uniformity, efficiency, calculability, and control, was an apt metonym[2] for the forces of modern capitalist globalization. More critically, Ritzer saw McDonald's strictly taste- and size-controlled hamburgers, scripted employee-customer interactions, generic friendliness, and unwavering emphasis on quantity at low prices over creativity and quality as pertinent symbols for an overly rationalized and homogenized culture. Hence, McDonaldization is not the story just of McDonald's per se, but a larger historical and social allegory. Historical forces create conditions in which a particular type of organizational structure becomes popular. McDonald's is a pioneering and iconic example of a specific type of organizational structure, which in turn is linked to the particular social and economic trends that gave rise to it. McDonaldization is Ritzer's term for the process by which other organizations adopt a similar structure in response to similar economic and social forces.

Since 1983, Ritzer's "McDonaldization" thesis has become widely influential and discussed – as evidenced by a recent Google search that retrieved over 91,000 hits for this term. In academic circles, the McDonaldization thesis has been most influential in sociology, where it has become a popular lens for looking at globalization (Falk 1999). The McDonaldization thesis has also received some attention in consumer research and marketing (Arnould and Thompson 2005; Holbrook 1999; Holt 2002; Thompson and Arsel 2004; Thompson and Tambyah 1999), since Ritzer claims that McDonaldization does as much to transform consumption as it does production.

McDonaldization was widespread across America and Europe for much of the twentieth century, and still continues to be an influential force there to a more limited extent today. Meanwhile, McDonaldization has followed modernization across the globe and is picking up speed in developing countries. However, we contend that the term McDonaldization is not illustrative of the way a growing number of institutions organize and compete in a truly global and highly information-driven marketplace. Nor do we believe that it captures the dominant cultural zeitgeist of postmodern societies in the USA and Europe (for reviews of postmodernism, see Brown 1995; Featherstone 1991; Fırat and Venkatesh 1993). Rather, we suggest the term *eBayization*, a postmodern form of economic and social organization powered by an information economy, as a fitting label for an emerging countertrend. In postmodern societies, McDonaldization and eBayization currently coexist and inform each other, and will likely do so in the future. Hence, in forwarding this argument, our goal is not to replace one grand narrative with another. Rather, we propose eBayization as an alternative theoretical lens with which to think about and evaluate the emerging economic practices and social relationships in post-industrial societies.

In presenting our analysis, the terms *McDonald's* and *eBay* refer to the specific businesses that serve as metonyms for the larger trends of which they are a part. *McDonaldization*, and our own term *eBayization*, refer to: (1) the growth of businesses and other institutions that have specified characteristics similar to McDonald's and eBay, respectively; and (2) the changes in society that both influence and are influenced by these McDonald's-like and eBay-like institutions. Finally, the terms *McDonaldization thesis* and *eBayization thesis* refer to the metaphoric tropes in which these businesses function as metonyms for larger social and economic changes. Within CCT (consumer culture theory) research (Arnould and Thompson 2005), such metaphoric tropes are often seen as a form of theory (Arndt 1985). As Alasuutari (1996: 376–7) explains, a "theory – as it is understood here – does not present a prediction of the results; it only suggest a particular, explicitly defined framework within which the details of a case and the data can be assessed." The terms *McDonaldization thesis* and *eBayization thesis* act as sensitizing propositions, enhancing scientific understanding by illuminating important aspects of reality.

This paper highlights three aspects of McDonaldization and eBayization: the organizational features that define McDonaldized and eBayized organizations, the historical forces that made McDonald's, and then later eBay, iconic exemplars of the prevailing American zeitgeist, and, finally, the social impacts of each, particularly of eBayization.

The paper is organized as follows. We first review Ritzer's McDonaldization thesis, which he defines mostly in terms of the organizational features of

McDonald's, and then discuss some criticism of this thesis in the literature. We then examine the historical conditions of twentieth-century modernity and their connection to McDonald's phenomenal popularity. This historical discussion continues with the shift in the later twentieth century to more postmodern forms of economic and social organization, and in particular the development of what Beck (1992) terms "risk society," which set the stage for eBay. Next, we examine eBayization in more detail, distinguishing eBayization from McDonaldization in three key areas: variety, unpredictability, and market-mediated control. Lastly, we discuss some social impacts of eBayization.

The McDonaldization thesis

Ritzer's McDonaldization thesis is a reframing and extension of Weber's theory of rationality. Taking a cue from how bureaucracies are organized, Weber (1946) distinguishes rationality as unique to the scientific and progressive mindset of Western societies. This form of rationality not only identifies the optimum ways of reaching ends and establishes those in specific processes, but also institutionalizes processes via rules and regulations so they can be transferred across time and space. Rationality, in turn, produces a bureaucratically organized social order that Weber terms an "iron cage." Expanding on Weber's theory, Ritzer contends that McDonaldization represents a more contemporary form of rationalization, as the process of McDonaldization extends well beyond formalization of production to rationalization of consumption.

More specifically, McDonaldization includes five main features. The first four features of McDonaldization are aspects of an organization. McDonald's was hugely successful as a business because it found particular ways to increase the: (1) *efficiency*; (2) *calculability*; (3) *predictability*; and (4) *control* of its operations. McDonaldization takes place when two criteria are met. First, the organization in question must strive to increase its efficiency, calculability, predictability, and/or control. Second, the organization must pursue these goals by using similar strategies and organizational processes to those used by McDonald's when it became a global icon. This second criterion is not explicitly stated by Ritzer, but it is implicit in the way the term McDonaldization is used. Without this caveat, any organizational change that, say, increases efficiency would be seen as McDonaldization; the concept of McDonaldization would become so broad as to be meaningless. A somewhat nuanced, but nonetheless important, point is that doing things "McDonald's style" does not refer so much to McDonald's current business practices as it does to the McDonald's of the public imagination. This is the image formed when McDonald's became a public icon in the 1960s and 1970s. The current McDonald's has not changed dramatically from its former self. However, as we will see, even McDonald's has made a few changes, which leave it slightly less McDonaldized than it used to be.

The fifth feature of McDonaldization is not an aspect of an organization, but rather an unintended negative social consequence from the spread of these organizational features. Ritzer calls this fifth feature the: (5) *"irrationality of rationality"* (Ritzer 2004: 134). It, along with the other features of McDonaldization, is explored in more detail below.

Efficiency

Ritzer (2004: 43) describes efficiency as a systematic approach of "choosing the optimum means to a given end" that minimizes cost and effort. More specifically, Ritzer pinpoints how modern institutions such as McDonald's, in their efforts to maximize such institutional gains as cost cutting and inventory control, not only maximize efficiency, but simultaneously promote this idea as a benefit to the consumer by keeping prices low and providing food with short wait times. In McDonald's case, efficiency in production is accomplished, in part, by streamlining the process of preparing the food and simplifying the menu. Yet, McDonald's strives for efficiency not only in production, but also in the process of consumption. Hence, McDonald's makes activities formerly associated with production part of the consumption experience, as tasks are shifted to consumers through self-ordering, self-service, and clean up. Customer flow is also strategically accelerated through uncomfortable seating assignments, easy-to-eat finger food, and drive-through service windows.

This process by which consumers take on tasks formerly performed by producers can easily be confused with Toffler's prosumption (Tapscott and Williams 2006; Toffler 1981), but the two are quite distinct and even somewhat opposed to each other. In McDonaldization, the producer engineers the process to maximize efficiency (e.g., chairs that are comfortable for a short sit but not a long time so as to increase customer throughput), whereas in prosumption the customer is given a certain level of creative input into the product design process, or at least is provided with information to facilitate mass customization. In work prescient of the current essay, Toffler (1981) argued that prosumption was a countertrend to what would later be called McDonaldization. In Toffler's view, human history could be divided into three waves. First wave economies developed out of the agricultural revolution and second wave economies developed out of the industrial revolution. In the following quote, we see that while the specifics are slightly different, there is a strong resemblance between Toffler's second wave societies and Ritzer's McDonaldization:

> The Second Wave Society is industrial and based on mass production, mass distribution, mass consumption, mass education, mass media, mass recreation, mass entertainment, and weapons of mass destruction. You combine those things with standardization, centralization, concentration, and synchronization, and you wind up with a style of organization we call bureaucracy.
>
> (Toffler 1981: 178)

McDonaldization is a metaphor for aspects of what Toffler termed second wave industrial economies. Prosumption, Toffler argued, was part of the emerging third wave society, which was a countertrend to second wave (i.e., McDonaldized) culture. Third wave societies were being born from the information revolution, which was creating a post-industrial economy in keeping with the new "information age" (yet another term he coined). eBayization is to Toffler's third wave as McDonaldization is to his second wave. Both "izations" refer to particular ways of structuring organizations, which take advantage of the technologies and social trends that existed at their birth.

Calculability

Calculability refers to the quantification of all aspects of production to ensure efficiency, quality, and control. In McDonald's case, calculability involves precisely measuring ingredients of each offering, controlling the portion size, and establishing the exact number of steps to be followed when employees prepare, package, and serve the food. In practice, the term McDonaldization refers not to all forms of calculability, but specifically to calculability à la McDonald's in which measurement and control are used to serve large numbers of consumers in a rapid and identical fashion. It has been argued that such practices eradicate the meaning of work and the pride of accomplishment for employees (Bergman 1983). In a similar vein, mass-produced goods and scripted service encounters do not always allow for unique consumer experiences, resulting in a loss of meaning and authenticity for consumers as elaborated in Holt (2002) and Kozinets (2002).

Ritzer argues that this form of calculability has led consumers to value quantity over quality. Drawing from such diverse examples as the impact of the publish-or-perish dictum regarding the declining quality of scholarship in academia, the overreliance on GRE or GMAT scores in college admissions, and the deteriorating quality of healthcare services due to time-capped patient-doctor consultations, Ritzer illustrates the McDonaldization of academia, education, and healthcare in the face of declining quality standards. In this respect, Ritzer's social criticism is reminiscent of Adorno and Horkheimer (2000 [1944]) in its concern that mass consumer culture is dumbing down society. Hence, the McDonaldization thesis is vulnerable to some of the same charges of elitism commonly aimed at this strain of critical theory (Scott 1993).

Predictability

Predictability is the assurance that the products and services modern institutions offer will be identical across time and place. Achieving predictability requires that "a rationalized society emphasizes discipline, order, system-atization, formalization, routine, consistency, and methodical operation" (Ritzer 2004: 86). More specifically, McDonaldized institutions achieve predictability by manufacturing controllable servicescapes, reducing the dialogue between service provider and client to scripted interactions, utilizing measures to routinize employee tasks, and creating predictable products.

While McDonaldized predictability offers everyone the peace of mind of knowing what to expect, it also eliminates the element of surprise in daily encounters. Building on this, Ritzer notes that predictability manufactures "plastic worlds" (Ritzer 2004: 102) or sterile consumer experiences that are bereft of risks, nuisances, and unpleasantness. For instance, Disney's Epcot entreats consumers to "(e)xplore the world in a day" (http://disneyworld. disney.go.com/) by offering today's armchair culture-vultures thematized pavilions (Fırat and Ulusoy 2011) that represent Mexico, Morocco, and China. Yet, these cultural encounters are strictly designed and manufactured with the principle of delivering a perfect consumer experience, where any sign of poverty, pollution, and crime that characterize many of these cosmopolitan countries are conveniently absent. It has been argued that in everyday life, such spatial and experiential ideals materialize in *Stepford*-like suburban towns, strategically designed to provide all the comforts of the good life while guaranteeing minimal interaction with the nuisances of nature and the dangers of inner-city neighborhoods (Beuka 2004). Likewise, this plasticity is said to engender a culture of fear based on a lack of tolerance for any person, culture, or idea that falls outside the norms of orderliness and safety, eventually pro-ducing a politics of fear (Furedi 2002). In sum, reminiscent of some cultural critiques (Adorno and Horkheimer 2000 [1944]; Baudrillard 1998 [1970]), Ritzer observes that predictability engenders false empowerment, duped consumers, and a manipulative consumer culture (Ritzer 1983, 2004).

Control

Historically, modern organizations have sought to exert greater control over the manufacturing process and employee behavior through scientific management (i.e., Taylorism) and the assembly line. Through the use of technology, automation, and other forms of institutional control (e.g., rules, regulations, and organizational hierarchies), the organizations break down and simplify the production process into a few repetitive tasks so that the work can be performed by anyone. In doing this, Ritzer contends that organizations not only render employees easily replaceable by either other low-cost workers or new technology, but they also engender "de-skilling" (Ritzer 2004: 115) by eliminating the need for expertise. As such, increasing the reliance of modern institutions on automated and high-surveillance work environments discour-ages and gradually eradicates employees' initiative and decision-making abilities. Ritzer maintains that as a consequence of McDonaldization, de-skilling extends beyond fast-food restaurants to hospitals, universities, and other institutions that societies entrust with training and employing individuals who possess the ability to critically analyze situations and information. Hence, the term McDonaldization refers to not all types of managerial control, but specifically to changes designed to enhance managerial control that results in deskilled and dehumanized work environments.

The irrationality of rationality

Ritzer argues that, taken together, the organizational characteristics of efficiency, calculability, predictability, and control produce a series of negative societal consequences, which he calls the irrationality of rationality. External-ities are the primary mechanism that links increased McDonaldization to these social ills. McDonaldization uses *control* to increase the *efficiency* with which measured (i.e., *calculated*) inputs (e.g., money invested, raw ingredients, labor hours, etc.) produce *predictably* saleable results. Anything that is not directly related to profitability is not measured. In addition, anything that is not measured is *external* to the calculations of efficiency, and therefore does not count in terms of decision-making. These unmeasured and hence external factors are called externalities and frequently bear the brunt of increases in efficiency. So, for example, increasingly predictable products and a small product line increase the efficiency of the business operations but also produce a less diverse and more homogenous culture. However, because the costs of a less diverse culture are external to the calculations used in decision-making, these costs are not taken into account in McDonaldized organizations.

Among the many adverse consequences of McDonaldization Ritzer cites are homogenization of cultures, dehumanization, and the potential dangers rationalization poses to the environment and human health. However, the most prominent of these costs seems to be the problems that the consumers and the environment have to bear as a result of organizational efficiencies. For example, increased traffic jams in metropolitan areas and greater fuel consumption are only a few of the externalized costs associated with just-in-time systems that allow for significant savings in inventory, management, and production. Research shows that while some organizations internally benefit from efficient inventory management, environmental costs are externalized, or passed on to the society, because:

> just-in-time techniques, such as smaller but more frequent deliveries, increase the number of vehicles needed, underutilize those vehicles, and (because of warehouse centralization) result in longer truck journeys . . . additional congestion and pollution . . . as well as extra packaging material that must also be disposed.
>
> (Zhu and Sarkis 2004: 271)

Among other costs of efficiency, critics also cite the considerable transformations undertaken in traditional agricultural practices to cope with food manufacturers' demand for highly standardized and affordable crops in greater quantities. Extensive use of chemical fertilizers and, most recently, the development of genetically modified organisms that may, in the long run, threaten human health and the environment are just some of the examples of how agricultural efficiency exacerbates environmental and human costs of production.

Critiques of the McDonaldization thesis

In keeping with the prodigious sales of Ritzer's *McDonaldization of Society*, the McDonaldization thesis has been a subject of scholarly criticism from such diverse fields as management, philosophy, sociology, communications, and political science (Alfino, Caputo, and Wynyard 1998). On theoretical grounds, the criticisms challenge the analytical value of the notion that McDonaldization provides an advanced understanding of rationality in modern life (Weinstein and Weinstein 1999), the theory's methodological reliance on newspaper sociology (Kellner 1999), and Ritzer's conceptual slippage in his interchangeable use of "McDonald's the fast-food business" with "'McDonaldization' as a complex economic process" (Smart 1999: 17). This theoretical criticism has been compounded by a growing body of empirical studies from marketing, anthropology, and sociology, which indicate that, contrary to Ritzer's homogenization claim, McDonald's is widely and diversely interpreted across cultures and socio-economic classes (Eckhardt and Houston 2002; Turner 2003).

Our critique of the McDonaldization thesis differs from these previous assessments. We argue that as a way of understanding contemporary reality in post-industrial information-based economies, McDonaldization is notably incomplete. In post-industrial societies, the social and economic forces that led to the rise of McDonald's-like organizations are, at best, holding steady and are arguably on the wane, while ascendant social and economic trends lead to a different type of production and consumption exemplified by eBay. For the foreseeable future, McDonald's-like and eBay-like firms will coexist, occupying different niches in the marketplace. Moreover, while McDonaldization may no longer be on the rise in the USA and Europe, it has become a good descriptor for major trends in China, India, and other rising industrial powers. In sum, though, we argue that eBayization captures the rising social, historical, and economic conditions that are shaping the new developments in the post-industrial societies of the USA and Western Europe. To better illustrate the divergences between the two, we next provide a brief review of the socio-historical conditions that brought about both McDonaldization and eBayization and how these socio-historical conditions relate to the actual business enterprises in question.

From McDonald's to eBay: historical forces at work

To understand the rise of McDonaldization, and later the rise of eBayization, it helps to begin with a discussion of the historical conditions that nurtured each one.

Industrial capitalism: post-war America and McDonald's

McDonaldization is a product of the industrialization and modernization that characterized early modern capitalism. Slater (1997) identifies the period of 1880–1930 as particularly significant in the emergence of a market society. Following the prosperous Victorian years, the period of 1880–1930 was marked by mass production and the first signs of the rationalization of production (Fraser 1981). While manufacturing goods such as textiles and steel were the first to be mass produced, the demand for these commodities gradually saturated, fostering an urgent need for new markets in consumer goods. This trend suitably corresponded with a population increasingly employed in industrial labor and no longer able to secure household consumption needs traditionally provided for through subsistence production. Consequently, the early twentieth century witnessed the shift in mass production from component material commodities to finished consumer goods. Meanwhile, the work process itself changed considerably; industrialists sought to maximize productivity by better utilizing the same amount of labor, rather than continuously boosting the labor force (Slater 1997). This new regime of efficiency was famously exemplified in the Fordist model of production that strategically combined the assembly line and principles of Taylorism for historically unprecedented levels of productivity.

Collectively, these social and economic transformations constituted a gradual shift from industrial capitalism to consumer capitalism (Bocock 1993; Gabriel and Lang 1995). Also known as the Fordist years (Slater and Tonkiss 2001), this period witnessed the emergence of a consumer class eager to purchase the ever-increasing variety of goods. McDonald's epitomized this zeitgeist. Whereas the current McDonaldization discourse depends for much of its power on the idea that McDonald's food is – to use a polite term – *junk*, in its early days McDonald's was known for the high quality of its food as compared to other producers in their price range. For instance, what interested a Multimixer[3] salesman named Ray Kroc[4] in the original McDonald's restaurant, owned by the McDonald brothers, were the lines of people queuing up for its renowned burgers, fries, and milkshakes. The McDonald brothers had applied the Fordist assembly line model to the restaurant business with what they called their "Speedee Service System." This system allowed them to serve customers hot off the grill, freshly made burgers for about half the price of their competitors. In a historical period of abundant optimism and optimism about abundance, McDonald's became an icon for how the benefits of modern rationalized production would reach average consumers.

It is in the nature of ideologies that they translate individual or group interests into moral virtues. During this historical period, the ideology of consumerism rendered consumption a "civic responsibility designed to improve the living standards of all" (Cohen 2004: 236). This view of consumption as a civic responsibility was based on both practical and moral claims. At a practical level, consumption was needed to maintain the economic recovery from the Great Depression and make the transition back to a civilian economy after

World War II. Consumerism also framed consumption as morally uplifting by claiming that increased accumulation of wealth would translate into a more egalitarian and peaceful society, as a growing number of individuals were able to satisfy their needs in a similar fashion through the modern market economy.

Within this historical context, McDonald's emerged not just as a symbol of how rationalized production would bring a better burger to the average consumer; it also became a potent moral symbol of *democratized* consumption. Uniting people of all economic strata to enjoy the quintessential American food under its roof, the fast-food restaurant quickly became the epitome of the post-war American cultural landscape. Conformist consumption in this period served as a passport to middle-class status for millions of Americans recovering from the Great Depression and World War II. Viewed from the cultural lenses of post-war America, it is evident how rationalist modern enterprises such as McDonald's, guided by principles of efficiency, calculability, predictability, and control, symbolized a more equitable culture – particularly for blacks, Hispanics, and women who felt excluded from the affluence and dynamism of a booming market society (Bagguley, Lawson, and Shapiro 1990). It is within this socio-historical conjuncture that we should understand the appeal of predictable products, standard service, and affordable goods that the process of McDonaldization, in Ritzer's term, came to provide.

Post-industrial risk society: setting the stage for eBay

As early as the 1970s, we saw the emergence of trends that would eventually render McDonaldization less culturally relevant, even as the McDonald's franchises continued to multiply. The anti-corporate counterculture of the late 1960s that began as a loose student movement was fueled by a mounting number of mainstream consumers fed up with what they saw as a homogenous marketplace and authoritarian marketers engaged in "cultural engineering" (Holt 2002: 70). Rejecting conformity, these consumers gradually sought more authenticity and social distinction through customized products that reflected their identities and unique lifestyles (Bourdieu 1984). Hence, an increasingly fragmented consumer society in terms of tastes, lifestyles, preferences, and a growing demand for differentiated market offerings marked this emerging postmodern consumer culture (Featherstone 1991).

On the economic front, the increasing saturation of consumer markets by the early 1970s reduced the profitability of "high output-low unit cost" mass production, as unsold inventories had to be liquefied at ever lower margins. Moreover, the growing demand for customized products and rapidly changing cultural trends no longer seemed to justify manufacturers' expensive capital investments. Facing a darkening economic outlook, industry leaders and businessmen began to realize the need for a new approach in manufacturing: flexible specialization (Piore and Sabel 1984). This new regime of flexible production, also known as post-Fordism, is characterized by novel technologies of production and information flow. Innovative techniques such as just-in-time management and electronic data interchange were developed during this period to support this new mode of accumulation.

Cultural tensions and economic uneasiness, as reflected in demonstrations, strikes, and absenteeism, also challenged the political harmony of the Fordist years (Friedman 1999; Glickman 1999). Initially gaining impressive momentum in business circles, the flexibility credo soon extended well beyond the firm to the political landscape as neo-liberal politics became popular; flexible manufacturing required deregulation and decentralization not just within the confines of the factory, but in the social and legal organization of the market society. Slater (1997: 191–2) describes the change as the "ending of the Fordist roles of the state," which symbolizes a shift toward "a devolution of all social decision making to the sphere of market-meditated consumption."

The dominance of markets over the social realm in the following two decades ushers in a new era in the evolution of the market society that is marked by new distributions of power, trade policies, and political arrangements. On the one hand, globalization, with a fervent primacy toward "informatization, informalization, and flexibility" (Pieterse 2000: 137), has pushed the pursuit of efficiency and the logic of rationalization to its limits. On the other hand, however, this relentless pursuit has produced a counter reaction; the human and ecological consequences of globalization lead to a self-awareness or reflexivity that is captured in Beck's (1992) notion of the risk society. Beck conceptualizes the risk society as a society significantly oriented around managing and responding to man-made risk. He sees these risks as an outcome of the modernization process and the priority it places on scientific development and rational industrialization. For Beck, the scientific organization of society and culture and the pursuit of rationalization have produced disasters, environmental hazards, and pollution. Increasing awareness of these collective risks creates a reflexive society ever cognizant and critical of the ecological and ethical consequences of its existence.

A testament to Beck's risk society has been the recent rise of a counter-consumer culture spurred by growing consumer awareness of the social, political, economic, and ecological ramifications resulting from outsourcing, unethical labor practices, and "Frankenfoods," among a host of others. More importantly, this counterculture is spreading from the shores of economically advanced Western markets to developing countries (Izberk-Bilgin 2006). Challenging the merits of rationalization and globalization, consumers react by mobilizing street demonstrations (Farro 2004; Klein 2000), organizing anti-market fests (Kozinets 2002), forming consumer-advocacy groups (Kozinets and Handelman 2004), fashioning alternative communities (Thompson and Coskuner-Balli 2007), creating virtual awareness platforms (e.g., www.clean clothes.org; www.organicconsumers.org), or simply altering consumption habits to reflect fundamentalist ideological stances (Izberk-Bilgin 2008). This counter-consumer culture has two strands; while voluntary simplicity advocates may reduce their overall level of consumerism, the other strand of counter-consumer culture simply shifts consumption away from McDonaldized brands toward customized offerings that allow for more individual expression, products from smaller producers with a homespun image, and an anti-McDonaldization ethos, or even corporate brands such as Apple that strike a rebellious anti-corporate pose. Hence, this counter-consumer culture can be just as consumerist as the McDonaldized cultural segments it disdains, and the move away from McDonaldization should not be equated with waning consumerism in general, but rather represents a shift toward a different style of consumerism.

From this historical perspective, it is evident that risk society poses a considerable ideological challenge to the process of McDonaldization and the long-held belief in rationalization. In addition to this ideological confrontation, the emergence of virtual marketplaces, novel forms of exchange (e.g., file sharing), Web 2.0, and cyber communities, when coupled with the shift toward experiential economies in the West, industrialization in the East, and the weakening of the nation state, require ever more flexible, openly accessible, mobile, and diverse, or, in Bauman's (2000) terms, "liquid" forms of social and economic organization. Such new forms of organizations not only challenge our extant notions of competition, productivity, and social responsibility, but also outline a new logic of post-industrial market society where the rationalization symbolized by McDonald's is no longer the assured formula for financial performance or cultural relevance. Indeed, in contrast to the pillars of standardization, regulation, and linearity on which McDonaldization is founded, risk society is characterized by "deregulation, differentiation, and liquidity" to deal with the economic, social, and cultural uncertainties and instabilities of post-industrial times (Turner 2003: 145). Accordingly, we suggest that eBayization, as a postmodern form of economic and social organization powered by information technology, better represents the deregulated, differentiated, and liquid nature of risk society, as well as the organizing principles of post-industrial enterprises.

The eBayization thesis

Building on Beck's conceptualization of risk society, we illustrate how eBayization diverges from previous modern forms of economic and social organization like McDonaldization. Whereas McDonald's functions as a metonym for Fordist, bureaucratic, centralized, hierarchical organizational structures, eBay serves as a metonym for organizations within post-industrial risk society, which are often considered part of the Web 2.0 phenomenon and utilize relatively distributed, networked, and market-mediated organizational structures. More specifically, the key differences between eBay and McDonald's can be seen in three features of eBay: variety, unpredictability, and market-mediated control. eBayization, as we define it, occurs when businesses and other institutions attempt to thrive through embracing these three features. These three features of eBayization do not always parallel Ritzer's McDonaldization features of efficiency, calculability, control, predictability, and irrationality of rationality. Broadly conceived, efficiency and calculability will be aspects of any successful large-scale business and are a heritage of modernization that remains prevalent in eBayization. However, as noted above, McDonaldization implies a particular style of efficiency and calculability based on narrow product lines and moderate quality offerings, neither of which is inherent to the processes eBay uses to achieve efficiency and calculability. Ritzer's notions of predictability and centralized control are directly contradicted by eBayization's embrace of variety and market-mediated control. These organizational features of McDonaldization and eBayization are summarized in Table 13.1. Finally, Ritzer's notion of the irrationality of rationality is not a designed-in feature of McDonaldization so much as an unintended consequence. eBayization, too, has its share of unintended consequences, and we address some of these in our conclusion.

Variety

While McDonald's sells essentially one product line through over 31,000 different brick-and-mortar locations (McDonald's Annual Report 2006), eBay offers over 2,500,000 different product lines from one virtual location. An eclectic hodgepodge of consumers seems to provide a market for even the most peculiar things. Indeed, eBay's first auction is renowned for fetching $14.83 for a broken laser pointer, sold to a collector of broken laser pointers (Row 2004). Today, the variety of products eBay offers can boggle even a jaded mind; recent items on sale have ranged from a charming historic Texas town, complete with its high school and library, to anatomical parts (www.npr.org). With apologies to Don Henley of The Eagles, eBayization is "life in the vast lane, everything, all the time."

By *variety*, we mean diversity of offerings experienced by any and all users of the business or other organization in question. There is a sense in which eBay offers a very limited variety of services, in that it is directly selling only access to its website to host an auction, and this access comes in a limited number of forms. However, our definition of variety includes both eBay's direct sale of website access to people hosting auctions and the wide variety of products offered to consumers through those auctions. Just as increases in efficiency only constitute McDonaldization when they are created à la McDonald's, so do increases in variety only constitute eBayization when they are implemented à la eBay. At a minimum, eBayization means using information technology to increase variety at what, by historical standards, would be considered very low costs. In more iconic cases, eBayization means increasing variety by linking together a network of actors. For example, the early Amazon.com was moderately eBayized in its approach to variety in that it used information technology to manage a huge inventory at relatively low costs. Later, however, Amazon.com became fully eBayized when, in addition to selling products from its own inventory, it became the public retail face for a large number of different sellers. This move further increased the already

Table 13.1 McDonaldization and eBayization as features of organizations

	McDonaldization	eBayization
Efficiency	*Efficiency is a core organizational objective.* It is achieved through centralized, hierarchical bureaucratic managerial control (see below).	*Efficiency is a core organizational objective.* It is achieved through information technology that supports, tracks, and collects revenues from many individual transactions.
Calculability	*Calculability is a primary tool used to achieve efficiency.* Almost all aspects of the business, from the physical dimensions of the products to customer satisfaction, are measured quantitatively and analyzed. This information gathering is a task that is over and above the work required to produce the products.	*Calculability is a primary tool used to achieve efficiency.* Almost all aspects of the business are measured quantitatively and analyzed. Much of this auditing and information gathering is a natural byproduct of the information technology used in the core functions of the business.
Control	*Centralized, hierarchical bureaucratic managerial control.* Most key decisions (e.g., what products to offer, what prices to charge) are made at headquarters (i.e., centralized) by formally recognized experts whose power stems from the fact that they are the organizational superiors of the people who will enact the decisions (i.e., hierarchical/bureaucratic).	*Decentralized, market-mediated control.* Most key decisions (e.g., what products to offer, what prices to charge) are made by a vast array of individuals around the world (i.e., decentralized) who may have no formal credentials (i.e., non-bureaucratic) and whose level of power to continue making future decisions is based on the market's response to their current offerings (i.e., market-mediated control).
Variety and predictability	*Low variety/high predictability.* A limited menu allows for low-cost production and for a high degree of standardization. This standardization yields a high level of predictability in the products offered and in the service experience.	*High variety/low predictability.* Because the cost of producing and/or managing inventory is born by the individual sellers, eBay's operating costs remain low while consumers experience a vast array of product choices. However, this decentralized process reduces the predictability of outcomes for all users of the organization.

staggering number of products Amazon offered. And it did so in an eBayized manner, via creating a network of actors such that variety was increased by expanding the scope of the network (i.e., every time a new seller became part of Amazon's network, the variety of offerings experienced by Amazon's users increased).

Similarly, McDonald's limited variety is not an incidental feature of its business strategy; it is a fundamental part of its structure. The original McDonald's started out as a barbeque restaurant that served a fairly wide variety of offerings. When the McDonald brothers realized that most of their profits where coming from hamburgers, they reduced the scope of their menu to nine items, which allowed them to reorganize their production process to use a hamburger assembly line. Henry Ford's famous quote that his customers "can have any color car they want, so long as it is black," also reflects the fact that assembly line production decreases in efficiency as the variety of products being produced increases. Hence, trading off reduced variety for increased efficiency (i.e., lower costs and lower prices) is an essential element of McDonaldization. This is because "McDonaldization" is not a value-neutral description (if there is such a thing); it is a critique that calls our attention to the social and cultural costs of using Fordist-style systems to increase efficiency. Were it possible to increase efficiency without decreasing variety or creating other negative outcomes, it would not be sensible to frame those increases in efficiency as McDonaldization.

As mentioned above, the same types of information technology that allow eBay to offer a wide variety of products have led to more flexible mass production systems, which make increased product variety and even mass customization (Pine 1993) more economically attractive. Using information systems to create more flexible manufacturing constitutes an eBayization of these production processes. Ironically, these flexible manufacturing and tracking systems now allow even McDonald's to be slightly eBayized and expand the variety of its menu from nine items in 1948 to over 50 main items[5] today, including salads and breakfast burritos.

eBay is a prominent example of what is being called a "long tail" business (Anderson 2006). The long tail has been described as "the end of the 80/20 rule" (Etheridge 2008: 1) because unlike many conventional businesses where a few hit products provide most of the profits, a long tail business has a vast array of infrequently purchased products that cumulatively become the mainstay of the enterprise. A former Amazon employee describes the long tail as, "We sold more books today that didn't sell at all yesterday than we sold today of all the books that did sell yesterday" (Brier 2005). Other examples include Tunecore and 101 Distribution, both Web-based businesses that allow independent musicians to produce and sell their music worldwide. It is no coincidence that many long tail businesses are Internet-based, as information technology makes them economically viable.

This difference in the level of variety provided by eBay and McDonald's also reflects a fundamental difference in the consumer problem each business is trying to solve. For McDonald's, the fundamental consumer problem was scarcity. McDonald's solution was efficient production, which delivered food in such abundance that today obesity, linked in no small part to McDonald's and similar businesses, has replaced hunger as America's key food-related health problem. In contrast, the central consumer problem that eBay helps solve for consumers is abundance: choices, information, and potential customers or suppliers. eBay and similar organizations earn their livings in essence as matchmakers, helping, for example, the potential buyer and seller of a good condition 1969 kid's Batman utility belt find each other from among hundreds of millions of others who have neither supply nor demand of that particular item. For many long tail businesses, helping consumers successfully sift through a vast variety of alternatives is a, or even *the*, core benefit they provide.

While information technology allows eBayized business to increase the *supply* of variety at affordable cost, it is changes in the social and cultural environment that complete the equation by generating increased *demand* for variety. Social differentiation, Beck observes, occurs because contemporary individuals have a myriad of social roles, making the construction of a coherent identity, in his view, impossible.[6] Instead, individuals continuously juggle a variety of roles, sometimes all at once (Thompson 1996), creating a highly differentiated society that is broken down into "separate functional spheres" and where "people are integrated into society only in their partial aspects as taxpayers, car drivers, students, consumers, voters . . . and are forced to take into their hands that which is in danger of breaking into pieces: their own lives" (Beck and Beck-Gernsheim 2001: 23). Not surprisingly, then, late modernity ushers in a period of reflection and self-discovery in which individuals are not "born into" an identity, but rather where "becoming" oneself is a lifelong process of self-evaluation, development, and assertion (Ahuvia 2005; Bauman 2001a; Turner 1999). In this endless pursuit of a coherent sense of self, prosperous consumers embrace even the most peculiar objects for their sign-value (Venkatesh, Peñaloza, and Fırat 2006) and their ability to construct and display flexible and complex identities (Ahuvia 2005).

Consumers' identity building through consumption is perhaps the single most pervasive and robust trend in contemporary consumer culture (Arnould and Thompson 2005). Yet, the McDonaldization thesis utterly fails to reflect this trend with its calculative logic that reproduces depersonalization and "dehumanization" (Ritzer 2004: 148). In contrast, eBay thrives on the individuation trend, or individuals' "practical capability for self-assertion" (Beck and Beck-Gernsheim 2001: xvi) by creating experiential and interactive platforms that bring together a zealous community of buyers and sellers, where an endless variety of products and props are offered to consumers busy scripting their own characters. This is not to say that eBay itself is the source of identity creation for great masses of consumers; as a metonym, it is only a small part of the process standing as a symbol for the whole. eBay is conducive to contemporary identity creation in a way that McDonald's is not, and is thus a better metonym for the identity-obsessed dominant zeitgeist of post-industrial societies.

In facilitating identity creation, eBay also serves as a consumption playground (Holt 1995), allowing consumers to devise products, create original commercial narratives, pursue ideological agendas, and make artistic statements while feeling empowered through the process (Modrak and Denfeld 2007; Siddiqui and Turley 2006). Just browsing eBay Pulse (eBay's popularity rating list) reveals many examples, such as the "Evil Kermit Needs a New Home," "I WAS ASSAULTED BY A GANG OF Oompa Loompas," or "Keith Olberman is IN MY PANTS" auctions, where consumers skillfully use their imaginations and creativity to construct unique products and personal narratives (Siddiqui, Turley, and Rifai 2008). In a particularly strong manifestation of this trend, the eBayaday project (Modrak, Ahuvia, and Denfeld 2007) presents eBay auctions by leading conceptual artists; the auction itself, along with the item being sold, share center stage as the creative product.

Such endeavors of identity building and personal narrative construction also allow consumers to perform both as producers and consumers. This dual role and the consumer empowerment it brings along is quite different than what Ritzer (1998) calls McDonald's modern quest to create passive and lifelong consumers, particularly out of children. Criticizing McDonald's marketing to children, Ritzer (1998: 185) writes that:

> McDonald's has historically been defined by its efforts to cater to children with a clown (Ronald McDonald) as its dominant symbol, its playgrounds, its carnival-like atmosphere, its child-oriented foods, and its promotional tie-ins with many movies and toys . . . In these and other ways, McDonald's has sought to make children lifelong consumers of its products.

In contrast, eBayized enterprises do not try to create passive consumers, believing instead that actively engaged consumers are a strong asset (Parise, Guinan, and Weinberg 2008). Rather, these institutions depend on interactive and creative consumers capable of performing as producers devising captivating narratives, inventing products (e.g., Evil Kermit), and providing authentic offerings. Even children become producers in these platforms, writing the adverts of the toys they sell on eBay or creating their profiles on social networking websites.

Unpredictability

One key to McDonald's success is predictability, which ensures that there are "no surprises and no risk in either the environment or food" and that only a "little decision-making is required" (Nancarrow, Vir, and Barker 2005). Taming reality by achieving predictability and control was always a component of the modernist project. While the scientific and technological developments of the modern period largely achieved this goal in certain technical domains, the events of 9/11 fully brought home the fact that the world at large is not a predictable place. Any pertinent metonym for the dominant American zeitgeist needs to capture the uncertainty and ambivalence entailed in risk society.

By unpredictability, we simply mean that as a viewer, shopper, buyer, or seller, you are never sure what is going to happen until it does happen. Part of the pleasure eBay provides is the excitement of exploration; consumers never know what unexpected product will pop up on the computer screen. When bidding on or selling through an auction, one never knows which bid will win or what the final price will be. On a less positive note, consumers are also never sure what the quality, condition, or even authenticity of the product will be when it arrives. For example, studies show that upwards of 90 percent of "Louis Vuitton" and 95 percent of the "Tiffany" items on eBay were counterfeit (Romani et al. 2008). From the seller's perspective, one never knows how long it will take to get paid, or even if one will ever get paid. It is sufficiently common for shoppers to change their minds after winning an auction and never submit payment for an item; eBay has instituted a system of second chance offers whereby the seller can contact other bidders and try to sell them the product if the auction winner fails to pay. All of these elements of surprise and serendipity, for better or worse, fit well with a post-industrial zeitgeist concerned with uncertainty and risk (Bauman 2001b; Beck 1992).

This unpredictability, while sometimes unpleasant, helps humanize eBayized organizations. Indeed, the gifts – both material and virtual – and product commentary serendipitously exchanged among complete strangers serve as social glue in the open access and anonymous platforms of eBay, Facebook, MySpace, and a myriad of other Web 2.0 contexts where consumers construct virtual social solidarity (Giesler 2006). While such solidarity is far removed from the ideal forms of socialization Putnam (2000) describes, virtual and temporal relationships are nevertheless typical of the kind of sociability that a risk society – with its "liquid" (Bauman 2000), in other words, continuously negotiated, fluctuating, and loose conceptions of identity and community responsibilities – engender.

Whether it is the surprise of what is in the box, the strange forms of commodity one comes across (e.g., "foreheads for sale for advertisement purposes," "25,000 friends delivered to your MySpace account in 2 days for a starting bid of $36" are among the recent auctions), or the possibility of mediatization (e.g., "Virgin Mary in Grilled Cheese" and "Tawny Peaks Breast Implants" auctions in Siddiqui, Turley, and Rifai 2008), eBay provides surprise, delight, disappointment, and occasional offense to consumers – and becomes successful in the process.

Market-mediated control

McDonald's is founded on the principle of controlling every part of the production process, right down to zealous efforts to grow standard-size potatoes. eBay also includes mechanisms of centralized control but limits them to a very restricted set of key areas, such as the sale of illegal or highly regulated products, and, of course, rules to ensure that eBay gets its share of the proceeds. But whereas centralized control is a primary strategy for McDonald's, eBay's primary strategy is to harness and ride the cacophony of billions of buyers and sellers by shifting direct control from a centralized bureaucracy to the market. For example, part of McDonald's early success was its reputation for cleanliness at a time when government regulation was somewhat lax. High standards for cleanliness at the local franchise outlets were enforced through inspections from the central headquarters. eBay faces a somewhat analogous issue with regard to fraud by people selling or buying through the eBay website. Online auctions are the single largest source of consumer fraud complaints reported to the Federal Trade Commission (Kuruvila 2006). Perhaps more surprisingly, sellers are also frequent victims of scams where payment is cancelled or reversed after the product is received (Tang 2006). This fraud is a serious problem for eBay and at least as much of a blight on its reputation as a dirty bathroom would have been for McDonald's. Yet, eBay chooses to respond not by tightening centralized control, but by introducing online reputational systems where buyers and sellers rate their interactions with the other party, in the hope that the cumulative voice of the market will limit the damage to tolerable levels. Indeed, eBay is so adamant on maintaining low levels of direct control over user postings that when luxury goods producers tried to force eBay to take action against people selling counterfeit goods through its website, eBay fought them in court to protect its policy of very loose control over what its users say and sell (Romani et al. 2008).

In this sense, eBayization is a fitting metonym for the dominant zeitgeist that is suspicious of large rationalized systems, and eBay very much reflects the deregulation trend of post-Fordist years and the period of intensified globalization that follows. The new global economic order and the deregulation of markets ensure that power and control are used to maintain a smooth functioning system and to increase the profitability of the enterprise, but not to influence the individual consequences for each party involved, placing the responsibility of each action squarely on the individual's shoulders.

The transfer of risks and responsibilities to the individual is a characteristic of the risk society. In postmodernity, individuals, relatively free from traditional roles, ties, and duties, are responsible for charting the course of their lives in the direction of their self-interest and "becoming" their self; the state has considerably scaled back its role of creating opportunities for employment, education, and health, outsourcing these responsibilities to private enterprises. Likewise, the flight of capital from one country to another in pursuit of cheap labor leaves both individuals and states on their own to tackle the economic and social problems of outsourcing.

In the socio-historical context of risk societies, economic organizations such as eBay excel in the global marketplace by facilitating commerce and information exchange. eBay provides consumers mechanisms through which they can control their transactions. For example, PayPal provides reasonable financial security of online payments, Skype allows buyers and sellers to communicate for free, and eBay's feedback tools allow consumers to rate the seller's performance while enabling vendors to build online reputations. In addition, eBay community blogs help disgrace unethical buyers, warn community members about scams, and partially relieve the frustration of cheated users. While these tools and mechanisms facilitate consumers' transactions and somewhat reduce the criminal risk involved, consistent with a market-driven risk society, eBay declines to actively participate in the resolution of most buyer-seller conflicts (Consumer Reports 2007), leaving individuals with the ultimate responsibility to conduct their own research about the authenticity of the items for sale and sellers' backgrounds. Unfortunately, evidence such as the pervasive fraud complaints and the astonishingly high level of counterfeit luxury goods being passed off as second-hand originals, as discussed above, suggests that this "buyer (and seller) beware" principle is simply not up to the task of providing a safe commercial environment.

From a macro-perspective, the societal and global consequences of market-mediated control are potentially quite serious. The policy preference for market-mediated control rests in free market economic theory, which rests in turn on the assumption that consumers can accurately assess the risks and rewards of their purchases. This assumption has long been disputed with regard to typical consumers (Ahuvia 2008; Gabriel and Lang 1995). However, the 2008 collapse of global financial markets made clear that this assumption does not always hold, even for the most sophisticated professional investors backed by the world's largest financial firms. The deregulation of financial markets in general, and mortgage markets in particular, led to eBayization of these markets. In this process, these markets became less homogenized, less predictable, and more market-mediated. The flourishing of new and innovative financial products caused a temporary boom in profits. However, it turned out that even the sophisticated professional investors who were purchasing these instruments were unable to accurately assess the risk associated with them. When the speculative bubble in US housing prices burst and home values fell, the losses to investors were far greater than they had anticipated, and the derivatives that these investors had purchased as a form of insurance turned out not to be solvent. In other words, the overreliance on financial markets' self-regulating capacity brought about a collapse of the global financial system, triggering a global recession.

While eBayization tends to flourish in the context of deregulation, eBayization is not synonymous with small government. Just as businesses can create eBayized systems to help them reach their profit objectives, governments can create eBayized systems to help them reach their policy objectives. eBayized government policies are likely to operate through what Sunstein and Thaler (2003) call "libertarian paternalism" – the use of government imposed incentives to influence behavior within a market without directly limiting choice.[7]

Global warming provides an example of how eBayization is both part of the problem and potentially also part of the solution in the context of libertarian paternalism. It is easy to see how eBayization is part of the problem of global warming. High levels of consumption are largely to blame for global warming, and since both McDonaldization and eBayization are processes that facilitate massive levels of consumption, both are implicated in rising world temperatures (Ritzer 2008). At the same time, carbon cap-and-trade systems provide an example of how eBayization may be part of the solution. Rather than a McDonaldized policy of centralized control producing a standardized solution, the eBayized carbon cap-and-trade policies are designed to maximize efficiency through the consciously crafted application of market forces. Through carbon trading, businesses are encouraged to limit carbon emissions because these emission "savings" can be sold for profit, just like stocks and futures, at Carbon Exchanges throughout the world. Advocates of cap-and-trade systems hope that once businesses have the financial incentive to reduce pollution, entrepreneurs will develop a plethora of innovative pollution reduction technologies. Cap-and-trade advocates also assume that businesses will choose wisely between these technologies so as to maximize pollution reduction and hence their profit. However, whether this system will provide the efficient solutions it promises, or another collapse like the mortgage meltdown, remains to be seen.

In sum, eBayization offers consumers of risk society market-mediated experiences with all the risks and rewards that it entails, both empowering and disempowering consumers in the process.

The scope of eBayization

We have stressed throughout the paper that the rise of eBayization does not imply the sudden death of McDonaldization, even in post-industrial societies. McDonaldization and eBayization are dominant in different sectors of the economy, influencing different segments of society. Currently, eBayization has primarily taken hold where information technology plays a core organizing role in functioning of the businesses or other institutions. As such, it might be argued that eBayization is likely to have less impact on the lives of people without Internet access, and therefore, eBayization's rise and influence will likely go hand in hand with the further diffusion of the Internet.

So long as current trends continue, in the post-industrial world we may see the retreat of McDonalization as it marches backwards along the same path that industrialization moved forwards many years ago. Industrialization began with the creation of large factories to refine raw materials and manufacture production inputs such as cloth, and only later moved into the final mass production of finished consumer goods such as clothing, still later in mass retail such as Sears or McDonald's. Today, the further back on the value chain one looks – from retailers, to distributors, to manufacturers – the less value tends to be placed on variety from a single source and the less tolerable risk becomes. Therefore, eBayization, which links variety to risk, is likely to influence consumer-oriented business more than industrial businesses. This will limit its social impact somewhat, but not as much as if the reverse pattern were true, since it is the retail businesses that interface with popular culture most directly.

Geographically, we have focused on eBay as a metonym for ascendant trends in post-industrial USA and Europe, and argued that McDonaldization is a better fit for ascendant trends in industrializing societies. Yet, it is also possible that just as eBay's reach is global, its utility as a metonym is not completely geographically limited to the post-industrial world. In countries around the globe, there is an emerging international class of global elites whose life experience combines elements of their geographic native culture with an individualistic global elite culture. It is possible that eBayization may extend to this group whatever their geographic location may be.

Concluding remarks

For many people beyond our shores, McDonald's remains the quintessential symbol of American-style modernity, at least for the time being. Yet, as industrialization moves from the USA and Europe to become more strongly associated with the developing world, a Fordist-style business such as McDonald's may no longer seem to capture the specifically American ethos, much less the dominant zeitgeist of contemporary Western society. As American culture shops abound for a new iconic institution to serve as a metonym for the dominant zeitgeist, we suggest we look where everything else can be found: eBay.

eBayization is a process by which social institutions become less predictable, less homogenized, and more market-mediated. From a theoretical perspective, we should note the symbiotic relationship that eBayization has with the intellectual shift from a product-dominant to a service-dominant logic for thinking about markets and marketing (Peñaloza and Mish 2008; Vargo and Lusch 2004, 2008). Whereas goods-dominant logic sees value as created by producers and then sold to consumers, service-dominant logic stresses that value is always co-created by sellers and buyers. This value co-creation is most visible in cases of prosumption,[8] but it occurs even in more typical consumption contexts because much of a product's value lies in the meanings it has for a consumer. In addition, these meanings are created through the consumers' interpretive process. This idea, that consumers are co-creators of value, fits well with the way many eBayized firms look to their customers as partners in their enterprise.

This, in turn, requires a relaxation of certain aspects of centralized control, which can at times be a difficult cultural shift for firms. For example, Parise, Guinan, and Weinberg (2008: 1) advise businesses seeking to profit from actively engaged consumers – "Don't control, let it go." In support of this point, they quote a businessperson as describing the secret to building online consumer communities as saying, "You have to let the members drive. When community members feel controlled, told how to respond and how to act, the community shuts down" (Parise, Guinan, and Weinberg 2008: 1). As Parise, Guinan, and Weinberg (2008: 1) further relate, this shift in thinking about consumers can be a difficult adjustment for some businesspeople:

> One marketing executive recalled the first time she let an online community created for a client interact with very little control or moderation, resulting in an animated discussion about the look of the company's product. The client, with great concern, asked. "Who told them [the consumers] they could do this, that they could go this far?" Of course, when this process resulted in totally new packaging that helped boost sales, the client was ecstatic.

As this example shows, the means by which eBayized institutions revolutionize the way we buy and sell is also bound up with interesting questions of who has the capital and the knowledge to sell and what is a sellable commodity. For instance, in the virtual marketplaces of eBay, individual sellers (housewives, teenagers, and seniors) and small business owners are gaining primacy over large organizations and corporations by giving consumers a sense of empowerment (Siddiqui, Turley, and Rifai 2008), while previously unthinkable and consumer-devised products and services (such as the "25,000 friends delivered to your MySpace account") emerge on a regular basis.

We have also discussed eBayization's role, particularly through its *variety* aspect, in consumer identity projects. eBayized institutions empower consumers by providing a variety of consumption choices and serving as playgrounds where individuals can script their identities. In other words, eBayized economic agents facilitate and support consumers' never-ending task of "becoming" individuals (Bauman 2001a; Beck and Beck-Gernsheim 2001). However, it is important to note that consumers' identity-building endeavors are not solely individualizing, but also collectivizing, as we elaborated in the *unpredictability* aspect of eBayization. As Beck and Beck-Gernsheim (2001: xxi) argue, in postmodern societies, "human mutuality and community rest no longer on solidly established traditions, but, rather, on a paradoxical collectivity of reciprocal individualization." This "collectivity of reciprocal individualization" is perhaps nowhere more readily observable than the open platforms of eBayized institutions, where individuals connect around individual yet shared tastes, experiences, and worries (e.g., online brand communities). Most importantly, these platforms are becoming more instrumental in bringing together and organizing groups of individuals, as evidenced by the success of virtual organizations lsuch as MoveOn.org and YouTube in both mobilizing the youth vote and determining the outcome of the 2008 US presidential elections. In short, whether by facilitating individualization or collectivization, eBayization empowers consumers in pursuing and achieving their goals, may that be crafting an authentic avatar in the virtual world or bringing social change in the real one.

Related to the issue of virtual solidarity, we wonder whether the popularity of eBay and its ability to bring together millions of individuals on a virtual platform – an ability facilitated by innovative technologies of search, security, and monetary exchange – indicate a comeback (although certainly not a full circle) to the festive and public marketplaces of early modernity. Slater and Tonkiss (2001: 12) note how earlier marketplaces are public and hence egalitarian simply because "all classes of people have access to it and might rub shoulders there" as opposed to the market societies that are firmly structured around a few large players and restricted networks. While eBay users physically do not rub shoulders, is not the fact that 2,250,000 Americans sold items, shared advice, wrote reviews, and participated in chats on eBay suggestive of certain elements of marketplaces past?

While we have tended to focus on the positive aspects of eBayization, it is important to note that, just like McDonaldization, this trend has its share of problems as well. Variety is a good thing, but it can also lead to information and choice overload (Schwartz 2003). Unpredictability can often be an annoyance, or worse. Moreover, market-mediated control shifts risks to consumers and small producers, both of whom suffer from fraud and other difficulties on eBay. Most dramatically, though, the global ecological and financial crises we have previously discussed show that the risks and rewards of eBayization go well beyond an individual getting a bargain or getting cheated in an online auction, suggesting that eBayization may be empowering and disempowering consumers at the same time.

Acknowledgments

The authors thank the three anonymous reviewers and editor (at the time of writing) Lisa Peñaloza for their valuable comments.

Notes

1   In a large diverse society such as the USA, there is no single zeitgeist shared by everyone. By "dominant zeitgeist," we do not refer to a universal experience or even necessarily the majority experience, but rather to a socially constructed view of "what's happening now," which reflects emerging social and economic trends and is portrayed by the mass media as representing the spirit of the times.
2   A metonym is a particular type of metaphoric trope in which part of a larger entity is used to represent the whole: for example, the use of the term *Washington* to refer to the US federal government. In the present discussion, McDonald's and eBay are used metaphorically to represent larger economic and social trends of which they are a part, and hence are metonyms.
3   Multimixers were blenders used in making milkshakes.
4   Ray Kroc is the person most associated with McDonald's business success, although all the key elements of the business were created by the McDonald brothers before he arrived. He began as a business partner of the McDonald brothers in 1954. Kroc originally ran the franchising of the business and later purchased the entire business in 1961.

5 This figure of 50+ main items only counts unique food and drink items. A complete list of McDonald's SKUs (i.e., stock keeping units, including different sizes of drinks and ancillary items such as margarine) comes to over 150 items. This data comes from the McDonald's menu, available at the company website.

6 For other views, Ahuvia (2005: 172) includes a brief review of the debate about whether construction of a coherent identity in contemporary post-industrial society is possible and/or desired by consumers.

7 A simple example of libertarian paternalism is placing high taxes on cigarettes to reduce smoking. This policy is "paternalistic" in that the government acts to influence consumers to behave in ways that are in the consumers' own long-term interest, even if the consumers might prefer a different behavior. This policy is "libertarian" in that it still allows consumers a measure of choice, rather than making cigarettes illegal altogether.

8 Prosumption refers to the merger of production and consumption. It occurs when the consumer plays an active role in helping produce the product.

References

Adorno, T.W., and M. Horkheimer. 2000 [1944]. "The culture industry: Enlightenment as mass deception." In *The consumer society reader*, edited by J.B. Schor and D.B. Holt. New York: The New Press, 3–19.

Ahuvia, A.C. 2005. "Beyond the extended self: Loved objects and consumers' identity narratives." *Journal of Consumer Research* 32 (1): 171–84.

Ahuvia, A.C. 2008. "If money doesn't make us happy, why do we act as if it does?" *Journal of Economic Psychology* 29 (4): 491–507.

Alasuutari, P. 1996. "Theorizing in qualitative research: A cultural studies perspective." *Qualitative Inquiry* 2 (4): 371–84.

Alfino, M., J.S. Caputo, and R. Wynyard. 1998. *McDonaldization revisited: Critical essays on consumer culture*. Westport, CT: Praeger.

Anderson, C. 2006. *The long tail: Why the future of business is selling less of more*. New York: Hyperion Press.

Arndt, J. 1985. "On making marketing science more scientific: Role of orientations, paradigms, metaphors, and puzzle solving." *Journal of Marketing* 49: 11–23.

Arnould, E., and C. Thompson. 2005. "Consumer culture theory (CCT): Twenty years of research." *Journal of Consumer Research* 31: 868–82.

Bagguley, P., J.M. Lawson, and D. Shapiro. 1990. *Restructuring: Place, class, and gender*. London: Sage.

Baudrillard, J. 1998 [1970]. *The consumer society: Myths and structures*. Thousand Oaks, CA: Sage.

Bauman, Z. 2000. *Liquid modernity*. Malden, MA: Blackwell.

Bauman, Z. 2001a. *The individualized society*. Malden, MA: Polity.

Bauman, Z. 2001b. "Individually, together." In *Individualization: Institutionalized individualism and its social and political consequences*, edited by Ulrich Beck and Elisabeth Beck-Gernsheim. Thousand Oaks, CA: Sage, xiv–xx.

Beck, U. 1992. *Risk society: Towards a new modernity*. Thousand Oaks, CA: Sage.

Beck, U., and E. Beck-Gernsheim. 2001. *Individualization: Institutionalized individualism and its social and political consequences*. Thousand Oaks, CA: Sage.

Bergman, F. 1983. *The future of work*. St Paul, MN: Praxis International.

Beuka, R. 2004. *SuburbiaNation: Reading suburban landscape in twentieth-century American fiction and film*. New York: Palgrave Macmillan.

Bocock, R. 1993. *Consumption*. New York: Routledge.

Bourdieu, P. 1984. *Distinction: A social critique of the judgment of taste*. Cambridge, MA: Harvard University Press.

Brier, N. 2005. "The long tail: A public diary on themes around a book." Available at: www.longtail.com.

Brown, S. 1995. *Postmodern marketing*. New York: Routledge.

Cohen, E. 2004. "A consumers' republic: The politics of mass consumption in postwar America." *Journal of Consumer Research* 31 (1): 236–9.

Consumer Reports. 2007. "Survey of eBay users reveals online auction seller deception and pitfalls can be hard to avoid." Available at: http://consumerreports.org.

Eckhardt, G.M., and M.J. Houston. 2002. "Cultural paradoxes reflected in brand meaning: McDonald's in Shanghai, China." *Journal of International Marketing* 10 (2): 68–82.

Etheridge, E. 2008. "The long tail: A public diary on themes around a book." Available at: http://longtail.typepad.com.

Falk, R. 1999. *Predatory globalization*. Cambridge: Polity.

Farro, A.L. 2004. "Actors, conflicts and the globalization movement." *Current Sociology* 52 (4): 633–47.

Featherstone, M. 1991. *Consumer culture & postmodernism*. Newbury Park, CA: Sage.

Firat, Fuat A., and Alladi Venkatesh. 1993. "Postmodernity: The age of marketing." *International Journal of Research in Marketing* 10 (3): 227–49.

Firat, Fuat A., and E. Ulusoy. 2011. "Living a theme." *Consumption Markets & Culture* 14 (2): 193–202.

Fraser, H.W. 1981. *The coming of the mass market, 1850–1914*. London: Macmillan.

Friedman, M. 1999. *Consumer boycotts: Effecting change through the marketplace and the media*. New York: Routledge.

Furedi, F. 2002. *Culture of fear: Risk-taking and the morality of low expectation*. New York: Continuum.

Gabriel, Y., and T. Lang. 1995. *The unmanageable consumer*. Thousand Oaks, CA: Sage.

Giesler, M. 2006. "Consumer gift systems." *Journal of Consumer Research* 33 (2): 283–90.

Glickman, L.B. 1999. "Born to shop? Consumer history and American history." In *Consumer society in American history: A reader*, edited by L. Glickman. Ithaca, NY: Cornell University Press, 1–17.

Holbrook, M.B. 1999. "Higher than the bottom line: Reflections on some recent macromarketing literature." *Journal of Macromarketing* 19 (1): 48–75.

Holt, D.B. 1995. "How consumers consume: A typology of consumption practices." *Journal of Consumer Research* 22: 1–16.

Holt, D.B. 2002. "Why do brands cause trouble? A dialectical theory of consumer culture and branding." *Journal of Consumer Research* 29 (1): 70–90.

Izberk-Bilgin, E. 2006. *Love it or hate it: Consumer resistance to global brands from a cross-cultural perspective*. PhD dissertation, University of Illinois at Chicago.

Izberk-Bilgin, E. 2008. "When Starbucks meets Turkish coffee: Cultural imperialism and Islamism as 'other' discourses of consumer resistance." In *Advances in consumer research*, vol. 35, edited by Angela Y. Lee and Dilip Soman. Duluth, MN: Association for Consumer Research, 808–9.

Kellner, D. 1999. "Theorizing/resisting McDonaldization: A multiperspectivist approach." In *Resisting McDonaldization*, edited by B. Smart. Thousand Oaks, CA: Sage.

Klein, N. 2000. *No logo*. New York: Picador.

Kozinets, R.V. 2002. "Can consumers escape the market? Emancipatory illuminations from burning man." *Journal of Consumer Research* 29 (1): 20–38.

Kozinets, R.V., and J.M. Handelman. 2004. "Adversaries of consumption: Consumer movements, activism, and ideology." *Journal of Consumer Research* 31 (3): 691–704.

Kuruvila, M.C. 2006. "Biting into online fraud: Complaints drop, but safety still up to consumers." *Knight Ridder Tribune Business News*, January 28, 1.

Living a Theme. Directed by F.A. Fırat and E. Ulusoy. Memphis, TN: Association for Consumer Research Conference Film Festival, 2007.

Modrak, R., A. Ahuvia, and Z. Denfeld. 2007. "eBayaday." Available at: www.ebayaday.com.

Modrak, R., and Z. Denfeld. 2007. "Artists and the online marketplace: Making a gesture, sharing an idea and carry out a plan in 34 categories." In *eBayADay exhibition catalog*, edited by R. Modrak, A. Ahuvia, and Z. Denfeld. University of Michigan School of Art and Design, 1–7.

Nancarrow, C., J. Vir, and A. Barker. 2005. "Ritzer's McDonaldization and applied qualitative marketing research." *Qualitative Market Research* 8 (3): 296–312.

Parise, Salvatore, Patricia J. Guinan, and Bricue D. Weinberg. 2008. "The secrets of marketing in a Web 2.0 world." *The Wall Street Journal*. Available at: www.wsj.com.

Peñaloza, Lisa, and Jenny Mish. 2008. "Sustainable services development: Insights and challenges for service dominant logic." Paper presented at the Australian Forum on Markets and Marketing: Extending the Services Dominant Logic, Sydney, Australia.

Pieterse, J.N. 2000. "Globalization north and south: Representations of uneven development and the interaction of modernities." *Theory, Culture & Society* 17 (1): 129–37.

Pine, Joseph. 1993. *Mass customization: The new frontier in business competition*. Cambridge, MA: Harvard Business School Press.

Piore, M.J., and C.F. Sabel. 1984. *The second industrial divide: Possibilities for prosperity*. New York: Basic Books.

Putnam, R. 2000. *Bowling alone: The collapse and revival of American community*. New York: Simon & Schuster.

Ritzer, G. 1983. "The McDonaldization of society." *Journal of American Culture* 6: 100–7.

Ritzer, G. 1998. *The McDonaldization thesis: Explorations and extensions*. Thousand Oaks, CA: Sage.

Ritzer, G. 2004. *The McDonaldization of society*. Thousand Oaks, CA: Pine Forge Press.

Ritzer, G. 2008. "A consuming passion: An interview with George Ritzer." *Consumption Markets & Culture* 11: 191–201.

Romani, S., G. Gistri, S. Pace, and A. Ahuvia. 2008. "What is the harm in fake luxury brands? Moving beyond the conventional wisdom." Working Paper.

Row, H. 2004. "The eBay experience." Available at: www.fastcompany.com.

Schwartz, B. 2003. *The paradox of choice: Why more is less*. New York: Ecco/HarperCollins.

Scott, L.M. 1993. "Spectacular vernacular: Literacy and commercial culture in the postmodern age." *International Journal of Research in Marketing* 3: 251–76.

Siddiqui, S., and D. Turley. 2006. "Cries from the goblin market: Consumer narratives in the marketplace." In *Asia-Pacific advances in consumer research*, edited by M.C. Lees, G. Gregory, and T. Davis. Provo, UT: Association for Consumer Research, 7.

Siddiqui, S., D. Turley, and F. Rifai. 2008. "Cries from the goblin market: Consumer narratives in the marketplace." In *Advances in consumer research*, vol. 35, edited by Angela Y. Lee and Dilip Soman. Duluth, MN: Association for Consumer Research, 810–11.

Slater, D. 1997. *Consumer culture and modernity*. Cambridge: Polity.

Slater, D., and F. Tonkiss. 2001. *Market society*. Malden, MA: Polity.

Smart, B. 1999. "Resisting McDonaldization: Theory, process, and critique." In *Resisting McDonaldization*. edited by B. Smart. Thousand Oaks, CA: Sage.

Sunstein, C., and R. Thaler. 2003. "Libertarian paternalism is not an oxymoron." The University of Chicago Law School, John M. Olin Law and Economics Working Paper No. 185. Available at: www.law.uchicago.edu/academics/publiclaw/index. html.

Tang, S. 2006. "The almighty customer." *Financial Times*, April 8, 9.

Tapscott, D., and A. Williams. 2006. *Wikinomics: How mass collaboration changes everything*. New York: Portfolio Hardcover.

Thompson, C.J. 1996. "Caring consumers: Gendered consumption meanings and the juggling lifestyle." *Journal of Consumer Research* 22 (4): 388–407.

Thompson, C.J., and S.K. Tambyah. 1999. "Trying to be cosmopolitan." *Journal of Consumer Research* 26: 214–41.

Thompson, C.J., and Z. Arsel. 2004. "The Starbucks brandscape and consumers' (anticorporate) experiences of glocalization." *Journal of Consumer Research* 31 (3): 631–43.

Thompson, C.J., and G. Coskuner-Balli. 2007. "Countervailing market responses to corporate cooptation and the ideological recruitment of consumption communities." *Journal of Consumer Research* 34 (2): 135–52.

Toffler, A. 1981. *The third wave*. New York: Bantam Books.

Turner, B.S. 1999. "McCitizens: Risk, coolness, and irony in contemporary politics." In *Resisting McDonaldization*, edited by B. Smart. Thousand Oaks, CA: Sage, 83–101.

Turner, B.S. 2003. "McDonaldization: Linearity and liquidity in consumer cultures." *The American Behavioral Scientist* 47 (2): 137–53.

Vargo, S.L., and R.F. Lusch. 2004. "Evolving to a new dominant logic for marketing." *Journal of Marketing* 68 (1): 1–17.

Vargo, S.L., and R.F. Lusch. 2008. "Service-dominant logic: Continuing the evolution." *Journal of the Academy of Marketing Science* 36 (1): 1–10.

Venkatesh, A., L. Peñaloza, and A.F. Firat. 2006. "The market as a sign system and the logic of the market." In *The service-dominant logic of marketing*, edited by R. Lusch and S. Vargo. New York: M.E. Sharpe, 251–66.

Weber, M. 1946. *From Max Weber: Essays in sociology*. New York: Oxford University Press.

Weinstein, D., and M.A. Weinstein. 1999. "McDonaldization enframed." In *Resisting McDonaldization*, edited by B. Smart. Thousand Oaks, CA: Sage.

Zhu, Q., and J. Sarkis. 2004. "Relationships between operational practices and performance among early adopters of green supply chain management practices in Chinese manufacturing enterprises." *Journal of Operations Management* 22 (3): 265–89.

14 Commentary

The consumer perspective on branding

Morris B. Holbrook

The present volume on *Brands: Interdisciplinary Perspectives* recognizes and celebrates the indubitable fact that the practice and study of branding has worked its way into every corner of our society. At the cultural level, brands provide some of the meanings that permeate social customs and the ethos of our times. At the corporate level, brands serve as tools whereby market-driven organizations manipulate promotional messages to create profits that maximize shareholder equity. At the consumer level, brands contribute cognitive-affective-and-behavioral influences that shape and enhance the fantasies-feelings-and-fun of consumption experiences. And at the critical level, various excesses in our cultural, corporate, and consumptive devotion to brands invite critiques that question the commercialistic, capitalistic, and materialistic nature of our commodified worldviews, free-enterprise economic systems, and self-interested personal lifestyles.

The present commentary focuses on four contributions that address the third of these concerns – namely, the role of brands in the enrichment of consumption experiences or, in other words, the penetration of branding into the day-to-day lives of consumers. Obviously, this broad issue lends itself to a large number of different potential approaches. From one point of view, brands have personalities that characterize the product offerings they signify: Ben & Jerry's = sweet and cuddly. From another viewpoint, brands carry images that rub off on the relevant items and that bolster or degrade the social status of those using them: Mercedes = classy; Kia = declassé. From a closely related perspective, we manipulate the brands we use as a form of conspicuous consumption: parading down the avenue with one's Labradoodle = elevated taste in canines. From still another orientation, brands serve as signifiers that contribute meanings to such cultural objects as novels, music, films, or television programs: first, Wild Turkey or, later, Knob Hill bourbon = the suave sophistication of Stone Barrington in the novels by Stuart Woods. From yet another vantage point, brands communicate to ourselves in ways that enhance or damage our own self-esteem: an Armani suit in the closet = pride in one's own affluence; a can of Pabst beer in the fridge = regret over one's lack of worldly success. In short, from any number of different perspectives, the brands with which we live shape the significance of our lives as consumers.

From my own point of view, everything we do involves consumption. And consumption entails a key role played by brands. So it follows that branding, in all its many guises, influences and informs the very core of our existence as human beings on the planet earth. Brands exist because we need them to give life meaning. Meanings arise, in part, because brands serve as signs all up and down the semiological spectrum of significance.

The four chapters under consideration here move from the more narrow to the more broad sphere of concerns with the connections between brands and consumers.

We begin with tattoos as a sort of self-administered brand by which one labels oneself as the embodiment of one or another episteme, ideology, or affiliation. Back in the days when brands originated, a cow had no choice about what brand the cattle rancher would burn into her skin. But, nowadays, people freely choose the tattoos they wear (for life), and these degrees of freedom open up choices whereby communicators such as those in the advertising profession can exploit the meanings of images on the skin to shape the significance of the brands they wish to promote.

From there, we move to a recognition that local-level manifestations of brand-related signification collect and compress various global- or international-level associations with meanings drawn from a variety of cultures from all around the world. The study of such variegated multivocality fits nicely into an essentially postmodern awareness of multicultural brand-based interpretations.

Moving farther toward wider issues, various macro-level aspects of morality surface in the broad question of how commodified celebrities serve as role models in the moral development of young viewers. In my own case, the relevant superhero was Jackie Robinson when, as a child, I saw *The Jackie Robinson Story* and, from there, moved toward an emotionally painful but nonetheless enlightening awareness of the evils fomented by racism in our early-1950s society. As explored in the present context, a more recent case involves the ethical implications for children of the celebrity-brand otherwise known as David Beckham.

Finally, at the cultural level, we might question the extent to which a brand-related phenomenon such as McDonaldization has permeated our society-wide ethos of consumption. Here, the dangers of standardized uniformity and mass-produced mediocrity embodied by, say, a Big Mac contrast with the glimmer of hope provided by the counter-cultural trend toward eBayization wherein variety enhances the chance to match diverse demands with differentiated offerings. Though I never fell for the ingenuous-if-not-cynical promise that, at Burger King, I could have it "my way," I am intrigued by the hope that someday, online (of course), it may be possible to bid for the hamburger of my dreams: thick, red, juicy, laden with onions, sweetened with ketchup, spiced with mustard, and glorified with extra garlic. The nuts-and-bolts delivery system for such a virtual delicacy remains to be perfected.

With these ramblings as a background, let me now say a few words about each chapter – not as a summary, much less a critique, but rather as an invitation for the reader to investigate further.

Consumer-brand assemblages in advertising: an analysis of skin, identity, and tattoos in ads

In this chapter, Bjerrisgaard, Kjeldgaard, and Bengtsson (BK&B) explore ways in which the self-imposed branding of one's own skin via tattoos provides meanings accessible to such marketing applications as advertising for a brand. Here, BK&B focus not so much on how the branding-of-self via tattoos communicates about one's own persona as on the ways in which such self-significations shape the meaning of a brand as portrayed by an ad or commercial.

Perhaps there is an important difference between these two viewpoints, but it might be more insightful to interpret branding as a skin- and advertising-related phenomenon that cuts across both vantage points, leaving open the issue of who or what is the relevant "brand" in question – the person wearing the insignia or the product advertised via insignia-linked imagery. Or – from my own perspective – both.

Perhaps the concept of "entanglement" skirts this issue by blurring it in a satisfying way. At any rate, it seems to me that BK&B focus primarily on the process of building brand meanings through advertising. In this, they raise questions about the extent to which tattoo-linked significations are imposed on an essentially passive audience, rather than negotiated with an actively resistant consumer. I cannot imagine any thoughtful postmodern or post-postmodern thinker opting for the former choice, so I shall confine my attention mostly to the question of how the relevant meanings are jointly manipulated by marketers (advertisers) and audiences (consumers).

In this connection, BK&B emphasize that consumers construct their bodies in ways that communicate about their own identities (cosmetic surgery, exercise regimens, body piercing, and – of course – tattoos). Such meanings then become available for the creation of consumer-brand "assemblages," of which BK&B recognize three major types.

First, the body potentially serves as a *canvas* for the inscription of various cultural or especially countercultural meanings. Second, the tattoo may represent a *fashion statement* whereby one attempts to integrate oneself with costume-related social norms. Third, as a *brand extended*, the tattoo may actually make reference to a particular commercial connection with a consumer product such as Mary Read, Eastpak, or Perrier Jouët.

The latter situation strikes me as a suitable point of departure for debunking any residual temptations to regard the consumer as a passive dupe, rather than as an actively resistant interpretive agent. With respect to this issue, we might conduct the following thought experiment. Imagine a world in which, like the cow branded by the proverbial cattle rancher, each individual was required by law to wear the brand of some sponsoring organization on his or her left shoulder – say, the Coca-Cola insignia for some folks or the Pepsi logo for others. We might safely bet that this initiative would encounter a rather obstreperous level of resistance – much of it connected to the celebration of freedom, with plentiful references to the first amendment and strong objections based on the mandates of life, liberty, and the pursuit of happiness. Indeed, the imposition of mandatory tattoos – as practiced, for example, by the Nazi prison camps – has become something of a cliché for capturing the essence of a repressive society.

Let us, therefore, celebrate a society in which I can wear the Nike swoosh on my forehead if I want to and Nike can picture me in their advertisements and – thanks to such assemblages and entanglements – we can wonder whether Nike labels me or I label Nike or, in short, how we can tell the dancer from the dance.

Consumer multiculturalism: consequences of multicultural identification for brand knowledge

Speaking of dancing, recent demographic data have shown a clear trend in which the Hispanic population in the USA has increased by 50 percent over the past decade and, given the relevant birth-rate statistics, will double again over the next 50 years until Latinos compose about one-third of the US population. Toss in the Asians, the Europeans, and those from other countries, and it becomes clear that dance bands had better start learning to play more sambas, mambos, rhumbas, boleros, and tangos – not to mention waltzes, yangges, syrtoi, and polkas. Further, we had all better start brushing up on our Spanish and Japanese – plus, as Kipnis, Broderick, and Demangeot (KB&D) would have it, being more sensitive to the multicultural meanings embedded in our vernacular sign systems, including those associated with brand imagery.

The point just made seems pretty obvious, but KB&D delve more deeply into the ways that local, global, and foreign multicultural meanings inter-penetrate in the formation of brand identities. Here, the relevant concept is "consumer multiculturalism" with its concern for "how consumers may develop affiliations with one, two, or multiple cultures, resulting in various types of cultural identities." In this connection, KB&D emphasize the culture of brand origin (COBO) in developing consumer brand knowledge (CBK) and stress the contrast between perspectives focused on "global" reach (one big world) versus "foreign" aspects (specific ethnic differences). The latter influences involve "identity discourses whereby individuals can simultaneously integrate composite identity links with several cultures that become interwoven within a given locale."

In other words, simplifying greatly, a brand identity emerges from the com-posite linkages of multiple cultures drawn from variegated local connections that extend internationally. Reverting to the example mentioned earlier, far from homogeneous, the "Hispanic" market embraces associations drawn from Mexico, Puerto Rico, Cuba, the Dominican Republic, Colombia, Argentina, and . . . any number of other Latin countries and cultures. Lumping all this under a single heading such as "Hispanic" or "Latin" involves a gross oversimplification. At any rate, responding to these and other multicultural differences, we acquire what KB&D (following anthropologist Arjun Appadurai) refer to as "hyphenated identities." For example, someone living near me on the Upper West Side of New York might draw upon the local influences of his neighbors to develop an American-Jewish-Dominican-Chinese-Russian identity. Obviously, with mixing and matching, the possibilities are endless:

> In culturally diverse societies, individuals may be strongly influenced by more than one FC [foreign culture]: the identity of an individual of Italian descent in the USA may be influenced, along with Italian and American cultures (ancestry/heritage and residence links), by French culture if he holds an affective bias towards France and by an African culture if he is in a relationship with someone of African origin (affiliative links).

Thus, we must study the identities of both people and brands from a perspective that acknowledges the interplay of diverse cultural influences (local, global, foreign) that converge at a given market location. This places the emphasis squarely on "hyphenated identities" within a multicultural environment.

From this, it follows that brand loyalties should reflect the particular mix of local-global-foreign influences adopted by a given consumer in the pursuit of CBK. KB&D present a table of possibilities – based on the $2 \times 2 \times 2$ possible combinations of local-global-foreign orientations. Further consideration of the local-global-foreign distinctions leads toward a further classification based on the differences between, say, cosmopolitanism, world-mindedness, cultural openness, xenocentrism, internationalism, ethnocentrism, patriotism, and nationalism.

But, here, my heart cries out for specific illustrations to give substance to the conceptual typology and classification scheme. For example, I might characterize my own consumption this afternoon of the music from a recording that features tangos by Astor Piazzolla (Argentinian) as performed by the New York-based Pablo Aslan (entitled *Piazzolla in Brooklyn*) as belonging to the category of "cultural openness." Surely, my consumption experience with this Soundbrush CD embodies meanings that jumble the New York and Argentinian cultures in ways that affect both my own identity as a consumer and the relevant brand identity of the offering consumed. At any rate, the provision of further examples – analyzed along the lines sketched by KB&D – appears to suggest a worthy topic for further research.

The role of commodified celebrities in children's moral development: the case of David Beckham

Even before reading the chapter by Wicks, Nairn, and Griffin (WN&G), I have long been a believer in the power that our identification as young consumers with celebrity role models can exert on our moral development as we approach adulthood. In my own case, a rather vivid example stems from my experience with a film about the early career of one of my own personal heroes – Jackie Robinson – entitled *The Jackie Robinson Story* (1950). I first saw this movie when I was a naive and innocent consumer of about 7 or 8 years in age. The experience distressed me deeply because I did not understand how a baseball player of such enormous talent could be subjected to the sorts of indignities portrayed on-screen by Jackie playing himself as the eponymous hero. When I returned home after the Saturday kiddie matinee where this film was screened, mystified, I asked the black lady who worked for us why the fans and players had treated Jackie so badly. She lovingly and patiently explained to me – at what cost to her own gentle sensitivities I will never know – a little bit about racial prejudice, not omitting some horrific details of how our own neigh-borhood children sometimes threw rocks at her when she left our house after work. I cannot begin to describe the agony I felt over these revelations that someone I loved so much could be treated with such cruelty. Suffice it to say that *The Jackie Robinson Story* encouraged my awakening to the moral calamities of racial prejudice in ways that have been with me ever since.

WN&G offer nuanced analyses of the sort of phenomenon just described. In this, they bypass the typical concern with the ethics of marketing to children (a worthy and extensively researched topic in itself) in favor of a focus on how child-targeted marketing can affect the moral development of young audience members. They focus on commodified celebrities as the locus for such moral influences in general and the special case of sports icon David Beckham as an ethical role model in particular.

It appears to worry WN&G that celebrity heroes typically reflect aspects of the market-driven culture by which they are, in part, created. I share WN&G's concerns about commodification as an influence on consumer culture. So I guess I, too, should worry that corporate greed or the profit motive might dictate which potential heroes get selected as the celebrity endorsers who champion what may turn out to be self-serving aspects of ethical values or social norms.

Such concerns arise in the case of David Beckham, whose success as a sports hero appears to be matched only by his fame as a spokesman for various brands of clothing, magazines, entertainment, and so forth. How, we might wonder, is his iconic appeal to children problematized by his connection with the process of commercialization?

In a refreshing departure from the norm of idle speculation, WN&G have collected interview data from children aged 7–8 and 10–11. The children themselves selected Beckham as a key target for discussion and chose to focus on "Beckham's participation in commercial spheres." Thus, as established by the children's own concerns, impressions concerning Beckham's sports-related heroism celebrate his perseverance, hard work, and courage. But, counterbalancing such good qualities, the children also comment on Beckham's self-promotion or even vanity – which WN&G link with impressions of "*(in)authenticity* and . . . *spectacularisation.*" Beckham's perceived tendency to show off is also connected with a perceived inclination toward greed – that is, being overcompensated for his otherwise estimable accomplishments. WN&G see such comments as a "critique of the increasing commercialisation of soccer players." Thus,

> In their debates around David Beckham the children grapple with the paradox of a man who epitomises the increasingly commercialised world *par excellence* and who can, at the same time, be construed as an active and engaged father and husband, a male pin-up, and furthermore, as a role model in relation to sporting achievement, perseverance and hard work, and as an ambassador of England and long-term captain of the national team in what is popularly construed as the national sport.

The point of all this seems to be that children display a surprisingly nuanced understanding of ethical issues in general and of those moral questions posed by the spectacle of celebrity role models in particular. Thus, by challenging the views of young audience members, a commodified sports hero and spokesperson such as David Beckham plays a role in their moral development. This role entails a process of understanding what WN&G characterize as "*ambivalent, contested, negotiated, located* and *mediated.*"

In other words, the interpretation of a commodified celebrity such as David Beckham involves a *struggle* between alternative meanings and ambiguous implications. Beckham brings to light various confusions that belong to a complex situation and that children apparently recognize as part of their interpretive work. All this leads toward a perspective that advocates our acceptance of complexity and tolerance for ambiguity in dealing with moral issues:

> following on from all of the above, an understanding of ourselves – both children and adults – as implicitly moral persons engaged in moral discourse and moral action in the messy contexts of our everyday lives signifies an explicit shift in the ways in which we might talk about ethical decision-making and value judgements with one another. We may help children to see that they will continually be faced with choices regarding how they interpret morality and themselves and others as moral persons, and that claims of uncertainty and confusion ("*I don't know what to think*") may represent not moral immaturity, but a moral self in the thick of critical engagement with complex questions and with opportunities for morality-in-the-making.

So, in retrospect, it appears that I was lucky. Confronted with a new innocence-shattering awareness of racial prejudice in the America of 1950, I did not find such ambiguities in the case of Jackie Robinson – whom, to this day, I prefer to regard as a pure hero, a worthy role model, admirable in every way. Who knows what confusion I might have suffered had I been required to base my moral judgments on the example set by, say, Alex Rodriguez or Tiger Woods. If I had a young child today, despite the embrace of ambiguity advocated by WN&G, I might advocate the adoption of a role model such as, say, Derek Jeter or Mariano Rivera – men for whom any temptations toward the commercial and ego-inflating side of celebrity (Derek in ads for Ford and Skippy peanut butter, Mariano as a spokesman for Acura and Arrid Deodorant) do not appear to compromise their stature as worthy sports heroes and estimable role models for young folks.

Limits of the McDonaldization thesis: eBayization and ascendant trends in post-industrial consumer culture

All of which brings us to the capstone chapter by Ahuvia and Izberk-Bilgin (A&I-B) on the topic of McDonaldization and various countervailing tendencies that A&I-B label "eBayization" in tribute to that somewhat fragmented or fractionated, if not fractured, manner of doing business when variegated suppliers greet diverse buyers online to swap stuff for money.

To me, McDonaldization emerges as the logical outcome of our potentially misguided push toward what the British like to call "Fordism" – that is, a deference to efficiencies of production achieved via standardization and an attempt to cater to the "average" consumer via the mass marketing of a cheap-but-functional product. As every marketing guru from Ted Levitt to Phil Kotler has proclaimed, pursuing a one-size-fits-all strategy – no matter how efficient in terms of production costs – commits a fallacy that ignores the diverse needs and wants of consumers. This sort of Fordism logic ultimately leads toward the creation of a Big Mac – everybody's favorite whipping boy as the hallmark of standardized production and mass-market selling gone amuck.

I personally wonder if McDonald's food is any worse for us than the stuff we cheerfully buy from the supermarket and cram down our greedy maws without a second thought. For example, is a grilled chicken sandwich at McDonald's any more caloric or less nutritious than a frozen cheese-sausage-and-mushroom pizza produced by Stouffer's and sold by Gristides or delivered by Fresh Direct? Probably not. Yet, McDonald's suffers from a special stigma that cannot be removed no matter how many "healthy salads" they try to offer.

To add insult to injury, A&I-B now tell us that the McDonald's model may be eroding or submerging in the face of a newer trend toward eBayization. I greeted this news with a bit of skepticism born from my experiences on the two or three occasions when I have succumbed to the temptation to purchase an expensive item online from eBay. The two most upsetting e-shopping experiences both involved my purchase of rather expensive vibraphones – each selling for over $500. The first one arrived in one piece but, somehow, was much smaller and dinkier than the tempting photos on the website had suggested. Ultimately, disappointed and frustrated, I donated it to a local music school and took a nice tax deduction. The second never arrived at all because I received a telephone warning from Western Union advising me that I had probably tried to wire money to the perpetrator of a scam. Either way – cheesy disappointment or costly scam – it strikes me that eBay may not provide the ideal retailing environment for yours truly.

But – blessed by an open mind that (according to a curmudgeonly friend), like a trashcan without its cover, invites the deposit of other people's garbage – I vowed to approach A&I-B's arguments for eBayization with an attitude of receptivity. Appealing to my credulity, near the outset, A&I-B offer the following well-articulated summary of their central thesis:

> We contend that the term McDonaldization is not illustrative of the way a growing number of institutions organize and compete in a truly global and highly information-driven marketplace. Nor do we believe that it captures the dominant cultural zeitgeist of postmodern societies in the USA and Europe. . . . Rather, we suggest the term eBayization, a postmodern form of economic and social organization powered by an information economy, as a fitting label for an emerging countertrend. In postmodern societies, McDonaldization and eBayization currently coexist and inform each other, and will likely do so in the future. Hence, . . . we propose eBayization as an alternative theoretical lens with which to think about and evaluate the emerging economic practices and social relationships in post-industrial societies.

The logic goes something like this. Suppose I want to purchase a table-model AM radio to listen to the Yankee games broadcast over CBS in New York City. As one option – the McDonaldized side of things – I can visit Radio Shack, where I will find a number of lookalike AM/FM tabletop sets that scream "digital" and "online" and "Bluetooth" at me. By comparison – in the spirit of eBayization – if I visit eBay.com, I will find a wide array of AM table radios ranging from a 1938 Zenith, to a 1946 RCA, to a 1948 Philco, to a 1951 General Electric, to a current-day Tivoli (designed by Henry Kloss), and a lot more besides. In short, at eBay, I will encounter a vast variety of offerings. And this variegated availability of unique products should better satisfy the diverse preferences of consumers from different market segments (electronics buffs in search of tube equipment, decorators looking for something campy, baseball aficionados who want to relive the authentic radio-broadcast experience, collectors of fine antiques, fans of Henry Kloss and his audio innovations, and so forth).

We should note that, here, the key difference depends on ways in which eBay, as opposed to McDonald's, can capture the passage of time. Each of the eBay offerings probably reflected the ethos of Fordism or McDonaldization at the time of its market introduction – that is, cranking out cheap-but-serviceable table radios at the lowest possible cost. But, over time, the continued availability of different models from different eras ensures a diversity of offerings on the second-hand market. By contrast, McDonald's cannot sell 50-year-old hamburgers, no matter how delicious they might taste to various segments of today's society. Hence, thanks to the march of time, eBay enjoys an "unfair advantage" in appealing to a variety of tastes.

Happily, A&I-B offer an analysis far more nuanced than that just presented by yours truly. The essence is that, with the "McDonaldization thesis," we trade variety for predictability whereas, with the "eBayization thesis," we trade uniformity for risk. Along with predictability go the evils of excessive standardization aimed at the lowest common denominator.

A&I-B register seemly resistance to the essentially elitist Adorno-like notion that catering to the largest possible clientele inevitably entails a reduction in the quality or aesthetic merit or complexity of an offering. But, on this front, I tend to side with Adorno. Face it, McDonald's produces an indubitably dumbed-down hamburger. I happen to enjoy McDonald's food (in small doses), but this speaks ill of me, not of Adorno.

However, under what A&I-B call the "irrationality of rationality," I must question whether McDonald's and similar organizations, all by themselves, have led toward a more homogenized, dehumanized society. To me, it seems more likely that the masses of people already lacked fine discrimination in their tastes for fast food before they ever walked through the doors of a McDonald's outlet. Conversely, bravely enduring false accusations of elitism, those folks who refuse to visit the golden arches may still be eating humble homegrown victuals that they themselves grew down on the farm.

However, A&I-B's main criticism of the McDonaldization thesis is that it is "notably incomplete" in its disregard for the emerging phenomenon of eBayization:

> We argue that as a way of understanding contemporary reality in post-industrial information-based economies, McDonaldization is notably incomplete. In post-industrial societies, the social and economic forces that led to the rise of McDonald's-like organizations are, at best, holding steady and are arguably on the wane, while ascendant social and economic trends lead to a different type of production and consumption exemplified by eBay. For the foreseeable future, McDonald's-like and eBay-like firms will coexist, occupying different niches in the marketplace . . . In sum, though, we argue that eBayization captures the rising social, historical, and economic conditions that are shaping the new developments in the post-industrial societies of the USA and Western Europe.

Here, A&I-B blame the decline of McDonaldization on the emergence of societal trends that favor a more fragmented consumer base – heterogeneous tastes in pursuit of tailor-made offerings as part of the shift from a modern to a postmodern ethos. According to A&I-B, these shifts move toward a greater acceptance of risk in the service of catering to heterogeneous consumer preferences via the availability of customized or at least diverse products.

Into the breach step eBay and like-minded organizations equipped to offer variety at the cost of unpredictability:

> Whereas McDonald's functions as a metonym for Fordist, bureaucratic, centralized, hierarchical organizational structures, eBay serves as a metonym for organizations within post-industrial risk society, which . . . utilize relatively distributed, networked, and market-mediated organizational structures. More specifically, the key differences between eBay and McDonald's can be seen in three features of eBay: variety, unpredictability, and market-mediated control. eBayization, as we define it, occurs when businesses and other institutions attempt to thrive through embracing these three features.

According to A&I-B, the ability of eBay-like businesses to target diverse individual preferences enhances the customer's efforts to construct and display an identity that captures his or her sense of self. Thus, a clear societal benefit accrues to the emergence of the eBay-related phenomenon. Specifically, "eBay is conducive to contemporary identity creation in a way that McDonald's is not, and is thus a better metonym for the identity-obsessed dominant zeitgeist of post-industrial societies."

The only problem with this otherwise reasonable argument is that I am not quite sure it is true. In my own case, for example, I tend to identify with the caramel sundae available at McDonald's – all the more if I can persuade the sometimes recalcitrant salesclerk to add some extra caramel (usually at a charge of 40 cents or so). By contrast, as A&I-B correctly anticipate, I do not fully appreciate the identity-enhancing element of risk encountered on eBay. For example, when my expensive vibraphone turned out to be a lot more rinky-dink than I had anticipated, I felt cheated, not humanized. Certainly, my sense of self was not enhanced by playing a tinny sounding toy-like musical instrument. Despite the risk-accepting zeitgeist of our time, if I were a woman, I do not think that I would buy my breast implants from eBay, opting instead for the potentially dehumanizing offerings made available by modern medicine.

A&I-B end by calling attention to the compatibility of eBayization with the service-dominant logic that has recently taken over so relentlessly in marketing circles. I agree, of course, that eBay users participate with the website's providers in the co-creation of value. But, frankly, I see the same process at work in fast-food outlets. Watching my wife Sally negotiate with the McDonald's employee for extra hot fudge at both the top and bottom of her sundae serves as a lesson in actively engaged consumption behavior. And, in this connection, it surprises me that A&I-B do not mention the counter-McDonaldization ethos of Burger King, which promised so memorably to let us have it "our way." True, this promise turned out to be largely illusive in nature or even a cynical scam – as anyone who has waited in line for an extra half-hour because he wanted to "hold the pickles, hold the relish" will gladly attest. But, in this age of value co-creation, there are ways of customizing one's Big Mac, even without the help of the McD's employees. One can remove the top of the bun, scrape off the gunky sauce, pick up the slice of pickle, and toss the offending accoutrements into the nearest trash receptacle. What is left is an approximation of what you wanted. It is not the same as a 1950s customized burger; it does not rival the goopy excess of the burgers at the now-defunct Big Nick's on Broadway; it does not touch the exorbitant extravagance of the 5 Napkins monster burger; but, hey, it is a lot easier and way more predictable than dining on eBay.

Part IV
Critical perspectives

15 Aesthetics awry

The Painter of Light™ and the commodification of artistic values

Jonathan E. Schroeder

We believe that the walls of the home are the new frontiers for branding.
(Thomas Kinkade, the Painter of Light—painter,
best-selling author, inspirational speaker,
CEO, real estate developer)

Art represents the highest goals of humans, and also the most crass commercialism, speculation, and ego gratification. Since the Renaissance, artists have been recognized as individual creators, valorized as expressive geniuses, and reified as heroes. With the rise of the artist as the acknowledged producer of acclaimed artwork, the art market provides compelling insight into organization—the managerial realm intersects with the art world in numerous ways. However, the separation of art and business—into high and low forms of cultural production—has had a profound influence on how art is viewed by researchers, cultural critics, and consumers alike (cf. Guillet de Monthoux 2000, 2004; Schroeder 1997, 2000; Venkatesh and Meamber 2006). This paper presents a case study of the tremendously successful American artist Thomas Kinkade, whose artistic output spans several industries, reaches thousands, and makes millions. I invoke Kinkade as a warning—or counter-case—for art and management, to question management studies' embrace of aesthetics, or, at least, a romantic notion of aesthetic endeavor.

Although often portrayed as transgressive tramps rallying against the oppressive system, many artists—particularly the famous ones—have, for centuries, participated in the persuasive mechanisms of the market, tapping sympathetic subjects, aggressive agents, and powerful patrons. The artist's critical role emerged later, heavily embroidered with myth, and today expresses itself in performance art, body art, and shock imagery—the kind that receives the wrath of the fanatical right. Suffice it to say that the last century revealed the intricate interconnections between the aesthetic and political realms. Artists do critique society, even if public recognition, fame, and appropriation mute that critique by the very objects of its reproach. However, market conditions often mitigate against critical commentary: "In today's art world the need to make a splash all too often overrides the idea of art as a long and difficult cultivation of art and soul" (Johnson 2001: B36). Art remains deeply entrenched with power. Museums celebrate affluence, images create wealth, and the art market remains a monetary machine (e.g., Benhamou-Huet 2001; Fry and Goodwin 1999; Stallabrass 2004).

Aesthetics, management, and marketing scholarship: a brief, interdisciplinary review

The growing field of aesthetics and management has reached a critical mass. In the practitioner arena, books extolling creativity, aesthetic experience, and vision come replete with insights from real live artists, and workshops are held regularly on creativity, reaching the artist within, and painting your way to power (OK, I made that one up). Management studies scholars write about theatrical insights (e.g., Austin and Devin 2003; Clark and Mangham 2004), morality and aesthetics (e.g., Borgerson 2002; Cairns 2002), markets and aesthetics (e.g., Joy and Sherry 2004; Schroeder 2000), arts management and aesthetics (Chong 2001), entrepreneurship and artists (Fillis 2004), and aesthetics and corporate responsibility (Küpers 2002), to name a few. Some question the rote application of aesthetics in organizations, worrying about new managerial dictates (e.g., Monin, Sayers, and Monin 2004; Warren 2002).

In the field of organization studies, Rafaël Ramirez's (1991) *Beauty of Social Organization* inspired many scholars in an aesthetic turn. *Organization and Aesthetics* by Antonio Strati (1999) has become well respected, its contribution resting on applying aesthetics to understanding organizations from a psychologically informed organizational theory point of view. Strati and Pierre Guillet de Monthoux have contributed two special journal issues on management and aesthetics, one in *Human Relations* (Strati and Guillet de Monthoux 2002) and another in *Consumption Markets & Culture* (Guillet de Monthoux and Strati 2002). Heather Höpfl and Stephen Linstead's (2000) edited volume *The Aesthetics of Organization* offers a useful, well-conceived introduction to the field. Adrian Carr and Philip Hancock's (2003) *Art and Aesthetics at Work* collection focuses on the ups and downs of aesthetics in and about the workplace. Dutch theorist Geip Hagoort (2004) collects his insights into arts management in *Art Management: Entrepreneurial Style* with a focus on managing cultural and arts firms. Guillet de Monthoux's (2004) *The Art Firm: Aesthetic Management and Metaphysical Marketing from Wagner to Wilson* traces the intellectual genealogy of aesthetic experience in the economy. Richard Caves (2002), like Guillet de Monthoux, writes about the organization of the "creative industries," with a focus on how artists interact with the market in his *Creative Industries: Contracts between Art and Commerce*, but without the historical sweep. Stephen Taylor and Hans Hansen (2005) provide a useful review of this emergent field, focused on aesthetic inquiry.

In the marketing milieu, Stephen Brown and Anthony Patterson's (2000) edited collection *Imagining Marketing: Art, Aesthetics, and the Avant-Garde* helped map new directions, offering interdisciplinary investigations into consumption and aesthetics. A more managerial oriented effort, *Marketing Aesthetics: The Strategic Management of Brands, Identity, and Image*, by Bernd Schmitt and Alex Simonson (1997), as the title suggests, covers practical implications, but it shares an interest in aesthetic production and value. My own *Visual Consumption* (Schroeder 2002) focuses on aesthetic issues, but is more concerned with contemporary visual aspects of the economy.

What unites these various efforts is an effort to take aesthetics seriously, and to find ways to approach, appreciate, and apply aesthetic concerns to management issues. Many draw upon classic aesthetic theories—even Kant— some call upon art history, and occasionally turn to weighty philosophical treatises. In doing so, a few end up reinforcing the very barrier they wish to collapse, by separating the economic and aesthetic realm as if commerce was divorced from culture (cf. du Gay, Allen, and Pryke 2001; Klamer 1996; Schroeder 2005). Much of the writing in management and marketing aesthetics offers earnest, hopeful, and appreciative paeans to the power of aesthetics to transform organization and consumers. Although I join this call, and undoubtedly I occasionally fall prey to this theoretical trap, I offer Kinkade— and the way his brand functions within the market—as a warning sign; his winsome art and wealth-generating product portfolios throw caution against reinventing the dualistic dilemma of art versus commerce, or glamorizing aesthetic endeavors.

Thomas Kinkade, the Painter of Light™

Thomas Kinkade is America's most commercially successful and wealthy artist. If you have missed him on your art museum visits and Left Bank gallery strolling, fear not, for Kinkade has not (yet) been embraced by the cultural elite. His works can be found at his worldwide chain of art galleries, on his website, and in online collectable forums such as eBay. He regularly appears on home shopping channels, talk shows, and in shopping malls. His art graces greeting cards, puzzles, mugs, calendars, night-lights—as well as canvas. One in 20 American homes proudly displays a Kinkade art-based product; his sales reached $131 million in 2001 (Miller 2002). His media savvy reveals itself on his website, where we learn a little about managing corporate identity and image:

> Media Arts Group, Inc. hereby grants you the limited right to reproduce in its entirety and without alteration of any kind the images listed below according to the following guidelines. You may not use these images in a manner which contains subject matter which Media Arts may deem, at its sole discretion, in poor taste or to be disparaging to Thomas Kinkade, Media Arts or its products or services. This right is revocable at Media Arts' sole discretion. Images may only be used for inclusion in news articles or other media outlets. Images cannot be used to promote, endorse

or sell and products, nor can they be used for advertising or inclusion in brochures or other sales materials. The following credit line must accompany image usage "Photograph courtesy Thomas Kinkade, Media Arts Group, Inc. Morgan Hill, CA 95037."

(Media Arts Group 2003a)

Kinkade's art, while not gracing many museums, has attracted the attention of art book publishers—the prestigious Bulfinch publishing firm brought out his retrospective catalogue and memoir, *The Thomas Kinkade Story: A 20 Year Chronology of the Artist*, in which we learn that Kinkade trained as a painter at Berkeley before venturing out into the commercial art world (Barnett and Kinkade 2003). He places his work firmly in the *plein air* tradition of the impressionists, tracing his artistic genealogy back to Monet and other masters of the form (Dougherty and Kinkade 2002).

The Thomas Kinkade Lifestyle Brand—that is the catchy, official phrase from his holding company Media Arts, Inc.—encompasses a highly developed product portfolio, including a chain of 350 Signature Galleries, limited edition prints, Master Highlighter Events, portfolio building workshops, crews of artistic assistants, a listing on the New York Stock Exchange, best-selling books, and real estate (Kinkade and Spencer 2002, 2003; Media Arts Group 2003b, 2003c). The master delights in discussing the intersections of art and management (cf. Brown 2002). Kinkade, The Painter of Light™, who believes that "the walls of the home are the new frontiers for branding," has turned his painting into big business—on a scale that demands attention from management scholars. He loves talking about his art firm, Media Arts Group, the largest art-based company in history, proudly announcing that *10 million* people have purchased a Kinkade product—generally syrupy, sentimental images that reify the rural past, and really do not interact with the contemporary world of performance art, body sculpture, and shock art (see his website: ThomasKinkade.com).

Thomas Kinkade provides a powerful case study of aesthetics gone awry, a warning about applying excessive art, or at least a romantic, historically uncontextualized vision of aesthetics, to management studies. In Kinkade's case, the connections between art and commerce are fairly (OK, very) clear, and it is easy to disparage his form of mass art. However, he seems to fulfill a need for aesthetic expression within a market mentality. Kinkade, while not accepted by the cultural gatekeepers, has nevertheless achieved considerable fame (and wealth) via his painting and related activities: "no matter what you might think of Kinkade's artistic merits, his celebrity suggests that he's tapped into a collective longing among Americans for real community" (Brown 2002: 1). He seems happy with his market-friendly strategy, and eagerly promotes his vision of the good life. Kinkade's aesthetic sensibility reflects his non-confrontational ethos: "Art can show us a way to lead simpler, richer, more satisfying life" (Kinkade 2005). However, Kinkade's optimistic intentions play small roles in his vast enterprise.

Figure 15.1 Thomas Kinkade, The Painter of Light™ with his original painting
Spring Gate (photograph courtesy Thomas Kinkade, Media Arts
Group, Inc. Morgan Hill, CA 95037)

Many artists and art dealers are business-focused; Kinkade may have just taken this commercial concern to its logical extreme. His analysis: "I created a system of marketing compatible with American art" (Orlean 2001: 128). Kinkade, like Andy Warhol, saw the value of mass production, branding, and celebrity to build his expansive empire (Schroeder 1997, 2005). Lest we chuckle that only Americans would fall for his schlocky sentimental work, rest assured that he has opened several galleries in Europe, the heartland of high art. Kinkade echoes the concerns of many a brand manager: "I want my work to be available but not common. I want it to be a dignified component of everyday life. It's good to dream about things. It's like dreaming of owning a Rolex – instead, you dream about owning a seventy-five-thousand-dollar print" (Orlean 2001: 128). A consummate image manager, Kinkade modestly remarks: "I have this certain ability to have in my mind an image that means something to real people." He obviously "touches" consumers. As one evangelist Christian website gushes:

> Thomas Kincade [sic] has become a modern-day Norman Rockwell, painting, in his words, "scenes that serve as places of refuge for battle-weary people." In this novel, he invites readers to enter a similar place of

Figure 15.2 Media Arts website (www.mediaarts.com/2003)

refuge: Cape Light. Nestled in Coastal New England, this picturesque little village is a seaside hamlet where folks still enjoy a strong sense of community, and everybody cares about their neighbors. They are friends and neighbors, doers and dreamers. They are the people who laugh and love and build their lives together in the town of Cape Light—and their story will capture readers' hearts forever.

(Covenant Bookstore online 2005)

Clearly, Kinkade has mastered the fine points of reaching a mass audience. However, critics continue to pan Kinkade's mushy, mainstream masterpieces: "With his appalling new novel, Thomas Kinkade, 'The Painter of Light™' makes a strong bid to become the world champion of vapid, money-grubbing kitsch" (Miller 2002: 1). In any case, Kinkade, not content to limit himself to art, writing, and special appearances at galleries around the US, has branched out into other ventures, extending the Kinkade lifestyle brand toward real estate, home construction, and town planning.

Figure 15.3 Thomas Kinkade, *Cape Light* book 2003, cover art by Kinkade, naturally

Thomas Kinkade, real estate brand

In his writings, interviews, websites, and in his wildly successful *plein air* painting oeuvre, Kinkade hews to a heartwarming vision of family, community, home, and hearth—"small town" values of yesteryear that seem to tap a huge sentimental reservoir, as they sell like hotcakes with homemade maple syrup and freshly churned butter (see Brown 2001). Kinkade's paintings fall into categories such as "Bridges," "Gazebos," "Seascapes," "Holidays," "Lighthouses," and so on (see Kinkade 2005). Close observers have noted that they never include people. Many are religious, in a light-handed way—no crucifixions here—and feature engraved Psalms, beams of sunlight, and cute country church steeples: "his work is sentimental, patriotic, quaint and spiritual" (Brown 2002: 2). Merchandizing Kinkade home furnishings, La-Z-Boy recliners, wallpaper, linens, and china preceded his recent move into the dynamic, challenging world of real estate development.

Kinkade had a unique chance to apply the aestheticized, romantic values of his wholesome paintings and books in building an entire community—the Village at Hiddenbrooke in Vallejo, California, just north of Berkeley in the bounteous Bay area. His latest brand extension was designed to "enrich homeowners' lives with endless visual surprises and delights" (Orlean 2001: 130). However, his development, or the one he lent the Thomas Kinkade Lifestyle Brand to, "ain't exactly ye olde quainte village it bills itself" (Brown 2002: 1). He might have strategically aligned his core values throughout this portfolio-enhancing venture, realizing his vision of the good life outside his faux-gilded frames. He did not. The Village at Hiddenbrooke might have been the culmination of Kinkade's lifework, a chance for an artist to manifest his aesthetic vision, joining art and commerce, bridging the divide between aesthetics and real estate management, and realizing the integration of material and immaterial goals. It is not.

The Village at Hiddenbrooke (2003) includes 10 planned communities on 1,300 acres, including the requisite gatehouse, golf course, and security patrol. In its marketing brochure, the Village represents "a vision of simpler times," with "extraordinary design and detail." However, in the words of one disappointed visitor, "none of the homes bear much resemblance to the stone-and-thatch roof cottages of Kinkade's paintings" (Brown 2002: 2). They look like all the other developments springing up in the booming Bay Area. Kinkade, it turns out, did not design the homes himself; he licensed his name and artistic vision to a development firm—commodifying his artistic brand. Fair enough, maybe his artistic abilities stop at chair designing, but how about the home interiors, the charmed walkways, the close-nit community that he, his books, and his paintings extol? Not here. Where are the "flowering bushes or graceful trees that are characteristic of Kinkade's paintings?" (Brown 2002). Where are the fireplaces with wispy smoke curling up into a sun-dappled sky (they are gas), or corner grocery stores, community squares, friendly banks, or local bakeries? Oh, sorry, Hiddenbrooke is zoned residential only. Kinkade might have shown how aesthetics and enterprise could work together, how artistic renown might translate into community respect:

> Imagine if the enormously famous Kinkade had brought his "artistic sensibilities" to a new-urbanist architect and an enlightened group of town planners instead of an enormous profit-seeking development conglomerate, and matched his cutesy aesthetics with their concepts of a new American suburb: he could have built something responsible and meaningful, and helped promote a community-building movement that is still struggling for widespread recognition.
>
> (Brown 2002: 1)

In my site visit to Hiddenbrooke, I was surprised to find it off interstate highway 80, the major east-west route of the densely populated San Francisco Bay Area. Once off the highway, following well-marked, folksy signs, I was amazed to come upon not just a development, but *an entire valley of custom Kinkade homes*. They looked eerily similar to each other. No one was outside; only the work crews busily constructing new models disturbed this suburban

Figure 15.4 Illustrative photographs from the Village at Hiddenbrooke real estate development, Vallejo, California (photographs courtesy Thomas Kinkade, Media Arts Group, Inc. Morgan Hill, CA95037)

vision. None of the hallmarks of Kinkade's painting, novels, and inspirational speeches were to be seen, anywhere. No meandering paths. No cute lighthouses. No rustic outbuildings. And no people, chatting amiably over a rough-hewn fence. Instead, I was faced with a typical California suburb, far away from the cares and crime of Vallejo, Oakland, or San Francisco. I am sure they are fine homes that families live happy—or unhappy—lives in, but I was disappointed.

Kinkade's foray into real estate provides an apocryphal warning to management scholars turning toward the aesthetic dimension—here is an artist with aesthetic vision whose "brand management" recapitulates the excesses of consumer culture and organizational dogma, providing us with a case study of crass. Here is an artist—with vision, aesthetic goals, and the power to "action this," yet this vision was almost completely obscured when translated to broader economic practices.

Many commentators have compared Hiddenbrooke to Celebration, the Florida town that Disney built on leftover land near Orlando. However, Celebration seems to have incorporated many "Disney" features, including strict zoning for appearance, upkeep, and general good behavior (see Ross 2000). Hiddenbrooke fails to reflect much of the small town, closely knit character of Kinkade's imaginary world—which seems to have had little impact on its success. Perhaps the vision of a single-family home, away from traffic, congestion, and noisy neighbors—a rarity in over-populated California— transcends other painterly virtues. However, I think Kinkade's brand portfolio offers larger lessons for those of us interested in potential intersections of art and commerce, as this case points to the unproductive dichotomy that often haunts management studies that embrace art and aesthetics. Furthermore,

Kinkade offers an illuminating case study of the market for art, and how artistic-based brands function outside artistic intention. In the next section, I turn to broader issues of the interrelationships between art and commerce, including branding, strategic image management, and value creation. I focus mainly on fine art and marketing, but the lessons may apply to the general arena of aesthetics and management.

Art in commercial context

Artists create images that abstract and reify things, people, and holy figures. They have honed these skills for centuries, building up a visual vocabulary that expresses our highest hopes and our deepest failures. Advertising, in turn, developed in close contact with fine art and continues to interact with the art world on a daily basis (cf. Gibbons 2005). It should be no surprise, then, that artists know a little about brand management, which is all about making emotional connections with images (see also Kreutz and Cantz 2003). As one of Andy Warhol's many biographers put it, "Andy Warhol's *Dollar Signs* are brazen, perhaps even insolent reminders that pictures by brand-name artists are metaphors for money, a situation that never troubled him" (Bourdon 1989: 384).

Just like products, artists are subject to market forces, management issues, substitution effects, and economic cycles (see Guillet de Monthoux 2000; Jensen 1994; Schroeder 2000). Emerging models of art training increasingly recognize the market-based nature of artistic production, and often include career management workshops. One such workshop, the Artist in the Market-place program at the Bronx Museum of Art, was started to help aspiring artists make it big, or at least make it in the art world. The 12-week workshop includes sessions on gallery representation, marketing, grant writing, accounting, and showing one's work (Johnson 2001). One art critic despairingly reviewed the workshop exhibition, lamenting that "Many young artists think of creating art as primarily a matter of strategic calculation" (Johnson 2001: B36). He seems shocked to find careerist thinking running rampant in art schools.

Researchers must come to terms with art's commercial underpinnings for fruitful inquiry in aesthetics and management. Art, like the corporate world, often celebrates wealth, power, and the status quo. Works of art that reflected the values, influence, and wealth of yesteryear's capitalists are now honored historically as great and valuable cultural artifacts, kept in elaborate museums, and form the basis of a thriving tourist industry—and can be considered an asset class (cf. Schroeder and Borgerson 2002). Indeed, art is a product in many respects, to be consumed through auction and gallery sales, museum patronage, reproductions, commercial art, and so forth. The line between art and commerce is blurry; many artists specifically produce things to be sold, artist's letters from the past are full of references to monetary matters, and advertising has incorporated the techniques, look, and producers of art—ad agencies, photography studios, and design firms are full of people with art history training (see Bogart 1995; Schroeder and Salzer-Mörling 2006).

Conclusion

Perhaps Kinkade's success offers insights to aspiring artists, writers—and real estate developers. Yet, for aesthetically inspired management researchers, I think he gently reminds us that art and commerce are fast friends. Kinkade, like Warhol, tamed the techniques of management to produce a corporate art firm extraordinaire—but not, seemingly, the kind called for by Guillet de Monthoux in his optimistic *Art Firm* treatise on creating aesthetic value (Guillet de Monthoux 2004). How, then, can we reconcile art and management? Many artists do provide cogent critiques of corporate culture, pointing out the dehumanizing process of commodification, the sameness of the branded environment, and the debilitating effects of celebrity and its quest. However, their works often sit comfortably within a celebratory, liberatory mode of consumption—paintings represent the most valuable objects in the world, corporations co-opt art for their own ends, and the art market injects economic considerations into cultural production. Yet, much management research clings to an appreciative, aesthetically elevated conception of aesthetics, combined with an essentialized, glamorized notion of The Artist, downplaying art's historical role in selling pictures, celebrating power, and serving patrons.

Acknowledgments

This chapter was brought to you by the Wallanders and Hedelius Foundation grant, "Brands, Companies, and Consumers: A Dynamic Perspective." I thank Janet Borgerson, Keith Borgerson, Mary Borgerson, Wendelin Küpers, Louise Wallenberg, Torkild Thanem, Pierre Guillet de Monthoux, Ian King, Adam Arvidsson, Ulrich Meyer, Stephen Brown, Christian DeCock, Christina Volkmann, Alan Bradshaw, Alf Rehn, and Samantha Warren for support and encouragement of this research project. I also thank the staff at the Thomas Kinkade Galleries in Petoskey, Michigan, and San Francisco, California, and whoever designed the billboard that directed me to the Village at Hiddenbrooke. An early version of this paper was presented at the Second Art of Management and Organisation Conference in Paris, September 2004; I wish to thank the staff at the Hotel Saint Sébastien, Paris, for their assistance during my stay.

References

Austin, Robert, and Lee Devin. 2003. *Artful making: What managers need to know about how artists work*. Upper Saddle River, NJ: Pearson.

Barnett, Rick, and Thomas Kinkade. 2003. *The Thomas Kinkade story: A 20-year chronology of the artist*. New York: Bulfinch.

Benhamou-Huet, Judith. 2001. *The worth of art*. Paris: Assouline.

Bogart, Michelle H. 1995. *Artists, advertising, and the borders of art*. Chicago, IL: University of Chicago Press.

Borgerson, Janet L. 2002. "Managing desire: Heretical transformation in Pasolini's Medea." *Consumption Markets & Culture* 5 (1): 55–62.

Bourdon, David. 1989. *Andy Warhol*. New York: Harry Abrams.

Brown, Janelle. 2002. "Ticky-tacky houses from 'The Painter of Light'." *Salon*, March 18. Available at: http://archive.salon.com/mwt/style/2002/03/18/kinkade_village/ (accessed June 25, 2003).

Brown, Stephen. 2001. *Marketing—The retro revolution*. London: Sage.

Brown, Stephen, and Anthony Patterson, eds. 2000. *Imagining marketing: Art, aesthetics, and the avant-garde*. London: Routledge.

Cairns, George. 2002. "Aesthetics, morality and power: Design as espoused freedom and implicit control." *Human Relations* 55 (7): 799–820.

Carr, Adrian, and Philip Hancock, eds. 2003. *Art and aesthetics at work*. New York: Palgrave.

Caves, Richard E. 2002. *Creative industries: Contracts between art and commerce*. Cambridge, MA: Harvard University Press.

Chong, Derrick. 2001. *Arts management: Critical perspectives on a new sub-discipline*. London: Routledge.

Clark, Timothy, and Iain Mangham. 2004. "From dramaturgy to theatre as technology: The case of corporate theatre." *Journal of Management Studies* 41 (1): 37–59.

Covenant Bookstore online. 2005. "Cape Light, by Thomas Kinkade and Catherine Spencer." Available at: www.covenantbookstore.com/calibythkika.html (accessed November 5, 2005).

Dougherty, Stephen, and Thomas Kinkade. 2002. *The artist in nature: Thomas Kinkade and the Plein Air movement*. New York: Watson-Guptill.

du Gay, Paul, John Allen, and Michael Pryke, eds. 2001. *Cultural economy: Cultural analysis and commercial life*. London: Sage.

Fillis, Ian. 2004. "The internationalising smaller craft firm: Insights from the marketing and entrepreneurship interface." *International Small Business Journal* 22 (1): 57–82.

Fry, Roger, and Craufurd D. Goodwin, eds. 1999. *Art and the market: Roger Fry on commerce in art*. Ann Arbor, MI: University of Michigan Press.

Gibbons, Joan. 2005. *Art & advertising*. London: I. B. Tauris.

Guillet de Monthoux, Pierre. 2000. "Performing the absolute. Marina Abramovic organizing the unfinished business of Arthur Schopenhauer." *Organization Studies* 21: 29–52.

Guillet de Monthoux, Pierre. 2004. *The art firm: Aesthetic management and metaphysical marketing from Wagner to Wilson*. Palo Alto, CA: Stanford Business Books.

Guillet de Monthoux, Pierre, and Antonio Strati, eds. 2002. "Special issue: Aesthetics and management—Business bridges to art." *Consumption Markets & Culture* 5 (1).

Hagoort, Giep. 2004. *Art management: Entrepreneurial style*. Chicago, IL: University of Chicago Press.

Höpfl, Heather J., and Stephen Linstead, eds. 2000. *The aesthetics of organization*. London: Sage.

Jensen, Robert. 1994. *Marketing modernism in fin-de-siècle Europe*. Princeton, NJ: Princeton University Press.

Johnson, K. 2001. "Newcomers ready for marketing, accounting . . . and, oh yes, creating." *New York Times*, August 10, B30, B36.

Joy, Annamma, and John F. Sherry, Jr. 2004. "Framing considerations of the PRC: Creating value in the contemporary Chinese art market." *Consumption Markets & Culture* 7 (4): 307–48.

Kinkade, Thomas. 2005. "Painter of light." Available at: www.thomaskinkade.com/magi/servlet/com.asucon.ebiz.home.web.tk.HomeServlet (accessed April 4, 2005).

Kinkade, Thomas, and Katherine Spencer. 2002. *Cape Light: A novel by the painter of light™*. New York: Berkley.

Kinkade, Thomas, and Katherine Spencer. 2003. *A gathering place: A Cape Light novel.* New York: Berkeley.

Klamer, Arjo, ed. 1996. *The value of culture: On the relationship between economics and arts.* Amsterdam: Amsterdam University Press.

Kreutz, Bernd, and Hatje Cantz. 2003. *The art of branding.* Ostfildern-Ruit: Hatje Cantz Verlag.

Küpers, Wendelin. 2002. "Phenomenology of aesthetic organizing—ways toward aesthetically responsive organisations." *Consumption Markets & Culture* 5 (1): 21–46.

Media Arts Group. 2003a. "Terms of use." Available at: www.mediaarts.com (accessed June 25, 2003).

Media Arts Group. 2003b. "First quarter results." Avaialble at: www.mediaarts.com (accessed June 25, 2003).

Media Arts Group. 2003c. "Third quarter results." Available at: www.mediaarts.com (accessed December 8, 2003).

Miller, Laura. 2002. "The writer of dreck." *Salon*, March 18. Available at: http://archive.salon.com/books/feature/2002/03/18/light/ (accessed December 8, 2003).

Monin, Nanette, Janet Sayers, and John Monin. 2004. "Quibble or QBL? Do we want another (aesthetic) bottom line?" Paper presented at the Second Art of Management and Organisation Conference, Paris, September.

Orlean, Susan. 2001. "Art for everybody: Thomas Kinkade, America's most profitable artist." *The New Yorker*, October 15, 124–46.

Ramirez, Rafaël. 1991. *The beauty of social organization.* Munich: Accedo.

Ross, Andrew. 2000. *The Celebration chronicles: Life, liberty and the pursuit of property value in Disney's new town.* New York: Ballantine.

Schmitt, Bernd, and Alex Simonson. 1997. *Marketing aesthetics: The strategic management of brands, identity, and image.* New York: The Free Press.

Schroeder, Jonathan E. 1997. "Andy Warhol: Consumer researcher." *Advances in Consumer Research* 24: 476–82.

Schroeder, Jonathan E. 2000. "Édouard Manet, Calvin Klein and the strategic use of scandal." In *Imagining marketing: Art, aesthetics, and the avant-garde*, edited by Stephen Brown and Anthony Patterson. London: Routledge.

Schroeder, Jonathan E. 2002. *Visual consumption.* London: Routledge.

Schroeder, Jonathan E. 2005. "The artist and the brand." *European Journal of Marketing* 39: 1291–305.

Schroeder, Jonathan E., and Janet L. Borgerson. 2002. "Innovations in information technology: Insights into consumer culture from Italian Renaissance art." *Consumption Markets & Culture* 5 (2): 154–69.

Schroeder, Jonathan E., and Miriam Salzer-Mörling, eds. 2006. *Brand culture.* London: Routledge.

Stallabrass, Julian. 2004. *Art incorporated: The story of contemporary art.* Oxford: Oxford University Press.

Strati, Antonio. 1999. *Organization and aesthetics*. London: Sage.

Strati, Antonio, and Pierre Guillet de Monthoux, eds. 2002. "Special issue: Organising aesthetics." *Human Relations* 55 (7).

Taylor, Steven S., and Hans Hansen. 2005. "Finding form: Looking at the field of organizational aesthetics." *Journal of Management Studies* 42 (6): 1211–31.

The Village at Hiddenbrooke. 2003. Available at: www.visithiddenbrooke.com/htmlpages/welcomeopt.html (accessed December 8, 2003).

Venkatesh, Alladi, and Laurie A. Meamber. 2006. "Arts and aesthetics: Marketing and cultural production." *Marketing Theory* 6 (1): 11–40.

Warren, Samantha. 2002. "'Show me how its feels to work here': Using photography to research organizational aesthetics." *Ephemera* 2 (3): 224–45.

16 Consuming the "world"

Reflexivity, aesthetics, and authenticity at Disney World's EPCOT Center

H. Rika Houston and Laurie A. Meamber

Introduction

> Nostalgia is memory with the pain removed.
>
> (Lowenthal 1985: 8)

As noted by Chronis (2005) and Goulding (2000, 2001), the late twentieth and the early twenty-first centuries have been marked by the increasing popularity of the past and a contemporary quest for history that are celebrated through countless consumption practices, many of which are experiential in nature. Goulding (2001) notes that postmodern consumers identify nostalgic-ally with people, places, and things from a bygone era as learned through lived experiences, books, and films (McCracken 1988). In addition, they may seek and find such nostalgia in themed attractions such as living heritage sites or other themed attractions (Goulding 2001).

The growing popularity of themed attractions as a means of consuming the past points to the recurring motivational theme of escape from the perceived fragmentation, instability, and inauthenticity of postmodern life (Chronis 2005; Goulding 2001; Lindholm 2008; Lowenthal 1985; MacCannell 1999, 2001). Embedded within this notion of escape lies the implicit search for an "authentic" past; one that is unsullied by the contemporary cloak of com-modification. The fact that the idyllic purity of temporal space does not now nor ever has before existed is somehow lost in the mindless hunger of the search. As a result, the producers of themed attractions must embrace the notion of an authentic past, even if it exists only within the magical realm of tourists' imaginations. Furthermore, they must do so with a full understanding that while many theme park tourists use authenticity as an experiential yardstick, they do so only in the context of their greater desires for comfort, safety, and cleanliness (Goulding 2000; Lindholm 2002, 2008).

In the process of socially constructing this "authentic" past, producers of themed attractions, as well as scholars of tourism and consumer research, have begun to recognize the important role of aesthetics. Chronis (2005), in his study of a heritage exhibition in Thessaloniki, Greece, identified aesthetic appreciation of the heritage site and its surrounding environment as one of the key experiential benefits realized by tourists at the site. In the same vein, Goulding (2000) discusses the heightened importance of aesthetics (of historical artifacts and objects) as the criteria for credibil ity and authenticity when a historical museum or site attempts to create an authentic past. And Lindholm (2008) notes that tourists are not paying an entrance fee to be reminded about the fallacies of history. Indeed, they are active agents seeking a connection to the past through the narratives they construct on their own. In this demanding context of co-production, close attention to the aesthetics of the authentic past becomes an increasingly important component of the "credibility armor" that historical museums and sites, as well as any themed experience that attempts to recreate the past, must manufacture (Lindholm 2008).

While the constructs of aesthetics and authenticity have been studied in the tourism literature, and to a lesser extent in the consumer research literature, much of our understanding of these constructs as they relate to each other, as well as the role their relationship plays in the consumption of themed attractions, remains unexplored. The specific role of aesthetics as it impacts and shapes experiential forms of consumption is also underexplored. This reflexive account begins to address this void by exploring the role and importance of aesthetics in the social construction of an "authentic" past at a themed attraction, the World Showcase at Walt Disney's EPCOT Center in Orlando, Florida.

Defining the constructs: aesthetics and authenticity

Aesthetics

In this reflexive account, we refer to aesthetics as experiences that include any sensorial content, as derived from the Greek "aesthesis," which means perceiving the world with the senses (Barilli 1989/1993; Björkegren 1996). We also recognize the aesthetic experience as a broad one that encompasses experiential, symbolic, sensory, and affective dimensions (Charters 2006). And finally, in our visualization of aesthetics, we include all architecture, service-scapes in general, exterior landscapes, interior environments, cultural artifacts, products, photographs, advertisements, clothing, costumes, music, paintings, cultural performances and actors, and any other physical and/or visual embodiments of an authentic past that are both produced and consumed in the context of a themed experience (Bruner 2001; Charters 2006; Chronis 2005; Goulding 2000, 2001; Kontogeorgopoulos 2003; Venkatesh and Meamber 2008; White 2007).

Authenticity

Authenticity, as it is defined in the tourism scholarship, is viewed as a social construction with a multiplicity of meanings that changes over time (Cohen 1988; Goulding 2000; Kontogeorgopoulos 2003; MacCannell 1999, 2001; McCabe 2005; Olsen 2002; Wang 1999, 2000; White 2007). There are many schools of thought, but the basic philosophy underlying the construct of authenticity is a dichotomous one. It implies that there is an original and authentic culture that is privileged in comparison to its counter-concept, the polluted and inauthentic copy (Olsen 2002; Schwartz 1996). An "authentic" culture, then, in short, is one that is viewed as pure and untainted by the polluting forces of modernity and capitalism. In this reflexive account, we will illustrate the role that aesthetics plays in the social construction of authenticity at Disney World's EPCOT World Showcase.

Disney World's EPCOT Center: a contextual overview

> From world travel to wide-eyed excitement, a day at EPCOT will set your imagination soaring. Blast off to Mars. Take flight on Soarin. Shift into high gear on Test Track. Sample cultures from around the globe. Watch the night erupt with a spectacular fire works finale.
>
> (Orlando/Orange County Convention and Visitors'
> Bureau, www.orlando.com/, February 2008)

Ever since its inception in 1982, Disney World's EPCOT Center in Orlando, Florida has heralded the utopian symbolism and futuristic vision of Walt Disney's imagination. EPCOT, an acronym for Experimental Prototype Community of Tomorrow, offers two venues of exploration to symbolize this utopian agenda, Future World and the World Showcase. Walt Disney's original vision for EPCOT was to create a thriving community of up to 20,000 residents who could shop at retail stores, attend school, and participate in civil services – all within a self-contained community. Within this utopian colony, everyone and everything was totally planned and controlled. Even transportation, with its inherent properties of noise and pollution, would be restricted to an underground monorail system called People Movers. Only pedestrian traffic would be allowed on the visible surface. EPCOT residents would be gainfully employed within the community and would rent, rather than own, their homes, thereby eliminating any opportunity to vote on issues regarding the community. Furthermore, retirees would not be allowed to live in EPCOT so as to not tarnish the manufactured reality of youth, vitality, and innovation. And finally, EPCOT was envisioned as a city that would evolve perpetually as new technology and innovations continued to improve the lives of EPCOT citizens (www.wdwhistory.com/FindFile.Ashx?/Epcot/; Mannheim 2002).

The spatial layout of the EPCOT Center is a juxtaposition of two worlds brought together through Walt Disney's overarching theme of diversity and (world) peace. Both attractions, Future World and the World Showcase, are patterned after World Fair exhibits that were popular during the first half of the twentieth century. The World Showcase, in fact, is essentially a permanent version of a world fair (Mannheim 2002).

Upon exiting Future World, guests enter the EPCOT World Showcase. In deep contrast to Future World, the World Showcase immerses guests into a static, historical, ancient, and exotic world of stereotypes grounded in carefully screened native employees, scaled-down architectural replicas, and culture-bound retail merchandise and dining experiences complemented by live cultural performances. The World Showcase features 11 different countries that reflect Walt Disney's view of the world in the late twentieth century. The countries represented include Mexico, Norway, China, Germany, Italy, the USA, Japan, Morocco, France, the UK, and Canada. Norway and Morocco were not part of the original World Showcase and pavilions for Russia, Spain, Venezuela, the United Arab Emirates, and Israel never made it past the planning phase of development. In addition, an African pavilion was planned but never built (Mannheim 2002). The exclusion of so many countries, cultures, and regions from the EPCOT World Showcase twentieth-century vision of the world – including but not limited to Australia, New Zealand, the Pacific Islands, and the countries of Central and South Africa, the Middle East, Southeast Asia, South America, Central America, and Eastern Europe – speaks volumes about the social construction of an "authentic" past that defies the historic and socio-political geographies of twentieth- and twenty-first-century reality. The World Showcase, in other words, symbolizes a socially constructed world frozen in the past – one that is notably inconsistent with our collective vision of the world as it exists today.

Consuming the "world": a reflexive account of Disney World's EPCOT World Showcase

Our introduction to the EPCOT World Showcase began with the not-so-subtle undertones of an "around the world" retail store. The shelves bulged with Disney merchandise that represented different countries of the world, many of which were embellished with the colorful "flags of the world" theme. Employees greeted us with happy smiles and "flags of the world" shirts that set the mood for our impending immersion into the "authentic" world of the past. With this brief introduction to the world as a unified image, we apprehensively began our journey around the circumference of a 40-acre, artificial lagoon surrounded by a global, "authentic" world of the past as envisioned by Walt Disney.

Like all EPCOT visitors, we were invited to travel the world experientially through the sights and sounds of architectural reproductions, culture-bound food and artifacts, and live cultural performances. During a pre-immersion discussion, we learned that employees working in each of the 11 world pavilions are hand-selected and carefully trained to project the stereotyped personification of local nationals (in a historic, traditional sense). World Showcase employees, in fact, are typically college students from the represented countries who work at the EPCOT World Showcase attraction for one year. During their year-long visit, they live in housing provided by the Walt Disney World College Program. Officially referred to as "cast members," these international students are more than mere employees. As their job title suggests, they are also cultural performers. The World Showcase cast members we encountered wore stereotypical, traditional costumes and entertained guests with live performances steeped in cultural tradition. In the Mexican pavilion, mariachi singers paraded the grounds with guitars in hand while singing traditional Mexican songs. In the Chinese pavilion, youthful Chinese acrobats entertained the outdoor crowds with amazing feats of flexibility and agility. In both form and function, the visual and behavioral aesthetics of performance at each of the successive country pavilions provided the necessary stage for the construction of an "authentic" world of the past.

The visual aesthetics of the respective country pavilions also imitated (historical) reality. Figures 16.1 and 16.2 show the scaled-down architectural replicas of Mexico's Chichén Itzá and China's Temple of Heaven, respectively. The China pavilion also included retail interiors designed in the fashion of the Forbidden Palace and an eerily realistic, albeit scaled-down, version of the Terra Cotta Warriors of Xian (see Figures 16.3 and 16.4). Other country pavilions displayed a Viking ship (Norway), a building vaguely reminiscent of the Imperial Palace (Japan), and a quaint provincial village with cafés emitting the heavenly aroma of freshly baked bread (France), to name just a few examples. The hyperreality of the setting created a practiced sensibility ripe for the construction and consumption of an "authentic" world of the past. From pavilion to pavilion, we immersed ourselves into the traditional sights and sounds of each country. Some nearby guests declared that by "traveling around the world" at EPCOT's World Showcase, it would no longer be necessary to actually travel around the (real) world. The perceived cultural authenticity of the pavilions at EPCOT World Showcase, it seems, was not only embraced without question, but also acknowledged as an adequate cultural proxy for visiting the selected countries. We were dismayed by the audacity of this possibility.

In the USA pavilion, the aesthetics of progress and culture were premised on an idealized representation of American history. The presentation of American history included the look, feel, sound, smell, and tastes of the exteriors and interiors of the pavilion, the "American Adventure" show, and the live cultural performances. To a lesser extent, the small colonial-themed retail store and restaurant also embraced the aesthetics of American history in the "authentic" past of the original 13 colonies and its brave, adventurous settlers. And without a doubt, the shows and performances at the USA pavilion dominated the entire World Showcase attraction. The shows were longer here than at the other sites (e.g., the film presentations in China and France were each under 30 minutes), and also were presented more frequently. The sights

Figure 16.1 Mexico pavilion, replica of Chichén Itzá, Disney World EPCOT
        Center, World Showcase (photograph by H. Rika Houston, 2006)

and sounds of American history (as selectively constructed) were predominant
at the performances. Colors were bright and patriotic (red, white, and blue),
and there were no distinctive smells in the environment, except for those in
the Liberty Inn (offering an "American" menu of hamburgers, hotdogs,
chicken, and salads). When we were experiencing the audio-animatronic/film
show, we were encouraged to turn off our twenty-first-century technology (e.g.,
cell phones, cameras, and camcorders) and, unlike in most other places at
EPCOT, we were strictly prohibited from taking photographs.

Figure 16.2 China pavilion, replica of the Temple of Heaven, Disney World EPCOT Center, World Showcase (photograph by H. Rika Houston, 2006)

Strategically located in the center of the World Showcase attraction, the exterior architecture of the main building (Liberty Theatre) in the USA pavilion was designed to portray a colonial town hall replete with its own town square that provided a staging area for the live and patriotically hued drum and fife corps performances. With its bold white pillars, the colonial-style house also resembled the main house of a southern plantation. The interior of Liberty Theatre was inspired by the architecture of Thomas Jefferson's Monticello and Richmond House and included a large domed ceiling and second story balcony. Aesthetically, it is apparent that Walt Disney's architects and designers combined the look and feel of many historic places throughout the USA (including any colonial period historic home that guests may have read about or seen in photographs, movies, or in person). Images such as George Washington's Mount Vernon, Thomas Jefferson's Monticello, Philadelphia's Independence Hall, and even the fictional antebellum Tara of Margaret Mitchell's *Gone with the Wind* came to mind. See Figure 16.5 for a look at the front of the Liberty Theatre and town square.

After entering the main building through the front entrance, we joined the crowd in the lobby to listen to the Voices of Liberty Choir singing a cappella renditions of uplifting, classic American folk songs (see Figure 16.6). Photographs of recognizable scenes and figures from American history were carefully placed on the perimeter walls of the main lobby and historical

Figure 16.3 China pavilion, interior view of retail store, Disney World EPCOT
Center, World Showcase (photograph by H. Rika Houston, 2006)

Figure 16.4 China pavilion, replicas of Terra Cotta Warriors, Disney World EPCOT
Center, World Showcase (photograph by H. Rika Houston, 2006)

artifacts could be viewed in the American Heritage Gallery. Newly recharged with the melody of American spirit, we were then directed up an escalator to the second-floor balcony where a World Showcase cast member dressed in a colonial period costume provided instructions for entering and exiting the theater. The auditorium was large, seating perhaps 2,000–3,000 people, and neo-classical statues (Spirits of Adventure) surrounded the sides of the theater proudly proclaiming the stalwart American values of individualism, innovation, independence, compassion, discovery, and heritage.

Through a combination of prominent figures and watershed events throughout American history, the American Adventure audio-animatronic/film show inspired us with displaced nostalgia. The powerful visual and audio aesthetics of Mayflower pilgrims fleeing religious prosecution, Thomas Jefferson struggling to write the Declaration of Independence, Frederick Douglas and Harriet Beecher Stowe talking with Mark Twain about slavery, the Civil War, Charles Lindberg's flight across the Atlantic, the 1929 stock market crash, the Great Depression, President Franklin Delano Roosevelt's animated advisory about the themes of revival and prosperity, and the iconic raising of the flag at Iwo Jima tugged at our very consciousness. After taking us on a visual journey through more recent events in American history, the story ended with Mark Twain speaking on the changes that he had never dreamed possible and Franklin Delano Roosevelt speaking on the dangers of success and taking things for granted. The resulting visual and audio tour through American history, albeit a sanitized and distorted one, left us with the resounding message that there

Figure 16.5 USA pavilion, replica of colonial town square, Disney World EPCOT Center, World Showcase (photograph by H. Rika Houston, 2006)

Figure 16.6 Lobby of USA pavilion, Voice of Liberty Choir, Disney World EPCOT
Center, World Showcase (photograph by H. Rika Houston, 2006)

was always a struggle before the USA lived up to its ideals. Americans have
come a long way in the struggle to make a free and democratic nation work,
and World Showcase's USA pavilion reminded us that there is still hope that
America can meet the challenges of tomorrow just as it has always overcome
the problems of the past.

Many of the guests at the American Adventure show in the USA pavilion
appeared to be enjoying the experience of the "authentic" American past,
including one consumer who we overheard telling her family that it was "the
best show in the park." However, as both Americans and consumer researchers,
we found it difficult to experience the site without feeling uncomfortable. In
addition to our previous travels through and experiential knowledge about many
of the represented countries, we had also read materials provided on a reading
list as an introduction to the Disney parks, most of which were written by
authors who were critical of Disney. So, at the outset, as researchers, we both
had difficulty enjoying the site as consumers (guests), rather than as researchers
who must maintain a certain distance from the experience in order to document
it and critique it through "objective" eyes. While we did admire the aesthetics
of the World Showcase pavilions, we remained critical of the narrative that
was constructed. For example, we were horrified beyond words as we viewed
the surreal scenes of World War II that displayed American planes dropping

bombs on Japan and the mushroom cloud of an atomic explosion engulfing Hiroshima, all to the empowering backdrop of patriotic American music. And true to any socio-political agenda of wartime propaganda, the same film neglected to show the resulting death of hundreds of thousands of innocent Japanese civilians and the utter devastation created by those same events. In short, we were not only speechless as we were herded out and away from this theatrical spectacle, but we also found ourselves stunned, depressed, and dismayed at what we had just experienced. To make matters even worse, this feeling of dismay was further extended to the nearby visitors (guests) who reveled in the experience in an unabashed and rather jubilant manner.

The World Showcase at Disney's EPCOT Center uses aesthetics to create a partic ular experience of the world of a bygone era for those who visit. As Langer (1953) argues, architecture represents an image of a place of habitation, real or imagined. Taking the USA pavilion as exemplar, it can be interpreted as a hyperreal (more real than reality) construction of the world of the past, as represented in the colonial architecture, which itself is a pastiche of designs from actual public and private buildings. The attractions also represented an amalgamation of different periods in American history – the drum and fife corps of the Revolutionary War period, the Voices of Liberty Choir who sang folk songs of the nineteenth and twentieth centuries, and the American Adventure film presentation itself with its narrative of struggle, achievement, and promise from the seventeenth century to the late twentieth century. The gift shop and restaurant showcased the markers of Americana – including souvenirs such as American flags from different periods in history (e.g., colonial flag, 48-state flag), and iconic American fast food offerings (e.g., hotdogs and hamburgers). The pavilion in its totality represented an imagined place of habitation from the past, a place that should be comfortable and familiar to Americans, and recognizable as "American" to non-Americans.

Kelleher (2004) notes and our observations confirm that, in the context of themed experiences such as EPCOT's World Showcase, claims to authenticity are constructed by the aesthetic details found in the historicized and sanitized hyperreality of the experience. As we navigated the carefully scripted terrain of each of the country pavilions, it was the aesthetics of our experience that sustained our idealized, postmodern notions of the "authentic" world of the past. In the China pavilion, for example, the historic fabric of Beijing's Temple of Heaven and Xian's Terra Cotta Warriors, in reality located in vastly different spatial and temporal geographies of China, were brought together in one place at one time. In addition, they were reinforced aesthetically with a short film on the history of China, a live performance of youthful Chinese acrobats, a restaurant menu of less-than-exotic Chinese delicacies, and a "Forbidden Palace" retail store filled with merchandise such as chopsticks, silk brocade coin purses, tea cups with Chinese motifs, and miniature replicas of the Forbidden Palace and the Great Wall. In this temporal gumbo of intermingled aesthetics, the difference between the "authentic" and the "inauthentic" world of the past became almost impossible to distinguish. Indeed, many critics of the "Disneyfication" of society point to the inevitable danger posed by the measured disappearance of "authentic" history as it is supplanted by Disney's sanitized interpretation of history and, perhaps even worse, the visitors' growing belief that this interpretation is, in fact, the accurate one (Boyer 1992; Bryman 2004; Kelleher 2004; Sorkin 1992; Zukin 1991).

Anthropologist Jennifer Robertson (2002: 791), in her social commentary on researcher reflexivity and positionality, notes that any self-conscious positioning in the field is pointless because most people in most places are quite proficient at assigning labels and creating positions of their own for others and themselves. Urry (1995) also notes the importance of "aesthetic reflexivity" in contemporary society as it relates to the ability of increasingly knowledgeable people to reflect upon their societies and place within the world, both historically and geographically. In the field of consumer research, Anderson (1986), Bristor and Fischer (1993), Firat and Venkatesh (1995), Hirschman (1993), Joy (1991), Murray and Ozanne (1991), and Peñaloza (2005), to name just a few, have also approached the topic of reflexivity and how it is invoked in the field.

As researchers, we felt that we stood apart from others because we could not just be "consumers" nor could we relate personally to the types of consumers that we found at the site. While we, as academics, have made great strides since the mid-1980s in challenging objective posturing in consumer research, there is much more work to be done in moving toward more subject-subject relations between the researcher(s) and those under study. Some potential challenges for researchers in achieving these subject-subject relations include common socio-demographic differences from many mainstream consumers, and other issues such as disparate beliefs about political ideologies, cultural authenticity, family values and dynamics, and leisure preferences, to name just a few.

In thinking about the impact of this distancing, perhaps this sense of awkwardness also comes across to consumers when researchers are observing or interviewing them. While "going native" may not be desirable in most cases, even when conducting ethnographic consumer research, developing more than just a rapport or an empathetic posture with subjects while conducting interviews or engaging in participant observations may be important in bridging subject-subject relations. We need to continue to develop methods and means of communicating and relating to consumers that address these perplexing issues. Some of these methods may include researcher immersion into the consumption activity and communication with others by whatever means feel appropriate, including dancing and performing (as we saw visitors do at EPCOT). In addition to relating to consumers in ways that consumers consume, we can also share our findings in ways that capture the most meaning, such as poetry and visual representations that include icons, photographs, videos, and performances, as many researchers in our field have been encouraging us to do in recent years (Belk and Kozinets 2006; Grayson 1998; Sherry and Schouten 2002; Schroeder 1998; Stern 1998). In this way we, as consumer researchers, can partake of everyday aesthetic experiences ourselves and our research can be informed by the process.

One of the basic tenets of consumer cultural research is exploiting researchers' subjective faculties in accessing and gaining understandings of consumers' lived experience as the context from which to develop the knowledge and theory of consumption (Arnould and Thompson 2005; Belk 2006; Belk, Sherry, and Wallendorf 1988; Despandé 1983; Moisander and Valtonen 2006). In making more explicit the impacts of our subject positions as researchers on the nature and content of these representations and on the processes of consumer research and its substantive findings, it is our hope that this discussion stimulates thought and contributes to previous work on reflexive consumer research (Joy 1991; Joy et al. 2006; Thompson 2002; Thompson, Stern, and Arnould 1998). We also hope that it will add to our understanding of the aesthetics of experience – including the criteria used to evaluate an aesthetic object (experience) – the sights, sounds, and other sensory material found at a themed environment, and the particular quality of the experience from the vantage point of both consumers and consumer researchers. As for the issue of authenticity, whether we are speaking of cultural authenticity or historical authenticity, this reflexive journey makes it clear that we, as consumer researchers, must accept the multiplicity of meanings and perspectives of this constantly changing, socially constructed notion. Instead of asking if authenticity exists, we might instead continue to investigate and interpret the experiences of authenticity that we and other consumers experience and to examine how these experiences are constructed through aesthetic content, much as we have done in this paper.

Consumer researchers, like all other social scientists, cannot presume a privileged vantage point, most especially when we are in search of an "authentic" past that never really existed in the first place and are further encumbered with aesthetic sensibilities that may differ greatly from those consumers who we seek to understand. Whether we are drenched in the guilt of "imperialist nostalgia" or not, we are nonetheless a part of the shifting social reality that we are attempting to observe (Rosaldo 1989). And so, as Shepherd (2003) has urged, we should all go about our fieldwork with neither guilt nor remorse. However, we should always do it with our eyes and minds wide open.

Conclusions: aesthetics and authenticity in themed environments

In this paper, we address the social construction of authenticity, an "authentic past" at Disney World's EPCOT World Showcase. We foreground the role of aesthetics, broadly defined as experiences that spring from sensorial content, in the creation of the themed experiences found at EPCOT's World Showcase. This sensorial material includes, but is not limited to, the architecture, costumed employees, restaurants, merchandise for sale in the gift shops, live cultural performances, and audio-animatronic/film shows. We discuss these elements in shaping a selective and sanitized cultural vision of the world rooted in the past at the theme park. Thus, in this account, we bridge the gap in the literature on aesthetics (Bloch 1995; Bloch, Brunel, and Arnold 2003; Charters 2006; Joy and Sherry 2003; Schroeder 2002; Venkatesh and Meamber 2006; Veryzer and Hutchinson 1998) that has largely ignored experience as the focal concern, and the literature on experiential consumption (Arnould and Price 1993; Kozinets 2002; Sherry 1998) that has not acknowledged aesthetics. For example, Bradshaw and Holbrook's (2008) and Holbrook and Anand's (1990) work on music consumption, by definition, does focus exclusively upon aesthetic experience, but not in themed environments. Peñaloza's (1999) study of consumption behavior at Nike Town is replete with rich, aesthetic descriptions of the visual elements within the store, with some attention to the textures, sounds, and smells encountered therein, yet this discussion does not frame these visual elements in aesthetic terms nor does it emphasize their essential role in the construction of the experience.

In addition, this paper contributes to the body of work on the consumption of themed attractions. Extant literature has identified aesthetics as being an important aspect of or motivation for the consumption of themed attractions (Cameron and Gatewood 2000; Chronis 2005; Goulding 2001), but has not examined the aesthetic elements that constitute the consumption experience. What is common across all of these studies is that aesthetics is an important aspect of the consumption of themed places, and yet these texts do not attempt to describe or understand the aesthetic material that comprises so much of the consumer experience.

The current study focuses almost exclusively on the aesthetic substance of the consumption experience in a themed environment. Aesthetic experiences are central to the social construction of the "authentic" past in EPCOT's World Showcase. As researchers, we indeed did experience the postmodern pastiche of sensorial content alongside other visitors to the park. We confronted our critical inner voices and reflected upon our reactions, which ran contrary to those that surrounded us. We hope our thoughts add to the growing discussion of reflexivity in research on consumption, consumers, and culture. As Urry (1990) writes when discussing existing research on popular pleasures, we in a postmodern (post-tourism) age, wholeheartedly and unselfconsciously embrace involvement in a cultural experience. And, it is in the consuming of the aesthetic environment that we, even as researchers, may experience the fantasy narrative of an "authentic" world of the past that spans the temporal and cultural boundaries of consumer imagination.

References

Anderson, Paul F. 1986. "On method in consumer research: A critical relativist perspective." *Journal of Consumer Research* 13 (September): 155–73.

Arnould, Eric J., and Linda L. Price. 1993. "River magic: Extraordinary experience and the extended service encounter." *Journal of Consumer Research* 20 (June): 24–45.

Arnould, Eric J., and Craig J. Thompson. 2005. "Consumer Culture Theory (CCT): Twenty years of research." *Journal of Consumer Research* 31 (March): 868–82.

Barilli, Renato. 1989/1993. *A course on aesthetics*. Translated by Karen E. Pinkus. Minneapolis, MN: University of Minnesota Press.

Belk, Russell W., ed. 2006. *Handbook of qualitative methods in marketing.* Cheltenham: Edward Elgar.

Belk, Russell W., and Robert V. Kozinets. 2006. "Videography in marketing and consumer research." *Qualitative Marketing Research* 8 (2): 128–41.

Belk, Russell W., John F. Sherry, Jr., and Melanie Wallendorf. 1988. "A naturalistic inquiry into buyer and seller behavior at a swap meet." *Journal of Consumer Research* 14 (March): 449–70.

Björkegren, Dag. 1996. *The culture business: Management strategies for the arts-related business*. New York: Routledge.

Bloch, Peter H. 1995. "Seeking the ideal form: Product design and consumer response." *Journal of Marketing* 9 (3): 16–29.

Bloch, Peter H., Frederic F. Brunel, and Todd J. Arnold. 2003. "Individual differences in the centrality of visual product aesthetics: Concept and measurement." *Journal of Consumer Research* 29 (March): 551–65.

Boyer, M. Christine. 1992. "Cities for sale: Merchandising history at the South Street Seaport." In *Variations on a theme park*, edited by Michael Sorkin. New York: Hill & Wang.

Bradshaw, Alan, and Morris B. Holbrook. 2008. "Must we have Musak wherever we go? A critical consideration of the consumer culture." *Consumption Markets & Culture* 11 (1): 25–43.

Bristor, Julia, and Eileen Fischer. 1993. "Feminist thought: Implications for consumer research." *Journal of Consumer Research* 19 (March): 518–36.

Bruner, Edward M. 2001. "The Maasai and the Lion King: Authenticity, nationalism, and globalization in African tourism." *American Ethnologist* 28 (4): 881–908.

Bryman, Alan. 2004. *The Disneyization of society*. Thousand Oaks, CA: Sage.

Cameron, Catherine M., and John B. Gatewood. 2000. "Excursions into the un-remembered past: What people want from visits to historical sites." *The Public Historian* 22 (3): 107–27.

Charters, Steve. 2006. "Aesthetic products and aesthetic consumption: A review." *Consumption Markets & Culture* 9 (3): 235–55.

Chronis, Athinodoros. 2005. "Our Byzantine heritage: Consumption of the past and its experiential benefits." *Journal of Consumer Marketing* 22 (4–5): 213–22.

Cohen, Erik. 1988. "Authenticity and commoditization in tourism." *Annals of Tourism Research* 15 (3): 371–86.

Despandé, Rohit. 1983. "Paradigms lost: On theory and method in research in marketing." *Journal of Marketing* 47 (Fall): 101–10.

Fırat, Fuat, and Alladi Venkatesh. 1995. "Liberatory postmodernism and the re-enchantment of consumption." *Journal of Consumer Research* 22 (December): 239–67.

Goulding, Christina. 2000. "The commodification of the past, postmodern pastiche, and the search for authentic experiences at contemporary heritage attractions." *European Journal of Marketing* 34 (7): 835–50.

Goulding, Christina. 2001. "Romancing the past: Heritage visiting and the nostalgic consumer." *Psychology & Marketing* 18 (6): 565–92.

Grayson, Kent. 1998. "The icons of consumer research: Using icons to represent consumers' reality." In *Representing consumers*, edited by Barbara B. Stern. New York: Routledge, 27–43.

Hirschman, Elizabeth. 1993. "Ideology in consumer research, 1980 and 1990: A Marxist and feminist critique." *Journal of Consumer Research* 19 (March): 537–55.

Holbrook, Morris B., and Punam Anand. 1990. "Effects of tempo and situational arousal on the listener's perceptual and affective responses to music." *Psychology of Music* 18 (2): 150–62.

Joy, Annamma. 1991. "Beyond the odyssey: Interpretations of ethnographic writing in consumer behavior." In *Highways and buyways*, edited by Russell W. Belk. Provo, UT: Association for Consumer Research, 216–33.

Joy, Annamma, and John Sherry. 2003. "Speaking of art as embodied imagination: A multisensory approach to understanding aesthetic experience." *Journal of Consumer Research* 30 (September): 259–82.

Joy, Annamma, John Sherry, Gabriele Troilo, and Jonathan Deschenes. 2006. "Writing it up, writing it down: Being reflexive in accounts of consumer behavior." In *Handbook of qualitative methods in marketing*. Cheltenham: Edward Elgar, 345–60.

Kelleher, Michael. 2004. "Images of the past: Historical authenticity and inauthenticity from Disney to Times Square." *CRM Journal*, Summer: 6–19.

Kontogeorgopoulos, Nick. 2003. "Keeping up with the Joneses: Tourists, travelers, and the quest for cultural authenticity in southern Thailand." *Tourist Studies* 3 (2): 171–203.

Kozinets, Robert V. 2002. "Can consumers escape the market? Emancipatory illuminations from burning man." *Journal of Consumer Research* 29 (1): 20–38.

Langer, Suzanne. 1953. "Virtual space." In *Aesthetics: A reader in philosophy of the arts*, edited by David Goldblatt and Lee B. Brown. Upper Saddle River, NJ: Prentice Hall, 155–9.

Lindholm, Charles. 2002. "Authenticity, anthropology, and the sacred." *Anthropological Quarterly* 75 (2): 331–8.

Lindholm, Charles. 2008. *Culture and authenticity*. Malden, MA: Blackwell.

Lowenthal, David. 1985. *The past is a foreign country*. Cambridge: Cambridge University Press.

McCabe, Scott. 2005. "Who is a tourist?" *Tourist Studies* 5 (1): 85–106.

MacCannell, Dean. 1999. *The tourist: A new theory of the leisure class*. Berkeley, CA: University of California Press.

MacCannell, Dean. 2001. "Tourist agency." *Tourist Studies* 1 (1): 23–37.

McCracken, Grant. 1988. *Culture and consumption: New approaches to the symbolic character of consumer goods and activities*. Bloomington, IN: Indiana University Press.

Mannheim, Steve. 2002. *Walt Disney and the quest for community*. Burlington, VT: Ashgate.

Moisander, Johanna, and Anu Valtonen. 2006. *Qualitative marketing research: A cultural approach*. London: Sage.

Murray, Jeff, and Julie Ozanne. 1991. "The critical imagination: Emancipatory interests in consumer research." *Journal of Consumer Research* 18 (September): 129–44.

Olsen, Kjell. 2002. "Authenticity as a concept in tourism research: The social organization of the experience of authenticity." *Tourist Studies* 2 (2): 159–82.

Peñaloza, Lisa. 1999. "Just doing it: A visual ethnographic study of spectacular consumption behavior at Nike Town." *Consumption Markets & Culture* 2 (4): 337–400.

Peñaloza, Lisa. 2005. "Have we come a long way baby? Negotiating a more multicultural feminism in the marketing academy in the U.S." In *Marketing and feminism*, edited by Miriam Catterall, Pauline McLaran, and Lorna Stevens. London: Routledge.

Robertson, Jennifer. 2002. "Reflexivity redux: A pithy polemic on 'positionality'." *Anthropological Quarterly* 75 (4): 785–92.

Rosaldo, Renato. 1989. *Culture and truth: The remaking of social analysis*. Boston, MA: Beacon Press.

Schroeder, Jonathan E. 1998. "Consuming representation: A visual approach to consumer research." In *Representing consumers: Voices, views and visions*, edited by Barbara B. Stern. New York: Routledge, 193–230.

Schroeder, Jonathan E. 2002. *Visual consumption*. New York: Routledge.

Schwartz, Hillel. 1996. *The culture of the copy: Striking likenesses, unreasonable facsimiles*. New York: Zone Books.

Shepherd, Robert. 2003. "Fieldwork without remorse: Travel desires in a tourist world." *Consumption Markets & Culture* 6 (2): 133–44.

Sherry, John F., Jr. 1998. "The soul of the company store: Nike Town Chicago and the emplaced brandscape." In *Servicescapes*, edited by J.F. Sherry, Jr. Lincolnwood, IL: NTC Business Books.

Sherry, John F., Jr., and John W. Schouten. 2002. "A role for poetry in consumer research." *Journal of Consumer Research* 29 (September): 218–34.

Sorkin, Michael. 1992. *Variations on a theme park*. New York: Hill & Wang.

Stern, Barbara. 1998. "Poetry and representation in consumer research: The art of science." In *Representing consumers*, edited by Barbara B. Stern. New York: Routledge, 290–307.

Thompson, Craig. 2002. "A re-inquiry on re-inquiries: A postmodern proposal for a critical-reflexive approach." *Journal of Consumer Research* 29 (June): 142–5.

Thompson, Craig, Barbara B. Stern, and Eric J. Arnould. 1998. "Writing the differences: Poststructuralist pluralism, retextualization, and the construction of reflexive ethnographic narratives in consumption and market research." *Consumption Markets & Culture* 2 (2): 105–60.

Urry, John. 1990. *The tourist gaze: Leisure and travel in contemporary societies*. Newbury Park, CA: Sage.

Urry, John. 1995. *Consuming places*. New York: Routledge.

Venkatesh, Alladi, and Laurie A. Meamber. 2006. "Art and aesthetics: Marketing and cultural production." *Marketing Theory* 6 (1): 11–39.

Venkatesh, Alladi, and Laurie A. Meamber. 2008. "The aesthetics of consumption and the consumer as an aesthetic subject." *Consumption Markets & Culture* 11 (1): 45–70.

Veryzer, Robert W., and J. Wesley Hutchinson. 1998. "The influence of unity and prototypicality on aesthetic responses to new product designs." *Journal of Consumer Research* 24 (March): 374–94.

Wang, Ning. 1999. "Rethinking authenticity in tourism experience." *Annals of Tourism Research* 26 (2): 349–70.

Wang, Ning. 2000. *Tourism and modernity*. Amsterdam: Pergamon Press.

White, Carmen M. 2007. "More authentic than thou: Authenticity and othering in Fiji tourism discourse." *Tourist Studies* 7 (1): 25–49.

Zukin, Sharon. 1991. *Landscapes of power: Western cityscapes and American culture after 1940*. Berkeley, CA: University of California Press.

17 Consuming caffeine

The discourse of Starbucks and coffee

Charlene Elliott

> It started on a gentle slope somewhere between the tropics of Cancer and Capricorn. Bright red coffee cherries plucked ripe from the trees—their prize extracted and delivered safely into the hands of our master roaster, an artist who changes their tiny forms by fire into something altogether different . . . something you now hold in your hand. Starbucks Coffee.
>
> Whether this Starbucks came from Africa, Arabia, Indonesia or Latin America, its destination is your cup.
>
> (Starbucks coffee package)

With the proliferation of academic texts on global culture, communication scholars have turned a critical eye to previous and emerging research. Debate about globalization—its appropriate definitions, theoretical underpinnings and practical impact—has not only "fed a boom in academic publishing during the 1990s" (Sreberny-Mohammadi et al. 1997: x), but has allowed scholars to redress some of the perceived shortcomings in the field of global communication. Annabelle Sreberny-Mohammadi (1997), for example, critiques the narrow and "reductionist" view of cultural imperialism that emphasizes the North-South flow of Western media and cultural industries at the expense of social and symbolic practices (such as map making, missionary activity, education and tourism). Peter Golding and Phil Harris extend this critique, arguing for the need to get beyond the "unduly limited dialogues of media research" to join "the wider conversation of international analysis" (Golding and Harris 1997: 9).

In spite of the call for symbolic analysis and interdisciplinarity, relatively few communication studies analyze global culture through the lens of a specific cultural commodity, artifact or "event." This seems largely the domain of anthropology, which offers a rich literature on topics such as the symbolic consumption of the tourist event (Little 1991), the role of clothing in "fashioning" African colonial subjects (Comaroff 1996) and the existence of "global" food identities in British cuisine (James 1996). Especially pertinent is the awareness of cross-cultural consumption—namely, that (symbolic) goods are often produced in one country and consumed in another: Thus, the "culture they 'substantiate' is no longer the culture in which they circulate"

(Howes 1996: 2). While this is not wholly unlike the notion of "cultural imperialism" (Tomlinson 1991) or "Coca-colonization" (Hannerz 1992), the cross-cultural consumption paradigm posits that *all* cultures transform or renegotiate the meanings of imported goods to fit a local context (Howes 1996). As such, goods moving from South to North (or Third World to First World) become objects of interest, which is rare in the case of the other two paradigms.

Hailing the call for interdisciplinarity and fresh approaches to studying global culture, the following analysis explores coffee as a form of transborder communication. This stimulant, which is widely circulated and mass consumed, has ample flavor *and* meaning. As one of the most valuable commodities in world trade and a key export product for developing countries (accounting for over 70 percent of foreign exchange earnings for some of the least developed countries) (ICO 2000), coffee has clear economic and political import—but as the preferred beverage of Americans and Canadians (second only to water), it has definite socio-cultural significance. Fifty-two percent of Americans and 62 percent of Canadians drink coffee daily (Cherney 1998, A6), and specialty coffeehouses adorn the First World landscape like bright confetti. Starbucks Coffee Company, the ubiquitous purveyor of specialty coffees, has retail stores throughout North America, the United Kingdom, the Pacific Rim and the Middle East. It competes with a host of other popular specialty retailers— including even the McDonald's Corporation, which recently joined the brouhaha with a $24-million chain of coffee bars in Britain (Stanley 1999: B3). Jamaican coffee producers also entered the retail market in January 1999, opening the "first of a planned 2,000 strong chain of coffee stores across the globe" (Jamaica boosts coffee 1999: C14).

Clearly, coffee is big business. Yet it is also symbolic business, dealing with the production, packaging and consumption of meaning. I am particularly interested in the cultural "text" of coffee, for it is multi-layered; meaning resides within the form itself (i.e., the "artifact" of the bean/beverage) and in the discourses surrounding that form (i.e., in its packaging and marketing). These discourses "blend" within the cup and are literally and figuratively consumed. Second, coffee is a unique artifact for analysis because the commodity flow is from South to North. While coffee has, from the onset, been stamped with a European thumbprint, there is no question that this ancient, *foreign* beverage has radically reshaped the social relations and complexion of *both* work and leisure within the consuming countries. Historically, coffeehouses served as forums for political discussion and learning (Naiman 1995: 52; Pendergrast 1999: 7–15); they have transformed over the years into "retail theaters" used primarily for socializing (MacLeod 1997: B4). The beverage itself has become integral to working and professional culture: it is simultaneously a pick-me-up that provides greater productivity and a pause (in the form of the coffee break). Arguably, coffee has transformed Western society through a kind of tempered coffeecolonialism, in which an imported commodity has been wholly embraced to become a fixture of Western consumer society and a marker of (Western) identity.

Consuming caffeine, then, entails more than brewing or buying. "Going for coffee" has global implications. Coffee beans, physically removed from their place of origin, have been conceptually repackaged, and the resulting discourse operating both through and about coffee proves fascinating. While it is possible to explore coffee's packaging and marketing from a political economy or consumption perspective,[1] this study follows Arjun Appadurai's s lead to focus on commodity itself, the "thing that is exchanged" (Appadurai 1986: 3). As such, the market becomes more than a commercial venue. It becomes the site for representation and discourse.

No market "site" is better suited for analyzing the discourse of coffee than Starbucks. It is the world's largest retailer, roaster and brand of specialty coffee. With over 3,300 stores operating in 15 international venues (Starbucks 2000, 2000a), Starbucks' coffee discourse circulates widely. Consequently, it provides a meaningful illustration of how one transborder commodity has been costumed for Western consumption. Starbucks' messages are steeped in the beverage itself, the names of the coffee blends, and the labeling of the beans. It thus becomes revealing to explore how Starbucks constructs, packages and presents coffee—for its messages implicate both global and *consumer culture*.

"Bean here, bean there . . ."

In their extensive study on the social role of advertising, communication scholars William Leiss, Stephen Kline and Sut Jhally reiterate the Marxist perspective of commodity fetishism, whereby all traces of production are erased from the object produced. "Goods reveal or 'show' to our senses their capacities to be satisfiers," they affirm, while "draw[ing] a veil across their own origins" (Leiss, Kline and Jhally 1990: 324). Since goods "do not bear the signatures of their makers" only the most astute shoppers realize the components of things and who made them (Leiss, Kline and Jhally 1990: 324–325). Fredric Jameson's analysis of postmodernity voices similar concerns, in which "the point" of consumerism, arguably, is to:

> forget about all those innumerable others for awhile; you don't want to have to think about Third World women every time you pull yourself up to your word processor or all the other lower class people with their lower class lives when you decide to use or consume your other luxury products.
> (Jameson 1991: 315)

Traditional coffee marketing does not belie these ideas. Starting from the 1920s, when coffee became a major consumer product, national corporations such as Standard Brands and General Foods advertised the stimulant as a regular part of the workaday world. By 1950, coffee was the favorite beverage of the American middle class (Pendergrast 1999: xviii), and in the decade that followed consumers could select from an array of coffees that masked their origins completely. *Maxwell House, Folgers, Nestle, Sanka*, and the inaptly named *Chock Full o' Nuts* certainly did little to connote their source or those producing the beans.[2] Origins were insignificant. As an American roaster of the 1960s claimed, US consumers simply wanted "normal" coffee in paper cups and "diluted to the tastes of the time, along with a hamburger and fries" (Pendergrast 1999: 271).

Arguments for commodity fetishism prove less convincing in contemporary culture, where fairly traded coffee and "environmentally friendly" coffee (such as shade grown and organic) are readily available—for an added price, of course. Transfair and Quality Mark labels *highlight* conditions within the producing countries to raise public awareness: these labels guarantee that coffee producers receive fair prices and consistent markets for their goods.[3] Shade grown and organic coffee marketing instead focus on the ecological impact of coffee harvesting, emphasizing either the alternatives to pesticides or water and soil conservation initiatives. Rather than veiling the wearisome information on where and how coffee is produced, then, fair trade, organic and shade grown products foreground such considerations. Shoppers know that their coffee had *bean there* before it became a *bean here*.

In Starbucks, the interplay between *global/local* and *producer/product* is much more intricate—and ironic. While Starbucks introduced organic coffee into its product line on April 20, 1999 (to commemorate Earth Day) and shade grown coffee in August (Starbucks 1999, 1999a), it is not a Transfair member company. And when Starbucks entered the Beijing market in January 1999 (Starbucks 1999b), it chose to serve imported coffee, even though China's southwestern province of Yunnan produces thousands of tons of dried coffee beans annually (Virant 1999). Moreover, Starbucks' promotional brochure, *The world of coffee*, highlights the role of the purveyor, not the producer. Our goals are "to do whatever it takes" to provide "a great cup of coffee," Starbucks declares in the flyer. This includes "finding and purchasing the best green beans in the world" and "listening and responding to the coffee and helping it reach its highest flavor potential" (Starbucks 1998). Here, Appadurai's s notion that "commodities have social lives" (Appadurai 1986: 3) gains added significance in that Starbucks personifies the bean as something to be "listened to" and conversed with. All told, these elements suggest that *Starbucks*, not source (i.e., producers/origin) is of primary concern—a suggestion confirmed by the maxim typed on every Starbucks package. *Whether this Starbucks came from Africa, Arabia, Indonesia or Latin America, its destination is your cup.*

Caffeinated cartography[4]

Although Starbucks proudly serves its coffee around the world, the company's sense of geography is refracted through a commodified Western lens. Reflecting on his Starbucks experience, one journalist carped that unsuspecting consumers must choose from "beans from countries that college graduates cannot find on a map" (Pendergrast 1999: 371). Indeed. Starbucks coffees embrace a range of growing locations, from Mexico, Guatemala, Colombia,

Indonesia and New Guinea, to Kenya, Ethiopia and Yemen. But consumers are not *expected* to find these places, merely to consume them symbolically. This is evidenced by Starbucks' *Coffee Categories*, which arrange the beans according to taste, not place. In this categorization, *Lively Impressions* subsume the "flavorful, bright and inviting" (Starbucks 1998) coffees from Costa Rica, Papua New Guinea and East Africa under one sprightly heading. *Rich Traditions*, in contrast, offers "wellrounded and balanced" flavors from sources as diverse as Kenya, Java and Guatemala. Finally, *Bold Expressions*— "assertive," "exotic" and "intense" coffees—stem from Arabia, Indonesia and Ethiopia. These "categories" add an entirely new dimension to Giddens' (1997) time/space distanciation, whereby societies are "stretched" over space. And while Starbucks' cartography of coffee may initially appear to substantiate David Harvey's view that global culture makes people "much more sensitized to what the world's spaces contain" (Harvey 1992: 294), the sensitivity is wholly superficial. "Sensitivity," in this case, is an awareness that the "world's spaces" of Java, Sulawesi, New Guinea or Guatemala "contain" one thing of import: the Starbucks coffee bean.

Starbucks' cartography of coffee is further problematized by its array of trademarked blends. Shoppers curious about a blend's origin can learn, through Starbucks edifying brochures, that the company's "master roasters" *create* these flavorful brews by combining various coffee beans to attain a desired "tasteprint." Thus, a commodity of Yemen is ground with a commodity of Indonesia to "create" Arabian Mocha Java™ and the beans of East Africa mix with those of Latin America to become Siren's Note Blend™. In this way, the world's coffees are "relocated" just like the other non-Western commodities imported into North American society—just like the Costa Rican bananas, Indonesian sweet potatoes and Chilean grapes housed in the local supermarket. But Starbucks' relocation has greater symbolic power. The commodity, identified by its location, has been fused with another; the country of Indonesia is symbolically annexed with Yemen. Even this is beguiling, for the marketing literature fails to identify Yemen as a source. Rather, it refers to the geographically vague Arabia, a place with no defined borders. Moreover, Starbucks blends are commonly packaged under vague or misleading names. Yukon Blend®, for example, is actually comprised of Indonesian and Latin American coffees. Caffe Verona® has the same distant ingredients, only in different proportions. And Italian Roast has nothing to do with the lovely red, white and green label that reminisces Italy's flag. As such, Starbucks "master roasters" function as modern bricoleurs, playing with commodity pieces to construct a tasty, *and trademarked*, text for consumption. Symbolically, the play is highly charged, as the beans *identified by their origins* are more than pieces. They index places.

Playing with the map

Geographic recombination also occurs within Starbucks' menu and in its store, where language, country and commodity all provide symbolic grist for the Starbucks mill. Customers do not purchase from servers, they order from *baristas*, and cup sizes do not come in small, medium or large, but in the equally Italian *short, grande* and *venti*. Popular espresso-based drinks such as cappuccino and cafe latte can be ordered *con panna* or as *macchiatos*. So while customers sip their grande cafe-au laits in a Seattle-based coffeehouse, they imbibe a style of coffee (espresso) invented in France, then perfected in Italy, but sourced from Latin America and Indonesia.[5] Worth noting, however, is the fact that Starbucks chooses not to identify the bean "origins" of Espresso Roast™, the blend used in every espresso drink on the menu. Espresso Roast™ is described simply as the "heart and soul of Starbucks . . . caramelly, smooth, great balance" (Starbucks 1988), suggesting that the essence of Starbucks could only have a corporate origin. This is also true of Starbucks' signature and most popular coffee, Starbucks House Blend, which is detailed solely as a "wonderful, round, balanced, straightforward cup of coffee" (Starbucks 1988). Here, the cloaking of origins is deliberate and supports the "veiling process" Leiss, Kline and Jhally (1990) deemed as characteristic of Western advertising. With this kind of naming and marketing, Starbucks reveals that "space" or "place" is merely a style, to be utilized for semantic purposes and discarded when not wanted.

Why mask certain countries of origin and articulate others? Literature on globalization is frustratingly silent on this question. It is more likely to explore *why* and *how* the global and the local are inextricably linked (in the spirit of Giddens) than to explain the semantic dimension and allure of transborder commodity forms. However, studies in anthropology and advertising theory prove very helpful, for the evocation of difference has both a strong cultural functionality and marketing value. Anthropologist Sidney Mintz (1985) reveals that today's "commonplace" imported commodities have shifted in meaning over time. Sugar, for instance, was first introduced to European society as a luxury item, and coveted precisely because of its distant origins. This is also the case for tea and chocolate, which only gradually became integrated through increased use and availability into wider society (Mintz 1985). These foreign goods ultimately transformed into staples and markers of both European and Western cultures; the physically deterritorialized commodities became *conceptually* deterritorialized into the realms of the familiar and the local. Thus for years consumers jump-started their mornings with the trusted, quotidian brands of Maxwell House, Folgers, or Nescafe. But the rise of specialty coffee worked to refresh this common staple, *to make the banal better*, to add what marketing guru Rosser Reeves calls a "Unique Selling Proposition" (Macrae 1991: 36)—the special perk that the competitors do not offer. Hence, the evocation of the exotic. Foreign beans, made common, are traced back to their roots to heighten coffee's consumer appeal. As Howes notes, "in general, the only time when the foreign nature of an imported product is emphasized in the West by its marketers . . . is when part of its appeal to Westerners lies in its exotic nature" (Howes 1996: 186).

"Foreignness" within the specialty coffee market allows consumers to conceptually partake of exotic locales. Coffee aficionados use geography to illustrate their taste preferences by ordering Brazil Ipanema Bourbon™, Kenya, Sumatra, Kona, New Guinea Peaberry, or Colombia Narino Supremo™. In short, they order a place in a cup. And since the coffee beans' origins are only a "spice" within Starbucks' marketing, they can be tinkered with. Kenya, the *country*, is a coffee name, but so is Kona, a *region* in western Hawaii. Ethiopia Sidamo, which Starbucks offers as a beverage, is both a place and a people: Sidamo refers to the Cushitic-speaking inhabitants of southwestern Ethiopia. Starbucks' Guatemala Antigua coffee is an inversion of the capital and country of Antigua, Guatemala. Finally, as merely a "spice," coffee's exotic origins can be omitted from the marketing at will. Reference to the foreign is used to make products appealing rather than threatening (Howes 1996: 187), and marketers strive to ensure their products (even those positioned as exotic) maintain a strong pull of familiarity so that they appeal to consumer lifestyles or lifestyle aspirations (Leiss, Kline and Jhally 1990). This explains why Starbucks' packaging, marketing and menu remain silent about the beans in the company's House Blend and Espresso Roast. There is the practical reason of wanting to appeal to the widest possible market by offering both exotic and familiar fare—but the logic extends deeper. Starbucks has established itself as an upscale, worldly, but pointedly American chain. Accuracy with regards to global details (such as geographical and source identification, or coffee names) sources proves secondary to Starbucks marketing and image. As Starbucks' promotional flyer affirms: *Starbucks works backwards from a cup of coffee.* It proudly considers the product first.

The rhetoric of Starbucks; or, "speaking of coffee . . ."[6]

Starbucks' "world of coffee" reaches beyond naming the beans. Coffee descriptors used in the company's marketing literature reveals Starbucks to be more than geographically challenged: it is steeped in racialized rhetoric. As earlier noted, Starbucks' house blends, those bearing company signature, are described in positive and non-threatening terms. They are "wonderful," "balanced," "straightforward" and "smooth"; they are the "heart and soul of Starbucks"; they are "bright" and "mild." The coffees with designed or entirely created names, such as Yukon Blend®, Caffe Verona®, Gold Coast Blend® or Italian Roast, present equally laudatory descriptors. Yukon Blend® is "bright" and "brisk" and "well-rounded"; Caffe Verona® is "classic" and "versatile." Gold Coast Blend© is "sophisticated, 'big city'," a "courageous cup of coffee" and Italian Roast, with its "sturdy, assertive flavor" is for connoisseurs. Contrast these descriptors with those of the "exotic" coffees— they have laudatory but loaded terms. Sulawasi is "exotic but approachable," Kenya is "intense" but "refreshing" and Arabian Mocha Java is "exotic" and "wild." Many of the words and phrases used are consistent with what Edward Said (1978) would classify as *Orientalist* discourse—the ethnocentric and stereotypic means of viewing, describing, restructuring and ultimately dominating over Muslim lands in Africa and Asia (Said 1978: 1–4). Orientalism pivots on the notion of the "mysterious East" (Said 1993: x) and often portrays the foreign as primitive. Starbucks falls right in line with this. Its exotic coffee descriptors convey those very categories.

Coffees are "magical," "intriguing," "fleeting," "elusive," "nearly indescribable" (i.e., mysterious), and "wild" and "earthy" (i.e., primitive). And as with Orientalism, these descriptors exist to be observed and consumed by the West. Thus, Guatemala Antigua coffee may seem "simple at the beginning" but promises "many levels of discovery" to the persistent connoisseur. Arabian Mocha Sanai's description brings many of these threads together, combining Starbucks' sense of the exotic and its Western gaze with the mysterious and primitive to create a coffee profile with multiple meanings:

> Arabian Mocha Sanani—A wild and wonderful coffee with an intense berry flavor and hints of spice, rum and cocoa. Sanani's s layers of exotic flavor appeal to the coffee adventurer as well as the sophisticated coffee connoisseur.
>
> (Starbucks 1998)

Orientalism also emerges in the sexually charged terminology Starbucks uses to define its "exotic" coffees. Taste descriptors refer to the body or female sexuality: coffees are "full-bodied," "well-rounded" and "soft" with "luxurious texture"; they are "smooth and satisfying." It is meaningful to contrast these descriptors with those of Starbucks' House Blend, Espresso Roast, Caffe Verona®, Italian Roast and French Roast—none of which make reference to the body.

Starbucks accentuates this racialized rhetoric by presenting the "wild side" of coffee. Said notes that "a principle dogma" of Orientalism is that the East is unpredictable, savage even, and "something to be feared" (Said 1978: 301). These random and savage elements emerge in the three Starbucks coffees labeled "Arabian"—they are the only Starbucks coffees deemed "wild." Arabian Mocha Java is "wild," "spicy" and "intense," and Arabian Mocha Sanani is all these things plus "unpredictable." "You never know how it's going to taste," affirms Starbucks' promotional brochure. To keep these elements under control, Starbucks offers the *Coffee Taster*—a service on its website that ensures these exotic elements will never offend a consumer's taste. By answering a series of questions, customers can receive a personal taste profile and a list of matching Starbucks coffees. Seven straightforward questions: *What does coffee do for you? What taste characteristics do you seek? What flavors do you enjoy? How do you describe yourself as a coffee drinker? How do you drink your coffee? How do you like your coffee brewed? What do you generally order in a restaurant?* The answers, from a semantic perspective, are complex. Again, Starbucks subordinates the commodity to personal taste, but even its taste profiles are symbolically charged. If consumers identify themselves as coffee-nervous or coffee-novice by answering in preference of mild flavors, consistent tastes and coffee with added cream and/or sugar, then the *Coffee Taster* affirms that House Blend, Siren's Note Blend or French Roast—in short, the non-exotic—are a "sure thing." For these consumers, it would be "adventurous" to try Colombia Narino Supremo or Guatemala Antigua, and "daring" to try Arabian Mocha Java. Yet, if consumers identify themselves as coffee-risk takers, who enjoy experimenting, "extremes" and the "wild," the *Coffee Taster* identifies Arabian Mocha Java as a "sure thing" and other exotic coffees as "adventurous." Regardless of the answers given, Starbucks' signature and "non-exotic" coffees never appear under the "daring" category. Starbucks' House Blend is listed either as a "sure thing" or not at all.

Consuming caffeine

It is with reference to the global but with thoroughly local representations that Starbucks markets its coffee. Coffee beans, distanced from their origins, have been relocated in an American chain, and it is fascinating to observe how Starbucks seemingly respects the imported commodity while managing to refashion it completely. In some regards, the "social life" of the coffee bean (in the fashion of Appadurai) parallels that of another imported commodity, sugar. Mintz's evaluation of sugar's complex history reveals that in Western society, the sweet "penetrated social behavior and, in being put to new uses and taking on new meanings, was transformed from curiosity and luxury into commonplace and necessity" (Mintz 1985: xxiv). This is equally true of coffee. However, specialty coffee purveyors have reintroduced its global dimension: Starbucks' savvy marketing has transformed the banal bean into something symbolically exciting. Yet the resulting issues of the palate are not confined within a bowl of Starbucks cappuccino or a mug of house blend. World geography has been remapped to sell a cup of coffee; Third World spaces have been equally appropriated. Kenya or Estate Java coffees may claim to substantiate Africa and Indonesia, respectively, yet the claim is rhetorical and the meaning provided by Starbucks. While globalism can be a powerful unifying discourse, sensitizing people to "what the world's spaces contain" (Harvey 1992: 294), Starbucks offers a packaged and refashioned global woven through a local representation.

Indeed, this symbolic reorganization of space *does* make the world seem smaller—but by no means does it truly display the characteristics of globalization, which "'stretches' social relations, removing the relationships which govern our everyday lives from local contexts to global ones" (Tomlinson 1997: 171). Quite the contrary, for Starbucks draws from a global context to create an image appealing for local consumption. The transborder commodity becomes a composite commodity, at times offering a metaphoric consumption of Third World space and elsewhere providing Starbucks consumers a "sophisticated," "big-city" Westernized blend. This has powerful implications. Coffee's commodity form has been made and remade in Western society, and while Starbucks' current marketing blends the exotic and familiar, and the local and global within its semantic coffeepot, the resulting brew is still poured from a Western perspective. Any increased awareness of global culture displayed within Starbucks is wholly tempered by local and stereotyped representations. This is confirmed, albeit unintentionally, by Starbucks' key slogan: "Starbucks—The World of Coffee." Indeed, it is *Starbucks' world of coffee*, rather than the world's coffees, being packaged for consumption.

Notes

1 Namely, how coffee "functions" within people's social lives (i.e., how the beverage helps to fashion an identity, create an image, etc.). See McCracken (1988) for excellent scholarship on the interplay between culture and consumption. Analyzing the consumption practices of coffee drinkers would lend fascinating insight to the communicative medium of coffee; however, this would require detailed ethnographic research that proves beyond the scope of this paper.

2 The exception is Juan Valdez, the mule-escorted, Sombrero-ed coffee grower invented by the National Federation of Coffee Growers of Colombia in the 1960s to laud Colombian coffee. This highly successful advertising campaign focused on Colombia's rich growing conditions and its hand harvesting methods, which ensured consumers a better tasting coffee (Pendergrast 1999: 284).

3 Although there is resistance to this concept. David Wilkes, president of the Coffee Association of Canada, argued that its 120 member companies have consistently "worked with farmers" to ensure equitable treatment, making the Transfair label unnecessary. "There are no coffee sweat shops," he claims (Longbottom 1998: N6).

4 Much of the following descriptive information is drawn from Starbucks' packaging and promotional brochures. Specific references will be provided where appropriate.

5 In this way, Starbucks stands as a clear expression of the postmodern affinity toward juxtaposing styles, mixing codes and presenting an "eclectic form of textuality" (Collins 1995: 2).

6 The following section draws its descriptive information on Starbucks beverages from the company's *World of Coffee* (1998) pamphlet and *Starbucks Passport*. Both marketing tools, available in the stores, describe the "features" of every Starbucks coffee.

References

Appadurai, Arjun. 1986. *The social life of things*. Cambridge: University of Pennsylvania.

Cherney, Elena. 1998. "Trends." *National Post*, November 9, A6.

Collins, James. 1995. *Architectures of excess*. New York: Routledge.

Comaroff, Jean. 1996. "The empire's old clothes: Fashioning the colonial subject." In *Cross-cultural consumption: Global markets, local realities*, edited by D. Howes. New York: Routledge,19–38.

Giddens, Anthony. 1997. *Sociology*, 3rd edition. Cambridge: Polity Press.

Golding, Peter, and Phil Harris, eds. 1997. *Beyond cultural imperialism*. London: Sage.

Hannerz, Ulf. 1992. *Cultural complexity: Studies in the social organization of meaning*. New York: Columbia University Press.

Harvey, David. 1992. *The condition of postmodernity*. Cambridge: Blackwell.

Howes, David, ed. 1996. *Cross-cultural consumption: Global markets, local realities*. New York: Routledge.

International Coffee Organization (ICO) 2000 "The story of coffee: Market information." September 9. Available at: www.icoffee.com/MainFrame.asp.

Jamaica boosts coffee industry with chain of shops. 1999. *National Post*, January 8, C14.

James, Allison. 1996. "Cooking the books: Global or local identities in contemporary British food cultures?" In *Cross-cultural consumption: Global markets, local realities*, edited by D. Howes. New York: Routledge, 77–93.

Jameson, Frederic 1991 *Postmodernism; or, the cultural logic of late capitalism*. Durham, NC: Duke University Press.

Leiss, William, Stephen Kline, and Sut Jhally. 1990. *Social communication in advertising*. Ontario: Nelson.

Little, Kenneth 1991 "On safari: The visual politics of a tourist representation." In *The varieties of sensory experience*, edited by D. Howes. Toronto: University of Toronto Press, 148–163.

Longbottom, Ross. 1998. "Church group goes to bat to improve lot of coffee farmers." *Hamilton Spectator*, March 28, N6.

MacLeod, Ian. 1997. "Beans with a premium: Rich exotica of specialty coffees sweeps continent." *Hamilton Spectator*, May 7, B4.

Macrae, Chris. 1991. *World class brands*. England: Addison-Wesley.

McCracken, Grant. 1988. *Culture and consumption*. Bloomington, IN: Indiana University Press.

Mintz, Sidney. 1985. *Sweetness and power*. New York: Viking.

Naiman, Sandy. 1995. "Spilling the beans." *Toronto Sun*, February 26, 52.

Pendergrast, Mark. 1999. *Uncommon grounds*. New York: Basic Books.

Said, Edward. 1978. *Orientalism*. New York: Vintage.

Said, Edward. 1993. *Culture and imperialism*. New York: Vintage.

Sreberny-Mohammadi, Annabelle. 1997. "The many cultural faces of imperialism." In *Beyond cultural imperialism*, edited by P. Golding and P. Harris. London: Sage, 49–68.

Sreberny-Mohammadi, Annabelle, Dwayne Winseck, Jim McKenna, and Oliver Boyd-Barrett, eds. 1997. *Media in global context*. London: Arnold.

Stanley, Bruce. 1999. "Coffee conquers British tastes." *Hamilton Spectator*, March 27, B3.

Starbucks Corporation. 1998. "The world of coffee." Coffee brochure.

Starbucks Corporation. 1999. "Coffee that's made in the shade." Press release, August 2. Available at: www.starbucks.com/company/archive.

Starbucks Corporation. 1999a. "Starbucks coffee company opens first store in Beijing, China." Press release, January 10. Available at: www.starbucks.com/company/archive.

Starbucks Corporation. 1999b. "Starbucks offers a new line of organic coffee." Press release, April 20. Available at: www.starbucks.com/company/archive.

Starbucks Corporation. 2000. "Starbucks coffee company opens first stores in Hong Kong and Shanghai; store openings reflect the momentum of the company's strategic growth in the Pacific Rim." Business wire 0012, May 2. Available at: www.businesswire.com/cnn/sbux.htm.

Starbucks Corporation. 2000a. "Starbucks reports August revenues." Business wire 2506, August 31. Available at: www.businesswire.com/cnn/sbux.htm.

Tomlinson, John. 1991. *Cultural imperialism*. London: Pinter.

Tomlinson, John. 1997. "Cultural globalization and cultural imperialism." In *International communication and globalization*, edited by A. Mohammadi. London: Sage, 170–190.

Virant, Christiaan. 1999. "Starbucks pours first coffee in China: 7 more outlets planned." *National Post*, January 12.

18 Compr(om)ising commodities in consumer culture

Fetishism, aesthetics, and authenticity

John F. Sherry, Jr.

Situating the commentary

The three preceding chapters that sketch the dark side (neglected and nefarious) of branding for us in such evocative fashion present a formidable challenge to the marketing imagination. They reveal the tension inherent in the brand and its relationship with stakeholders, in a way that invites introspection, not simply recognition, in the reader. Collectively, they remind me of Robert Frost's estimation of the value of poetry (Kilcup 1998: 50): "Nothing is quite honest that is not commercial. Mind you I don't put it that everything commercial is honest."

There is something both contradictory and righteous about the commingling of realms of value. The pecuniary and the profound, the fungible and the beautiful, and the populist and the professional seem at once independent and contingent. All may be "seared with trade," but Hopkins (1953) reminds us that still "[t]here lives the dearest freshness deep down things." One of our tasks as researchers is to understand this interpenetration of art and asset, and the animism that binds them.

Before parsing the chapters, let me position my essay in the following way. I have dropped parentheses into my title to underline the ambivalence I feel about our relationship to the world of goods that is made palpable in my reading of these provocative chapters, and use this partitioned word as both an adjective and a verb to capture my understanding of the stuff of life the authors have worried so tenaciously.

Back in the day, we made a covenant with the material world to repress our animistic tendencies (Sherry 2013) and to treat "goods" as simple utilitarian solutions to our problems, delivered to us by marketers who labored to understand our needs. The arc of this covenant has changed dramatically over time. Today, we expect to be co-creators of a transformative experience that marketers facilitate in large measure by inviting the return of the repressed in the realization of our wants (Fırat and Venkatesh 1995; Gilmore and Pine 2007; Pine and Gilmore 1999; Vargo and Lusch 2004). We are purveyors and consumers not merely of used goods, but of used *gods*. As the numinous manifests in the material world, fetish, art, and authenticity interact in fascinating fashion. The quest for authenticity appears to have become a principal preoccupation in our – and here I mean researcher, consumer, and practitioner – negotiation of consumer culture.

The mystic syllable I have lodged amidword hints at the play of meaning in which marketers and consumers are engaged, in their joint creation of our experience of culture. The mantric word "*om*," voiced in three sounds and clipped in resonant silence, transports its chanter from the material world through the spiritual world to fulfillment, embodying and unifying the essence of the universe in the breath. As life is breathed into commodities, they comprise a host of cognitive, emotional, and visceral meanings, even as they comprise our world (Appadurai 1986; Douglas and Isherwood 1979). With this same breath that transmogrifies them from *materia* to *prima materia*, commodities are compromised, even as they compromise our world. "Goods" become "bads" more often than we care to admit, as the unanticipated and unintended consequences of their deployment rack our existence. I hope your interrupted reading of my title trips a meditative pause of the kind our three authors conjured in me, and that your subsequent musing goes similarly agley.

Most of us adopt a curious posture toward this profane trinity of fetishism, aesthetics, and authenticity (which I abbreviate hereafter as FAA, in recognition of the flight of fancy that is my essay) that mediates our transactions with stuff. As consumers, we are often embarrassed to admit that we animate the material world, but as marketers, we treat goods animistically, as a palimpsest, overwriting origin myths and user projections with managerial narratives of image and essence, bodying forth the brand for further quickening (Holt and Cameron 2010; Levy 1978). As consumers, we often under-appreciate design and the embodied resonance that allows us to delight in our accomplishment of mundane tasks, but as marketers we use art strategically, to seduce and persuade (Simonson and Schmitt 2009). As consumers, we do not risk looking too closely at the commercial roots of authenticity, but as marketers we have no doubt that authenticity can be created through commercial means (Beverland 2009; Beverland and Ferrelly 2010), and artfully deployed to assist people in their quest to experience immanence and transcendence.

We – researchers and consumers – often behave in "as if" fashion with FAA (Cluley and Dunne 2012), deceiving ourselves about the nature of our comprehension, skimming the semiotic surface of the complex, rather than diving deeply into its meanings and consequences. Such skating allows us to preserve illusions and prevent disruptions, keeping consideration of the extent and implication of extra-economic dimensions of our marketplace behavior at arm's length. I resume this critique later in my essay.

The commentary

Chapter 15 entitled "Aesthetics awry," in which Jonathan Schroeder writes about brand Kinkade, is offered as a cautionary tale, a morality play of sorts, of the abduction and corruption of aesthetic value by commerce, and of the artistic perils of abdication to management theory. My own dim understanding of this latter vibrant area is informed only by a cursory immersion in the impressive collection of Minahan and Cox (2007), whose volume I commend to CCT (Consumer Culture Theory) researchers of managerial inclination.

The translation of vision across media or genres, a daunting challenge even for a versatile artist, seems destined to be garbled when delegated to a brand extension team bent on sacralizing commodities with no intrinsic (and often little extrinsic) resonance with the original vision. Schroeder presents a negative case of the potential for synergy between aesthetics and management, while still recognizing the historical interdependence of art and commerce. It is one thing to imagine the Painter of Light (Kinkade) in an unholy alliance with the Bringer of Light (Lucifer) to degrade art, but quite another to condemn the dalliance of aesthetics with the market; where the former may simply be a reflection of personal taste and prejudice, the latter is an exercise in misplaced cultural criticism.

If we accept the author's conclusion that there is a wrong way, can we imagine a proper way (or ways) to harness art to commerce, beyond the simple expedient of enlightened patronage? Must the artist succumb to the clutter-busting call of novelty, arrest consumers adrift in a sea of distraction, go big or go home? Does the market encourage the artist to foreswear the seasoning, annealing and cultural immersion essential to "authentic" creation and criticism? Can cross-training in management and venturing with qualified (and cultivated) partners ensure affective implementation of uncorrupted vision? Can aesthetics and marketing strategy be synergists, rather than antagonists?

My colleagues and I (Joy et al. 2014) have described a phenomenon we call "M(Art)Worlds," reflecting a trend of luxury brand stores becoming hybrid venues that incorporate both art gallery and museum orientations into a retail ideology. Companies such as Louis Vuitton use architecture, interior design, lighting, curatorial merchandising, artisanal products, and collaboration with artists to embody aesthetics into their brand's commercial essence, such that consumers come to regard the brand's offerings as *objets d'art* in their own right. This fusion of aesthetics with marketing strategy constructs the product as a cultural artifact meriting appreciation, ensuring an ongoing relationship of co-creation between managers, consumers, and artists.

While this M(Art)World phenomenon (Joy et al. 2014) might seem to be peculiar to luxury brands, there is no reason to assume that other forms of art could not be drawn into the orbit of more mundane brands. In the Kinkade case, the democratization of luxury – in the form of the accessible sophistication afforded by folk art or kitsch, depending upon the critic's disposition – and the reassurance of the familiar (Marling 1988) might readily be translated into alliances with artists, designers, and planners, such that the vernacular architecture of communities might embody the values of the brand and be perceived by consumers as authentic. The extension and the core must reinforce one another's value. I resume this theme later in connection with Starbucks.

In Chapter 16 entitled "Consuming the 'World'," Rika Houston and Laurie Meamber don their critical marketing goggles and take us on an academic walkabout through the Disneytopia of EPCOT Center, ostensibly in search of ways in which aesthetics creates and validates authenticity. The tour is set against the historic backdrop of the rise of all things retro stemming from the postmodern condition (Reynolds 2011). The theming of built environments is itself in part a reaction to consumers' need to escape the experience of inauthenticity supposedly characterizing said condition (Brown and Sherry 2003). The authors paint a top-down picture of cultural production, and "[a]s American consumer researchers," their discomfort and discomfiture are on display throughout their tour of the sanitized semiotics of placemaking.

The ethos of CMC (and of the Heretical Consumer Research project that birthed this investigation) is critical, and incites my inner exegete to rail against the chapter's positioning. The study is neither an analysis of aesthetic experience nor a reflexive account of the research enterprise. Where it could be auto-ethnographic, it is simply impressionistic – which is still an accepted, if less satisfying, genre of tale telling – and, occasionally, reflective. Brief disclosures hint at the preconditioning (infrastructural analysis and critical reading) the authors experienced prior to what seems to have been a short exposure to the venue, in contrast to the immersive strategy of prolonged contact that characterizes most CCT work on servicescapes, and assertions about others' experience are offered in lieu of phenomenological interview verbata. Finally, their account is rendered in a single voice, effacing distinctive insight into research subject, object and process, a particular pity given the visceral and perhaps aesthetic response the site and their fellow travelers (in each case, revulsion is not too strong a characterization) seem to have elicited. The better positioning, it seems to me, lies in the authors' impassioned plea for reflexivity in research, and their recommendation that "we should always do it [fieldwork] with our eyes *and* minds open."

What appeals to me most about this chapter is its provocation to explore the bracketing process to which CCT researchers routinely profess to subscribe, but which they (and I mean we) honor more often in the breach, much as our experimental brethren fail to exploit the debriefing process to maximum effect. In particular, this chapter is an open invitation to meditate upon the nature of authenticity, and its relationship to aesthetics. The pornographic criterion ("I know it when I see it") is not an effective touchstone for cultural analysis when it comes to a construct as crucial as authenticity. We need a precise calibration of its nuances, and their reverberation in our principal social scientific instrument – our self – if we are to understand consumers' lived experience of authenticity. As I have maintained elsewhere (Sherry 2003), one man's anthropological recrudescence (McMurtry 2001) is another's architecture of reassurance (Marling 1988). I pursue this argument a bit later in my essay.

The cultural shift in the image of women betokened by the recent huge success of Disney's animated blockbuster film *Frozen* – featuring a princess named Anna who embodies the traits of a much more realistic, empowered, and self-reliant female than the brand's traditional depiction of femininity – suggests that an evolving conception of authenticity is being embraced by some of the marketing imagineers. Perhaps this conception might be generalizable in some measure to themed environments. Disney's Celebration experiment in planned community may have been too ambitious an undertaking, or "city" too large and enduring a unit of implementation (unlike the ephemeral Black Rock City of the Burning Man Project), for the effective transfer of core brand values from center to periphery. Or, our academic concept of "authenticity" may require significant rethinking.

Chapter 17, "Consuming caffeine: the discourse of Starbucks and coffee" by Charlene Elliott, is an early contribution to a CCT coffee literature that has since burgeoned (Holt and Cameron 2010; Kjeldgaard and Östberg 2007; Sherry 1995; Simon 2011; Thompson, Rindfleisch, and Arsel 2006; Venkatraman and Nelson 2008). There is perhaps no sturdier platform for staging an exploration of commodity fetishism than coffee, nor a more notorious poster firm than Starbucks for attracting an application of that same theory. The consumption of the drink is so ubiquitous, the masking of its myriad meanings so pervasive, and the marketing of its branded formulations so compelling that category dynamics virtually cry out for analysis. The author tracks the material flow of the commodity from South to North, and its subsequent infusion of branded meaning from North *through* South, charting a "cartography of coffee" that results in the drinker's consumption of "tasteprints" that evoke exotic (and ersatz) images of ostensible origins. While actual origins and conditions of production may be masked, the semiotic appeal of the "foreign" and the "ethical" are promoted to enhance consumers' enjoyment. Starbucks' Orientalist discourse suffuses coffee drinking with an adventurousness unavailable elsewhere in the category. The lived experience of coffeeworld – and the bowdlerized version of globalization therein comprised – encouraged by the brand is its competitive advantage. Starbucks is authentic insofar as consumers are eager to pay a remarkable premium for a semiotic surplus, the privilege of intertwining an aesthetic of moral cosmopolitanism with their own life narratives in a way that apotheosizes brand and self.

Starbucks acts as both a fetish and a totem for the legion of the devoted (Sherry 2005), providing consumers an experience both of personal transcendence and tribal merger. Holt and Cameron (2010: 91–105) have demonstrated the ways in which Starbucks has been able to massify its niche position by migrating subcultural values to the mainstream market. Employing a "trickle-down" approach to cultural capital, the brand has "democratized elite sensibility" by creating a myth of "accessible sophistication" that taps into the trending cultural ideology of "artisanal-cosmopolitan" foods. Aesthetics has played a pivotal role in the servicescape redesign – to "sanitized bohemian" (Holt and Cameron 2010: 176–179) – that has driven consumer engagement with the brand. Visual, aural, olfactory, and gustatory props animate the retail theatrics that have made the venue a compelling site of ritual socialization, the third place to which we gain admission through our facile manipulation of symbols.

A striking display of authenticity dynamics occurred at the Sochi Winter Olympic Games in 2014. NBC funded a private commissary-style Starbucks café where employees received beverages at no charge (Sonne and Troianovski 2014a). Soon, these employees were supplying off-site friends with gifts of the precious substance – serving as "mules" for "addicts" in one account (Sonne and Troianovski 2014b) – and bearing their branded cups as status symbols on journeys throughout Sochi; the nearest Starbucks franchise was over 350 miles away. Since Starbucks was not an official Olympic sponsor, these public displays of affection and conspicuous consumption constituted a serious breach of protocol, infringing, for example, on the aura of McDonald's legitimate (i.e., sponsored) coffee. To combat this gift economy and brand flaunting, NBC instituted a policy requiring employees to consume beverages in branded cups on-site only, barring the visible circulation of the brand beyond the café. To-go beverages were served in plain cups, no siren logo certifying to the world the authenticity of the contents (Sonne and Troianovski 2014b). One can imagine a brisk trade emerging in smuggled used branded cups as vessels of counterfeit Starbucks coffee, and in that same fake brand coffee hawked in plain cups as the real deal. Authenticity is as fluid as the contents of the cup to which the siren's song summons us.

The authenticating power of brand narrative can erode over time, especially if motivated consumerists perceive a gap between talk and walk and start to circulate disauthenticating meanings, as Starbucks has experienced in the past decade (Thompson, Rindfleisch, and Arsel 2006). The "authenticity dilemma" that Starbucks faces in the disaffection of Bobo loyalists may require a revised mythical charter, or perhaps a new brand extension, to pacify critical consumers and prevent them from moving to a perceptually more authentic brand. Ironically, the financial success of Starbucks has antagonized its original base of cosmic capitalists (Brooks 2001), rendering them dispensable to the brand's future. The relative influence of commerce (corrupting for the Bobos, corroborating for the mainstream, confounding for consumer researchers) on authenticity remains problematic.

Corollary of the commentary

For the sake of argument, I assert that the FAA complex depicted by our authors seems to revolve around the construction of authenticity, with fetishism and aesthetics becoming primary inputs into and shapers of this complex construct. I spend the balance of this essay seeking to unpack this relationship.

As an anthropologist myself, I am captivated by Lindholm's (2008: 141–145) anthropological apologia for authenticity. Riven by our conflicting roles as observers and participants, somewhat estranged from our home values but unable to go native in host cultures, my tribe is ultra-sensitive to the context-dependence of identity in a way that makes authenticity a kind of spiritual anchor in what Bauman (2000) has described as a liquid world, a source of transcendence that energizes culture (Lindholm 2002). Mid-career, a study of retro branding (Brown, Kozinets, and Sherry 2003) caused me regretfully to conclude that we are not searching for authenticity in an inauthentic world, but rather that there is no such thing as authenticity, only varying degrees of inauthenticity.

And yet, sophisticated interpreters of consumer experience such as Gilmore and Pine (2007) maintain that there is no such thing as an inauthentic experience, and that marketers are in the paradoxical business of rendering inauthentic offerings authentic. In fact, Beverland (2009) has provided us a narrative template – couched in a delicate dance of avowal of tradition and disavowal of industrial modernity – for accomplishing just such an authentica-tion program. So have Holt and Cameron (2010), as I have already indicated. From these polar perspectives, authenticity's anthropological appeal is the *belief* that it exists. From that belief, a host of other interesting features of authenticity cascades. The contestation of its essence, its animating tensions, its plasticity, its evolution, and the interplay of internal discovery and external validation all excite the anthropological imagination, and, by extension for me, the marketing imagination.

Broadly sketched, the trajectory of authenticity is widely recognized. Arising from the dislocations of modernism, fueled by the re-enchantment agenda of romanticism, buffeted by the forces of state and market co-optation, subjected to the abasement of inexorable commodification, and gradually refined as a politico-aesthetic enterprise, authenticity is often regarded as the re-emergence of the sacred in our contemporary world (Lindholm 2002, 2008; Potter 2010). The dynamics of the authentic can be summarily detailed. There is an intrinsic component, internal or integral to the offering. There is an extrinsic component, a socially constructed aspect of the offering, which emplaces both the ideology of the dominant interest and the imagination of the stakeholder. Finally, there is a transactional component, wherein the intrinsic and extrinsic interact to motivate the processes of quest (internal and external), meaning investiture and recovery. Recent work on the nature of vibrant matter (Bennett 2010) and object-oriented ontology (Bogost 2012; Harmon 2011; Morton 2013) promises to help us better understand these dynamics, especially as actor network theory in its various forms diffuses into consumer research.

In critical and popular discussions of authenticity, it seems as if the aesthetic and sacred dimensions of the condition are celebrated, and that the political and commercial dimensions are derogated. In managerial and governance circles, these tensions are less acutely felt, and are more a matter of reconciliation. In the former case, if a traditional aesthetic (and its implied system of values) is discernible in an offering, that offering is readily sacralized; the offering may be *in* the market (or polity), but it is not *of* the market (or polity). The offering transcends these mundane realms to become sublime. In the latter case, the issue is how best to aestheticize the offering so that its commercial or political origins do not interfere with the desired consumer experience, which may incidentally include sacralization.

Potter (2010: 4, 13) has boldly proclaimed that authenticity is a hoax, and has become a status game driven by invidious comparison. The quest for authenticity needs to be redirected, he maintains, in a way that recognizes the reality of the material world and the vibrancy of the market as a source of human value. He asks us to imagine how we might take the concept of authenticity more seriously. One answer might lie in a hybrid approach to understanding that Outka (2009: 4–5) has called the "commoditized authentic." Such an approach requires that we view our penchant for unmasking inauthenticity as a roadblock to our comprehension of authenticity, and consider the consequences of the long historical co-construction of authenticity by art and commerce.

The concept of the commoditized authentic *preserves*, rather than *resolves*, contradiction; it delivers tension in a way that allows us to appreciate both noncommercial aura and commercial availability. Thus, we are able, in a completely modern fashion, to tap into values we associate with authenticity. As an "antidote" to the anxiety it generates, the commoditized authentic summons forth its own critique, revealing itself to be at once a "marketing technique" and a "cultural strategy" (Outka 2009: 4, 16, 21). In this light, marketing and authenticity may sometimes actually comprise a holy alliance (Beverland 2009; Holt 2004).

How might we guide new research into authenticity? Beverland and Farrelly (2010) suggest two directions: comprehensive investigation of the infrastructure of different interpretations of authenticity, and exploration beyond dichotomous categorization to such dimensions as reconciliation of alternative interpretations of authenticity. Outka's (2009) work suggests that we suspend inquiry into resolution, and focus on understanding the lived experience of paradox, and possibly encourage marketers to call more attention to the tension between aura and accessibility, provoking intensified introspection among consumers. Potter's (2010) work suggests that to take authenticity seriously, we will need to understand the commingling of the spiritual and the commercial in a way that is not unreflexively critical, suspending our disbelief and bracketing our intellectual prejudices until we better understand consumers' lived experience of the marketplace.

My own favorite starting point for rethinking conventional wisdom is to map the central construct into Greimas' (1990) semiotic square, and, in this case, explore the multiplex relationships between the authentic and inauthentic, the not inauthentic and the not authentic, the authentic and the not authentic, and the inauthentic and the not inauthentic. I defer this exercise to another essay and to a classroom workshop with my MBA students.

Conclusion

I hope my colleagues will forgive my misprisions in using their work inspirationally to riff on the themes their ideas touched off in me. Deep thinkers all, my margin notes have flattened their perspectives to a narrow focus, but

362 *John F. Sherry, Jr.*

I hope my comments will provoke another round of conversation as we all nudge the field toward extended exploration of these powerful cultural forces.

Read together, the preceding chapters are an inspirational work of speculative fiction, insofar as they invite us to consider the multifaceted ways in which marketers make culture, and how, in essence, marketing becomes culture (Sherry 2014). Branding is the principal tool of this becoming. It is this making that affords us so many practical and interpretive possibilities. We began by ruminating on the use and abuse of aesthetics in marketing. We moved to a mulling of the very possibility of authenticity in the tug of war between aesthetics and commerce. We concluded by exploring how the fetishization of commodities can be redirected by aesthetics to engender a sense of authentic experience. What economists efface, marketers rejuvenate; while each mystifies and conceals, marketing seeks also to reveal, whether through aesthetic artifice, careful consumer research, or both. Our authors peel this ontological onion in several interesting ways.

For all practical purposes, Kinkade™, Disney®, and Starbucks® stand for everybrand in summing up the learning from our authors' treatises. Thrown into a post-Enlightenment world and condemned to roam its brandscapes for eternity, haunted by the false memory of an authentic life conditioned by aesthetics and not commerce, we either struggle futilely to resolve our cultural contradictions or embrace the paradox of irreducibly ambivalent standards and get on with our plumbing of consumers' lived experience, as theoreticians and practitioners. We live in an era of great brandwith and much branditry. We need to be relentlessly critical of our critical frameworks, even as we hold the market and the state accountable for their shortfalls. But most of all, we need an accurate and empathic understanding of our subjects.

In seeking to account for willful consumer misbehavior, Cluley and Dunne (2012: 253) describe the "as if" moment of commodity consumption – "at the very moment at which consumers consume, they often act *as if* they did not know what they know only all too well" – not as a contradiction of the nature of the consuming subject, but as constitutive of that subject. Consumption takes place not in spite of, but because of, moral contradictions. They extend theorizing beyond commodity fetishism to what they call commodity "narcissism," proposing that consumption be understood less as an "other-denying act of self-interest," and more of an "other-abasing self-love."

The self-deception Marx identifies is tougher to maintain in our critical era of information ubiquity, but we cling to disavowal in order to continue to enjoy the benefits we demand that producers deliver, choosing to believe we are "beyond the grasp" of commodity fetishism (Cluley and Dunne 2012: 255). In Freudian perspective, Cluley and Dunne (2012) assert that desire, rather than knowledge or experience, drives our engagement with the world, that narcissistic desires routinely inhibited because of their unacceptability are allowed expression through consumption, and that consumption allows us to realize sadistic pleasure, such that our "knowledge of other people's suffering" affords us satisfaction of being able to think ourselves "better than others."

We fetishize the narcissism, repressing the notion that we consume, at least in part, to injure others (Cluley and Dunne 2012: 258–260).

The thought that our next order of non-fat half-caff-triple-grande quarter-sweet sugar-free vanilla non-fat-lactaid extra-hot extra-foamy caramel macchiato is placed with intent to harm is even more sobering than our complicity in the exotic tasteprints Elliot tracks (Sherry 2014). If so, for simple coffee, how much more so for the myriad consumption choices we make within our un-reflexive bubble? To the extent that we are all painters of lite and set designers of others' private Idaho, the quality of our scholarship, indeed of our life, remains imperiled.

References

Appadurai, Arjun, ed. 1986. *The Social Life of Things: Commodities in Cultural Perspective*. Cambridge: Cambridge University Press.

Bauman, Zygmunt. 2000. *Liquid Modernity*. Malden, MA: Blackwell.

Bennett, Jane. 2010. *Vibrant Matter: A Political Ecology of Things*. Durham, NC: Duke University Press.

Beverland, Mark. 2009. *Building Brand Authenticity: 7 Habits of Iconic Brands*. New York: Palgrave.

Beverland, Mark, and Francis Ferrelly. 2010. "The Quest for Authenticity in Consumption: Consumers' Purposive Choice of Authentic Cues to Shape Experienced Outcomes." *Journal of Consumer Research* 36 (February): 838–856.

Bogost, Ian. 2012. *Alien Phenomenology, Or What It's Like to Be a Thing*. Minneapolis, MN: University of Minnesota Press.

Brooks, David. 2001. *Bobos in Paradise: The New Upper Class and How They Got There*. New York: Simon & Schuster.

Brown, Stephen, and John F. Sherry, Jr., eds. 2003. *Time, Space, and the Market: Retroscapes Rising*. New York: M. E. Sharpe.

Brown, Stephen, Robert Kozinets, and John F. Sherry, Jr. 2003. "Teaching Old Brands New Tricks: Retro Branding and the Revival of Brand Meaning." *Journal of Marketing* 67 (3): 19–33.

Cluley, Robert, and Stephen Dunne. 2012. "From Commodity Fetishism to Commodity Narcissism." *Marketing Theory* 12 (3): 251–265.

Douglas, Mary, and Baron Isherwood. 1979. *The World Of Goods: Towards and Anthropology of Consumption*. New York: Basic Books.

Fırat, A. Fuat, and Alladi Venkatesh. 1995. "Liberatory Postmodernism and the Reenchantment of Consumption." *Journal of Consumer Research* 22 (December): 239–267.

Gilmore, James, and Joseph Pine. 2007. *Authenticity: What Consumers Really Want*. Cambridge, MA: Harvard Business School Press.

Greimas, Algirdas. 1990. *Du Sens*. Paris: Seuil

Harmon, Graham. 2011.*The Quadruple Object*. Alresford, Hand, UK: Zero Books.

Holt, Douglas. 2004. *How Brands Become Icons*. Cambridge, MA: Harvard Business School Press.

Holt, Douglas, and Douglas Cameron. 2010. *Cultural Strategy: Using Innovative Ideologies to Build Breakthrough Brands*. New York: Oxford University Press.

Hopkins, Gerard Manley. 1953. "God's Grandeur." In *Poems and Prose*, edited by W. H. Gardner. New York: Penguin, 27.

Joy, Annamma, Jeff Jianfeng Wang, Tsang-Sing Chan, John F. Sherry, Jr., and Gene Cui. 2014. "M(Art)Worlds: Consumer Perceptions of How Luxury Brand Stores Become Art Institutions." *Journal of Retailing* 90 (3): 347–364.

Kilcup, Karen. 1998. *Robert Frost and Feminine Literary Tradition*. Ann Arbor, MI: University of Michigan Press.

Kjeldgaard, Dannie, and Jacob Östberg. 2007. "Coffee Grounds and the Global Cup: Glocal Consumer Culture in Scandinavia." *Consumption Markets & Culture* 10 (2): 175–187.

Levy, Sidney J. 1978. *Marketplace Behavior: Its Meaning for Management*. New York: AMACOM

Lindholm, Charles. 2002. "Authenticity, Anthropology and the Sacred." *Anthropological Quarterly* 75 (2): 331–338.

Lindholm, Charles. 2008. *Culture and Authenticity*. New York: Wiley-Blackwell.

Marling, Karal Ann. 1988. *Designing Disney's Theme Parks: The Architecture of Reassurance*. Paris: Flammarion Press.

McMurtry, Larry. 2001. *Walter Benjamin at the Dairy Queen: Reflections on Sixty and Beyond*. New York: Simon and Schuster.

Minahan, Stella, and Julie Cox. 2007. *The Aesthetic Turn in Management*. Burlington, VT: Ashgate.

Morton, Timothy. 2013. *Realist Magic: Objects, Ontology, Causality*. Ann Arbor, MI: Open Humanities Press.

Outka, Elisabeth. 2009. *Consuming Traditions: Modernity, Modernism, and the Commodified Authentic*. Oxford: Oxford University Press.

Pine, Joseph, and James Gilmore. 1999. *The Experience Economy*. Boston, MA: Harvard Business School Press.

Potter, Andrew. 2010. *The Authenticity Hoax: How We Get Lost Finding Ourselves*. New York: Harper.

Reynolds, Simon. 2011. *Retromania: Pop Culture's Addiction to Its Own Past*. New York: Faber and Faber.

Sherry, John F., Jr. 1995. "Bottomless Cup, Plug in Drug: A Telethnography of Coffee." *Visual Anthropology* 7 (4): 355–374.

Sherry, John F., Jr. 2003. "Past is Prologue: Retroscapes in Retrospect." In *Time, Space, and the Market: Retroscapes Rising*. New York: M. E. Sharpe, 313–320.

Sherry, John F., Jr. 2004. "We Might Never be Post-Sacred: A Tribute to Russell Belk on the Occasion of His Acceptance of the Converse Award." In *The Sixteenth Paul D. Converse Symposium*, edited by Abbie Griffen and Cele Otnes. Chicago, IL: American Marketing Association.

Sherry, John F., Jr. 2005. "Brand Meaning." In *Kellogg on Branding*, edited by Alice M. Tybout and. Timothy Calkins. New York: John Wiley, 40–69.

Sherry, John F., Jr. 2013. "Reflections of a Scape Artist: Discerning Scapus in Contemporary Worlds." In *Spirituality and Consumption*, edited by Diego Rinallo, Linda Scott, and Pauline Maclaran. London: Routledge, 211–230.

Sherry, John F., Jr. 2014. "Slouching Toward Utopia: When Marketing Is Society." In *Marketing and the Common Good: Essays on Societal Impact from Notre Dame*, edited by Patrick Murphy and John F. Sherry, Jr. New York: Routledge, 43–60.

Simon, Bryant. 2011. *Everything but the Coffee: Learning about America from Starbucks*. Berkeley, CA: University of California Press.

Simonson, Alex, and Bernd Schmitt. 2009. *Marketing Aesthetics*. New York: The Free Press.

Sonne, Paul, and Anton Troianovski. 2014a. "Pssst! Here's the Skinny on NBC's Olympic Latte Secret." *Wall Street Journal*, February 15–16: A1, A10.

Sonne, Paul, and Anton Troianovski. 2014b. "NBC's Starbucks Lockdown." *Wall Street Journal*, February 21: D4.

Thompson, Craig, Aric Rindfleisch, and Zeynep Arsel. 2006. "Emotional Branding and the Strategic Value of the Doppelgänger Brand Image." *Journal of Marketing* 70 (1): 50–64.

Vargo, Stephen L., and Robert F. Lusch. 2004. "Evolving to a New Dominant Logic for Marketing." *Journal of Marketing* 68 (January): 1–17.

Venkatraman, Meera, and Teresa Nelson. 2008. "From Servicescape to Consumptionscape: A Photo Elicitation Study of Starbucks in the New China." *Journal of International Business Studies* 39 (6): 1010–1026.

Index

For Product Safety Concerns and Information please contact our EU
representative GPSR@taylorandfrancis.com
Taylor & Francis Verlag GmbH, Kaufingerstraße 24, 80331 München, Germany

www.ingramcontent.com/pod-product-compliance
Ingram Content Group UK Ltd.
Pitfield, Milton Keynes, MK11 3LW, UK
UKHW021021180425
457613UK00020B/1020